Amongst the earliest Volumes published

1. The Confessions of S. Augustine.
2. The Five Empires. R. Wilberforce.
3. À Kempis's Imitation of Christ.
4. George Herbert's English Poems, &c.
5. Select Sermons from S. John Chrysostom.
6. Selections from S. Bernard.
7. Bp. Jeremy Taylor's Holy Living.
8. The Shepherd of Hermas and the Epistles of SS. Clement, Ignatius, and Polycarp.
9. Baxter's Saint's Rest.
10. S. Athanasius' Orations.
11. Andrewe's Sermons on the Incarnation.
12. Giles Fletcher's Victory of Christ.
13. Sermons by Massillon.

These will be followed by other volumes selected from the sources indicated above. To what extent we may be able to increase the series must necessarily depend upon the amount of support accorded to the earlier issues of the enterprise. Our belief is that the great authors, whose living voices stirred the Christian World, and who by their eloquence and knowledge of Scripture upheld the Faith in times of difficulty and assault, have their message for to-day, and that their definiteness and the vigour of their teaching will still prove attractive, as we trust it may prove serviceable to the cause of Christ's Church. In this belief we commend our venture to the sympathy and support of the people.

For the convenience of those who may wish to receive the volumes regularly as they appear, subscribers' names to the first Twelve Books will be received by the Publishers, or by any retail Bookseller, and the books will be sent post-free, as published, on prepayment of 12/-.

GRIFFITH, FARRAN, OKEDEN & WELSH,
Corner of St. Paul's Churchyard, London.

SEVENTEEN SERMONS

ON THE

NATIVITY

BY THE

RIGHT HONOURABLE AND REVEREND FATHER IN GOD

LANCELOT ANDREWES

Sometime Lord Bishop of Winchester.

A NEW EDITION

LONDON:

GRIFFITH, FARRAN, OKEDEN & WELSH

(SUCCESSORS TO NEWBERY AND HARRIS)

WEST CORNER OF ST PAUL'S CHURCHYARD.

E. P. DUTTON & CO., NEW YORK

PREFACE.

LANCELOT ANDREWES was born in Thames Street, London, in the year 1555; educated at Cooper's Free School, Radcliffe, and at Merchant Taylors. His industry and ability attracted the notice of Dr Watts, Canon of St. Pauls, who had lately founded some scholarships at Pembroke Hall, Cambridge, to one of which he presented this promising scholar. In the year 1576 he became a fellow of his college, and about the same time was made fellow of the newly founded Jesus College at Oxford. His reputation as a scholar was very high, and he is said to have been master of no less than fifteen languages, and to have been thoroughly acquainted with the writings of fathers, schoolmen, casuists, and jurists.

After some few years' occupation at the University he accepted the invitation of the Earl of Huntingdon, "President of the North," to visit him; and his preaching in various places attracted much notice. The favour of Sir Francis Walsingham, minister of Queen Elizabeth, obtained for him preferment first to the parsonage of Alton, then to St. Giles', Cripplegate, London; to which was shortly added a stall at St. Pauls, and another at Southwell, and the mastership of Pembroke Hall at Cambridge. He found this college at a low ebb, and raised it by his diligence to a much better position, leaving it at last with £1000 in its coffers, which had been empty at his entry upon the office.

His next step upwards was his promotion to be chaplain in ordinary to Queen Elizabeth, who greatly admired his preaching, and caused offers of a mitre to be made to him more than once. These offers, however, he was constrained by his conscience to refuse, as they were hampered with some conditions as to alienation of revenues, which he was unable to accept. The spoliation of the monasteries by Henry VIII. had greatly disturbed the settlement of church property, and Andrewes was for a time excluded from the position to which his qualities entitled him by his rigid determination not to injure the heritage of the church. In 1601 he was made Dean of Westminster, and the accession of James opened to him afresh the channels of high preferment. In 1605 he was consecrated Bishop of Chichester, translated to Ely in 1609, and to Winchester in 1618, when he was also made Dean of the Royal Chapel. He continued to hold a high place in the regard of James I., whom he outlived by a couple of years only, and died at Winchester, on his birthday, in 1626, aged seventy-one years. Charles I. esteemed him so highly that after his death he commanded Bishops Laud and Buckeridge to collect and publish his sermons; and it is to their care that we owe the preservation of them to us.

The private character of Andrewes was marked by a peculiar sanctity, charity, and integrity, upon which in this brief preface it is impossible to dwell. His place in the history of the English Church is of deep interest and high importance. When Andrewes obtained his fellowship, Laud was but three years old, and he had attained to the highest dignity of his life, namely, the see of Winchester, three years before Laud's consecration as Bishop of St. Davids. In the teaching and religious practice of Lancelot Andrewes, however, we find all those doctrines and customs for which Laud contended, and which some seem to fancy he forced upon the Church. It cannot, however, fail to amend notions of this kind, to find what were the doctrines and ritual of this Elizabethan court chaplain and Jacobean bishop; and an interest apart from that which must be created by his genius, learning, and character, belongs to him as the exponent of the mind and practice of the English Church in the years that intervened between the Reformation and the Revolution. The noisy faction of the Puritans was beginning to be troublesome even in the later years of Elizabeth; and their controversial clamour has seemed to drown other voices of the time, fuller of a truer harmony; but in the pages of Andrewes we find a clear and lucid exposition of sound Church doctrine, while the puritan description of his chapel, when Bishop of Ely, with its "credence, lavabo basin, altar candles, censer, &c.," and his ritual notes upon the Prayer Book (printed in Nicholls' Commentary on the Book of Common Prayer), show us with what reverent and ceremonious circumstance the worship of that time was rendered.

In this volume of sermons preached upon Christmas Day, his firm grasp of the Doctrine of the Incarnation is clearly manifested; and the close relation between the apprehension of this Verity, and the place in worship of the Blessed Eucharist, is particularly illustrated. To treat with freshness the same topic on seventeen different occasions is, as most preachers will allow, no mean test of power; but in these sermons of Bishop Andrewes no reader can fail to be charmed with the constant variety of treatment displayed in them, the great wealth of Scriptural illustration, and the profound depth of insight, which detects in the most seemingly insignificant details, matter of rich dogmatic truth. He cuts and polishes a text, like a jeweller a diamond, and the rays of truth from its heart of light flash from every facet. As models of division and treatment, and as mines of learning and eloquent illustration, these sermons are invaluable to a preacher, and with a view to specially emphasising this value, an index of Scriptural references has been added to this edition. To the general reader they appeal as devout homilies, which gather many truths about the central doctrine of the Holy Incarnation, and build up Christian conduct and temper upon the sure foundation of dogmatic instruction.

As for the Puritan charge that his puns and quips made the sermons worthless, it may be said that it is easier to attack the manner than the matter of his discourses; and that in common with the men of his day he had a quick ear to detect similarities of sound, and made use of this skill to display similarities and dissimilarities of sense. But no one who has read the sermons could assert that they are marred by the slightest levity of expression. The pithy, balanced phrases would dwell in the memories of those that heard them, but would be the despair of those too dull to imitate them; especially when we remember that the Bishop's delivery was extolled by his contemporaries as highly as his composition. The church at any time would be enriched by the genius of such a preacher; and both preachers and congregations of to-day may learn much from him. That these, his Christmas day sermons, may influence an ever widening audience with their practical, devotional, and doctrinal teaching, is the hope of the   EDITOR.

CONTENTS.

Sermons on the Nativity.

—o—

SERMON I.

A Sermon Preached before the King's Majesty, at Whitehall, on Tuesday, the Twenty-fifth of December, a.d. mdcv., being Christmas-day.

For He in no wise took the Angels'; but the seed of Abraham He took. Hebrews ii. 16.

[*Nusquam enim Angelos apprehendit; sed semen Abrahæ apprehendit.* Latin Vulg.]

AND even because this day He took not the Angels' nature upon Him, but took our nature in "the seed of Abraham," therefore hold we this day as a high feast; therefore meet we thus every year in a holy assembly, even for a solemn memorial that He hath as this day bestowed upon us a dignity which upon the Angels He bestowed not That He, as in the chapter before the Apostle setteth Him forth, That is "the brightness of His Father's glory. the very character of His substance, the Heir of all things, by Whom He made the world," (Heb. i. 3); He, when both needed it—His taking upon Him their nature—and both stood before Him, men and Angels, "the Angels He took not," but men "He took;" was made Man, was not made an Angel; that is, did more for them than He did for the Angels of Heaven.

Elsewhere the Apostle doth deliver the very point positively, and that, not without some vehemency; "Without all question great is the mystery of godliness: God is manifested in the flesh." (1 Tim. iii. 16.) Which is in effect the

A

same that is here said, but that here it is delivered by way of comparison ; for this speech is evidently a comparison.   If He had thus set it down, 'Our nature He took,' that had been positive ; but setting it down thus, 'Ours He took, the Angels' He took not,' it is certainly comparative.

1. Now the masters of speech tell us that there is power in the positive if it be given forth with an earnest asseveration, but nothing to that that is in the comparative.   It is nothing so full to say, 'I will never forget you,' as thus to say it ; " Can a mother forget the child of her own womb? well, if she can, yet will not I forget you." (Isa. xlix. 15.) Nothing so forcible to say thus, 'I will hold my word with you,' as thus, " Heaven and earth shall pass, but My word shall not pass." (Luke xxi. 33.)   The comparative expressing is without all question more significant ; and this here is such.   Theirs, the Angels', *nusquam*, 'at no hand' He took, but ours he did.

2. Now the comparison is, as is the thing in nature whereunto it is made ; if the thing be ordinary, the comparison is according ; but then is it full of force, when it is with no mean or base thing, but with the chief and choice of all the creatures as here it is, even with the Angels themselves ; for then it is at the highest.   1. That of Elihu in Job, that God "teacheth us more than the beast, and giveth us more understanding than the fowls of the air," (Job xxxv. 11) ; that is, that God hath been more gracious to us than to them, being made of the same mould that we are ; that yet He hath given us a privilege above them—this is much.   2. That of the Psalmist, "He hath not dealt so with every nation," (Ps. cxlvii. 20) nay, not with any other nation, in giving us the knowledge of His heavenly truth and laws ; even, that we have a prerogative, if we be compared with the rest of mankind ;—more than the beasts, much ; more than all men besides, much more.   3. But this here *nusquam Angelos*, &c., that He hath given us a pre-eminence above the Angels themselves, granted us that that he hath not granted the Angels—that is a comparison at the very highest, and farther we cannot go.

3. One degree yet more ; and that is this.   As in comparisons making it skilleth much the excellency of the thing wherewithal it is compared, so doth it too the manner how the comparison is made, the pitch that is taken in it.

It is one thing to make it *in tanto*, another, *in toto.* One thing when it is in degrees—that more, this less; this not so much as that, yet that somewhat though—another, when one is, the other is not at all. So is it here; *Assumpsit; non assumpsit;* 'us He did take; the Angels, οὐδήπου, not in any wise;' not in a less, or a lower degree than us, but them 'not at all.' So it is with the highest, and at the highest. So much is said here: more cannot be said.

The only exception that may be made to these comparisons is, that most-what they be odious; it breedeth a kind of disdain in the higher to be matched with the lower, especially to be overmatched with him. We need not fear it here. The blessed Spirits, the Angels, will take no offence at it; they will not remove Jacob's ladder for all this, or descend to us, or ascend for us, (Gen. xxviii. 12) ever a whit the slower because He is become "the Son of Man." (John i. 51.) There is not in them that envious mind that was in the elder brother in the Gospel, when the younger was received to grace after his riotous course. (Luke xv. 28.)

When the Apostle tells us of the "great mystery," that "God was manifested in the flesh," immediately after he tells that He was "seen of the Angels," (1 Tim. iii. 16); and lest we might think they saw it, as we do many things here which we would not see, St Peter (1 Pet. i. 12) tells us that *desiderant prospicere*, that with 'desire and delight' they saw it, and cannot be satisfied with the sight of it, it pleaseth them so well. And even this day, the day that it was done, an Angel was the first that came to bring news of it to the shepherds; and he no sooner had delivered his message, but "presently there was with him a whole choir of Angels," singing, and joying, and making melody, for this εὐδοχία ἐν ἀνθρώποις, this "good-will of God towards men." (Luke ii. 9-14.) So that, without dread of any disdain or exception on the Angels' parts, we may proceed in our text.

I. Wherein first, of the parties compared; Angels and Men.

II. Then, 1. of that, wherein they are compared, 'assumption,' or 'apprehension;' in the word 'taking:' 2. And not every 'taking,' but *apprehensio seminis*, 'taking on Him the seed.'

III. Lastly, of this term, "Abraham's seed;" the choice

of that word, or term, to express mankind by, thus taken on by Him. That He saith not, ' but men He took ; ' or ' but the seed of Adam,' or 'the seed of the woman He took ; ' "but the seed of Abraham He took."

I. Of the parties compared, Angels and men. These two we must first compare, that we may the more clearly see the greatness of the grace and benefit this day vouch-safed us. No long process will need to lay before you, how far inferior our nature is to that of the Angels ; it is a comparison without comparison. It is too apparent ; if we be laid together, or weighed together, we shall be found *minus habentes,* ' far too light.' They are in express terms said, both in the Old and in the New Testament, "to excel us in power," (Ps. ciii. 20, and 2 Pet. ii. 11) ; and as in power, so in all the rest. This one thing may suffice to shew the odds ; that our nature, that we, when we are at our very highest perfection—it is even thus expressed—that we come near, or are therein like to, or as an Angel. Perfect beauty in St Stephen ; " they saw His face as the face of an Angel." (Acts vi. 15.) Perfect wisdom in David ; "my Lord the King is wise, as an Angel of God." (2 Sa. xiv. 20.) Perfect eloquence in St. Paul ; "Though I spake with the tongues of men, nay of Angels." (1 Cor. xiii. 1.) All our excellency, our highest and most perfect estate, is but to be as they ; therefore, they above us far.

But to come nearer ; What are Angels ? Surely, they are Spirits, (Heb. i. 14) ;—Glorious Spirits, (Heb. ix. 5) ;—Heavenly Spirits, (Mat. xxiv. 36) ;—Immortal Spirits. (Luke xx. 36.) For their nature or substance, Spirits ; for their quality or property, glorious ; for their place or abode, Heavenly ; for their durance or continuance, immortal.

And what is " the seed of Abraham " but as Abraham himself is ? And what is Abraham ? Let him answer himself ; " I am dust and ashes." (Gen. xviii. 27.) What is " the seed of Abraham ? " Let one answer in the persons of all the rest ; *dicens putredini,* &c. " saying to rottenness, Thou art my mother ; and to the worms, Ye are my brethren." (Job xvii. 14.) 1. They are Spirits ; now, what are we—what is " the seed of Abraham ? " (Gal. vi. 8.) Flesh. And what is the very harvest of this seed of flesh ? what, but corruption, and rottenness, and worms ? There is the substance of our bodies.

2. They, glorious Spirits; we, vile bodies—bear with it, it is the Holy Ghost's own term; "Who shall change our vile bodies," (Phil. iii. 21)—and not only base and vile, but filthy and unclean; *ex immundo conceptum semine,* 'conceived of unclean seed.' (Job xiv. 4.) There is the metal. And the mould is no better; the womb wherein we were conceived, (Ps. li. 5) vile, base, filthy, and unclean. There is our quality.

3. They, Heavenly Spirits, Angels of Heaven; that is, their place of abode is in Heaven above. Ours is here below in the dust, *inter pulices, et culices, tineas, araneas, et vermes;* Our place is here 'among fleas and flies, moths and spiders, and crawling worms.' There is our place of dwelling.

4. They, immortal Spirits; that is their durance. Our time is proclaimed in the Prophet: flesh; "all flesh is grass, and the glory of it as the flower of the field," (Isa. xl. 6);—from April to June. The scythe cometh, nay the "wind but bloweth and we are gone," withering sooner than the grass which is short, nay "fading" sooner than the "flower of the grass" which is much shorter; nay, saith Job, "rubbed in pieces more easily than any moth." (Job iv. 19.)

This we are to them, if you lay us together. And if you weigh us upon the "balance," we are "altogether lighter than vanity itself," (Ps. lxii. 9); there is our weight. And if you value us, "Man is but a thing of nought," (Ps. cxliv. 4); there is our worth. *Hoc est omnis homo,* this is Abraham, and this is "Abraham's seed;" and who would stand to compare these with Angels? Verily, there is no comparison; they are, incomparably, far better that the best of us.

Now then, this is the rule of reason, the guide of all choice; evermore to take the better and leave the worse. Thus would man do; *Hæc est lex hominis.* Here then cometh the matter of admiration: notwithstanding these things stand thus, between the Angels and "Abraham's seed;"—they, Spirits, glorious, Heavenly, immortal;—yet "took He not" them, yet "in no wise took He them, but the seed of Abraham." "The seed of Abraham" with their bodies, "vile bodies," earthly bodies of clay, bodies of mortality, corruption, and death;—these He took, these He took for all that. Angels, and not men ; so in reason it should be. Men, and not Angels ; so it is ; and, that granted to us, that denied to them. Granted to us, so base, that denied them, so glorious. Denied, and strongly denied ; *οὐ, οὐδήπου*, "not, not in any wise, not at any hand," to them. They, every way, in every thing else, above and before us ; in this, beneath and behind us. And we, unworthy, wretched men that we are, above and before the Angels, the Cherubim, the Seraphim, and all the Principalities, and Thrones, in this dignity. This being beyond the rules and reach of all reason is surely matter of astonishment ; *Τοῦτο*, &c. saith St. Chrysostom, 'this it casteth me into an ecstacy, and maketh me to imagine of our nature some great matter, I cannot well express what.' Thus it is ; "It is the Lord, let Him do what seemeth good in His own eyes." (1 Sam. iii. 18.)

II. And with this, I pass over to the second point. This little is enough, to show what odds between the parties here matched. It will much better appear, this, when we shall weigh the word *ἐπιλαμβάνεται*, that therein they are matched. Wherein two degrees we observed ; 1. *Apprehendit*, and 2. *Apprehendit semen*.

1. Of *apprehendit*, first. Many words were more obvious, and offered themselves to the Apostle, no doubt ; *suscepit*, or *assumpsit*, or other such like. 'This word was sought for, certainly, and made choice of,' saith the Greek Scholiast ; and he can best tell us it is no common word, and tell us also what it weigheth ; *Δηλοῖ δὲ*, saith he, *ὅτι ἡμεῖς ἐφεύγομεν, ὁ δὲ ἐδίωκε, καὶ διώκων ἔφθασε, καὶ φθάσας ἐπελάβετο*, 'this word supposeth a flight of the one party, and a pursuit of the other—a pursuit eager, and so long till he overtake ;' and when he hath overtaken, *ἐπιλαμβανόμενος, apprehendens*, 'laying fast hold, and seizing surely on him.' So two things it supposeth ; 1. a flight of the one, and 2. a hot pursuit of the other.

I. It may well suppose a flight. For of the Angels there were that fled, that kept not their original, but forsook and fell away from their first estate. (Jude, ver. 6.) And man fell, and fled too, and "hid himself in the thick trees" (Gen. iii. 8.) from the presence of God. And this is the first issue. Upon the Angels' flight He stirred not, sat still, never vouchsafed to follow them ; let them go whither they would, as if they had not been worth the while. Nay, He never assumed aught by way of promise for them; no promise in the Old, to be born and to suffer; no Gospel in the New Testament, neither was born nor suffered for them.

But when man fell He did all; made after him presently with *Ubi es?* (Gen. iii. 9.) sought to reclaim him, 'What have you done? Why have you done so?' Protested enmity to him that had drawn him thus away, made His *assumpsit* of " the woman's seed." (Gen. iii. 14, 15.)

And, which is more, when that would not serve, sent after him still by the hand of His Prophets, to solicit his return.

And, which is yet more, when that would not serve neither, went after him Himself in person; left His " ninety-and-nine in the fold," and got Him after the " lost sheep;" never left till He " found him, laid him on His own shoulders, and brought him home again." (Luke xv. 4-5.)

It was much even but to look after us, to respect us so far who were not worth the cast of His eye; much to call us back, or vouchsafe us an *Ubi es?*

But more, when we came not for all that, to send after us. For if He had but only been content to give us leave to come to Him again, but given us leave to " lay hold " on Him, to " touch but the hem of His garment "—Himself sitting still, and never calling to us, nor sending after us— it had been favour enough, far above that we were worth. But not only to send by others, but to come Himself after us; to say, *Corpus apta Mihi, Ecce venio;* " Get Me a body, I will Myself after Him," (Ps. xl. 7);—this was ex-ceeding much, that we fled, and He followed us flying.

2. But yet this is not all, this is but to follow. He not only followed, but did it so with such eagerness, with such earnestness, as that is worthy a second consideration. To follow is somewhat, yet that may be done faintly, and afar off; but to follow through thick and thin, to follow hard and not to give over, never to give over till He overtake— that is it.

And He gave not over His pursuit, though it were long and laborious, and He full weary; though it cast Him into a " sweat," a " sweat of blood." *Angelis suis non pepercit,* saith St Peter, " The Angels offending, He spared not them," (2 Pet. ii. 4): man offending, He spared him, and

to spare him, saith St Paul, "He spared not His own Son."
Nor His own Son spared not Himself, but followed His
pursuit through danger, distress, yea, through death itself.
Followed, and so followed, as nothing made Him leave
following till He overtook.

3. And when He had overtaken, for those two are but presupposed, the more kindly to bring in the word ἐπελάβετο,
when, I say, He had overtaken them, cometh in fitly and
properly ἐπιλαμβάνεται. Which is not every "taking," not
suscipere or *assumere*, but *manum injicere, arripere, appre-
hendere;* "to seize upon it with great vehemency, to lay
hold on it with both hands as upon a thing we are glad we
have got, and will be loath to let go again." We know
assumpsit and *apprehendit* both 'take'; but *apprehendit*
with far more fervour and zeal than the other. *Assumpsit,*
any common ordinary thing; *apprehendit,* a thing of price
which we hold dear, and much esteem of.

Now, to the former comparison, of what they, and what
we, but specially what we, add this threefold consideration;
1. That He denied it the Angels, οὐ: denied it "peremp-
torily," οὐδήπου, neither looked, nor called, nor sent, nor
went after them; neither took hold of them, nor suffered
them to take hold of Him, or any promise from Him;
denied it them, and denied it them thus. 2. But granted
it us, and granted it how? That He followed us first, and
that, with pain; and seized on us after, and that, with great
desire: we flying and not worth the following, and lying
and not worth the taking up. 1. That He gave not leave
for us to come to Him; or sat still, and suffered us to
return, and take hold: yet this He did. 2. That he did
not look after us, nor call after us, nor send after us only:
yet all this He did too. 3. But Himself rose out of His
place, and came after us, and with hand and foot made
after us—followed us with His feet, and seized on us with His
hands; and that, *per viam, non assumptionis, sed appre-
hensionis,* the manner more than the thing itself. All these
if we lay together, and when we have done weigh them
well, it is able to work with us. Surely it must needs
demonstrate to us the care, the love, the affection, He had
to us, we know no cause why; being but, as Abraham was,
"dust," (Gen. xviii. 27); and as Abraham's seed Jacob
saith, "less," and not worthy of any one of these; no, not

of the "meanest of His mercies." (Gen. xxxii. 10.)
Especially, when the same thing so graciously granted us
was denied to no less persons than the Angels, far more
worthy than we. Sure He would not have done it for us,
and not for them, if He had not esteemed of us, made more
account of us than of them.

2. And yet, behold a far greater than all these; which is,
apprehendit semen. He took not the person, but "He took
the seed," that is, the nature of man. Many there be that
can be content to take upon them the persons, and to
represent them, whose natures nothing could hire them
once to take upon them. But the seed is the nature; yea,
as the philosopher saith, *naturæ intimum,* 'the very internal
essence of nature is the seed.' The Apostle showeth what
his meaning is of this 'taking the seed,' when the verse next
afore save one he saith, that "Forasmuch as the children
were partakers of flesh and blood, He also would take part
with them by taking the same." (Heb. ii. 14.) To take
the flesh and blood he must needs take the seed, for from
the seed the flesh and blood doth proceed; which is nothing else but the blessed 'apprehension' of our nature by this
day's nativity. Whereby He and we become not only "one
flesh," (Eph. v. 31, 32), as man and wife do by conjugal
union, but even one blood too, as brethren by natural
union; *per omnia similis,* saith the Apostle, in the next verse
after again, sin only set aside; "Alike and suitable to us in
all things" (Heb. ii. 17), flesh and blood, and nature and
all. So taking "the seed of Abraham," as that He became Himself "the seed of Abraham;" so was, and so
is truly termed in the Scriptures. Which is it that doth
consummate, and knit up all this point, and is the head of
all. For in all other 'apprehensions' we may let go, and
lay down when we will; but this—this 'taking on the seed,'
the nature of man—can never be put off. It is an 'assumption' without a deposition. One we are, He and we, and
so we must be; one, as this day, so for ever.

And emergent or issuing from this, are all those other
'apprehendings,' or seizures of the persons of men—by
which God layeth hold on them, and bringeth them back
from error to truth, and from sin to grace—that have been
from the beginning, or shall be to the end of the world.
That of Abraham himself, whom God laid hold of, and

brought him out of Ur of the Chaldeans, (Gen. xv. 7), and
the idols he there worshipped. That of our Apostle St.
Paul, that was 'apprehended' in the way to Damascus.
(Acts ix. 4.)   That of St. Peter, that in the very act of sin
was 'seized on' with bitter remorse for it. (Luke xxii. 61,
62.)   All those, and all these, whereby men daily are laid
hold of in spirit, and taken from the bye-paths of sin and
error, and reduced into the right way ; and so their persons
recovered to God, and seized to His use.   All these 'apprehensions of the branches' come from this 'apprehension of
the seed,' they all have their beginning and their being from
this day's 'taking,' even *semen apprehendit ;* our receiving
His spirit, for ' His taking our flesh.'   This seed wherewith
Abraham is made the son of God, from the seed wherewith
Christ is made the Son of Abraham.

And the end why He thus took upon Him "the seed of
Abraham" was, because He took upon Him to deliver
"the seed of Abraham."   Deliver them He could not except
He destroyed "death, and the lord of death, the devil."
(Heb. ii. 14.)   Them He could not destroy unless He died;
die He could not except He were mortal ; mortal He could
not be except He took our nature on Him, that is, "the
seed of Abraham."   But taking it He became mortal, died,
destroyed death, delivered us ; was Himself 'apprehended,'
that we might be let go.

One thing more then out of this word *apprehendit*.   The
former toucheth His love, whereby He so laid hold of us,
as of a thing very precious to Him.   This now toucheth
our danger, whereby He so caught us, as if He had not it
had been a great venture but we had sunk and perished.
One and the same word, *apprehendit*, sorteth well to express
both His affection whereby He did it, and our great peril
whereby we needed it.   We had been before laid hold of
and 'apprehended' by one, mentioned in the fourteenth
verse, he that hath "power of death, even the devil ; " we
were in danger to be swallowed up by him, we needed one
to lay hold on us fast, and to pluck us out of his jaws.   So
He did.   And I would have you to mark, it is the same
word that is used to St. Peter in like danger, when, being
ready to sink, ἐπελάβετο, Christ "caught him by the hand,"
(Matt. xiv. 31), and saved him.   The same here in the
Greek, that in the Hebrew is used to Lot and his daughters

in the like danger, when "the Angels caught him, and by strong hand plucked him out of Sodom." (Gen. xix. 16.) One delivered from the water, the other from the fire.

And it may truly be said, inasmuch as all God's promises, as well touching temporal as eternal deliverances, and as well corporal as spiritual, be "in Christ yea, and Amen " (2 Cor. i. 20)—yea, in the giving forth, Amen in the performing —that even our temporal delivery from the dangers that daily compass us about, even from this last [1] so great and so fearful as the like was never imagined before; all have their ground from this great 'apprehension,' are fruits of this Seed here, this blessed Seed, for Whose sake and for Whose truth's sake that we (though unworthily) profess, we were by Him caught hold of, and so plucked out of it; and but for which Seed *facti essemus sicut Sodoma,* "We had been even as Sodom," (Rom. ix. 29), and perished in the fire, and the powder there laid had even blown us up all.

And may not I add to this *apprehendit ut liberaret,* the other in the eighth chapter following, (Heb. viii. 9), *apprehendit ut manu duceret ;* to this of 'taking us by the hand to deliver us,' that 'of taking us by the hand to guide us ;' and so out of one word present Him to you, not only as our Deliverer, but as our Guide too? Our Deliverer to rid us from him that hath "power of death," our Guide to Him that hath 'power of life.' To lead us even by the way of truth to the path of life, by the stations of welldoing to "the mansions in His Father's House." (John xiv. 2.) Seeing He hath signified it is His pleasure not to let go our hands, but to hold us still till He hath brought us, "that where He is, we may also be." (John xiv. 3.) This also is incident to *apprehendit,* but because it is out of the compass of the text I touch it only, and pass it.

And can we now pass by this, but we must ask the question that St. John Baptist's mother sometime asked on the like occasion? *Unde mihi hoc ?* (Luke i. 43) saith she; *Unde nobis hoc ?* may we say. Not, *quod mater Domini,* but *quod Dominus Ipse venit ad nos :* 'Whence cometh this unto us, that the Lord Himself thus came unto us and took us, letting the Angels go ?' Angels are better than the best of us, and reason would ever the better should be taken; how then were we taken that were not the better?

[1] [The Gunpowder Conspiracy.]

Sure, not without good ground, say the Fathers, who have adventured to search out the theology of this point; such reasons as might serve for inducements to Him that is *pronus ad miserendum,* 'naturally inclined to pity;' why upon us He would rather have compassion. And divers such I find; I will touch only one or two of them.

1. First, Man's case was more to be pitied than theirs, because man was tempted by another—had a tempter. The Angels had none—none tempted them; none but themselves. *Et levius est alienâ mente peccâsse quam propriâ,* saith Augustine; 'the offence is the less if it grow from another, than if it breed in ourselves;' and the less the offence, the more pardonable.

2. Again, Of the Angels, when some fell, other some stood, and so they all did not perish. But in the first man all men fell, and so every mother's child had died, and no flesh been saved, for all were in Adam; and so, in and with Adam, all had come to nought. Then cometh the Psalmist's question, *Nunquid in vanum, &c. ?* "What hast Thou made all men for nought?" (Ps. lxxxix. 47.) That cannot be, so great wisdom cannot do so great a work in vain. But in vain it had been if God had not shewed mercy, and therefore was man's case rather of the twain matter of commiseration. (This is Leo.)

3. And thus have they travailed, and these have they found, why He did 'apprehend' us rather than them. It may be not amiss. But we will content ourselves for our *unde nobis hoc ?* 'whence cometh this to us?' with the answer of the Scriptures. Whence, but from "the tender mercies of our God, whereby this day hath visited us?" (Luke i. 78.) *Zelus Domini,* saith Esay, "the zeal of the Lord of Hosts shall bring it to pass." (Isa. ix. 7.) *Propter nimiam charitatem,* (Eph. ii. 4), saith the Apostle; *Sic Deus dilexit,* (John iii. 16), saith He—He Himself; and we taught by Him to say, "Even so, Lord, for so it was Thy good pleasure thus to do." (Luke x. 21.)

III. All this while we are about "taking the seed,"—the seed in general. But now, why "Abraham's seed?" Since it is Angels in the first part, why not men in the second but seed? Or, if "seed" to express our nature, why not "the seed of the woman," but "the seed of Abraham?" It may be thought, because he wrote to the Hebrews, he rather used this term of "Abraham's seed," because so they were, and so loved to be styled, and he would please them. But I find the ancient Fathers go farther, and out of it raise matter both of comfort and direction, and that, for us too.

1. Of comfort, first, with reference to our Saviour, Who taking on Him "Abraham's seed," must withal take on Him the signature of Abraham's seed, and be, as he was, circumcised. There is a great matter dependeth even on that. For being circumcised, He "became a debtor to keep the whole Law of God," (Gal. v. 3) ; which bond we had broken, and forfeited, and incurred the curse annexed, and were ready to be apprehended and committed for it. That so, He keeping the Law might recover back the *chirographum contra nos,* "the handwriting that was against us," (Col. ii. 14), and so set us free of the debt. This bond did not relate to "the seed of the woman," it pertained properly to "the seed of Abraham ;" therefore that term fitted us better. Without fail, two distinct benefits they are : 1. *Factus homo,* and 2. *Factus sub lege ;* and so doth St. Paul recount them. "Made man," that is, "the seed of the woman ;" and "made under the Law," that is, "the seed of Abraham." (Gal. iv. 4.) To little purpose He should have taken the one, if He had not also undertaken the other, and as "the seed of Abraham" entered bond for us, and taken our death upon Him. This first.

2. And besides this, there is yet another ; referring it to the nation, or people, whom He took upon Him. It is sure they were of all other people the most "untoward ;" both of the "hardest hearts," and of the "stiffest necks," (Deut. ix. 6) ; and as the heathen man noteth them, of the worst natures. God Himself telleth them so ; it was no virtue of theirs, or for any pure naturals in them, that He took them to him, for they were that way the worst of the whole earth. And so then the taking of "Abraham's seed" amounteth to as much as that of St. Paul, no less true than "worthy of all men to be received," that He "came into the world to save sinners," (1 Tim. i. 15), and that chief sinners, as it is certain they were ; even "the seed of Abraham," of all the seed of Adam.

2. But not for comfort only, but for direction too doth He use Abraham's name here. Even to entail the benefit coming by it to his seed, that is, to such as he was. For, "for

his sake were all nations blessed." (Gen. xxii. 18). And
Christ, though He took " the seed of the woman," yet doth
not benefit any but " the seed of Abraham," even those that
follow the steps of his faith.   For by faith Abraham (Gen.
xv. 6) took hold of Him by Whom he was in mercy taken
hold of: *Et tu mitte fidem et tenuisti*, saith St Augustine.
That faith of his to him was " accounted for righteousness."
(Rom. iv. 3.)   To him was, and to us shall be, saith the
Apostle, if we be in like sort ' apprehensive' of Him.   Either
as Abraham, or as the true " seed of Abraham " Jacob was,
that took such hold on Him as He said plainly, *Nom dimit-
tam Te, nisi benedixeris mihi ;* " without a blessing he would
not let Him go." (Gen. xxxii. 26.)   Surely, not the Hebrews
alone ; nay, not the Hebrews at all, (Rom. ix. 7), for all their
carnal propagation.   They only are " Abraham's seed,"
that lay hold of the word of promise.   And the Galatians so
doing, though they were mere heathen men as we be, yet
he telleth them they are " Abraham's seed," and shall be
blessed together with him. (Gal. iii. 9.)

But that is not all ; there goeth more to the making us
" Abraham's seed," as Christ Himself, the true Seed,
teacheth both them and us.   Saith He, " If ye be Abraham's
sons, then must you do the works of Abraham," (John viii.
39), which the Apostle well calleth " the steps " (Rom. iv.
12), or impressions of " Abraham's faith ; " or we may call
them the fruits of this seed here.   So reasoneth our Saviour : *Hoc non fecit Abraham ;* " This did not he ; " if ye do
it, ye are not " his seed."   ' This did he ;—do ye the like,
and his seed ye are.'   So here is a double ' apprehension ; '
1. one of St. Paul, 2. the other of St. James (James ii. 22)—
work for both hands to apprehend.   Both 1. *charitas quæ ex
fide ;* and 2. *fides quæ per charitatem operatur.* (Gal. v. 6.)
By which we shall be able, saith St. Paul, " to lay hold of
eternal life," (1 Tim. vi. 12) ; and so be " Abraham's seed "
here at the first, and come to " Abraham's bosom " there at
the last.   So have we a brief of *semen Abrahæ.*

Now what is to be commended to us out of this text for
us to lay hold of?   Verily first, to take us to our meditation,
the meditation which the Psalmist hath, and which the
Apostle in this chapter voucheth out of him at the sixth
verse.   " When I consider," saith he, " the Heavens " (Ps.
viii. 3)—say we, the Angels of Heaven—and see those

glorious Spirits passed by, and man taken, even to sigh with
him, and say, "Lord, what is man," either Adam or Abraham, "that Thou shouldest be thus mindful of him, or the
seed, or sons of either, that Thou shouldest make this do
about him!" The case is here far otherwise—far more
worth our consideration. There, "Thou hast made him a
little lower;" here, 'Thou hast made him a great deal higher
than the Angels.' For they, this day first, and ever since,
daily have and do adore our nature in the personal unity
with the Deity. Look you, saith the Apostle, "when He
brought His only-begotten Son into the world, this He proclaimed before Him, Let all the Angels worship Him,"
(Heb. i. 6); and so they did. And upon this very day's
"taking the seed" hath ensued, as the Fathers note, a great
alteration. Before, in the Old Testament, they suffered David
to sit upon his knees before them, (1 Chron. xxi. 26); since,
in the New, they endure not St. John should fall down to
them, (Rev. xxii. 9), but acknowledge the case is altered now,
and no more superiority, but all fellow-servants. And even
in this one part two things present themselves unto us; 1.
His *humility*, *Qui non est confusus*, as in the eleventh verse
the Apostle speaketh, "Who was not confounded" thus to
take our nature. 2. And withal, the honour and happiness
of Abraham's seed, *ut digni haberentur*, that were 'counted
worthy to be taken so near unto Him.' (Luke xx. 35.)

The next point; that after we have well considered it we
be affected with it, and that no otherwise than Abraham was.
"Abraham saw it," even this day, and but afar off, "and he
rejoiced at it," (John viii. 56); and so shall we on it, if we
be his true seed. It brought forth a *Benedictus* and a *Magnificat*, from the true seed of Abraham; if it do not the
like from us, certainly it but floats in our brains—we but
warble about it; but we believe it not, and therefore neither
do we rightly understand it. Sure I am, if the Angels had
such a feast to keep, if He had done the like for them, they
would hold it with all joy and jubilee. They rejoice of our
good, but if they had one of their own, they must needs do
it after another manner, far more effectually. If we do not
as they would do were the case theirs, it is because we are
short in conceiving the excellency of the benefit. It would
have surely due observation, if it had his due and serious
meditation.

Farther, we are to understand this, that " to whom much is given, of them will much be required," (Luke xii. 48) ; and as Gregory well saith, *Cum crescunt dona, crescunt et rationes donorum,* ' As the gifts grow, so grow the accounts too ;' therefore, that by this new dignity befallen us, *Necessitas quædam nobis imposita est,* saith St. Augustine, ' there is a certain necessity laid upon us' to become in some measure suitable unto it ; in that we are one—one flesh and one blood—with the Son of God. Being thus " in honour," we ought to understand our estate, and not fall into the Psalmist's reproof that we " become like the beasts that perish." (Ps. xlix. 12.) For if we do indeed think our nature is ennobled by this so high a conjunction, we shall henceforth hold ourselves more dear, and at a higher rate, than to prostitute ourselves to sin, for every base, trifling, and transitory pleasure. For tell me, men that are taken to this degree, shall any of them prove a devil, as Christ said of Judas? (John vi. 70) ; or ever, as these with us of late, have to do with any devilish or Judasly fact? Shall any man, after this ' assumption,' be as " horse or mule that have no understanding," (Ps. xxxii. 9), and in a Christian profession live a brutish life ? Nay then, St. Paul tells us farther, that if we henceforth "walk like men" (1 Cor. iii. 3), like but even carnal or natural men, it is a fault in us. Somewhat must appear in us more than in ordinary men, who are vouchsafed so extraordinary a favour. Somewhat more than common would come from us, if it were but for this day's sake.

To conclude ; not only thus to frame meditations and resolutions, but even some practice too, out of this act of ' apprehension.' (Phil. iii. 12.) It is very agreeable to reason, saith the Apostle, that we endeavour and make a proffer, if we may by any means, to ' apprehend ' Him in His, by Whom we are thus in our nature ' apprehended,' or, as He termed it, ' comprehended,' even Christ Jesus ; and be united to Him this day, as He was to us this day, by a mutual and reciprocal ' apprehension.' We may so, and we are bound so ; *vere dignum et justum est.* And we do so, so oft as we do with St. James lay hold of, ' apprehend,' or receive *insitum verbum,* the " word which is daily grafted into us." (James i. 21.) For " the Word " He is, and in the word He is received by us. But that is not the proper of this day, unless there be another joined unto it. This day *Verbum caro factum est,* (John i. 14), and so must be ' apprehended' in both. But specially in His flesh as this day giveth it, as this day would have us. Now "the bread which we break, is it not the partaking of the body, of the flesh, of Jesus Christ?" (1 Cor. x. 16.) It is surely, and by it and by nothing more are we made partakers of this blessed union. A little before He said, " Because the children were partakers of flesh and blood, He also would take part with them," (Heb. ii. 14)—may not we say the same? Because He hath so done, taken ours of us, we also ensuing His steps will participate with Him and with His flesh which He hath taken of us. It is most kindly to take part with Him in that which He took part in with us, and that, to no other end, but that He might make the receiving of it by us a means whereby He might " dwell in us, and we in Him ;" He taking our flesh, and we receiving His Spirit ; by His flesh which He took of us receiving His Spirit which He imparteth to us ; that, as He by ours became *consors humanæ naturæ,* so we by His might become *consortes Divinæ naturæ,* "partakers of the Divine nature." (2 Pet. i. 4.) Verily, it is the most straight and perfect ' taking hold' that is. No union so knitteth as it. Not consanguinity ; brethren fall out. Not marriage ; man and wife are severed. But that which is nourished, and the nourishment therewith—they never are, never can be severed, but remain one for ever. With this act then of mutual ' taking,' taking of His flesh as He hath taken ours, let us seal our duty to Him this day, for taking not " Angels," but " the seed of Abraham."

Almighty God, grant, &c.

SERMON II.

A Sermon Preached before the King's Majesty, at Whitehall, on Wednesday, the Twenty-fifth of December, a.d. mdcvi. being Christmas-Day.

*For unto us a Child is born, and unto us a Son is given;
and the government is upon His shoulder; and He shall
call His Name Wonderful, Counsellor, the Mighty God,
the Everlasting Father, the Prince of Peace.* Esay ix. 6.

[*Parvulus enim natus est nobis, et Filius datus est nobis, et factus est
principatus super humerum ejus: et vocabitur nomen ejus, Admira-
bilis, Consiliarius, Deus, fortis, Pater futuri sæculi, Princeps
Pacis.* Latin Vulg.]

THE words are out of Esay; and, if we had not heard him named, might well have been thought out of one of the Evangelists, as more like a story than a prophecy. " Is born," " is given," sound as if they had been written at, or since the birth of Christ; yet were they written more than six hundred years before.

There is no one thing so great a stay to our faith, as that we find the things we believe so plainly foretold so many years before. " Is born," " is given ? " nay—' shall be ;' speak like a Prophet: nay—" is ; " *loquens de futuro per modum præteriti,* ' speaking of things to come as if they were already past.' (Rom. iv. 17.) This cannot be but of God, " Who calleth things that are not as if they were," and challengeth any other to do the like. (Isa. xli. 23.) It is true, miracles move much ; but yet even in Scripture we read of "lying miracles," (2 Thess. ii. 9), and the possi-bility of false dealing leaveth place of doubt, even in those that be true. But for One, six hundred years before He is born, to cause prophecies, plain direct prophecies to be written of Him, that passeth all conceit; cannot be ima-gined, how possibly it may be, but by God alone. There-fore Mahomet and all false prophets came—at least boasted to come—in signs. But challenge them at this ; not a word, no mention of them in the world, till they were born. True therefore that St. John saith ; " The testimony," that is, the great principal testimony, " of Jesus, is the spirit of pro-phecy." (Rev. xix. 10.) It made St. Peter, when he had recounted what he himself had heard in the Mount (yet as if there might be even in that, *deceptio sensus*), to add *Habemus etiam firmiorem sermonem prophetiæ* (2 Pet. i. 19), "We have a word of prophecy besides;" and that *firmiorem*, the "surer" of the twain.

This prophecy is of a certain Child. And if we ask of this place, as the Eunuch did of another in this Prophet, "Of whom speaketh the Prophet this?" (Acts viii. 34), we must make the answer that there Philip doth, "of Christ;" and "the testimony of Jesus is the spirit of this prophecy." The ancient Jews make the same. It is but a fond shift to draw it, as the latter Jews do, to Ezekias; it will not cleave. It was spoken to Ahaz, Ezekias' father, now King; and that after the great overthrow he had by the kings of Syria and Israel, in the fourth of his reign. But it is deduced by plain supputation out of the eighteenth of the second of Kings, Ezekias was nine years old before Ahaz his father came to the crown. It was by that time too late to tell it for tidings then that he was born, he then being thirteen years of age.

Beside, how senseless is it to apply to Ezekias that in the next verse; that "of His government and peace there should be none end," that "His throne should be established from thenceforth for ever," (Isa. ix. 7); whereas his peace and government both had an end within few years.

To us it is sufficient that the fore-part of the chapter is by St. Matthew expressly applied to our Saviour, (Mat iv. 14); and that this verse doth inseparably depend on that, and is alleged as the reason of it; "For, unto us." Of Him, therefore we take it, and to Him apply it that cannot be taken of any, or applied to any other but Him.

But how came Esay to speak of Christ to Ahaz? Thus: Ahaz was then in very great distress; he had lost in one day eighty thousand of his people, and two hundred thousand of them more, carried away captives. And now the two Kings were raising new power against him, the times grew very much overcast. And this you shall observe. The chiefest prophecies of Christ came ever in such times, that St. Peter did well to resemble the word of prophecy to a candle in *loco caliginoso*, "a dark room." (2 Pet. i. 19.) Jacob's of Shiloh, in Egypt, a dark place, (Gen. xlix. 10); Daniel's of Messias, in Babylon, a place as dark as Egypt, (Dan. ix. 24, 25); this of Esay, when the ten tribes were on the point of carrying away, under Hoshea. That of Jeremy, "a woman shall enclose a man," (Jer. xxxi. 22), when Judah in the same case, under Jechonias. Ever in dark times, who therefore needed most the light of comfort.

But what is this to Ahaz' case? He looked for another message from him, how to escape his enemies. A cold comfort might he think it to be preached to of Immanuel. Indeed, he so thought it; and therefore he gave over Esay, and betook him to Shebna, who wished him to seek to the King of Ashur for help, and let Immanuel go. Yet for all that, even then to speak of Christ, being looked into, it is neither impertinent, nor out of season. With all the Prophets it is usual in the calamities of this people, to have recourse still to the fundamental promise of the Messias. For that, till He were come, they might be sure they could not be rooted out; but must be preserved, if it were but for this Child's sake, till He were born. And yet, if they could believe on Him, otherwise it is no match, (Isa. vii. 9) : *Nisi credideritis.* Then—thus the Prophets argue—He will not deny you this favour, for He will grant you a far greater than this, even His own Son, and by Him a far greater deliverance; and if He can deliver you from the devouring fire of hell, much more from them; and if give you peace with God, much more with them. So teaching those that will learn, the only right way to compass their own safety is by making sure work of "Immanuel, God with us." To the true regard of Whom God hath annexed the "promises as well of this, as of the other life." (1 Tim. iv. 8.) All are as lines drawn from this centre, all in Him "yea and Amen." (2 Cor. i. 20.) Which all serve to raise Ahaz up, and his people, to receive this Child, and "to rejoice in His day," as their "father Abraham" (John viii. 56) did.

Thus the occasion you have heard. The parts, *ad oculum,* 'evidently,' are two; I. a Child-birth, and II. a Baptism. I. The Child-birth in these, "For unto you," &c. II. The Baptism in these, "His Name," &c.

In the former; I. First of the main points, the Natures, Person, and Office; 1. Natures in these, "Child" and "Son." 2. Person in these, "His shoulders," "His name." 3. Office in these, "His government." II. Then of the deriving of an interest to us in these,—"to us," two times. And that is of two sorts: 1. By being "born;" a right by His birth. 2. By being " given ;" a right by a deed of gift.

In the latter, of His Baptism, is set down His style, consisting of five pieces, containing five uses, for which He was thus given ; each to be considered in his order.

I. It is ever our first care to begin with, and to settle the main point of the mystery ; 1. Nature, 2. Person, and 3. Office ; and after, to look to our own benefit by them. To begin with the natures, of God and Man, they be *super hanc petram*, (Mat. xvi. 18) ; upon them lieth the weight of all the rest, they are the two shoulders whereon this government doth rest.

We have two words, " Child," and " Son ;" neither waste. But if no more in the second than in the first, the first had been enough ; if the first enough, the second superfluous. But in this Book nothing is superfluous. So then two diverse things they import.

Weigh the words : " Child " is not said but *in humanis*, ' among men.' " Son " may be *in divinis*, ' from Heaven ;' God spake it, " This is My Son," (Mat. xvii. 5) ; may, and must be, here.

Weigh the other two ; 1. " born," and 2. " given." That which is born beginneth then first to have his being. That which is given presupposeth a former being ; for be it must that it may be given.

Again, when we say " born," of whom ? of the Virgin His mother ; when we say " given," by whom ? by God His Father.

Esay promised the sign we should have should be from the " deep " here " beneath," and should be from the " height above," (Isa. vii. 11) ; both " a child " from " beneath," and " a Son " from " above." To conclude ; it is an exposition decreed by the Fathers assembled in the Council of Seville, who upon these grounds expound this very place so ; the Child, to import His human ; the Son, His divine nature.

All along His life you shall see these two. At His birth ; a cratch for the child, a star for the Son ; a company of shepherds viewing the Child, a choir of Angels celebrating the Son. In His life ; hungry Himself, to shew the nature of the Child ; yet " feeding five thousand," to shew the power of the Son. At His death ; dying on the cross, as the "Son of Adam;" at the same time disposing of Paradise, as the "Son of God."

If you ask, why both these? For that in vain had been the one without the other. Somewhat there must be borne, by this mention of shoulders; meet it is every one should bear his own burden. The nature that sinned bear his own sin; not Ziba make the fault, and Mephibosheth bear the punishment. Our nature had sinned, that therefore ought to suffer; the reason, why a Child. But that which our nature should, our nature could not bear; not the weight of God's wrath due to our sin: but the Son could; the reason why a Son. The one ought but could not, the other could but ought not. Therefore, either alone would not serve; they must be joined, Child and Son. But that He was a Child, He could not have suffered. But that He was a Son, He had sunk in His suffering, and not gone through with it. God had no shoulders; man had, but too weak to sustain such a weight. Therefore, that He might be liable He was a Child, that He might be able He was the Son; that He might be both, He was both.

This, why God. But why this Person the Son? Behold, "Adam would" have "become one of us," (Gen. iii. 22)—the fault; behold, one of Us will become Adam, is the satisfaction. Which of Us would he have become? *Sicut Dii scientes,* 'the Person of knowledge,' (Gen. iii. 5). He therefore shall become Adam; a Son shall be given. Desire of knowledge, our attainder; He in "Whom all the treasures of knowledge," (Colos. ii. 3), our restoring. Flesh would have been the Word, as wise as the Word—the cause of our ruin; meet then the "Word become flesh," (John i. 14), that so our ruin repaired. There is a touch given in the name "Counsellor," to note out unto us which Person, as well as the "Son."

One more; if these joined, why is not the "Son" first, and then the "Child;" but the "Child" is first, and then the "Son." The Son is far the worthier, and therefore to have the place. And thus too it was in His other name Immanuel. (Isa. vii. 14.) It is not *Elimanu;* not *Deus nobiscum,* but *nobiscum Deus.* We in His Name stand before God. It is so in the Gospel; the "Son of David" first, the "Son of God" (Luke iii. 31-38) after. It is but

this still, *zelus Domini exercituum fecit hoc*, (Isa. ix. 7); but
to shew His zeal, how dear He holdeth us, that he pre-
ferreth and setteth us before Himself, and in His very name
giveth us the precedence.

The Person, briefly. The "Child," and the "Son;"
these two make but one Person clearly; for both these
have but one name, "His Name shall be called," and both
these have but one pair of shoulders, "Upon His shoulders."
Therefore, though two natures, yet but one Person in both.
A meet person to make a Mediator of God and man, as
symbolizing with either, God and man. A meet person, if
there be division between them, as there was, and "great
thoughts of heart" for it, to make an union; *ex utroque
unum*, (Eph. ii. 14), seeing He was *unum ex utroque*. Not
man only; there lacked the shoulder of power. Not God
only; there lacked the shoulder of justice; but both together. And so have ye the two Supporters of all, 1. Justice,
and 2. Power. A meet Person to cease hostility, as having
taken pledges of both Heaven and earth—the chief nature
in Heaven, and the chief on earth; to set forward commerce
between heaven and earth by Jacob's ladder, "one end
touching earth, the other reaching to Heaven," (Gen. xxviii.
12); to incorporate either to other, Himself by His birth
being become the "Son of man," by our new birth giving
us a capacity to become the "sons of God." (John i. 12.)

His office; "The kingdom on His shoulders." For
He saw when the child was born, it should so poorly be
born, as, lest we should conceive of Him too meanly, He
tells us He cometh *cum principatu*, 'with a principality,' is
born a Prince; and beautifieth Him with such names as
make amends for the manger. That He is not only *Puer*,
"a Child;" and *Filius*, "a Son;" but *Princeps*, "a
Prince."

Truth is, other offices we find besides. But this you
shall observe, that the Prophets speaking of Christ, in good
congruity ever apply themselves to the state of them they
speak to, and use that office and name which best agreeth
to the matter in hand. Here, that which was sought by
Ahaz, was protection; that we know is for a King; as a
King therefore he speaketh of Him. Elsewhere He is
brought forth by David as a Priest; and again elsewhere by
Moses, as a Prophet. If it be matter of sin for which

sacrifice to be offered, He is "a Priest for ever after the order of Melchizedek." (Ps. cx. 4.) If the will of God, if His great counsel to be revealed, "A Prophet will the Lord raise, &c. hear Him." (Deut. xviii. 18.) But here is matter of delivery only in hand ; here therefore he represented Him *cum principatu*, 'with a principality.'

"A principality, not of this world." Herod need not fear it, nor envy it. If it had, his officers, as they would have seen Him better defended at His death, so would they have seen Him better lodged at His birth, than in a stable (Luke ii. 7) with beasts ; for if the inn were full, the stable we may be sure was not empty. Of what world then ? of that He is Father, *futuri sæculi*. Of that He is Father, and He is a Prince of the government That guideth us thither.

Yet a Prince He is, and so He is styled ; "born" and "given" to establish a "government," that none imagine they shall live like libertines under Him, every man believe and live as he list. It is Christ, not Belial, that is born to-day, He bringeth a government with Him ; they that be His must live in subjection under a government ; else neither in Child nor Son, in Birth nor Gift, have they any interest.

And this "government" is by name a principality, wherein neither the popular confusion of many, nor the factious ambition of a few, bear all the sway, but where One is Sovereign. Such is the government of Heaven, such is Christ's "government."

With a principality, or government, and that upon His shoulders ; somewhat a strange situation. It is wisdom that governs ; that is in the head, and there is the crown worn ; what have the shoulders to do with it ? Certainly somewhat by this description. The shoulder as we know is the bearing member, and unless it be for heavy things, we use it not. Ordinary things we carry in our hands, or lift at the arms' end ; it must be very heavy if we must put shoulders and all to it. Belike, governments have their weight—be heavy ; and so they be ; they need not only a good head, but good shoulders, that sustain them. But that not so much while they be in good tune and temper, then they need no great carriage ; but when they grow un-wieldly, be it weakness or waywardness of the governed, in that case they need ; and in that case, there is no governor

but, at one time or other, he bears his government upon
his shoulders.   It is a moral they give of Aaron's apparel;
he carved the twelve tribes in his breast-plate next his heart,
(Ex. xxviii. 29), to shew that in care he was to bear them;
but he had them also engraven in two onyxstones, and those
set upon his very shoulders, (Ex. xxviii. 12, &c.), to shew,
he must otherwhile bear them in patience too.   And it is
not Aaron's case alone; it was so with Moses too.   He
bare his government as a 'nurse doth her child,' as he
saith, (Numb. xi. 12); that is, full tenderly.   But when
they fell a murmuring, as they did often, he bare them upon
his shoulders, in great patience and long-suffering.   Yea he
complained, *Non possum portare,* "I am not able to bear
all this people," &c. (Numb. xi. 14.)

It were sure to be wished that they that are in place
might never be put to it.   Bear their people only in their
arms by love, and in their breast by care.   Yet if need be,
they must follow Christ's example and patience here, and
even that way bear them; not only bear with them, but
even bear them also.

Yet is not this Christ's bearing, though this He did too;
there is yet a farther thing, He hath a patience paramount,
beyond all the rest.   Two differences I find between Him
and others.   1. The faults and errors of their government,
others do bear, and suffer—indeed suffer them; but suffer
not for them.   He did both; endured them, and endured
for them heavy things; a strange superhumeral, the print
whereof was to be seen on His shoulders.   The Chaldee
Paraphrast translateth it thus, 'The Law was upon His
shoulders;' and so it was too.   A burden, saith St. Peter,
neither he, nor the Apostles, nor their "fathers, were able
to bear." (Acts xv. 10.)   This He did, and bare it so evenly
as He brake, nay bruised not a commandment.   But there
is another sense, when the Law is taken for the punishment
due by the Law.   It is that which our Prophet meaneth
when he saith, *Posuit super humeros,* "He hath laid upon
his shoulders the iniquities of us all." (Isa. liii. 6, &c.)
And not against His will; "Come," saith He, "you that
are heavy laden, and I will refresh you," (Matt. xi. 28), by
loading Myself; take it from your necks, and lay it on
Mine own.   Which His suffering, though it grew so heavy
as it wrung from Him plenty of tears, a strong cry, (Heb. v.

7), a sweat of blood, (Luke xxii. 44),—such was the weight of it;—yet would He not cast it off, but there held it still, till it made Him "bow down His head and give up the ghost." (John xix. 30.) If He had discharged it, it must have light upon us; it was the yoke of our burden, as in the fourth verse He termeth it: if it had light upon us, it had pressed us down to hell, so insupportable was it. Rather than so, He held it still and bare it; and did that which never Prince did—died for His government. It was not for nothing, we see, that of the Child born no part but the shoulders is mentioned; for that, we see, in this Child, is a part of special employment.

2. The other point of difference between Him and other governors. When we say, "On His shoulders," this we say; on no other shoulders but His. For others, by Moses' example upon Jethro's advice and God's own allowance, (Ex. xviii. 23), may, and do lay off and translate their burden, if it be too heavy, upon others, and so ease it in part. Not so He. It could not be so in His. He, and He alone; He, and none but He: upon His own shoulders, and none but His own, bare He all. He "trod the wine-press," and bare the burden *solus*, "alone;" *et vir de gentibus*, "and of all the nations, there was not a man with Him." (Isa. lxiii. 3.) Upon His only shoulders did the burden only rest.

3. Now from these two doth the Prophet argue to a third, to the point here of principal intendment. That if, for His government sake, He will bear so great things; bear their weaknesses as the lost sheep (Matt. xviii. 13, 14), bear their sins as the scapegoat, (Lev. xvi. 8, 9); He will over the government itself, as in Deut. xxxii. (11). He maketh the simile, stretch forth His wings, "as the eagle over her young ones," and take them, and bear them between His pinions—bear them, and bear them through. They need take no thought; "No man shall take them out of His hands," (John x. 28), no man reach them off His shoulders. He had begun so to carry them, and through He would still carry them; at least-wise, till this Child Immanuel were born. Till then He would; and not wax weary, nor cast them off. And, like the scape-goat, bear their sins; and like the eagle, bear up their estate, "till the fulness of time came," (Gal. iv. 4), and He in it, with the

fulness of all grace and blessing. And this point I hold so material as *Puer natus*, nothing, and *Filius datus*, as much, without *Princeps oneratus;* for that is all in all, and of the three the chief.

II. And now, what is this to us? Yes—"to us" it is; and that, twice over, for failing. We come now to look another while into our interest to it, and our benefit by it. *Nobis* is *acquisitive positus;* we get by it—we are gainers by all this.

"To us;" not to Himself. For a far more noble Nativity had He before all worlds, and needed no more birth.— Not to be born at all; specially, not thus basely to be born. Not to Him therefore, but to us and our behoof.

"To us," as in bar of Himself, so likewise of His Angels. *Nusquam Angelos*, not to the Angels (Heb. ii. 16) was He "born," or "given;" but "to us" He was both. Not an Angel in Heaven can say *nobis*. *Vobis* they can, the Angels said it twice. (Luke ii. 11.) *Nobis natus* or *datus* they cannot, but we can, both.

Nobis exclusive, and *nobis inclusive*. Esay speaks not of himself only, but taketh in Ahaz. Both are in *nobis;* Esay, an holy Prophet, and Ahaz, a worse than whom you shall hardly read of. Esay includeth himself as having need though a saint, and excludeth not Ahaz from having part though a sinner. Not only Simeon the just (Luke ii. 25), but Paul the sinner (1 Tim. i. 15), of the *quorum*, and the first of the *quorum*.

Inclusive, not only of Esay, and his countrymen the Jews, it is of a larger extent. The Angel so interpreteth it this day to the shepherds, *Gaudium quod erit omni populo*, "Joy that shall be to all people." (Luke ii. 10.) Not the people of the Jews, or the people of the Gentiles, but simply "to all people." His name is Jesus Christ, half Hebrew, half Greek; Jesus, Hebrew; Christ, Greek; so sorted of purpose to shew Jews and Greeks have equal interest in Him. And now, so is His Father's name too, "Abba, Father," (Mark xiv. 36 and Rom. viii. 15); to shew the benefit equally intended by Him to them that call Him Abba, that is, the Jews; to us that call Him Father, that is, the Gentiles.

But yet, it is *inclusive* of none but those that include themselves—"that believe," (Rom. iii. 22), and therefore say, *nobis,* 'to us He is born, to us He is given.' Which excludes all those that include not themselves. St. Ambrose saith well, *Facit multorum infidelitas ut non omnibus nasceretur qui omnibus natus est;* 'Want of faith makes that He, That is born to all, is not born to all though.' The Turks and Jews can say, *Puer natus est;* the devil can say, *Filius natus est,* too; but neither say *nobis,* but *Quid nobis et Tibi?* They have not to do with Him; and for lack of it, of this, neither Child nor Son, Birth nor Gift, doth avail them: we must make much of this word and hold it fast, for thereby our tenure and interest groweth. Which interest groweth by a double right, and therefore is *nobis* twice repeated. 1. The one, of His birth, *natus;* 2. the other, by a deed of gift, *datus.* Of which the one, His birth, referreth to Himself; the other, the gift, to His Father; to shew the joint consent and concurrence in both, for our good. "So Christ loved us, that He was given," (Eph. v. 2); "so God loved us, that He gave His Son." (John iii. 16.)

By His very birth there groweth to us an interest in Him, thereby partaker of our nature, our flesh, and our blood. That which is *de nobis,* He took of us, is ours; flesh and blood is our own, and to that is our own we have good right.

His humanity is clearly ours; good right to that. But no right to His Deity. Therefore His Father, Who had best right to dispose of Him, hath passed over that by a deed of gift. (John iii. 16.) So that, what by participation of our nature, (Gal. iv. 4), what by good conveyance, both are ours. Whether a Child, He is ours; or whether a Son, He is ours. We gave Him the one; His Father gave us the other. So both ours; and He ours, so far as both these can make Him. Thus, "God, willing more abundantly to shew to the heirs of promise the stableness of His counsel," (Heb. vi. 17), took both courses; that, by two strong titles, which it is impossible should be defeated, we might have strong consolation, and ride as it were at a double anchor.

I want time to tell of the benefit which the Prophet calleth the "harvest" or "booty" (Isa. ix. 3) of His Nativity. That it is in a word: if the tree be ours, the fruit is; if He be ours, His birth is ours, His life is ours, His death is ours; His satisfaction, His merit, all He did, all He suffered, is ours. Farther, all that the Father hath is

His, He is Heir of all, (Heb. i. 2, John iii. 35, Matt. xxviii.
18); then, all that is ours too. (1 Cor. iii. 22, and Rom. viii.
32.) St Paul hath cast up our account. Having given Him,
there is nothing but He will give us with Him ; so that by
this deed we have title to all that His Father or He is
worth.

And now, shall we bring forth nothing for Him That was
thus born? No *Quid retribuam,* (Ps. cxvi. 12)—no giving
back—for Him That gave Him us? Yes—"thanks to the
Father for His great bounty in giving." (2 Cor. ix. 15, and
Col. i. 12.) Sure, so good a giving, so perfect a gift, there
never came down "from the Father of lights." (Jas. i. 17.)
And to the Son, for being willing so to be born, and so to
be burdened as He was. For Him to condescend to be
born, as children are born, to become a child—great
humility ; great, *ut Verbum infans, ut tonans vagiens, ut
immensus parvulus ;* 'that the Word be not able to speak a
word, He that thundereth in Heaven cry in a cradle, He
that so great and so high should become so little as a child,'
and so low as a manger. Not to "abhor the Virgin's
womb," not to abhor the beasts' manger, not to disdain to
be fed with "butter and honey ;" all, great humility. All
great, and very great ; but that is greater is behind. *Puer
natus,* much ; *Princeps oneratus,* much more ; that which he
bare for us, more than that He was born for us : for greater
is *mors crucis* (Phil. ii. 8) than *nativitas præsepis ;* worse to
drink vinegar and gall, than to eat butter and honey ; worse
to endure an infamous death, than to be content with an
inglorious birth.

Let us therefore sing to the Father with Zachary, *Benedictus,* (Luke i. 68) ; and to the Son, with the blessed Virgin,
Magnificat, (Luke i. 46) ; and, with the Angels, *Gloria in
excelsis,* (Luke ii. 14), to the Prince with His "government
on His shoulders."

Nothing but thanks? Yes, by way of duty too, to render
unto the Child, confidence ; *Puer est, ne metuas :* to the Son,
reverence ; *Filius est, ne spernas :* to the Prince, obedience ;
Princeps est, ne offendas. And again, to *natus ;* Is He born?
then cherish Him. I speak of His spiritual birth wherein
we, by hearing and doing His Word, are, as Himself saith,
His mothers. (Matt. xii. 49, 50.) To *datus ;* Is He given?

then keep Him. To *oneratus;* Is He burdened? favour
Him, lay no more on than needs you must.

This is good moral counsel. But St Bernard gives us
politic advice ; to look to our interest, to think of making
our best benefit by Him. *De nobis nato et dato faciamus id
ad quod natus est et datus ; utamur nostro in utilitatem nostram, de Servatore nostro salutem operemur ;* 'with this born
and given Child, let us then do that for which He was born
and given us ; seeing He is ours, let us use that that is ours
to our best behoof, and even work out our salvation out of
this our Saviour.' His counsel is to make our use of Him ;
but that is not to do with Him what we list, but to employ
Him to those ends for which He was bestowed. Those are
four :

1. He is given us, saith St Peter, εἰς ὑπογραμμὸν, "for an
example" (1 Peter ii. 21) to follow. In all ; but—that which
is proper to this day—to do it in humility. It is that
which the Angel set up for a sign and sample, upon this
very day. It is the virtue appropriate to His birth.   As
faith to His conception, *beata quæ credidit;* so humility to
His birth, *et Hoc erit signum. Fieri voluit in vitâ primum,
quod exhibuit in ortu vitæ,* (it is Cyprian ;) that 'He would
have us first to express in our life, that He first shewed us
in the very entry of His life.'   And to commend us this
virtue the more, *Placuit Deo majora pro nobis operari,* ' It
hath pleased Him to do greater things for us in this estate '
than ever He did in the high degree of His Majesty ; as we
know the work of redemption passeth that of creation by
much.

2. He is given us *in pretium,* ' for a price.' A price
either of ransom, to bring us out *de loco caliginoso,* (2 Peter
i. 19) ; or a price of purchase of that, where without it we
have no interest—the Kingdom of Heaven. For both He
is given ; offer we Him for both.   We speak of *quid retribuam ?* we can never retribute the like thing. He was given
us to that end we might give Him back.   We wanted, we
had nothing valuable ; that we might have, this He gave
us as a thing of greatest price to offer for that which
needeth a great price—our sins, so many in number, and
so foul in quality. We had nothing worthy God; this
He gave us that is worthy Him, which cannot be but
accepted, offer we it never so often.   Let us then offer Him

and in the act of offering ask of Him, (Matt. vii. 7, 8), what is meet; for we shall find Him no less bounteous than Herod (Mat. xiv. 6, 7), to grant what is duly asked upon His birth-day.

3. He is given us, as Himself saith, as "the living Bread from Heaven," (John vi. 51), which bread is His "flesh" born this day, and after "given for the life of the world." For look how we do give back that He gave us, even so doth He give back to us that which we gave Him, that which He had of us. This He gave for us in Sacrifice, and this He giveth us in the Sacrament, that the Sacrifice may by the Sacrament be truly applied to us. And let me commend this to you; He never bade, *accipite*, plainly "take," (Mat. xxvi. 26, 1 Cor. xi. 24), but in this only; and that, because the effect of this day's union is no ways more lively represented, no way more effectually wrought, than by this use.

4. And lastly, He is given us *in præmium*; not now to be seen, only in hope, but hereafter by His blessed fruition to be our final reward, when 'where He is we shall be,' and what He is we shall be; in the same place, and in the same state of glory, joy, and bliss, to endure for evermore.

At His first coming, you see what He had "on His shoulders." At His second He shall not come empty, *Ecce venio, &c.* "Lo, I come, and My reward with Me," (Rev. xxii. 12); that is, a "kingdom on His shoulders." And it is no light matter; but, as St. Paul calleth it, αἰώνιον βάρος, "an everlasting weight of glory." (2 Cor. iv. 17.) Glory, not like ours here feather-glory, but true; that hath weight and substance in it, and that not transitory and soon gone, but everlasting, to continue to all eternity, never to have end. This is our state in expectancy. St. Augustine put all four together, so will I, and conclude; *Sequamur* 1. *exemplum*; *offeramus* 2. *pretium*; *sumamus* 3. *viaticum*; *expectemus* 4. *præmium*; 'let us follow Him for our pattern, offer Him for our price, receive Him for our sacramental food, and wait for Him as our endless and exceeding great reward,' &c.

SERMON III.

A SERMON PREACHED BEFORE THE KING'S MAJESTY, AT
WHITEHALL, ON THURSDAY, THE TWENTY-FIFTH OF
DECEMBER, A.D., MDCVII., BEING CHRISTMAS-DAY.

*And without controversy great is the mystery of godliness,
which is, God is manifested in the flesh, justified in the
Spirit, seen of Angels, preached unto the Gentiles, believed
on in the world, and received up in glory.* I TIM. iii. 16.

[*Et manifeste magnum est pietatis sacramentum, quod manifestatum est
in carne, justificatum est in Spiritu, apparuit Angelis, pœdicatum
est Gentibus, creditum est in mundo, assumptum est in gloria.*
Latin Vulg.]

" THE mystery " here mentioned is the mystery of this
feast, and this feast the feast of this mystery ; for as
at this feast " God was manifested in the flesh." In that it
is a great mystery, it maketh the feast great. In that it is a
mystery of godliness, it should make it likewise a feast of
godliness ; great we grant, and godly too we trust. Would
God, as godly as great, and no more " controversy " of one
than of the other !

The manifestation of God in the flesh the Evengelists set
down by way of an history ; the Apostle goeth farther, and
findeth a deep mystery in it, and for a mystery commends
it unto us. Now there is difference between these two,
many—this for one ; that a man may hear a story, and
never wash his hands, but a mystery requireth both the
hands and heart to be clean that shall deal with it.

Speaking of it then as a mystery, the Apostle doth here
propound two things ; I. First, that it is one ; " without
controversy," &c. II. Then, what it is ; " God manifested,"
&c. III. And out of these a third will grow necessarily,
because mysteries will admit a fellowship, how to order the
matter that we may have our " fellowship in this mystery."
(Eph. iii. 9.)

In the first part, four things he affirmeth ; 1. that it is a
" mystery ; " 2. a " mystery of godliness ; " 3. that it is a
" great " one ; 4. a " great one without controversy."

Then doth he, as it were, rend the veil in sunder, and

shew us what it is : 1. " God manifested ; " 2. "manifested in the flesh."

Which mystery, how it may concern us, will be our third and last consideration. And that two ways : 1. by the operation of it in us ; 2. by the initiation of us into it.

A mystery it is, presented to us in that term by the Apostle to stir up our attention. *Omnes homines naturâ scire desiderant,* 'all men even by nature love to be knowing.' The philosopher hath made it his ground, and set it in the front of his metaphysics. So saith philosophy.

And even to this day, saith divinity, doth the "tree of knowledge" (Gen. iii. 6) still work in the sons of Eve ; we still reckon the attaining of knowledge a thing to be desired, and be it good or evil, we love to be knowing, all the sort of us. Knowing ; but what ? Not such things as every one knoweth that goeth by the way, vulgar and trivial ; tush, those are nothing. But metaphysics that are the arcana of philosophy ; mysteries that are the secrets of divinity ; such as few besides are admitted to ; those be the things we desire to know. We see it in the Bethshemites, they longed to be prying into the Ark of God, (1 Sam. vi. 19) ; they were heathen. We see it in the people of God too, they pressed too near the Mount, (Ex. xix. 12) ; rails were fain to be set to keep them back. It is because it is held a point of a deep wit to search out secrets, as in Joseph. (Gen. xli. 45.) At least of special favour to be received so far, as *Vobis datum est nosse mysteria.* (Luke viii. 10.) All desire to be in credit. The mention of mysteries will make us stand attentive ; why then, if our nature like so well of mysteries, *Ecce ostendo vobis mysterium,* " Behold I shew you a mystery," (1 Cor. xv. 51), saith the Apostle.

A " mystery of godliness." The world hath her mysteries in all arts and trades, (yea, mechanical, pertaining to this life ;) which are imparted to none but such as are *filii scientiæ,* 'apprentices to them.' These have their mysteries ; have them, nay are nothing but mysteries. So they delight to style themselves by the name of such and such a mystery. Now *Pietas est quæstus,* and *ad omnia utilis,* a " trade of good return " (1 Tim. vi. 6), to be in request with us ; whether we look " to this life present," saith he, " or to that to come." (1 Tim. iv. 8.) Therefore to be allowed her mysteries ; at least as all other trades are. The rather, for that there is *mysterium iniquitatis*. (2 Thes. ii. 7.) And it were somewhat hard that there should not be *mysterium pietatis*, to encounter and to match it; that "Babylon" should be allowed the name of a "mystery," (Rev. xvii. 5), and Sion not. It were an evident *non sequitur*, that there should be *profunda Satanæ*, "deep things of Satan," (Rev. ii. 24); and there should not be "deep and profound things of God and godliness, for the Spirit to search out." (1 Cor. ii. 10.) But such there be—mysteries of godliness. And we will, I trust, stand affected as in all other trades, so in this, to be acquainted with these; and, as the Apostle speaketh, to pierce *ad interiora velaminis*, "to that which is within the veil," (Heb. vi. 19), to the very "mystery of godliness."

3. It is not only a "mystery of godliness," but a "great" one. The Apostle, where he saith, "If I knew all mysteries," (1 Cor. xiii. 2), giveth us to understand, there be more than one; there is a plurality of them. And here in this place telleth us, they be not all of one scantling; there is *magis* and *minus* in them; some little, some great. 1. Some great, if you will, according to all the dimensions, length and breadth, (Eph. iii. 18), &c. 2. Or great, *virtute, non mole*, 'of greater value, more precious than other.' (2 Pet. i. 4.) 3. Or great, a third way, that is, *gravida mysteriis*, 'one mystery, but hath many mysteries with it.' That such there are, and that this here is one of them, "great." Now that which leadeth us to make account of mysteries, will likewise lead us to make great account of great mysteries, such as this is.

Yet have we not all—one point further. It is a "great" one—a "great one without controversy." For even of those mysteries that are great, all are not great alike. Many great there are, yet is not the greatness of all generally acknowledged *in confesso*. Doubts are made, questions arise about them; all are not *manifeste magna*. We see in our days how men languish about some points, which they would have thought to be great; and great controversies there be, and great books of controversies about them. Well, howsoever it is with other, it is not so with this. This is ὁμολογουμένως, taken *pro confesso*, "great;" "great without controversy;" the manifesting of God in the flesh is a mystery manifestly great. Being then one of the mysteries of religion, a great one among them; so great, as though questions grow about the greatness of others, none may about this; I hope there will be no more question, or controversy of our account, and our great account of it, than there is of the mystery itself, and the greatness of it.

But before we go any further to remove the veil, and shew what it is, let us pause here awhile, till we have rendered thanks to God, and said with Nazianzen, Χάρις τῷ μακαρίῳ Θεῷ, &c. Now yet, blessed be God That, among divers other mysteries about which there are so many mists and clouds of controversies raised in all ages, and even in this of ours, hath yet left us some clear and without controversy; manifest and yet great; and again, great and yet manifest. So great as no exception to be taken; so manifest, as no question to be made about them.

Withal, to reform our judgments in this point. For a false conceit is crept into the minds of men, to think the points of religion that be manifest to be certain petty points, scarce worth the hearing. Those—yea those be great, and none but those, that have great disputes about them. It is not so; Τὰ μὲν ἀναγκαῖα, &c. Those that are necessary He hath made plain; those that [are] not plain not necessary. What better proof than this here? This here a mystery, a great one—religion hath no greater—yet manifest, and *in confesso,* with all Christians. Zachary's prophecy and promise touching Christ, wherewith he concludeth his *Benedictus,* (we hear it every day,) shall not deceive us for this mystery; He came " to guide our feet into the way of peace." (Luke i. 79.) A way of peace then there shall be whereof all parts shall agree, even in the midst of a world of controversies. That there need not such ado in complaining, if men did not delight rather to be treading mazes than to walk in the ways of peace. For even still such a way there is, which lieth fair enough, and would lead us sure enough to salvation; if leaving those other rough labyrinths, we would but be " shod with the preparation of the Gospel of peace." (Eph. vi. 15.)

Yea further the Apostle doth assure us, that if whereunto we are come and wherein we all agree, we would constantly proceed by the rule, those things wherein we are "otherwise minded," (Phil. iii. 15), even them would God reveal unto us. That is, He maketh no controversy but controversies would cease, if conscience were made of the practice of that which is out of controversy. And I would to God it were so; and that this here, and such other *manifeste magna* were in account. With the Apostle himself it was so. He sheweth plainly what reckoning he made of this plain mystery; in that having been " ravished in spirit up to the third heavens, and there heard wonderful high mysteries, past man's utterance," (2 Cor. xii. 2); yet reckoned he all those nothing, in comparison of this plain mystery here, nay "esteemed himself not to know any thing at all," (1 Cor. ii. 2), but this.

And as he esteemed it himself, so would he have us. It is his express charge we see in the verse next before, where he tells his Bishop Timothy how he would have him, his Priests, and Deacons, occupy themselves in his absence. This he commends to them; wills them to be doing with this mystery. That you may know what to do, saith he, what? do but deal with this point; thoroughly deal with it. Howsoever it is manifest, it is great; great regard to be had to it, great pains to be bestowed about it. And even so then let us do, and see now another while this mystery what it is.

II. "God is manifested in the flesh." Being one of the mysteries of godliness, it cannot be but God must be a part, and a chief part of it. And God's being a part maketh it great. For great must that needs be whereof He is a part, of 'Whose greatness there is no end.' And mark first, that it is not *aliquid Dei*, but DEUS; not any thing divine, or of God, but God Himself. Divers things, divers "invisible things of God" (Rom. i. 20) had been formerly made manifest; His eternal power, wisdom, providence, in and since the creation. They be no mysteries, but this is; that not the things of God, but God's own self; not the ἀπαυ-γάσματα, 'the beams of His brightness,' (Heb. i. 3), but the very character of His Substance, the very Nature and Person of God. This is a great mystery.

Of God the Prophet Esay saith, *Vere Deus absconditus es tu,* (Isa. xlv. 15); God is of Himself a mystery, and hidden; and, that which is strange, hidden with light, (1 Tim. vi. 16), which will make any eyes past looking on Him. But a hidden God our nature did not endure. Will you hear them speak it plainly? *Fac nobis deos,* "make us visible gods who may go before us" (Ex. xxxii. 1), and we see them. Mystical, invisible gods we cannot skill of. This we would have ; God to be manifested. Why then, "God is manifested."

"Manifested" wherein ? Sure, if God will condescend to be manifested, there is none but will think it is meet to be, and it would be, in the most glorious creature that is under or above the sun; none, good enough. Yea, in what thing soever, be it never so excellent, for God to manifest Himself in, is a disparagement too. What say you to flesh? is it meet God be manifested therein? "Without controversy" it is not. Why, what is flesh? It is no mystery to tell what it is; it is "dust," (Gen. xviii. 27), saith the Patriarch Abraham. It is "grass," (Isa. xl. 6), saith the Prophet Esay ; *fænum*, "grass cut down, and withering." It is "corruption," (1 Cor. xv. 54), not corruptible, but even corruption itself, saith the Apostle Paul. There being then, as Abraham said to him, χάσμα μέγα, 'so great a gulf, so huge a space, so infinite a distance' (Luke xvi. 26) between those two, between God and dust, God and hay, God and corruption, as no coming of one at the other ; *sileat omnis caro*, "talk not of flesh." (Zech. ii. 13.) Were it not a proud desire and full of presumption, to wish things so remote to come together? to wish that the Deity in the flesh may be made manifest? Yet we see wished it was, by one in a place in reasonable express terms; "O that thou wert as my brother, that sucked the breasts of my mother!" (Cant. viii. 1.) That is, O that He might be "manifested in the flesh!" O that He might be ! and so He was. Not only manifest at all; that is great : but manifest in the flesh; that is greater. For if gold mixed though it be with silver is abased by it, what if it be mixed with the rust of iron or dross of lead? This must needs be great in itself, but greater with us ; with us especially that make such ado at any though never so little disparagement; and that if any, though not much our inferior, be ranked with us, take ourselves mightily wronged. We cannot choose but hold this mystery for great, and say with St Augustine, *Deus ; quid gloriosius ? Caro; quid vilius ? Deus in carne ; quid mirabilius ?* 'God ; what more glorious? flesh ; what more base? Then, God in the flesh ; what more marvellous ?'

But I ask further, "manifested in the flesh?" what flesh? or how manifested? In what flesh? What! in the pride and beauty of our nature? No; but in the most disgraceful estate of it that might be. And how manifested? *Ad glóriam,* 'for His credit or glory?' No; but *ad ignominiam,* 'to His great contempt and shame.' So to have been manifested as in the holy mount, "His face as the sun," His garments as "lightning," (Matt. xvii. 2); between Moses and Elias, in all glory and glorious manner—this had not been so great an impeachment. Was that the manner? No; but how? In clouts, in a stable, in a manger. The God Whom "the heavens and the heaven of heavens cannot contain," in a little child's flesh not a span long; and that flesh of a child not very well conditioned, as you may read in the sixteenth of Ezekiel. (Ezek. xvi. 4, 5, &c.)

So to-day, but after much worse. To-day, in the flesh of a poor babe crying in the cratch, *in medio animalium;* after, in the rent and torn flesh of a condemned person hanging on the Cross, *in medio latronum,* in the midst of other manner persons than Moses and Elias; that men even hid their faces at Him, not for the brightness of His glory, but for sorrow and shame. Call you this manifesting? Nay, well doth the Apostle call it the "veil of His flesh," (Heb. x. 20), as whereby He was rather obscured than any way set forth; yea eclipsed in all the darkest points of it. Verily the condition of the flesh was more than the flesh itself, and the manner of the manifestation far more than the manifestation itself was. Both still make the mystery greater and greater.

And now to weigh the word "manifested" another while; because that may seem to be *terminus diminuens,* 'a qualified term,' rather abating than any way tending to make great the mystery; in that a thing may be manifested and not be that for which it is manifested, be manifested for one thing and be another. Would to God we had not too plain examples of these even in that we are about, in godliness itself; that there were not that manifested themselves ἐν μορφώσει, "in the vizor or mask of godliness," (2 Tim. iii. 5), but be nothing less. Well this, how or wheresoever it may be with men, with God it is not; He is not like to us; and howsoever, not here in this. For first, it is not in the shadow, show, or shape of flesh, but in very flesh itself. Then it is not, saith the Greek Scholiast, φανθεις, but φανερωθεις: φανθεις, which importeth but 'an apparition, transitory, for a season, and then vanisheth again;' but φανερωθεις, 'a manifestation;' such as is, say they, permanent, which passeth not, but lasteth for ever. And to put all out of question that here is *nihil personatum,* but even *persona,* He that here is said to be "God manifested in the flesh," is in another place said to be *Verbum caro factum,* "the Word made flesh." (John i. 14.) So manifested that made; so taking our nature, as His and it are grown into one person, never to be severed or taken in sunder any more. And in sign thereof that flesh wherein He is manifested in the beginning of the verse, in the end of the verse in the very same flesh He is "received up into glory," and in the same shall appear again at His second manifestation.

And yet to go further; I say that this word "manifested" is so far from being *terminus diminuens,* that it doth greatly ampliate and enlarge the mystery yet still. To be and to be manifested, *esse* and *videri, dici de* and *esse in,* are two things. And as in some cases it is more to be than to be manifested, so in some other it is more to be manifested than to be; and namely in this here. More for God to be manifested, than to be in the flesh. It is well known, when a great high person doth fall into low estate, he careth not so much for being so, as for appearing such; manifest him not, and you do him a pleasure. More it is for him to be made known, than to be that he is. O it is naturally given us to hide our abasing what we can. Our misery must be kept in a mystery, and that mystery not manifested in any wise. "Blow a trumpet in Sion," (Joel ii. 1), if any good come to us; but whist, "let it not be heard in Gath, nor in Ascalon," (2 Sam. i. 20), if any evil fall upon us. Not so much as Naomi, we see, but when she was fallen into poverty, she could not endure to be called by that name (Ruth i. 20); no, her name was Mara, as if she had been some other party; so loath was she to have her misery made manifest. Humility intrinsical is not so much; it is the manifesting our humility that poseth us. That David should have been humble in heart before God and His Ark, that Michal could have borne well enough. This was the grief; that David must make it manifest, "uncover himself, wear an ephod," and thereby as she thought mightily disgrace and make himself "vile in the eyes of his servants." (2 Sam. vi. 20.) That was it she took so ill; not to be so much as to be manifest; that same manifesting marred all. And why would Nicodemus come to Christ but not but by candlelight, (John xix. 39), but that to be seen manifestly to come, was with him a far greater matter than to come. By all which it appeareth, that in case of abasement to seem is more than to be; *dici de* than *esse in ;* and so here *nosci* more than *nasci.* And I make no question but we may reckon these two as two distinct degrees. 1. He abhorred not to become flesh. 2. He abhorred not to have it manifestly known. It was not done, this, in a corner, (Acts xxvi. 26), in an out-corner of Galilee; but in the city of David. His poor clouts manifested by a star, (Matt. ii. 10, 11); His shameful death published by a great eclipse; yea that it might be manifest indeed, (as it followeth after in the verse), He would have it preached over all the world.

But when we have done and said all that ever we can, if we had all mysteries and no love, (1 Cor. xiii. 1), the Apostle tells us it is nothing. We can have no mystery except love be manifest. So is it. Two several times doth the Apostle tell us, 1. *apparuit gratia,* (Tit. ii. 11); 2. *apparuit amor erga homines.* (Tit. iii. 4.) At the opening of this mystery there appeared the 1. grace of God, and the 2. love of God toward mankind. *Velatio Deitatis, revelatio charitatis ;* ' as manifest as God was in the flesh, so manifest was His love unto flesh.' And then, because great love a great mystery, *Dilexit* goeth never alone, but with *sic ;* so Christ, (John iii. 16); *ecce quantam charitatem ;* so St. John. (1 John iii. 1.) Sure, how great and apparent humility, so great and apparent love. And His humility was too apparent. So we have "God manifested in the flesh," *Deus charitas,* (1 John iv. 8); for if ever He were love or shewed it, in this He was it, and shewed it both. God that is "love" was "manifested in the flesh."

To make an end, one question more. To what end? *Cui bono?* 'who is the better for all this?' God that is manifested, or the flesh wherein He is manifested? Not God; to Him their groweth nothing out of this manifestation. It is for the good of the flesh, that "God was manifested in the flesh." 1. For the good present: for we let go that of the Psalmist now, "Thou that hearest the prayer, to Thee shall all flesh come," (Ps. lxv. 2); and much better and more properly say, 'Thou that art manifested in the flesh, to Thee shall all flesh come; with boldness entering into the holy place, by the new and living way prepared for us through the veil, that is, His flesh.' (Heb. x. 19, 20.) 2. And for the good to come; for we are put in hope that the end of this manifesting God in the flesh will be the manifesting of the flesh in Him, even as he is; and that which is the end of the verse be the end of all, "the receiving us up into His glory." To this haven arriveth this mystery of the manifestation of it.

III. The end of this second part is but the beginning of the third. For hearing that it is so great and of so great avail rising by it, that it is *quæstus multo uberrimus*, 'a trade so beneficial;' it makes us seek how to incorporate ourselves, as in the third of the Ephesians he speaketh, how to have our part and fellowship in this trade or mystery. (Eph. iii. 6, 9.) And that may we do, saith he in the same place, *si operetur in nobis*, (Eph. iii. 7), that is, 'if it prove to us, as it is in itself, a mystery.' I know it were a thing very easy for a speculative Divine to lead you along, and let you see that this mystery is the substance of all the ceremonies, and the fulfilling of all prophecies; that all Moses' veils, and all the Prophets' visions, are recapitulate in it. But it is a point of speculation; we hear those points too often, and love them too well: points of practice are less pleasing, but more profitable for us; namely, how we may get into the partnership of this mystery.

There is this difference between a ceremony and a mystery. A ceremony represents and signifies, but works nothing; a mystery doth both. Beside that it signifieth, it hath his operation; and work it doth, else mystery is it none. You may see it by the mystery of iniquity; that doth *operari*, 'was at work' (2 Thes. ii. 7) in the Apostles' time; and it is no way to be admitted, but that the "mystery of godliness" should have like operative force.

If you ask what it is to work? It is to do, as all other agents; *ut assimulet sibi passum*, 'to make that it works on like itself;' to bring forth in it the very same quality. This the rather, for that this day being a birth-day, and the mystery of it a birth or generation; in that, we know, the natural and most proper work is *sui simile procreare,* 'to beget and bring forth the very like to itself.' And what should the "mystery of godliness" beget in us but godliness? What the "mystery of godliness" in this chapter, but the exercise of godliness in the next? (1 Tim. iv. 7.) To shew, we must make St. Basil's ἀσκητικὰ of it; for his ἀσκητικὰ and St. Paul's γυμναστικὰ I take to be all one.

First within, after the manner of a mystery, by entering into ourselves and saying with St. Peter, "Seeing then God hath so dealt with us, what manner of persons ought we to be, in all holy conversation and godliness?" (2 Pet. iii. 11.) How ought we to esteem Him that so esteemed us? How to esteem ourselves whom He hath so esteemed? How without soil or spot (Jam. i. 27) to keep that flesh wherein God hath "manifested" Himself, that nothing come from it but such as may become that flesh which is now all one with the flesh of the Son of God.

Provided that it be not all within; for we deal not with a mystery alone, but with a manifestation too. That therefore our godliness be not only mystical but manifest, as God was. As the mystery, so the godliness of it; "great" and conspicuous, both. For that is the complaint, that in our godliness, nowadays, we go very mystically to work indeed; we keep it under a veil, and nothing manifest but *opera carnis.* (Gal. v. 19.) Which maketh St. James cry, *ostende mihi,* "shew it me," (Jam. ii. 18); and St. Paul tells us, that the life of Jesus must not only be had in our spirit, but manifest in our flesh. (2 Cor. iv. 10, 11.) For godliness is not only faith, which referreth to the mystery as we have it directly at the ninth verse, the "mystery of faith;" but it is love too, which referreth to the manifestation. For in *hoc cognoscimus,* saith St. John, "by this we know, ourselves," (1 John iii. 14, and iv. 13); and, in *hoc cognoscent omnes,* saith Christ, "by this shall all men know" (John xiii. 35) that we are His. And if faith work by love, the mystery will be so manifest in us, as we shall need no prospective glasses, or optic instruments, to make it visible; all men shall take notice of it.

And yet remaineth there one point, than which there is not one more peculiar to a mystery. That which the Apostle calleth initiating, (Heb. x. 20); whereby we grow into the fellowship of this and what mysteries soever. For this we are to understand, that mysteries go not all by hearing; no, they be dispensed also : and men are to esteem of us, saith he, not only as of the unfolders, but, as of "the stewards," or dispensers "of the mysteries of God." (1 Cor. iv. 1.) *Operari mysteriis* is a phrase well known to the very heathen themselves; that mysteries, as they work, so they are to be wrought. That they are to be handled, and that our hands are to be clean washed yet we offer to touch them.

By which I understand the mystery of godliness, or exercise of godliness—call it whether ye will—which we call the Sacrament ; the Greek hath no other word for it but Μυστήριον, whereby the Church offereth to initiate us into the fellowship of this day's mystery. Nothing sorteth better than these two mysteries one with the other ; the dispensation of a mystery with the mystery of dispensation. It doth manifestly represent, it doth mystically impart what it representeth. There is in it even by the very institution both a manifestation, and that visibly, to set before us this flesh ; and a mystical communication to infeoffe us in it or make us partakers of it. For the elements ; what can be more properly fit to represent unto us the union with our nature, than things that do unite themselves to our nature? And if we be to dispense the mysteries in due season, what season more due than that His flesh and blood be set before us that time that He was "manifested in flesh and blood" for us? Thus we shall be initiate.

You look to hear of a consummation of it too ; and consummate it shall be, but not yet ; not till the days of the voice of the seventh Angel. Then shall the mystery of God be finished. (Rev. x. 7.) So we find it directly, but not before. When He that was this day "manifested in the flesh," shall manifest to the flesh the fulness of this mystery, His eternity, glory, and bliss. So, still it remaineth a mystery in part ; a part thereof there still remaineth behind to be manifested. What He is appeareth ; what we shall be doth not yet appear, but shall at the second appearing. Two veils we read of : 1. The veil of His flesh, (Heb. x. 20) ; 2. And the veil where our hope hath cast anchor, even within the veil, meaning Heaven itself. The first is rent ; these mysteries are remembrances of it. The second also shall be, as we also with it ; and as He, in the end of the verse, so we with Him in the end shall be "received up into glory." To the consummation of which great mystery, even that great manifestation, He vouchsafe to bring us all, That was this day for us all "manifested in the flesh," "Jesus Christ the righteous," (1 John ii. 1), &c.

———o———

SERMON IV.

A Sermon Preached before the King's Majesty, at Whitehall, on Monday, the Twenty-fifth of December, a.d. mdcix., being Christmas-day.

When the fulness of time was come, God sent His Son, made of a woman, made under the Law.
That He might redeem them that were under the Law, that we might receive the adoption of sons. Gal. iv. 4, 5.

[*At ubi venit plenitudo temporis, misit Deus Filium suum factum ex muliere, factum sub Lege,*
Ut eos, qui sub lege erant, redimeret, ut adoptionem filiorum reciperemus.
Latin Vulg.]

IF, when the "fulness of time" cometh, "God sent His Son," then when "God sent His Son," is "the fulness of time" come. And at this day "God sent His Son." This day therefore, so oft as by the revolution of the year it cometh about, is to us a yearly representation of "the fulness of time." So it is; and a special honour it is to the feast that so it is. And we ourselves seem so to esteem of it. For we allow for every month a day—look how many months so many days—to this feast, as if it were, and we so thought it to be, the full recapitulation of the whole year.

This honour it hath from Christ who is the Substance of this and all other solemnities. Peculiarly, *a Christi missa,* 'from Christ's sending.' For they that read the ancient writers of the Latin Church, Tertullian and Cyprian, know that *missa* and *missio,* and *remissa* and *remissio,* with them are taken from one. So that *Christi missa,* is the sending of Christ. And when then hath this text place so fit as now? Or what time so seasonable to entreat of it as this? of the sending of His Son, as when "God sent His Son;" ot "the fulness of time," as on the yearly return and memorial of it?

To entreat of it then. The heads are two: I. Of "the fulness of time." II. And of that wherewith it is filled. I. Time's fulness in these, "When the fulness of time came." II. Time's filling in the rest, "God sent His Son, made of a woman, made under the Law," &c.

In the former, *Quando venit plenitudo temporis*, there be four points: 1. *Plenitudo temporis*, 'that time hath a fulness;' or, 'that there is a fulness of time.' 2. *Venit plenitudo*, 'that that fulness cometh by steps and degrees;' not all at once. 3. *Quando venit;* that it hath a *quando*, that is, 'there is a time when time thus cometh to this fulness.' 4. And when that *when* is? and that is "when God sent His Son." And so pass we over to the other part in the same verse, *Misit Deus;* "God sent His Son."

For the other part, touching the filling of time. There be texts, the right way to consider of them is to take them in pieces, and this is of that kind. And if we take it in sunder, we shall see as it is of fulness so a kind of fulness there is in it, every word more full than other; every word a step in it whereby it riseth still higher, till by seven several degrees it cometh to the top and so the measure is full. 1. "God sent," the first. 2. "Sent His Son," the second. 3. "His Son made," the third. 4. And that twice made; "made of a woman," the fourth. 5. "Made under the law," the fifth; every one fuller than other, still.

And all this, for some persons, and some purpose; the persons *ut nos*, "that we." The purpose, *reciperemus*, "that we might receive." Nay, if you mark it, there be two *uts*, 1. *ut ille;* 2. *ut nos*, "that He might," and that "we might." He might redeem, and we might receive; that is, He pay for it, and we reap the benefit. 6. A double benefit, of 1. Redemption, first, from the state of persons cast and condemned under the Law, which is the sixth. 7. And then, of 2. Translation into the state of adopted children of God, which is the seventh, and very filling up of the measure.

All which we may reduce to a double fulness: God's as much as He can send; ours as much as we can desire. God's in the five first. 1. "God sent." 2. "Sent His Son." 3. "His Son made." 4. "Made of a woman." 5.

"Made under the Law." And ours in the two latter ; 6. "We are redeemed," the sixth. 7. "We receive adoption," the seventh.

In that of God's every point is full. The thing sent, full ; the sending, and the manner of sending, full. The making, and the two manners of making, 1. "of a woman," and 2. "under the Law," both full. And our fulness in the two latter, the effects of those two acts or makings, 1. "of a woman," 2. "under the Law," redemption and adoption, which make up all. That when we were strangers from the adoption, and not that only, but lay under the Laws, as men whom sentence had passed on ; from this latter we are redeemed—He "under the Law," that we from under the Law—that being so redeemed we might further "receive the adoption of children," and as He the "Son of Man," so we might be made the "sons of God"—which two are as much as we can wish. And this is our fulness.

And to these I will crave leave to add another fulness of ours, rising out of these, and to make a motion for it. That as it is the time when we from God receive the fulness of His bounty, so it might be the time also when He from us may likewise receive the fulness of our duty. The time of His bountifulness, and the time of our thankfulness : that it may be *plenitudo temporis, qua ad illum, qua ad nos ;* 'downward and upward, from Him to us and from us to Him again ;' and so be both ways "the fulness of time."

Quando venit plenitudo temporis.

I. First there is a fulness in time. The term "fulness" carrieth our conceit to measure straight from whence it is borrowed ; which is then said to be full when it hath as much as it can hold. Now "God hath made all things in measure," (Wis. xi. 20) ; and if all things then time. Yea time itself is by the Apostle called *mensura temporis,* "the measure of time." (Eph. iv. 13.) As then all other measures have theirs ; so the measure of time also hath his fulness, when it receiveth so much as the capacity will contain no more. So time is a measure ; it hath a capacity ; that hath a fulness. That there is such a thing as "the fulness of time."

But nothing is full at first ; no more is time by and by.

Venit plenitudo, it cometh not at once or straightways, but by steps and paces, nearer and nearer; fills first a quarter, and then half, till at last it come to the brim. And degrees there be by which it cometh. *Ecce palmares posuisti dies meos,* (Ps. xxxix. 5); from which word [*palmares*] it is an observation of one of the Fathers, "a man may read his time." In his own hand visibly there is an ascent, the fingers rise still till they come to the top of the middle finger; and when they be come thither, down again by like descent till they come to the little which is the lowest of all. So is it in our time. It riseth still by degrees till we come to the full pitch of our age, and then declineth again till we grow to the lower end of our days. But, howsoever it may be—as it oft falls out—the descent is sudden, we go down headlong without degrees, go away in a moment; yet ever this holdeth, to our fulness we come not but by degrees.

Now thirdly, this coming hath a *quando venit,* 'a time when it cometh thither.' As a time there is a great while when we say, *nondum venit hora,* "the time is not yet come" (John vii. 8), while the measure is yet but in filling; so at the last a time too that we may say *venit hora,* "the time is now come," (John xii. 23), when the measure is full; that is, a time there is when time cometh to the full. As in the day, when the sun cometh to the meridian line; in the month, when it cometh to the point of opposition with the moon; in the year, when to the solstice; in man, when he cometh to his full years; for that is the "fulness of time" the Apostle allegeth in three verses before.

And when is that *when* that time thus cometh to his fulness? *Quando misit Deus,* 'when God sends it;' for time receives his filling from God. Of itself time is but an empty measure, hath nothing in it. Many days and months run over our heads, *Dies inanes,* (Ps. lxxviii. 33), saith the Psalmist; *Menses vacui,* (Job vii. 3), saith Job, "empty days," "void months," without any thing to fill them.

That which filleth time is some memorable thing of God's pouring into it; or, as in the text, of His sending to fill it withal. *Misit Deus* is it; and so cometh time to be more or less full, thereafter as that is which God sends to fill it.

Now many memorable missions did God make before this here, whereby in some measure He filled up certain times of the year under Moses and the Prophets ; all which may well be termed, The implements of time.

But for all them, the measure was not yet full ;—filled perhaps to a certain degree, but not full to the brim ; full it was not, seeing it might be still fuller, till God sent That than Which a more full could not be sent.

And That He sent when "He sent His Son," a fuller than Whom He could not send, nor time could not receive. Therefore with the sending Him when that was, time was at the top, that was the *quando venit*, then it was *plentitudo temporis* indeed.

And well might that time be called "the fulness of time." For when He was sent into the world, "in Whom the fulness of the Godhead dwelt bodily," (Col. ii. 9) ; in Whom "the Spirit was not by measure," (John iii. 34) ; in Whom was "the fulness of grace and truth," (John i. 14) ; "of Whose fulness we all receive," (John i. 16) ;— when He was sent That was thus full, then was time at the full.

And well also might it be called "the fulness of time" in another regard. For till then all was but in promise, in shadows and figures and prophecies only, which fill not, God knows. But when the performance of those promises, the body of those shadows, the substance of those figures, the fulfilling or filling full of all those prophecies came, then came "the fulness of time," truly so called. Till then it came not ; then it came.

And well might it be called "the fulness of time" in a third respect. For then the heir, that is, the world, was come to his full age ; and so that the fittest time for Him to be sent. For to that compareth the Apostle their estate then ; that the former times under Moses and the Prophets were as the nonage of the world, *sub pædagogo*, (Gal. iii. 24), ὑπὸ στοιχεῖα, at their A. B. C. or rudiments, (as in the very last words before these). Their estate then, as of children in their minority, little differing from servants. For all this while, *nondum venit*, "the fulness of time" has not yet come. But a time there was, as for man, so for mankind to come to his full years ; that time came with Christ's coming, and Christ's coming with it, and never till then was "the fulness of time ;" but then it was.

And let this be enough for this point ; more there is not

in the text. But if any shall further ask why then, at that age of the world the world was at his full age, just then and neither sooner nor later? I know many heads have been full of devices, to satisfy men's curiosity in that point. But I hold it safest to rest with the Apostle, in the second verse, on God's ὑποθεσμία. Let that content us. Then was the time, for that was *tempus præfinitum a Patre*, "the time appointed of the Father." For even among men, though— the father being dead—the law setteth a time for the son to come to his heritage; yet the father living, no time can be prefixed, but only when it liketh him to appoint; and the Father here liveth; and therefore let His προθεσμία stay us. "The times and seasons He hath put in His own power, it is not for us to know them." (Acts i. 7.) This is for us to know, that with His appointment, we must come to a full point. So doth the Apostle, and so let us, and not busy ourselves much with it; time is but the measure or cask, that wherewith it is filled doth more concern us. To that therefore let us come.

II. The degrees are seven, as I said. To take them as they rise. *Misit Deus*, "God sent." That standeth first, and at it let our first stay be. That will fall out to make the first degree. For even this, that God sent at all, *ipsum mittere Dei*, this very sending itself is a degree. It is so; and so we would reckon of it, if we knew the Sender, and Who He is; the Majesty of His presence how great it is, and how glorious, how far surpassing all we can see on earth.

For Him—for such an one as He—to condescend but to send, is sure a degree. For enough it had been, and more than enough for Him, to be sent to; and not to send Himself. To have sit still, and been content that we might send to Him, and have our message and petition admitted, and not He send to us. That had been as much as we could look for, and well if we might have been vouchsafed but that. But it was He that sent; not we to Him first, nay not we to Him at all, but He to us.

He to us! And what were we that He to us? Us, as elsewhere He termeth us, "mere aliens" (Eph. ii. 12) from Him and His Household; not that only, but us, in case of men whom the law had passed upon. So is our estate described in the end of the text. For Him to send to us, so great as He to such as we; to think us *tanti*, 'so much

D

worth,' as to make any mission, or motion, or to disease any about us—this may well be the first. Be it then so ; that to us, or for us, or concerning us, God would trouble Himself to make any sending; a fulness there is in this. Full He was ; a fulness there was in Him—even the fulness of compassion in His bowels over our estate—else such a Sender would never once have sent.

" God sent ;" " sent," and " sent His Son." That I make no question will bear a second. Others He might have sent; and whosoever it had been He had sent, it might well have served our turns. If sent by the hand of any His servants, any Patriarch, Prophet, any ordinary messenger, it had been enough. So hitherto had been His sending. So, and no otherwise, ever till now.

Then, if to send by any may seem sufficient, to send " His Son" must needs seem full. For ever the more excellent the person sent, the more honourable the sending ; the greater he, the fuller it. Now greater there is not than " His Son," His first, His only-begotten Son, " in Whom the fulness of the Godhead dwelt, (Col. ii. 9) ; in sending Him He sent the greatest, the best, the fullest thing He had.

To heap the measure up yet more with the cause of His sending, in the word ἐξαπέστειλε. It was voluntary. He sent him not for need ; but for mere love to us, and nothing else. There was no absolute necessity that he should have sent Him. He might have done what He intended by the means and ministry of some besides. God could have enabled a creature ; a creature enabled by God, and the power of His might, could soon have trod down Satan under our feet. But if it had been any other He had sent, His love and regard to us had not shewed so full. It had been, *Ostendit Deus charitatem*, but not *Ecce quantam charitatem ostendit Deus*. (1 John iii. 1.) Whomsoever He had sent besides, His love had not been full ; at least, not so full as it should have been, if He had sent His Son. That therefore it might be full, and so appear to us for full, *Misit Deus Filium suum*. Enough it was, in compassion of our estate, to have relieved us by any. Men that are in need to be relieved care not who they be that do it. Enough then for compassion ; but not enough to manifest the fulness of His love unless to relieve us He sent His own Son.

This is full one would think; yet the manner of His sending Him is fuller still. *Misit Filium; Filium factum.* "Send His Son;" "His Son made." Sent Him, and sent Him "made." This is a third. For if He would have sent Him, He should not have sent Him "made;" but as He was, "neither made nor created," but like Himself in His own estate, as was meet for the Son of God to be sent. To make Him anything is to mar Him, be it what it will be. To send Him made, is to send Him marred, and no better. Therefore I make no doubt Christ's sending is one degree, His making is another; so to send as withal to make are two distinct measures of this filling. As He is, He is a Maker, a Creator. If God make Him any thing, He must be a thing made, a creature, and that is a great disparagement. So that howsoever the time is the fuller for this, He is the emptier; πλήρωμα χρόνου κένωμα Χριστοῦ, 'the fulness of time is His emptiness;' the exalting of that, His abasing. And this very *exinanivit seipsum,* "emptying Himself" (Phil. ii. 7) for our sake, is a pressing down the measure; and so even by that still the measure is more full.

Yea the very manner of this making hath his increase too, addeth to it still. In the word γενόμενον, which is not every making, but 'making it His nature.' To have made Him a body and taken it upon Him for a time till He had performed His embassage, and then laid it off again, that had been much; but so to be made as once made and ever made; so to take it as never lay it off more, but continue so still, γενέσθαι, 'it to become His very nature;' so to be made is to make the union full. And to make the union with us full, He was content not to be sent alone but to be made; and that γενέσθαι, 'to be made so as never unmade more.' Our manhood becoming His nature, no less than the Godhead itself. This is *Filium factum* indeed.

"Made," and twice "made," for so it is in the verse. 1. *Factum ex,* and 2. *Factum sub;* "made of," and "made under;" "of a woman," "under the Law." So two makings there be; either of them of itself a filling to the measure, but both of them maketh it perfectly full.

"Made," first, "of a woman;" that I take it clearly to be one. For if He, if the Son of God must be made a creature, it were meet He should be made the best creature of all. And if made of anything, if any one thing better than another, of that; made some glorious Spirit, some of the orders of the Angels. Nay "made," but made no Spirit; *Verbum caro factum est*, "The Word became flesh," (John i. 14); "made," but made no Angel; *nusquam Angelos*, "He in no wise took the Angels' nature upon Him." (Heb. ii. 16.)

But "made" man. First I will ask with David, *Domine, quid est homo?* "Lord, what is man?" And then tell you his answer. *Homo quasi res nihili*, "Man is like a thing of nought." (Ps. cxliv. 3, 4.) And this He was "made," this He became "made" man, "made of a woman;" "did not abhor the virgin's womb," as we sing daily to the high praise of the fulness of His humility, to which His love brought Him for our sakes. For whatsoever else He had been "made," it would have done us no good. In this then was "the fulness" of His love, as before of His Father's—that He would be made, and was made, not what was fittest for Him, but what was best for us; not what was most for His glory, but what was most for our benefit and behoof.

"Made of a woman." For man He might have been "made," and yet have had a body framed for Him in Heaven, and not "made of a woman." But when He saith, *Factum ex muliere*, it is evident He passed not through her as water through a conduit pipe, as fondly dreameth the Anabaptist. "Made of," *Factum ex; ex dicit materiam.* "Made of her;" she ministered the matter, "flesh of her flesh." *Semen mulieris*, "the seed," (Gen. iii. 15); and *semen intimum substantiæ*, 'that is the principal and very inward chief part of the substance.' Made of that, made of her very substance.

And so have we here now in one both twain His natures. "God sent His Son"—there His divine; "made of a woman"—here His human nature. That, from the bosom of His Father before all worlds; this, from the womb of His mother in the world. So that as from eternity God His Father might say that verse of the Psalm, *Filius Meus es Tu, hodie genui Te*, "Thou art My Son, this day have I begotten Thee," (Ps. ii. 7): so, in "the fulness of time" might the Virgin His mother no less truly, *Filius meus es Tu, hodie peperi Te*, 'Thou art my Son, this day have I brought Thee into the World.'

And here now at this word, "made of a woman," He

beginneth to concern us somewhat. There groweth an alliance between us; for we also are made of a woman. And our hope is as He will not be confounded to be counted *inter natos mulierum,* (Heb. ii. 11): no more will He be, saith the Apostle, to say, *in medio fratrum,* (Rom. viii. 29), "to acknowledge us His brethren." And so by this time He groweth somewhat near us.

This now is full for the union with our nature, to be "made of a woman." But so to be "made of a woman" without He be also "made under the Law," is not near enough yet. For if He be out of the compass of the law that the law cannot take hold of him, *factum ex muliere* will do us small pleasure. And He was so born, so "made of a woman." As the verity of His conception is in this *factum ex muliere,* so the purity is in this, that it is but *ex muliere,* and no more; of the Virgin alone by the power of the Holy Ghost, without mixture of fleshly generation. By virtue whereof no original soil was in him. Just born He was, and *Justo non est lex posita,* "no law for the just," (1 Tim. i. 9)—no law could touch Him. And so we never the better for *factum ex muliere.*

For if one be in debt and danger of the law, to have a brother of the same blood, made of the same woman, both as we say lying in the one belly, will little avail him, except he will also come "under the law," that is, become his surety, and undertake for him. And such was our estate. As debtors we were by virtue of *chirographum contra nos,* "the handwriting that was against us." (Col. ii. 14.) Which was our bond, and we had forfeited it. And so, *factus ex muliere,* to us, without *factus sub Lege,* would have been to small purpose.

No remedy therefore, He must be new made; made again once more. And so He was, cast in a new mould; and at His second making "made under the Law;" under which if He had not been made, we had been marred; even quite undone for ever, if this had not been done for us too. Therefore He became bound for us also, entered bond anew, took on Him not only our nature but our debt, our nature and condition both. Nature as men, condition as sinful men, expressed in the words following, "them that were under the Law;" for that was our condition. There had indeed been no capacity in Him to do this, if the former had not gone before, *factum ex muliere ;* if He had not been, as we "made of a woman." But the former was for this ; "made of a woman" He was, that He might be "made under the Law :" being *ex muliere,* He might then become *sub Lege,* which before He could not, but then He might and did ; and so this still is the fuller.

And when did He this? When was He "made under the Law ?" Even then when He was circumcised. For this doth St. Paul testify in the third of the next chapter, "Behold, I Paul testify unto you whosoever is circumcised," *factus est debitor universæ Legis,* "he becomes a debtor to the whole Law." (Gal. v. 3.) At His Circumcision then He entered bond anew with us ; and in sign that so He did He shed then a few drops of His blood, whereby He signed the bond as it were, and gave those few drops then, *tanquam arrham universi sanguinis effundendi,* 'as a pledge or earnest,' that "when the fulness of time came," 'He would be ready to shed all the rest ;' as He did. For I would not have you mistake ; though we speak of this *sub Lege,* being "under the Law," in the terms of a debt sometimes, yet the truth is this debt of ours was no money debt ; we were not *sub Lege pecuniariâ,* but *capitali ;* and the debt of a capital law is death. And under that, under death He went, and that the worst death law had to inflict, "even the death of the cross," the most bitter, reproachful, cursed death of the cross. So that upon the matter, *factus sub Lege,* and *factus in cruce,* come both to one ; one amounts to as much as the other. Well, this He did undertake for us at His circumcision, and therefore then and not till then He had His Name given Him, the name of Jesus, a Saviour. (Luke ii. 21.) For then took He on Him the obligation to save us. And look, what then at His Circumcision He undertook, at His Passion He paid even to the full ; and having paid it, *delevit chirographum,* "cancelled the sentence of the Law" (Col. ii. 14) that till then was of record and stood in full force against us.

Howbeit, all this was but one part of the Law ; but He was made *sub Lege universâ,* 'under the whole Law ;' and that not by His death only, but by His life too. The one half of the Law, that is, the directive part—He was made under that, and satisfied it by the innocency of His life, without breaking so much as one jot or tittle of the Law ;

and so answered that part, as it might be the principal. The other half of the Law, which is the penalty—He was under that part also, and satisfied it by suffering a wrongful death, no way deserved, or due by Him ; and so answered that, as it might be the forfeiture. So He was made under both, under the whole Law. Satisfying the principal, there was no reason He should be liable to the forfeiture and penalty ; yet, under that He was also. And all, that the whole Law might be satisfied fully, by His being under both parts ; and so no part of it light upon us.

These two then, 1. " Made of a woman," 2. " Made under the Law," ye see, are two several makings, and both very requisite. Therefore either hath a several feast, they divide this solemnity between them. Six days apiece to either ; as the several moieties of this "fulness of time." This day, *Verbum caro factum*, " the Word made flesh," (John i. 14) ; that day, " Him that knew no sin, He made sin," (2 Cor. v. 21), that is, made Him undertake to be handled as a sinner, to be " under the Law," and to endure what the Law could lay upon Him. And so now the thing sent is full ; and fully sent, because made ; and fully made, because made once and twice over ; fully made ours, because fully united to us. " Made of a woman," as well as we ; " made under the Law," as deep as we ; both *ex muliere* and *sub Lege*. So of our nature " of a woman," that of our condition also "under the Law." So, fully united to us in nature and condition both.

And so we are come to the full measure of His sending. And that we are come to the full ye shall plainly see by the overflowing, by that which we receive from this fulness, (Gal. iv. 5) ; which is the latter part of the verse and is our fulness, even the fulness of all that we can desire. For if we come now to ask, For whom is all this ado, this sending, this making, over and over again ? It is for us. So is the conclusion, *ut nos*, that we might from this fulness receive the full of our wish. For in these two behind, 1. Redemption, and 2. Adoption ; to be redeemed and to be adopted are the full of all we can wish ourselves.

The transcendent division of good and evil is it that comprehendeth all. And here it is. Our desire can extend itself no farther than to be rid of all evil, and to attain all that good is. By these two, being redeemed and being adopted, we are made partakers of them both. "To be redeemed from under the Law," is to be quit of all evil. "To receive the adoption of children," is to be stated in all that is good. For all evil is in being "under the Law" from whence we are redeemed, and all good in being invested in the Heavenly inheritance whereunto we are adopted. Thus stood the case with us, 'aliens we were from God, His covenant, and His Kingdom.' (Eph. ii. 12.) More than that, prisoners we were, fast laid up under the Law. From this latter we are freed ; of the former we are seized ; and what would we more ?

Only this you shall observe that in the idiom of the Scriptures it is usual, two points being set down, when they are resumed again, to begin with the latter and so end with the former. So is it here. At the first, "made of a woman, made under the Law." At the resuming, He begins with the latter, "made under the Law, that He might redeem them that were under the Law." And then comes to the former, "made of a woman," made the Son of man, "that we by adoption might be made the sons of God." But this we are to mark, it is He that is at all the cost and pain ; and we that have the benefit by it. At the redeeming it is, *ut ille ;* at the receiving it is, *ut nos.*

Briefly of either. And first, of our redeeming. Redeeming, as the word giveth it, is a second buying, or buying back of a thing before aliened or sold. Ever, a former sale is presupposed before it. And such a thing there had gone before. A kind of alienation had formerly been whereby we had made away ourselves, for a sale I cannot call it, it was for such a trifle ; our nature aliened in Adam for the forbidden fruit, a matter of no moment. Our persons likewise ; daily we ourselves alien them for some trifling pleasure or profit, matters not much more worth. And when we have thus passed ourselves away, by this "selling ourselves under sin" (Rom. vii. 14), the Law seizeth on us, and under it we are συγκεκλεισμένοι, even "locked up" (Gal. iii. 23) as it were in a dungeon, "tied fast with the cords of our sins," (Prov. v. 22) ; the sentence passed on us, and we waiting but for execution. What evil is there not in this estate, and on every soul that is in it ? Well then, the first *ut*, the first end is to get us rid from under this estate.

He did it; not by way of entreaty, step in and beg our pardon; that would not serve. Sold we were, and bought we must be;—a price must be laid down for us. To get us from under the Law it was not a matter of intercession, to sue for it and have it. No, He must purchase it and pay for it. It was a matter of redemption.

And in redemption or a purchase we look to the price. For if it be at any easy rate, it is so much the better. But with a high price He purchased us; it cost Him dear to bring it about. *Non auro, nec argento;* neither of them would serve: at an higher rate it was, even *pretioso sanguine,* "His precious Blood was the price we stood Him in." (1 Pet. i. 18, 19.) Which He paid, when "He gave His life a ransom for many." (Matt. xx. 28.)

It stood thus between Him and us in this point of redemption. Here are certain malefactors under the Law, to suffer—to be executed. What say you to them? Why, I will become "under the Law," suffer that they should, take upon Me their execution, upon condition they may be quit. In effect so much at His Passion He said, *Si ergo Me quæritis,* "If you lay hold on Me," if I must discharge all, *sinite hos abire,* "let these go their way." (John xviii. 8.) Let the price I pay be their redemption, and so it was. And so we come to be "redeemed from under the Law."

And this is to be marked, that "them that were under the Law" and "we that are to receive" are but one, one and the same persons both; but being so redeemed, then we are ourselves. Till then the Apostle speaks of us in the third person, "them that were under the Law," as of some strangers, as of men of another world, none of our own. But now being redeemed, the style changeth. He speaketh of us in the first person *ut nos,* 'that we.' For till now, we were not our own, we were not ourselves; but now we are. Till this it was the old year still with us, but with the new year cometh our new estate.

Being thus redeemed, we are got from under the Law; and that is much. Till a party come to be once under it and feel the weight of it, he shall never understand this aright; but then he shall. And if any have been under it, he knows what it is, and how great a benefit to be got thence. But is this all? No, He leaves us not here; but to make the measure complete, yea even to flow over, He

gives us not over when He had rid us out of this wretched
estate, till He have brought us to an estate as good as He
Himself is in.   After our redemption we stood but as
prisoners enlarged ; that was all : but still we were as
strangers ; no part nor portion in God or His Kingdom,
nor no reason we should hope for any.   He now goeth one
step farther, which is the highest and farthest step of all.
For farther than it He cannot go.

"That we might receive the adoption," that is, from the
estate of prisoners condemned be translated into the estate
of children adopted.   Of adopted, for of natural we could
not.   That is His peculiar alone, and He therein only above
us ; but else, fully to the joint fruition of all that He hath,
which is fully as much as we could desire.   And this is our
fieri out of His *factum ex muliere*.   We made the sons of
God, as He the Son of man ; we made partakers of His
divine, as He of our human nature. (2 Pet. i. 4.)   To purchase our pardon, to free us from death and the law's sentence, this " seemed a small thing " (2 Sam. vii. 19) to Him,
yet this is *lex hominis*.   Man's goodness goeth no farther,
and gracious is the prince that doth but so much.   For who
ever heard of a condemned man adopted afterward, or that
thought it not enough and enough if he did but scape with
his life ?   So far then to exalt His bounty to that fulness as
pardon and adopt both, *non est lex hominis hæc* "no such
measure amongst men ; " *zelus Domini exercituum*, "the
zeal of the Lord of Hosts" was to perform this, (Isa. ix. 7) ;
"the fulness of the Godhead dwelt in Him" that brought
this to pass.

For, to speak of adopting, we see it daily ; no father
adopts unless he be orbe, have no child ; or if he have one,
for some deep dislike have cast him off.   But God had a
Son, "the brightness of His glory, the true character of His
substance." (Heb. i. 3.)   And no displeasure there was ; no,
in Quo complacitum est, "in Whom He was absolutely well
pleased," (Matt. xvii. 5) ; yet would He by adoption for all
that "bring many sons to glory." (Heb. ii. 10.)   Is not
this full on His part ?

We see again no heir will endure to hear of adoption, nay,
nor divide his inheritance ; no, not with his natural brethren.
Then, that "the Heir of all things" (Heb. i. 2) should
admit "joint-heirs" (Rom. viii. 18) to the Kingdom He was

born to ; and that admit them not out of such as were near
Him, but from such as were strangers ; yea, such as had
been condemned men under the law—is not this full on His
part ? To purchase us, and to purchase for us, both at
once ? And not to do this for us alone, but to assure it to
us. For as His Father in this verse sends Him, so in the
next verse " He sends the Spirit of His Son " to give us
seisin of this our adoption ; whereby we now call Him, the
Jews *Abba,* the Gentiles *Pater,* as children all and He our
Father, which is the privilege of the adoption we here receive.

III. And now are we come to the fulness indeed. For this
adoption is the fulness of our option ; we cannot extend—
we our wish, or He—His love and goodness any farther.
For what can we ask, or He give more, seeing in giving this
He giveth all He is worth ? By this time it is full sea ; all
the banks are filled. It is now as Ezekiel's waters that he
saw " flow from under the threshold of the Temple ; " that
took him to the ancles first, then to the knees, after to the
loins ; at last, so high risen there was no more passage.
(Ezek. xlvii. 3-5.)

1. From the fulness of His compassion, He " sent " to
release us. 2. From the fulness of His love, " He sent His
Son." 3. In the fulness of humility, " He sent Him made."
4. " Made of a woman," to make a full union with our
nature. 5. " Made under the Law," to make the union yet
more perfectly full with our sinful condition. 6. " That
we might obtain a full deliverance from all evil, by being
redeemed." 7. " And a full estate of all the joy and glory of
His Heavenly inheritance, by being adopted." So there is
fulness of all hands. And so much for the fulness of the
benefit we receive.

IV. Now, for the fulness of the duty we are to perform
this day. For, " in the fulness of time " all things are to be
full. *Plenitudo temporis, tempus plenitudinis.* And seeing
God hath suffered us to live, to see the year run about to
this *plenitudo temporis ;* if it be so on God's part, meet also it
be so on ours ; and that we be not empty in this " fulness of
time." It is not fit, if He be at the brink that we be at the
bottom. But, as we be willing to yield Him of ours again,
of our duty, I mean ; that it to Him in a measure and proportion be like full, as His bounty hath been full above
measure toward us. That so from us, and on our parts, it

may be *plenitudo temporis,* or *tempus plenitudinis,* "the fulness of time," or 'time of fulness,' choose you whether.

I. And a time of fulness it will be, I know, in a sense ; of
fulness of bread, of fulness of bravery, of fulness of sport
and pastime ; and this it may be. And it hath been ever a
joyful time in appearance, for it should be so. "With the
joy," saith Esay a verse or two before *Puer natus est nobis,*
"unto us a Child is born," "that men rejoice with in
harvest." (Isa. ix. 3.) Not to go from our text here, with
the joy of men that are come out of prison, have escaped
the law ; with the joy of men that have got the reversion of
a goodly heritage. Only, that we forget not the principal ;
that this outward joy eat not up, evacuate not our spiritual
joy proper to the feast ; that we have in mind in the midst
of our mirth the cause of it, Christ's sending, and the
benefits that come thereby. And it shall be a good sign
unto us if we can thus rejoice, if this our joy can be full,
if we can make a spiritual blessing the object of our
mirth. *Beatus populus qui scit jubilationem,* "Blessed is the
people that can rejoice on this manner." (Ps. lxxxix. 15).

2. And after our joyfulness or fulness of joy, our fulness
of thanks or thankfulness is to ensue ; for with that fulness
we are to celebrate it likewise. Our minds first, and then
our mouths, to be filled with blessing, and praise, and
thanks to Him, That hath made our times not to fall into
those empty ages of the world, but to fall within this "fulness of time," which "so many Kings and Prophets desired
to have lived in," (Luke x. 24), but fell short of ; and lived
then when the times were full of shadows, and promises,
and nothing else. How instantly they longed to have held
such a feast, to have kept a Christmas, it is evident by
David's *Inclina Cælos,* (Ps. cxliv. 5), by Esay's *Utinam
disrumpas Cælos,* (Isa. lxiv. 1), "Bow the Heavens," and
"Break the Heavens :" how much, I say, they longed for
it ; and therefore, that we make not light account of it.

To render our thanks then, and to remember to do it
fully, to forget none ; to Him that was sent, and to Him
that "sent ;" "sent His Son" in this, "the Spirit of His
Son" in the next verse. To begin with *Osculamini Filium,*
it is the first duty enjoined us this day, to "kiss the Babe,"
(Ps. ii. 12), new born, That when His Father would send
Him, said, *Ecce venio,* (Ps. xl. 7), so readily ; and when He

would make Him, was content with *Corpus aptasti Mihi,* to
have a body made Him, meet for Him to suffer in; who
willingly yielded to be our Shilo, (Gen. xlix. 10)—to this
ἀπέστειλε here; yea, to be not only Christ but an Apostle
for us, even " the Apostle of our profession." (Heb. iii. 1).

And not to Him that was sent and made alone; but to
the Father that sent Him, and to the Holy Ghost that made
Him, as by Whom He was conceived. To the Father for
His mission, the Son for His redemption, the Holy Ghost
for His adoption; for by Him it is wrought. He that made
Him Son of Man, doth likewise regenerate us to the state
of the sons of God. And this for our thankfulness.

3. And to these two, to make the measure full, to join
the fulness of duty, even whatsoever dutiful-minded persons
may yield to a bountiful-minded and a bountiful-handed
Benefactor. And with this to begin, to consecrate this first
day of this fulness of time even with our service to Him at
the full; which is then at the full when no part is missing,
when all our duties of preaching, and praying, of hymns, of
offering, of Sacrament and all, meet together. No fulness
there is of our Liturgy or public solemn Service, without
the Sacrament. Some part, yea the chief part is wanting, if
that be wanting. But our thanks are surely not full without
the Holy Eucharist, which is by interpretation, thanksgiving
itself. Fully we cannot say, *Quid retribuam Domino?* but
we must answer, *Calicem salutaris accipiam,* " we will take
the Cup of salvation," (Ps. cxvi. 12, 13), and with it in our
hands give thanks to Him, render Him our true Eucharist,
or real thanksgiving indeed. In which Cup is the Blood
not only of our redemption, of the covenant that freeth us
from the Law and maketh the destroyer pass over us; but
of our adoption, of the New Testament also which entitles
us and conveys unto us, testament-wise or by way of legacy,
the estate we have in the joy and bliss of His Heavenly
Kingdom whereto we are adopted. (Mat. xvi. 28). We are
then made partakers of Him, and with Him of both these
His benefits. We there are made " to drink of the spirit,"
(1 Cor. xii. 13), " by which we are sealed to the day of our
redemption," (Eph. iv. 30), and adoption both. So that our
freeing from under the Law, our investiture into our new
adopted state, are not fully consummate without it.

And what? Shall this be all? No, when this is done,

there is allowance of twelve days more for this "fulness of time;" that we shrink not up our duty then into this day alone, but in the rest also remember to redeem some part of the day, to adopt some hour at the least, to bethink ourselves of the duty the time calleth to us for; that so, we have not Job's *dies vacuos,* "no day quite empty" in this fulness of time. Hereof assuring ourselves, that what we do in this "fulness of time" will have full acceptance at His hands. It is the time of His birth, which is ever a time, as accepted, so of accepting, (2 Cor. vi. 2); wherein, what is done will be acceptably taken to the full—fully accepted, and fully rewarded by Him, "of Whose fulness we all receive," (Joh. i. 16); with this condition "of grace for grace," ever one grace for another.

And so, growing from grace to grace, finally from this "fulness" we shall come to be partakers of another yet behind, to which we aspire. For all this is but "the fulness of time." But that, the fulness of eternity, when time shall be run out and his glass empty, *et tempus non erit amplius,* (Rev. x. 6), which is at His next sending. For yet once more shall God send Him, and He come again. At which coming we shall then indeed receive the fulness of our redemption, not from the Law—that we have already—but from corruption to which our bodies are yet subject, and receive the full fruition of the inheritance whereto we are here but adopted. And then it will be perfect, complete, absolute fulness indeed, when we shall all be filled with "the fulness of Him that filleth all in all." (Eph. i. 23.) For so shall all be, when nothing shall be wanting in any; for "God shall be all in all." (1 Cor. xv. 28.) Not as here He is, something and but something in every one; but then, *omnia in omnibus.* And then, the measure shall be so full as it cannot enter into us, we cannot hold it. We must enter into it; *Intra in gaudium Domini tui.* (Mat. xxv. 21.)

To this we aspire, and to this in the fulness appointed of every one of our times Almighty God bring us by Him, and for His sake, That in this "fulness of time" was sent to work it for us in His Person; and work it in us by the operation of His blessed Spirit. To Whom, &c.

SERMON V.

A Sermon Preached before the King's Majesty, at
Whitehall, on Tuesday, the Twenty-fifth day of
December, a.d. mdcx., being Christmas-day.

The Angel said unto them, be not afraid; for behold, I bring
you good tidings of great joy, which shall be to all people.
That there is born unto you this day a Saviour, Which is
Christ the Lord, in the city of David. LUKE ii. 10, 11.

[*Et dixit illis Angelus: Nolite timere: ecce enim evangelizo vobis*
gaudium magnum, quod erit omni populo:
Quia natus est vobis hodie Salvator, Qui est Christus Dominus in
civitate David. Latin Vulg.]

THERE is a word in this text, and it is *hodie*, by virtue
whereof this day may seem to challenge a special
property in this text, and this text in this day.   Christ was
born, is true any day; but this day Christ was born, never
but to-day only.   For of no day in the year can it be said
hodie natus but of this.   By which word the Holy Ghost
may seem to have marked it out, and made it the peculiar
text of the day.

Then it will not be amiss, *donec cognominatur hodie*, as the
Apostle speaketh, "while it is called to-day," (Heb. iii. 13),
to hear it.   To-morrow the word *hodie* will be lost; this day
and not any day else it is in season.   Let us then hear it
this day which we can hear no day besides.

It is then the first report, the very first news that came,
as this day, of that which maketh this day so high a feast;
the birth of Christ.

It came by an Angel then; no man was meet to be the
messenger of it.   And look, how it came then so it should
come still, and none but an Angel bring it, as more fit for
the tongues of Angels than of men.   Yet since God hath
allowed sinful men to be the reporters of it at the second
hand, and the news never the worse; for that good news is
good news and welcome by any, though the person be but
even a foul leper that brings it, (2 Kings vii. 9); yet, that
the meanness of the messenger offend us not, ever we are
to remember this; be the party who he will that brings it,
the news of Christ's birth is a message for an Angel.

This had been news for the best prince in the earth.

That these *illis* here, these parties were shepherds, that this message came to them, needs not seem strange. It found none else at the time to come to; the Angel was glad to find any to tell it to, even to tell it the first he could meet withal; none were then awake, none in case to receive it but a sort of poor shepherds, and to them he told it.

Yet it fell not out amiss that shepherds they were; the news fitted them well. It well agreed to tell shepherds of the yeaning of a strange Lamb, such a Lamb as should "take away the sins of the world," (John i. 29); such a Lamb as they might "send to the Ruler of the world for a·present," *mitte Agnum Dominatori terræ*—Esay's Lamb. (Isa. xvi. 1.) Or, if ye will, to tell shepherds of the birth of a Shepherd, Ezekiel's Shepherd; *Ecce suscitabo vobis Pastorem*, "Behold, I will raise you a Shepherd," (Ezek. xxxiv. 23); "the Chief Shepherd," (1 Peter v. 4), "the Great Shepherd," (Heb. xiii. 20), and "the Good Shepherd that gave His life for His flock." (John x. 11.) And so it was not unfit news for the persons to whom it came.

For the manner; the Angel delivereth it *evangelizando*, 'church-wise,' and that was a sign this place should ever be the exchange for this news. Church-wise, I say, for he doth it by a sermon, here at this verse; and then by hymn or anthem after, at the 14th verse. A sermon; the Angel himself calls it so, *evangelizo vobis*, 'I come to evangelize, to preach you a gospel;' that first. And presently after he had done his sermon, there is the hymn, *Gloria in excelsis*, taken up by the choir of Heaven. An Angel makes the one; a multitude of Angels sing the other. The whole service of this day, the sermon, the anthem, by Angels, all.

Now the end of both sermon and anthem, and of the Angels in publishing it, and of the shepherds and us in hearing it, is *gaudium*, "joy," for the benefit and honour; *gaudium magnum*, "great joy," for the great benefit and great honour vouchsafed our nature and us this day. "Joy" is in the text, and if joy be in the time, it is no harm. We keep the text, if we hold the time with joy, for so the Angel doth warrant us to hold it.

Of this angelical or evangelical message, or, as not I but the Angel calleth it, sermon, these two verses I have read are a part. Whereof the former is but an *ecce*, exciting them to hear it by magnifying the message as well worth their hearing, "Be not afraid, for behold I bring you good tidings of great joy, which shall be to all people." The latter is the very message itself, "that there is born unto you this day a Saviour, Which is Christ the Lord, in the city of David."

I. In the former are these points; 1. "Fear not," it is no ill news I bring you. 2. Nay, it is "good news." 3. Good, for it is "news of joy." 4. Joy, and that no ordinary but "great joy." 5. Not to some few, but "to the whole people." 6. And not *toti populo*, 'to all one people,' but *omni populo*, "to all people whatsoever." 7. And them, not for the present, but *quod erit omni populo*, "that is and so shall be to all, as long as there shall be any people upon earth." And by virtue of this *quod erit*, to us here this day. *Ecce*, "behold," such is the news I bring.

II. In the latter, the message itself. The sum whereof is the birth of a Child, a Child is born. Three things are proposed of Him. 1. This Child is "a Saviour." 2. "A Saviour, Which is Christ." 3. "Christ the Lord," *Christus Dominus*. For every saviour is not Christ, nor every christ *Christus Dominus*, "Christ the Lord, or the Lord Christ." He is all three.

Then have we besides three circumstances, of the 1. Persons, 2. Time, and 3. Place. 1. The persons for whom all this is, twice repeated; 1. *evangelizo vobis* in the first verse, 2. *natus vobis* in the second. But this I make some doubt of whether it be a circumstance or no; I rather hold it a principal part of the substance, as the word of conveyance whereby it passeth to us. And sure there is no joy either *in evangelizo* 'the message,' or *natus* 'the birth' without it, without *vobis*. But if the message and the birth itself both be ours, then it is *gaudium magnum* indeed. Specially, if we add 2. the time when, not many days hence, but even this very day. And 3. the place where, that it is in no remote region far hence, but "in the city of David," even here hard by.

III. And then lastly in a word; what our parts are to perform, to these two parts, 1. this day's message, and 2. this day's birth of our "Saviour Christ the Lord."

I. "Be not afraid." Here is a stop, that the message cannot proceed; for the sight of the messenger hath almost marred the hearing of the message. The parties to whom

E

it comes be in such fear as they be not in case to receive it. "They were afraid," and that "sore afraid," as is said in the verse before, at the sight of the Angel that came with the news.

And this was not the case of these poor men only; others, and other manner of people were so, as well as they. This Gospel of St. Luke is scarce begun, we are yet but a little way in the second chapter, and we have already three *noli timeres* in it; and all, as here, at the coming of an Angel. 1. "Fear not, Zachary." (chap. i. 13.) So he was afraid. 2. "Fear not, Mary." (chap. i. 30.) So she was afraid. 3. And now "Fear not" these here, that it seems to be general to fear at an Angel's appearing.

What was it? It was not the fear of an evil conscience; they were about no harm. Zachary was at Church at his office; the blessed Virgin, I doubt not, blessedly employed; these here doing their duty, "watching over their flocks by night;" yet feared all. What should the matter be? It is a plain sign our nature is fallen from her original; Heaven and we are not in the terms we should be, not the best of us all.

Angels are the messengers of Heaven. Messengers ever come with tidings, but whether good or bad we cannot tell. Here comes an Angel with news from Heaven; what news he brings we know not, and therefore we fear because we know not. Which shews all is not well between Heaven and us, that upon every coming of an Angel we promise ourselves no better news from thence, but still are afraid of the messages and messengers that come from that place.

That the message then may proceed, this fear must be removed. In a troubled water no face will well be seen, nor by a troubled mind no message received, till it be settled. To settle them then for it; no other way, no other word to begin with but *nolite timere,* "fear not," and that is ever the Angel's beginning. Such is our infirmity, ever he must begin with these two words, *noli timere,* "fear not;" and so he doth seven times in this Gospel.

But fear will not be cast out with a couple of words, till they see some reason to quiet them. And no better reason, than to shew they have no reason to fear. For fear is the expectation of evil, and there is no evil toward them; and so they have no reason to fear, *quod trepidaverunt timore ubi*

non erat timor. (Ps. liii. 5.) As if he should say, Angels
have come with weeping news, as Judges ii. 1. If I were
such an one, if I came with sad tidings, ye had reason, ye
might fear. But now your terror groweth out of error.
You are mistaken in me, I am no such Angel ; I am *Angelus
evangelizans*, ' an Angel with a Gospel,' one that comes with
no bad news. " Fear not " then. There is no evil toward.

No evil ; and that were enough for " fear not." But here
is a farther matter ; not only *privative*, ' I bring no ill,' but
positive, " I bring you good news." And good news is
nolite timere and somewhat besides, that is, " fear not " but
be of good cheer. They be two degrees plainly, though
one be inferred of the other. Fear no ill, there is none to
fear ; there is no ill, nay there is good towards. For good
news is good, in that it represents the good itself to us
before it come. It is but words. True—but such words
made Jacob " revive again," (Gen. xlv. 27) when he was
more than half dead, even the good news of Joseph's wel-
fare. " If I might but hear good tidings," saith David,
when his bones were broken, " it would make me well
again," (Ps. li. 8) ; that Solomon said well, " A good
messenger is a good medicine." (Pro. xiii. 17.)

Specially, this here which is so good as it carrieth away
the name from the rest, to be called the Gospel or the glad
tidings, as if none so glad, nay none glad at all without it.
It is, saith the Apostle, *odor suavitatis*, " a comfortable
sweet savour." (2 Cor. ii. 15.) It is, saith the Wise Man,
dulcedo animæ, et sanitas ossium, " the sweetness of the soul,
the very health of the bones." (Pro. xvi. 24.) It is such,
saith the Prophet, (Isa. lii. 7), " as the lips are precious, and
the feet beautiful, of them that bring it," that a Saviour is
born, as by Whom " things in Heaven and things in earth,"
(Col. i. 20), men and Angels—which were in fear one of
another—" are set at peace, and love ; " and " love casteth
out fear," (John iv. 18), giveth the true *noli timere*.

Good news of joy ; for of good news there are more sorts
than one. Good news it had been, if it had been but *evangelizo vobis spem*, ' news of good hope ; ' that had been enough
for *nolite timere*. This is more, it is of joy. I wot well there
is a joy in hope, *Spe gaudentes*, (Rom. xii. 12), saith the
Apostle ; but that joy is not full, (John xvi. 24), " till the
fulness of time come." (Gal. iv. 4.) Nor it is not perfect,

for it is allayed somewhat with an unpleasing mixture, which is *spes differtur*, and that, as the Wise Man saith, *affigit animam*, "hope deferred afflicteth the soul." (Pro. xiii. 12.) *Gaudium spei* is nothing to *gaudium rei;* the hope *de futuro*, of a thing to come hereafter, nothing to the actual fruition of a thing present.

And indeed, this day's news it was ever *evangelium spei*, ever in the future tense before. Even the very last before this to the blessed Virgin, *Ecce concipies*, (Luke i. 31), "Thou shalt conceive"—"Shalt." So it was yet to come. This is the first in the present tense; not, 'is to be born,' 'is to be sent,' 'is to come,' but *natus est, missus est, venit*, "is born," "is sent," "is come." *Hodie*, even "to-day" takes no time; "in the city of David," not far hence, but even hard by. This is *evangelizo gaudium*, "this is joy indeed."

But even in joy there be divers degrees. All are not of one size. Some there are lesser; some as this here, *gaudium magnum*. The fire is as the fuel is, and the joy is as the matter is. There is not like joy to a shepherd when his ewe brings him a lamb as when his wife brings him a son; yet that of a lamb is a joy, such as it is. But then if that son should prove to be *princeps pastorum*, 'the chief shepherd in all the land,' that were somewhat more. But then, if he should prove to be a Cyrus, or a David, a prince, then certainly it were another manner of joy, *gaudium magnum* indeed. As the matter is, so is the joy. If great the benefit, great the person, then great the joy. And here the benefit is great, none greater; as much as the saving of us all, as much as all our lives and souls are worth; therefore great. And the person great, none so great—it is the Lord Himself—therefore *primæ magnitudinis*, 'great even as He is.' Indeed so great it is, that the Prophet bids us plainly "remember no more former things, nor regard matters of old." (Isa. xliii. 18.) This passeth them all, the joy of it puts them all down ; so that none of them shall once be mentioned with it. Therefore well said the Angel, *Evangelizo gaudium magnum*.

And great it may be *intensive*, in the parties themselves; yet not great *extensive*, nor extend itself to many, not be *gaudium magnum populo*. Yes, even that way also it is great; it is public joy, it is "joy to the people." And well fare that joy where it is merry with all. It is added purposely

this, that they might not mistake when he said, *Evangelizo
vobis*, " he brought them good news; " that though he
brought it them, yet not them only ; it was not appropriate
to them it was common to others. They had their parts in
it, but so should others have no less than they. And every
good shepherd will like it the better for that, will be *pro
grege*, and still prefer the joy of the whole flock.

In other joys it falls out as Esay tells, "multiply the
nation, and ye shall not increase their joy," (Isa. ix. 3); for
that which one wins another loses : but this joy, the joy of
Puer natus est nobis, in it " they shall all rejoice before Thee,
as men make merry in harvest, and be joyful as men that
divide the spoil." " In harvest ; " and a good harvest all
the country is the better for. " At a spoil ; " wherein every
one hath his share. That is *gaudium populi*, and such is
this. Well figured in the place of His birth, an inn, which
is *domus populi*, ' open to all passengers' that will take it up ;
juris publici, ' wherein every one hath right.' Yea, and the
most common part of the inn. For though they sort themselves and have every one their several chambers, in the
stable (Luke ii. 7) all have interest ; that is common. And
as the place public, so is the benefit, and so is the joy public
of His birth : Christmas joy right ; all fare the better for
this day. *Salus populi* is the best, and so is *gaudium populi*
too ; and every good mind will like it so much the better
that all the people have their part in it,

And this were much, *toti populo*, ' to the whole people,' if it
were but one ; but it is *omni populo*, say Theophylact and
Beda, that is, " to all people," which is a larger extent by far.
And if ye speak of great joy, this is great indeed, for it is
universal, it is as great as the world is great ; when not the
Jew only but the Gentile, nor the Gentile but the Jew, not
one people but all, keep a feast. And at this word *omni
populo, nec vox hominem sonat*, ' it is not man that speaketh
now,' whose goodness commonly when it is at the greatest
extendeth no farther but to one nation ; but with God it is
never great, till it come to *omni populo*. " It is but a
small thing (saith He by Esay) to raise the tribes of Jacob,
or to restore the decays of Israel ; I will give a light to
the Gentiles, and a salvation to the end of the world."
(Isa. xlix. 6.)

As we said of the inn even now the place of His birth, so

say we here of the time of it. It is well set down by St. Luke to have been at the description of the whole world, (Luke ii. 1); for that was a meet time for the Saviour of the whole world to be born, " the dew of Whose birth is of the womb of the morning," (Ps. cx. 3)—the Psalmist in passion of joy misplacing his words, the meaning is, " His birth from the womb is as the morning dew" which watereth and refresheth the face of the whole earth ; not Gideon's fleece alone, (Judg. vi. 37), but the whole earth ; not one part, not the Jews only, no partition now but *utraque unum,* (Eph. ii. 14), " one of two ;" nay, one of all, (Eph. i. 10), all recapitulate in Himself, and from Him as a centre lines of joy drawn to all, and every part of the circle.

And we may not pass by *quod erit,* "which shall be," which not only is but shall be. For by this word we hold ; it is our best tenure. Not only to all that then were—then had we been out—but that were or ever should be to the world's end. *Omni populo,* " all people," is the latitude or extent ; *quod erit,* " that shall be," is the longitude or continuance of the joy. *Quod erit,* that it should be a feast of joy, so long as any people shall be to hold a feast on the face of the earth. In a word, that same *evangelium æternum* that St. John saw in the Angel's hand we now hear from the Angel's mouth, " to be preached to every nation, kindred, tongue, and people," (Rev. xiv. 6), that be, or shall be while the world endureth.

So, if we read *quod erit* with *omni populo.* But some read *gaudium* with *quod erit,* (*gaudium quod erit*), and make a note of that ; the joy *quod erit,* " that is and shall be." For commonly all our earthly joy is *gaudium quod est, et non erit,* " that is for the present, but continueth not ;" is, but shall not be, like the blaze of a brush faggot, all of a flame and out again suddenly in a moment. (Eccl. vii. 6). *Gaudium quod erit,* " the joy that so is as it shall be still," is grounded upon the joy of this day—Christ and His birth. Without which our joy is as the joy of men in prison, merry for a while, but within a while sentence of death to pass upon them. Without which *extrema gaudii luctus occupat,* "the end of all our mirth will be but mourning." (Pro. xiv. 13.) All joy else is, but shall not be within a while ; at leastwise, *erit quando non erit,* a time shall be when it shall not be. *Sed gaudium Meum nemo tollet a vobis ;* " but My joy"—

Mine, grounded on Me—"none shall ever take from you,"
(Joh. xvi. 22); not sickness, not death itself. Other it shall,
this it shall not; but now ye shall this day, and evermore
ye shall rejoice in the holy comfort of it.

And this is the magnifying of the message. 1. No evil
news, "fear not." 2. Nay "good," be of good cheer. 3.
"Good news of joy," 4. "Of great joy." 5. "Public joy,"
toti populo. 6. "Universal joy," *omni populo.* 7. "Joy to
all" that are or shall be; and again, "joy which now is, and
shall be so for ever."

Now upon all these he setteth an *ecce,* and well He may;
and that is never set by the Holy Ghost but *super res magnæ
entitatis,* 'upon matters of great moment.' But upon this
hill, upon the top of it that hath so many ascents, a beacon
would do well. For look, how many *ecces* in the Scriptures,
so many beacons; and between them, as between these, ye
shall observe a good correspondence still. This *ecce* here,
to the last, *Ecce concipies* (Luke i. 31) of the blessed Virgin;
that, to Esay's *Ecce concipiet Virgo,* (Isa. vii. 14); that to
David's *Ecce de fructu ventris tui,* (Ps. cxxxii. 11); that to
Abraham's *Ecce in semine tuo,* (Gen. xxii. 18); and so up
till ye come to *semen mulieris.* (Gen. iii. 15.) There they
first begin, and take light one from another, till they come
to the *Ecce natus est hodie,* the *ecce* of all *ecces,* the last and
highest of them all. And as a beacon serveth to call up
and stir up men to have regard, so is this here to excite
them, and in them us all, with good attention to hear and
to heed these so great good tidings. And indeed, who is
not excited with it? whose eye is not turned to behold this
ecce? whose ear standeth not attent to hear this *evangelizo?*
whose heart doth not muse, "what manner of message this
should be?" (Luke i. 29.)

II. This it is then, *quod natus est.* The Birth of a
Child, "That there is One born this day" the cause of all
this joy.

There is joy at every birth. "Sorrow in the travail,"
saith our Saviour, "but after the delivery the anguish is no
more remembered, for joy that a man is born into the world."

But the greater he is that is born, and the more beneficial his birth, the greater ado is made. And among men,
because there are none greater than princes, and great
things are looked for at their hands, their births are ever

used to be kept with great triumph. Pharaoh's in the Old, (Gen. xl. 20), Herod's in the New, (Mark vi. 21); both their *natus ests* days of feasting.

Now of him that is born here it may truly be said, *Ecce major hîc,* "Behold a greater is born here." (Matt. xii. 42.) One, whose birth is good news even from the poorest shepherd to the richest prince upon the earth.

Who is it? Three things are said of this Child by the Angel. 1. He is "a Saviour." 2. "Which is Christ." 3. "Christ the Lord." Three of His titles, well and orderly inferred one of another by good consequence. We cannot miss one of them; they be necessary all. Our method on earth is to begin with great; in Heaven they begin with good first.

First then, "a Saviour;" that is His name, Jesus, *Soter;* and in that Name His benefit, *Salus,* 'saving health or salvation.' Such a name as the great Orator himself saith of it, *Soter, hoc quantum est? Ita magnum est ut latino uno verbo exprimi non possit.* 'This name Saviour is so great as no one word can express the force of it.'

But we are not so much to regard the *ecce* how great it is, as *gaudium* what joy is in it; that is the point we are to speak to. And for that, men may talk what they will, but sure there is no joy in the world to the joy of a man saved; no joy so great, no news so welcome, as to one ready to perish, in case of a lost man, to hear of one that will save him. In danger of perishing by sickness, to hear of one will make him well again; by sentence of the law, of one with a pardon to save his life; by enemies, of one that will rescue and set him in safety. Tell any of these, assure them but of a Saviour, it is the best news he ever heard in his life. There is joy in the name of a Saviour. And even this way, this Child is a Saviour too. *Potest hoc facere, sed hoc non est opus Ejus,* 'This He can do, but this is not His work;' a farther matter there is, a greater salvation He came for. And it may be we need not any of these; we are not presently sick, in no fear of the law, in no danger of enemies. And it may be, if we were, we fancy to ourselves to be relieved some other way. But that which He came for, that saving we need all; and none but He can help us to it. We have therefore all cause to be glad for the Birth of this Saviour.

I know not how, but when we hear of saving or mention of a Saviour, presently our mind is carried to the saving of our skin, of our temporal state, of our bodily life, and farther saving we think not of. But there is another life not to be forgotten, and greater the dangers, and the destruction there more to be feared than of this here, and it would be well sometimes we were remembered of it. Besides our skin and flesh a soul we have, and it is our better part by far, that also hath need of a Saviour; that hath her destruction out of which, that hath her destroyer from which she would be saved, and those would be thought on. Indeed our chief thought and care would be for that; how to escape the wrath, how to be saved from the destruction to come, whither our sins will certainly bring us.

Sin it is will destroy us all. And to speak of a Saviour, there is no person on earth hath so much need of a Saviour as hath a sinner. Nothing so dangerous, so deadly unto us, as is the sin in our bosom; nothing from which we have so much need to be saved, whatsoever account we make of it. From it cometh upon us all the evil of this life, and from it all the evil of the life to come; in comparison whereof these here are not worth the speaking of. Above all then we need a Saviour for our souls, and from our sins; and from the everlasting destruction which sin will bring upon us in the other life, not far from us, not from him of us that thinketh it farthest off.

Then if it be good tidings to hear of a Saviour, where it is but a matter of the loss of earth, or of this life here; how then, when it cometh to the loss of Heaven, to the danger of hell, when our soul is at the stake, and the well-doing or un-doing of it for ever? He that could save our souls from that destroyer—were not the birth of such an one good news trow? Is not such a Saviour worth a hearkening after? Is He not? Is it then because we have not that sense of our souls and the dangers of them, that we have of our bodies; nor that fear of our ghostly enemies, nor that lively apprehension of the eternal torments of that place, and how near we are to it, nothing being betwixt us and it but this poor puff of breath which is in our nostrils. Our carnal part is quick and sensible, our spiritual is dead and dull. We have not the feeling of our sins that we have of our sickness; if we had, we would hear this news with greater cheerfulness, and hold this day of the birth of such a Saviour with joy indeed. We cannot conceive it yet, this destruction is not near enough to affect us. But *in novissimo intelligetis plane,* "in the end," when the destroyer shall come and we shall find the want of a Saviour, "we shall plainly understand this," (Jer. xxx. 24), and value this benefit and the joy of it as we ought, and find there is no joy in the earth to the joy of a Saviour.

"There is born a Saviour," is the first. The Angel addeth farther, "A Saviour Which is Christ." For, many saviours had been born, many had God sent them that at divers times had set them free from divers dangers of their enemies; Moses, from the Egyptians; Joshua, from the Canaanites; Gideon, from the Midianites; Jephtha, from the Ammonites; Sampson, from the Philistines. And indeed, the whole story of the Bible is nothing else but a calendar of saviours that God from time to time still stirred them up.

But these all were but petty saviours, there was One yet behind that was worth them all. One, that "should save His people from their sins," (Mat. i. 21); save not their bodies for a time, but their souls for ever, which none of those saviours could do. One therefore much spoken of, wished for, and waited for, a Saviour Which was Christ. When He came they looked for great matters, as said the woman at the well's side, (John iv. 25), for he was the most famous and greatest Saviour of all. And this is He, "a Saviour Which is Christ." He, of Whom all the promises made mention, and He the performance of them all; of Whom all the types under the Law were shadows, and He the substance of them all; of Whom all the prophecies ran, and He the fulfilling of them all; He, of Whom all those inferior saviours were the figures and forerunners, and He the accomplishment of all that in them was wanting. This is He; Jacob's "Shiloh," (Gen. xlix. 10), Esay's "Immanuel," (Isa. vii. 14), Jeremy's "Branch," (Jer. xxiii. 5), Daniel's "Messias," (Dan. ix. 25), Zachary's *Oriens ab alto,* (Zech. vi. 12), Aggei's *desideratus cunctis gentibus,* "the desire of all the nations," (Hag. ii. 7), then, and now the joy of all nations, a Saviour Which is Christ.

And what is meant by this term Christ? a Saviour anointed ; or, as in another place it is said more agreeable to our phrase of speaking, a Saviour "sealed," (John vi. 27) —a Saviour under God's Great Seal. That is, not as those other were, saviours raised up of a sudden upon some occasion, to serve the turn for the present, and never heard of till they came; but a Saviour in God's fore-counsel resolved on, and given forth from the beginning; promised and foretold, and now signed and sent with absolute commission and fulness of power to be the perfect and complete Saviour of all.

And to be it, *ex officio;* His office, His very profession, to be one, that all may have right to repair unto Him, and find it at His hands. Not a Saviour incidentally, as it fell out; but one *ex professo,* anointed to that end, and by virtue of His anointing appointed, set forth, and sent into the world to exercise this function of a Saviour; not for a time, but for ever; not to the Jews, as did the rest, but even to all the ends of the earth. So runs His bill, *Venite ad Me omnes,* "come all," (Mat. xi. 28); and *qui ad Me venerit non ejiciam foras,* "of them that come to Me, I will cast none out." (John vi. 37.) *Servator omnium hominum,* "the Saviour of all men," (1 Tim. iv. 10), and as the Samaritans said of Him, *Servator mundi,* "the Saviour of the world," (John iv. 42), of Samaritans, Jews, Gentiles; of kings, of shepherds, and all.

And there is yet more particularity in this word Christ: three offices did God from the beginning erect to save His people by; and that by three acts—the very heathen took notice of them—1. *Purgare,* 2. *Illuminare,* 3. *Perficere.* 1. Priests, to purge or expiate; 2. Prophets, to illuminate or direct them; 3. Kings, to set all right, and to keep all right in that perfection which this world admitteth. And all these three had their several anointings. Aaron the Priest, (Lev. viii. 12), Elisha the Prophet, (1 Kings xix. 16), Saul the King. (1 Sam. x. 1.) In the Saviour Which is Christ, His will was all should meet, that nothing in Him might want to the perfecting of this work. That He might be a perfect Saviour of all, He was all. "A Priest after the order of Melchizedek," (Ps. cx. 4); a Prophet to be heard when Moses should hold his peace, (Deut. xviii. 18); a King to save His people, "Whose name should be *Jehova Justitia nostra.*" (Jer. xxiii. 6.) David's Priest, Moses' Prophet, Jeremy's King.

And these formerly had met double, two of them in some

other ; Melchizedek, King and Priest ; Samuel, Priest and Prophet ; David, Prophet and King. Never all three but in Him alone ; and so, no perfect Christ but He ; but He all, and so perfect. By His Priesthood to purge, expiate, and "save us from our sins, being a propitation to God for them," (1 John ii. 2) ; by His prophecy to illuminate and save us from the by-paths of error, "guiding our feet in the way of peace," (Luke i. 79) ; by His Kingdom protecting and conducting us through the miseries of this life, till He perfect us eternally by Himself in the joys of His Heavenly Kingdom. Rightly then, "a Saviour Which is Christ."

Now, as in the name Saviour there was, so is there like-wise joy in this name Christ ; and that, many ways : 1. First, that we shall hang no more in expectation, we shall be no longer, *Vincti spei*, "Hope's prisoners." (Zech. ix. 12.) He that should come is come. The promised Saviour, the Saviour Which is Christ is now born, and when *spes* becomes *res* then our joy is full. 2. That now there is a saving office erected, One anointed to that end, a professed Saviour to Whom all may resort. We shall not be to seek, "there is a name given under Heaven" (Acts iv. 12) whereby we may be sure of salvation, the Name of Christ. 3. That to this our saving we have the joint consent and good-will of all parties, in this name Christ. Christ, that is, the Anointed, what Person is He? The Son, the second Person. Anointed by whom? By the Father (*Quem unxisti*) (Acts iv. 27) the first Person. Anointed with what? With the Holy Ghost, (Acts x. 38), the third Person. So a concurrence of all Persons in this Name, all willing and well-pleased with the work of our salvation. 4. If we would be saved, we would be saved *unctione*, 'by oil,' not by vinegar. *Et unguentum effusum Nomen ejus ;* "and His name is Christ, one that saveth by anointing." (Cant. i. 3.) 5. And if by oil—there be hot oils—with a gentle lenitive oil. And the oil which He useth, wherewith He is anointed, is the oil of gladness. Gladness therefore must needs go with this Name. Which oil of gladness is not for Himself but for us, not for His use but for ours. So He saith Himself in His first sermon at Nazareth, upon His text out of Esay. (Isa. lxi. 1). The anointing, this oil of gladness, was upon Him to bestow it upon us, and of us ; upon them especially that through a wounded conscience were troubled with the spirit of heaviness, to turn their heaviness into joy. Glad then that He is come that by His office is to save, and come with the good liking of all; to save us by oil, and that the oil of gladness.

And yet to make our joy more full the Angel addeth the third. "A Saviour Which is Christ, Christ the Lord." For neither is this all. He is not Christ only. We must not stay there. For the name of Christ will agree, hath been, and may be imparted to others besides. Many a king in Scripture hath had the honour to carry the name of Christ, but with a difference. The king, *christus Domini,* 'the Lord's christ;' He *Christus Dominus,* "the Lord Christ," or "Christ the Lord." Consider then, how great this Child is, (Heb. vii. 4), Whose anointed kings themselves are. For if they be *christi Domini,* 'the Lord's anointed;' His they are, for He is the Lord. The Lord absolute, without any addition; ye may put it to what ye will—Lord of men and Angels, Lord of Heaven and earth, and all the hosts of them, *Dominus Christorum,* and *Dominus Dominorum,* "Lord paramount over all."

But why the Lord? Because this name of Christ will sort with men. Nay, as He is Christ, that is anointed, He is man only. It is His name as Man, for God cannot be anointed. But He that should save us would be more than Man; and so, more than Christ. Indeed, Christ cannot save us. He that must save us must be the Lord. For "such a Saviour it behoveth us to have," (Heb. vii. 26), as might not begin the work of our salvation and leave it in the midst, but go through with it and make an end too, which the former saviours could not do. Formerly, ever their complaint was, that their saviours, their christs died still, and left them to seek; their kings, and priests, and prophets, dropped away still, for "they were not suffered to endure by reason of death." (Heb. vii. 23, 24.) But this Saviour, this Christ, because He is the Lord, "endureth for ever, hath an everlasting Priesthood," Kingdom, and Prophecy, and so "is able perfectly to save them that come to God by Him." This is one reason, why hither we must come at the last to Christ the Lord, and till we be at it we be not where we should. Else, our saviours will die and leave us destitute.

But the main reason is set down by Esay, *Ego sum, Ego sum,* saith God Himself, *et præter Me non est Servator;* "It

is I, I that am the Saviour, I am, and besides Me there is
no Saviour," (Isa. xliii. 11) ; none indeed, no true Saviour
but the Lord. All other are short, *Vana salus hominis,* saith
the Psalm, " Man's salvation is vain," any salvation is vain
if it be not the Lord's. 1. Those christs that were not the
Lord could save but the body, and not one of them quicken
his own soul ; Christ that is the Lord can save souls and
bodies, His own and others both. Those christs that were
not the Lord, could save but from carnal enemies, with
arms of flesh ; He, from our ghostly enemies, even " spiritual
wickednesses in heavenly places," from Abaddon the great
destroyer of the bottomless pit. 3. They that were not the
Lord could save but from worldly calamities, could but
prune and take off the twigs, as it were; He, from sin itself,
and so plucketh it up by the roots. 4. They that were not
the Lord, put it off but for a time, and after it came again
—temporal only. He for ever, once for all ; and is become
" Author of eternal salvation " (Heb. v. 9) to all that depend
on Him. And mark that word " eternal," for none but the
Lord can work eternal salvation. 5. They all had need of
a Saviour themselves, and of this Saviour ; He needs none,
receives of none, imparts to all, as being not a Saviour only
but *Salus ipsa in abstracto,* " Salvation itself," (Luke ii. 30)
as Simeon calleth Him " of Whose fulness we all receive."
(John i. 14.) To save may agree to man ; to be salvation
can agree to none but to Christ the Lord. To begin and
to end; to save soul and body from bodily and ghostly
enemies ; from sin the root, and misery the branches ; for a
time and for ever ; to be a Saviour and to be salvation
itself ; Christ the Lord is all this, and can do all this. Now
then we are right, and never till now. " A Saviour Which
is Christ the Lord."

But the name " Lord " goeth yet further, not only to save
us and set us free from danger, to deliver us from evil ; but
to state us in as good and better condition than we forfeited
by our fall, or else though we were saved we should not save
by the match. To make us then savers, and not savers only
but gainers and that great gainers by our salvation, He doth
further impart also the estate annexed of this last title, even
whatsoever He is Lord of Himself. And He is " Lord of
life," (Acts iii. 15), saith St. Peter ; life then He imparts.
And He is " Lord of Glory," (1 Cor. ii. 8), saith St. Paul ;

glory then He imparts. And He is Lord of joy, *intra in gaudium Domini,* "enter into the joy of the Lord," (Mat. xxv. 21); joy then He imparts. Life and glory and joy; and makes us lords of them, and of whatsoever is within the name and title of Lord. For having thereto a double right, 1. by inheritance as the Son, (Heb. i. 2), 2. and by purchase as a Redeemer, (for "therefore He died and rose again, that He might be Lord of all,"), (Rom. xiv. 9) ; contenting Himself with the former, He is well pleased to set over the latter to us, and admit us with Himself into His estate of joint-purchase of Heaven, or whatsoever He is owner of ; that in right of it we may enter into the life, glory, and joy of our Lord, and so be saved and be savers, and more than savers every way. This also is in the word "Lord," this benefit farther we have by it.

And now, if we will put together *natus* and *Servator, Servator* and *Christus, Christus* and *Dominus, Dominus* and *natus ;* 'born and Saviour, Saviour and Christ, Christ and the Lord, the Lord and born;' take them which way you will in combination, any of the four, then have we His two natures in one Person. In *Servator,* His Godhead ; none but God is a Saviour. In *Christus,* His Manhood; God cannot be anointed, man may. In *Dominus,* His Divine again, "the Lord from Heaven." In *Natus,* His human nature directly, born of a woman ; both ever carefully joined, and to be joined together. When St. Matthew had begun His Gospel thus, "The Book of the Generation of Jesus Christ the Son of David," (Mat. i. 1)—one nature, His humanity ; St. Mark was careful to begin his thus, "The beginning of the Gospel of Jesus Christ the Son of God," (Mark i. 1)—the other nature, His divinity. But St. John he joins them, *Verbum caro factum est,* "the Word became flesh." (John i. 14.) *Verbum,* "the Word," there is *Dominus ;* and *caro,* "the flesh," that is *natus.*

And even this very conjunction is a new joy. For that such an one, that the Lord would condescend to be born, besides the benefit there is also matter of honour. Even that He, so great a person, would become such as we are, would so esteem our nature as to take it upon Him—this certainly is a great dignity and exaltation of our nature, and it is matter of new joy that He would so highly value it as to assume, associate, and unite it into one Person with the Son of God. By this we see why "a Saviour," why "Christ," why "the Lord." "A Saviour," His name of benefit whereby He is to deliver us; "Christ," His name of office whereby He is bound to undertake it; "the Lord," His name of power whereby He is able to effect it. We see also why Man, and why God. First, so it should be, for of right none was to make satisfaction for man but man; and in very deed none was able to give satisfaction to God but God. So that being to satisfy God for man, He was to be God and man. Secondly, so we would wish it ourselves: if we would be saved, we would be saved by one of our nature, not by any stranger. He is born, and so one of our own nature. Again, if we would be saved, we would be saved by no inferior, but by the best; He is the Lord, and so the very best of all. And so, our desire is satisfied every way.

This blessed birth of this "Saviour Which is Christ the Lord" thus furnished in every point to save us throughly, body and soul, from sin and destruction, and Satan the destroyer of both, and that both here, and for ever—this blessed and thrice blessed birth is the substance of this day's solemnity of the Angel's message, and of our joy.

And now to the circumstances; and first of the persons, *vobis;* "I bring you good tidings, that to you is born," &c.

We find not any word through all but there is joy in it, and yet all is suspended till we come to this one word, *vobis;* this makes up all. This word therefore we shall do well ever to look for, and when we find it to make much of it. Nothing passeth without it; it is the word of application. But for it, all the rest are loose; this girds it on, this fastens it to us, and makes it ours. But for it, we are but in their case, *Quid nobis et Tibi,* "What have we to do with Thee?" (Matt. viii. 29.) This "Saviour Christ the Lord," in this good time and fit place, *quid ad nos?* "what are we the better?" *Omni populo,* is somewhat too general, and the hundredth part of them shall not be benefited by Him. We would hear it in more particularity. Why *vobis,* "for you it is," born for you. Yea, now ye say somewhat.

And twice it is repeated for failing, in either verse once. *Evangelizo vobis,* and *natus vobis,* that ye may know the message is yours, and the birth is yours; therefore the message is sent to you, because the birth concerneth you. But yours they be, both.

May we then be bold to change the person, and utter it in the first which he doth in the second, and say, *nobis!* We may sure—*Puer natus est nobis;* Esay hath said it before us. (Isa. ix. 6.) And thereby lieth a mystery. The Angels they say, *vobis:* the Prophets were men; men say, *nobis.* Bid the Angel say, *nobis,* he cannot—neither sing nor say it; *Angelis* he cannot, ' to Angels,' (*Nusquam Angelos,*) (Heb. ii. 16); but *hominibus* "unto men," (Luke ii. 14), he can and doth. And this is a special high prerogative; that which the Angels can neither sing nor say, we can do both.

If then He be born to us, it is to some end. Esay tells us what it is, when he expoundeth *natus* by *datus,* "born to us" by "given us." Born, to be bestowed upon us. And if given us, bestowed upon us, then He is ours. Ours His benefit, His office, His power. His benefit to save us, His office to undertake us, His power to assure us. Ours, His salvation as Jesus, His anointing as Christ, His dominion as the Lord. And if He be ours, then all His are ours; *Omnia Ejus nostra sunt,* (Luke xv. 31); His birth ours, and if His birth, all that follow His birth, ours too.

Now then, seeing He and they be ours, will it not be well done to make our entry, to take *seisin* of Him and them, and dispose them to our best benefit? And how can we do that better than as God hath offered Him to us this day that He was born for us, so we reciprocally this day that He is born offer Him again to God as the best pleasing oblation that we can offer Him. To-day, as in the Temple alive for our morning oblation; and when the time cometh of His death, offer Him as on the Cross slain for our evening sacrifice. So shall we, as Bernard wisheth us, *uti Nostro in utilitatem nostram, et de Salvatore salutem operari,* 'employ, or make use of Him for our best behoof; draw His proper extract from Him, and work salvation out of this our Saviour.'

III. Now a word only, what is to be done on our parts and that respectively to these two points, what we are to return to them; what to this message, and what to this birth.

To the message, *Evangelizo vobis,* this we are to return;

this is due to a message—to hear it. And that we do, and
this is all; we come to the Sermon, we hear it, and little
we do besides. But we hear it but heavily, with a faint
affection, God knoweth; we hear it not as an *ecce,* as matter
of high admiration; we hear it not as *gaudium magnum,*
with that alacrity and cheerfulness we should. We hear it
not as *nobis,* as if it nearly touched us, but as a matter that
little concerned us, it skilled not much whether we heard it
or no. Many meaner things affect us more, but this should
be the joyfullest hearing that we ever heard.

And shall we not likewise perform some duty to *natus
est?* Yes, even to that also. And not hear of Him, and
let Him alone; hear His tidings, and let Himself go.

He was "born for us and given us," *natus nobis* and
donatus nobis—both go together in the Prophet. To a gift
the duty that belongeth properly, is to receive it. If He
be *natus nobis* and *donatus nobis,* I trust we will take order
He be *acceptus a nobis.* If "born for us, and given us," it
is our part then, we can do no less than receive Him. We
evacuate the gift, disgrace both the Giver and it, if we
vouchsafe not to accept of it.

How is that? how shall we receive Him? who shall give
Him us? That shall One That will say unto us within a
while, *Accipite,* "Take, this is My Body," "by the offering
whereof ye are sanctified." (Heb. x. 10.) "Take, this is
My Blood," by the shedding whereof ye are saved. Both
in the holy mysteries ordained by God as pledges to assure
us, and as conduit pipes to convey into us this and all other
the benefits that come by this our Saviour.

Verily, upon His memorable days, of which this is the
first, we are bound to do something in memory, or remembrance of Him. What is that? Will ye know what it is?
Hoc facite, "Do this in remembrance of Me."

Something would be thought on "to return Him for all
His benefits," and this day for this first, the fountain of all
the rest—His birth. Some thanks would be rendered Him
for it. And how can we do that better than as we are
taught by him that studied the point of *quid retribuam,* and
resolved it thus; no way so well as by *accipiam Calicem,*
"I will take the Cup of salvation." (Ps. cxvi. 13.) And so
do it; so, with it taken into our hands, "give thanks to the
name of the Lord." And when better than to-day, *hodie,*

as we are here directed? What better day than on this day, the very day He was bestowed on us? To defer Him no longer than He did us. He deferred not us at all, but as soon as He was born sent us word the same instant; and shall we defer Him to hear of us another time, and not be as ready on our part to receive Him instantly as He was on His to bestow Himself; even presently, as soon as He was born? Sure, somewhat would be done more than ordinary this day of His birth; the day itself is more than ordinary.

And let this move us. If ever there be a day of salvation, *ecce hic est dies salutis*, behold this is it when a Saviour is born unto us. If ever an accepted time *ecce tempus acceptum*, behold, now it is, this is that time. The birth-day hath ever been a time accepted. Then, one king forgave the trespass of his servant and received him to grace. (Gen. xl. 21.) Another, being pleased, was ready in his bounty to have given away the one half of his kingdom. (Mark vi. 23.) Our Saviour Christ, our Lord, on His birth-day will be no worse than they. His bounty *then* no less than theirs.

Let us then make this so accepted a time in itself twice acceptable by our accepting, which He will acceptably take at our hands. Let us honour this day with our receiving, which He hath honoured by His first giving; yielding Him evermore (but this day, the day of it, chiefly,) our unfeigned hearty thanksgiving for this so good news, for this so great a gift, both of them this day vouchsafed us; in Him and for Him, Who was Himself the gift, our "Saviour, Christ the Lord." To Whom, with the Father, and the Holy Ghost, three Persons, one immortal, ever-living, invisible, only wise God; be all honour, glory, blessing, praise, and thanksgiving, this day and for ever.

SERMON VI.

A Sermon Preached before the King's Majesty, at
Whitehall, on Wednesday, the Twenty-fifth of
December, a.d. mdcxi., being Christmas-day.

*And the Word was made flesh and dwelt among us, (and we
saw the glory thereof, as the glory of the only-begotten Son
of the Father), full of grace and truth.* John i. 14.

[*Et Verbum caro factum est, et habitavit in nobis: et vidimus gloriam
ejus, gloriam quasi unigeniti a Patre plenum gratiæ, et veritatis.*
Latin Vulg.]

THERE is in the Old Testament, in the tenth of Ezekiel,
(Ezek. x. 14), and in the New, in the fourth of the
Revelation, (Rev. iv. 6, 7), a vision of four sundry
shapes, a man, a lion, an ox, and an eagle. It hath been
usually received, to apply these four to the four Evangelists,
and of them the eagle to St. John. The nature of the eagle
is by God Himself described by two properties, 1. *elevare ad
ardua,* (Job xxxix. 27), no fowl under Heaven towereth so
high; 2. and *ubicunque fuerit cadaver statim adest,* (Matt.
xxiv. 28); none so soon or so suddenly down upon the body
as he. Both these do lively express themselves in St. John,
and no where more lively than in this Gospel. Wherein, as
an eagle in the clouds, he first mounteth wonderfully high
beyond Moses and his *in principio,* with an higher *in principio*
than it; beyond Genesis and the world's creation, (Gen. i.
1): and "the Word was then with God, and was God."
(John i. 1.) This may well be termed the eagle's flight, so
exceeding high as the clearest eye hath much ado to follow
him. Yet so far as they can follow him, the very philosophers have been driven to admire the penning of this
Gospel. But after this, as an eagle again, (*ubi corpus, ibi
aquila,*) (Luke xvii. 37), down he cometh directly from the
height of Heaven, and lights upon the body of His flesh,
the mystery of his incarnation; and tells us, that He that
"in the beginning was *apud Deum* and *Deus*"—He "in the
fulness of time" was *apud homines* and *homo.* He dwelt not
long aloft, He knew it was not to purpose; *Verbum Deus*
is far above our reach. *Verbum caro* that concerns us. No

time but it concerns us, but this time above others. This feast is held, this assembly met, for no other end but to celebrate the contents of the text, that the Word being made flesh this day came to dwell among us.

Two parts there be in the text, sensibly parted by a parenthesis. I. That without the parenthesis is that he would have us believe *Verbum caro, &c.* II. That within is the affidavit, *vidimus &c.* In the former three things are affirmed of the Word. 1. *Factum a nobis;* 2. *habitavit in nobis;* 3. *plenum pro nobis;* 1. that the Word was made flesh of us ; 2. dwelt with us ; 3. was full for us.

Then followeth the affidavit of these. That St. John, and other more besides, saw, and so spake no more than they knew ; nor testify no more than they had seen. (1 John i. 2.) The best proof that can be. They saw (though not the Word Himself, yet) His glory : we saw His glory. And that glory such as would suit with none but Him ; and so, every way sufficient to demonstrate Him the only Son of God.

And, after all this one more there is without which His making, dwelling, and seeing, were to little purpose ; that is, that as He came not obscurely but was seen, so He came not empty but "full of grace and truth." (John i. 14.) This fulness was not for Himself, but for us ; *et de plenitudine Ejus omnes accepimus.*

There is not any thing that concerneth this mystery, but is within this text. His two natures, "the Word," and "flesh :" 1. "Word," divine ; 2. "flesh," human. The union of them in *factum est;* union into a Person, in *habitavit; habitare, est personæ.* 3. Then, His office also— ἐσκήνωσε, which is not only *habitavit,* but *castrametavit in nobis;* not only, took a house, but "pitched a pavilion in us ;" not only, *factus incola,* 'made our neighbour,' but made a champion for us to undertake our quarrel and to fight a combat. 4. And last, the benefit; "made," that He might " dwell ; " and "dwell," that He might impart to us, and we derive from Him, that whereof He was full, and we were empty—we had need, and He had store ; "grace and truth."

All reducible to these three: I. *Quod Verbum caro;* II. *Quid Verbum carni;* III. *Quid caro Verbo.* I. 'That the Word became flesh ;' the mystery. II. 'What the Word did for flesh;' the benefit.   III. 'And what flesh is to do to the Word again;' the duty.

I. We are in a deep point, and a dangerous.   It will not be amiss to pause a little on the three terms, *Verbum, caro,* and, *factum est.*   "The Word."   1. There be that take this name to be given Him, as who should say; He, of Whom so many excellent words are spoken all along this book, so many words of promise and prophecy, and all of Him—so the word, *objective.*   2. Others; for that He discloseth to us all God's counsel, even as the word openeth the mind of man; by Whom as His Word, we know whatsoever we know of the Father's mind: so the word *effective.*   3. A third; for that he cometh not only as Jesus to save us but as the Word to teach us, we as to honour Him so learn His word as the way to our salvation: so the word *præceptive.*

4. These are all well and true all, but all short.   We may have use of them, but there is a farther matter than all these.   This Word, as we find in the affidavit, is " the Only-begotten of the Father."   These two are one and the same, but need to be set in two terms, that what is wanting in the one may be supplied by the other; (so high is the divine nature above our reach as no one term is able to express it; it is well if divers will do it).   In this they agree; as the Son is to the Father, so is the word to the mind.   The Son, *Proles parentis;* the word, *proles mentis.*   They proceed both.   The Son from the Father, the word from the mind; and so note out unto us a party proceeding, a second Person from the first; from Him that begetteth, the Son; from Him that speaketh, the word; against Sabellius.

The Son referreth to a living nature, the Word addeth farther an intellectual nature; *generare est viventium, loqui intelligentium;* that there is in Him not only the nature and life, but the wisdom of the Father.

Both proceed.   The Word sheweth the manner; the Son, the truth of His proceeding.   With us the son is not begot but by flesh, by propagation; the Word therefore requisite to shew His proceeding was after no carnal manner, but as the word from the mind.   A better term could not be devised.   For there is not in all the world a more pure, simple, inconcrete procreation than that whereby the mind conceiveth the word within it, by *dixit in corde.*   For in itself and of itself doth the mind produce it without help of any mixture of ought, without any passion stirring or agitation at all. Such was the issue of the Word eternal. But then, lest we might imagine God's Word to be to Him no other than ours is to us, not of our substance; He makes amends for that and tells us He is "the Only-begotten," and so of the substance of His Father, ("very God, of very God"), as all begotten sons be. The Word, to shew His proceeding pure and merely spiritual; the Son, to shew that for all that it is true and substantial. Truly consubstantial with the Father, as the Son; but in all clean and pure manner conceived, as the Word.

The Son though He be consubstantial, yet the Person of His Father may have a being long before Him. The Word makes amends for that. For the mind's conceiving and the mind cannot be severed a moment; if one be eternal, both are. So then as the Son He is consubstantial, as the Word He is coeternal.

But He begins with the Word. His care being first to tell us of the pureness of His generation before of His generation itself; but after, by little and little unfoldeth Himself and tells, He is so the Word as the Son also. Indeed, it was best beginning with the Word. That term the heathen wise men, the philosophers, would never stumble at, but brook it well enough; as indeed they did not with approbation only, but with high admiration, read and magnify the beginning of this Gospel. Witness Tertul. in Apol., Euseb. in Præpar., August. de Civit. 10., and Theodoret. It was conform to their reason, *Quod Deus ab æterno intelligit*, and that Νοῦς and Λόγος, 'the conceiving of the mind,' and 'the mind' must needs be coeternal—the mind never without it; as the Prophet saith, *Egressus Ejus a diebus æternitatis.* (Mic. v. 2.) This for the Word of much more that might be said of it.

As the Word and the Only-begotten refer to One, so doth *caro* and *in nobis*, flesh and in us; that is, such flesh as is in us, human flesh. 1. To express the union fully, a better word could not be chosen. It is a part for the whole, and the worser part for the whole of purpose. For in this case our nature is best set out by the worser part. For this we know; if the worse be taken, the better will not be left behind. If He abhor not the flesh, of the spirit there will be no question. More forcible it is to say, " He was made flesh," than " He was made man ; " though both be true. He vouchsafed to become man, nothing so much as to become flesh, the very lowest and basest part of man.

Besides, from the flesh, as from Eve, came the beginning of transgression—longing after the forbidden fruit, refused the Word quite ; so, of all other, least likely to be taken. The Word not refusing it, the rest have good hope.

But there is a kind of necessity to use the term flesh. If He had said ' man,' man might be taken for a person. He took no person, but our nature He took. Flesh is no person but nature only, and so best expresseth it. And if soul, it might have been taken, as if He took not the flesh but *mediante anima ;* but so He did not but as immediately and as soon the flesh as the soul, in one instant both.

Yet one more. It will not be amiss to tell you; the word that is Hebrew for flesh the same is also Hebrew for good tidings—as we call it, the Gospel ; sure, not without the Holy Ghost so dispensing it. There could be no other meaning but that some incarnation, or making flesh, should be generally good news for the whole world. To let us know this good tidings is come to pass He tells us, The Word is now become flesh.

Thus, why flesh; now, why the Word, flesh. *Caro Verbum* was our bane. Flesh would be the Word ; nay, wiser than the Word, and known what was evil better than it. If *caro Verbum* our bane, then *Verbum caro* our remedy.

Surely, if the Word would become flesh, it were so most kindly. The Word was *Pars læsa,* ' the Party that was most offended.' If He would undertake it, if He against Whom the offence was would be Author of the reconciliation, there were none to that. It were so most proper.

But in another respect He were fit too. He had said above, " all things were made by Him," (John i. 3) ; a kind of meetness there were *ut per quem facta omnia per eumdem refecta,* (Colos. i. 16, 17), ' He that first made them should restore them ; He that built, repair '—so is best ever.

And indeed, *sic oportet implere omnem justitiam,* " that were the way to fulfil all justice," (Matt. iii. 15) ; if the Word would take flesh, He might make full amends for the flesh's fault in rejecting the Word. So is justice ; that flesh for flesh, and not the flesh of oxen and sheep but even that flesh that sinneth (our flesh) should suffer for it, and so suffering make satisfaction to justice.

Why then, *factum est caro*, "the Word is made flesh;" this makes up all. For, *factum est, ergo est;* 'He is made flesh, therefore is flesh.' *Fieri terminatur ad esse,* 'the end of making is being.' And *per modum naturæ*, (so is ἐγένετο, the Greek word :) 'this being is natural;' *et nativitas est via ad naturam,* 'and nativity is the way to nature.' So, to be born; as this day He was. *Venit per carnem, sanat per verbum,* "that all flesh may see the salvation of God." (Luke iii. 6.) "Made" it was; against Manicheus holding that He had no true body; as if *factum* had been *fictum*, or making were mocking. Made it was, but how made? Not *convertendo*, 'the Word converted into flesh,' as Cerinthus; or 'flesh converted into the Word,' *Verbum caro facta est*, as Valentinus; for the Deity cannot be changed into any thing, nor any thing into it. Nor made *conciliando*, as friends are made, so as they continue two several persons still; and while the flesh suffered the Word stood by and looked on, as Nestorius. That is *cum carne*, not *caro;* 'made with flesh,' not 'flesh;' and never was one person said to be made another. Nor made by compounding; and so a third thing produced of both, as Eutyches. For so, He should be neither of both, Word nor flesh, neither God nor man.

But "made" He was; St. Paul tells us how; *assumendo,* "by taking the seed of Abraham." (Heb. ii. 16.) His generation eternal, as *Verbum Deus*, is as the inditing the word within the heart. His generation in time, *Verbum caro*, is as the uttering it forth with the voice. The inward motion of the mind taketh unto it a natural body of air, and so becometh vocal : it is not changed into it, the word remaineth still as it was, yet they two come one voice. Take a similitude from ourselves. Our soul is not turned into nor compounded with the body, yet they two though distinct in natures grow into one man. So, into the Godhead was the Manhood taken ; the natures preserved without confusion, the person entire without division. Take the definition of the fourth General Council : *Sic factum est caro ut maneret Verbum, non immutando quod erat, sed suscipiendo quod non erat; nostra auxit, sua non minuit; nec Sacramentum pietatis detrimentum Deitatis;* 'He was so made flesh that he ceased not to be the Word, never changing that He was, but taking that He was not; we were the better, He was never the worse; the mystery of godliness was no detriment to the Godhead, nor the honour of the creature wrong to the Creator.'

And now, being past these points of belief I come to that which I had much rather stand on, and so it is best for us; that which may stir up our love to Him That thus became flesh for us.

First, comparing *factum* with *dictum*. For if we were so much beholden for *verbum dictum*, " the word spoken," the promise; how much more for *Verbum factum*, 'the performance?' If for *factum carni*, 'the word that came to flesh,' how then for *factum caro*, 'became flesh?'

Then, taking *factum* absolutely. The Word " by Whom all things were made," (John i. 3), to come to be made Itself. It is more for Him, *fieri*, 'to be made' anything, than *facere*, 'to make' another world, yea many worlds more. There is more a great deal in this *factum est*, than in *omnia per Ipsum facta sunt;* in ' He made,' than in " All things by Him were made."

Factum est, with what He was made. For if made, made the most complete thing of all that ever He had made; made a Spirit, for God is a Spirit, (John iv. 24)—some degree of nearness between them; but what is man that He should be made him, or the son of man that He should take His nature upon Him! (Ps. viii. 4, and Heb. ii. 7.)

If man, yet the more noble part, the immortal part, the soul; what else? There are some points of His image in that; it understandeth, it loveth, hath a kind of capacity of the word. So hath not the flesh. It is *res bruta*, ' common to them with us;' neither able to understand, or love, or in any degree capable of it. Make it the soul, " the precious soul," (Prov. vi. 26)—so calleth it Solomon ; not the body, " the vile body," (Phil. iii. 21)—so the Apostle calleth it. Of the Word He said ever, *vidimus gloriam Ejus*, " we saw the glory of It." Of the flesh we may say *vidimus sordes ejus*, ' we daily see that comes from it ;' as *non est vilius sterquilinium*, 'on the dung-hill worse is not to be seen.' Set not so precious a stone in so base metal.

But this is not all. If He must be made, for love of God make Him something wherein is some good, for " in our flesh" St. Paul saith "there dwelleth no good," (Rom. vii. 18) ; yea, " the very wisdom of the flesh at flat defiance with the word." (Rom. viii. 7.) Make it somewhat else. For there is not only a huge distance, but main repugnancy between them. Yet for all this *non potest solvi Scriptura*, (John x. 35), " the Word was made flesh."

I add yet farther ; what flesh ? The flesh of an infant. What, *Verbum infans*, the Word an infant ? The Word, and not be able to speak a word ? How evil agreeth this ! This He put up. How born, how entertained ? In a stately palace, cradle of ivory, robes of estate ? No ; but a stable for His palace, a manger for His cradle, poor clouts for His array. This was His beginning. Follow Him farther, if any better afterward ; what flesh afterward ? *Sudans et algens*, in cold and heat, hungry and thirsty, faint and weary. Is His end any better ? that maketh up all : what flesh then ? *Cujus livore sanati*, (Isa. liii. 5), black and blue, bloody and swollen, rent and torn, the thorns and nails sticking in His flesh ; and such flesh He was made. A great *factum* certainly, and much to be made of. To have been made *caput Angelorum* had been an abasement ; to be made *minoratus Angelis* (Heb. ii. 7) is more ; but, to be *novissimus virorum*, " in worst case of all men," (Isa. liii. 3), nay, " a worm and no man," (Ps. xxii. 6) ; so to be born, so arrayed, and so housed, and so handled—there is not the meanest flesh but is better. So to be made, and so unmade ; to take it on and lay it off,with so great indignity : weigh it and wonder, at it that ever He would endure to be made flesh, and to be made it on this manner. What was it made the Word thus to be made flesh ? *Non est lex hominis ista*, ' flesh would never have been brought to it.' It was God, and in God nothing but love ; *dilexit* with *sic*, (John iii. 16) *charitas* with an *ecce*, (1 John iii. 1) ; *fecit amor ut Verbum caro fieret ; Zelus Domini exercituum fecit hoc.* (2 Kings xix. 31.) Love only did it. *Quid sit, possit, debeat, non recipit jus amoris*, ' That only cares not for any *exinanivit*, any *humiliavit se*, any emptying, humbling, loss of reputation ; love respects it not, cares not what flesh He be made, so the flesh be made by it.'

" And dwelt." *Factum est* is the word of nature ; *habitavit* of person ; *habitare est personæ.* And two there are not. It is not *habitaverunt* ; therefore, but one person,

And *habitavit* is a word of continuance; that which was begun in *factum*, is continued in *habitavit*. Not only made, but made stay, made His abode with us; not appeared and was gone again straight, but for a time took up His dwelling; *factus caro, factus incola.* And this word concerns this day properly. This is the day, the first day of *habitavit in nobis.* Incarnate He was in the Virgin's womb, His taking flesh could not be seen. But this draweth after it a *vidimus*, dwelt and was seen visibly.

And this leadeth us to a third, *conversatus est. Factum*, and *factum familiare;* that He withdrew not Himself into some solitary place, but was *Verbum prope nos*, "near us," (Rom. x. 8), near neighbours to us. *Habitu inventus ut homo*, "in His habit, and in His habitation, found as a man." (Phil. ii. 7.) One might ask Him as they at verse 38, *ubi habitas*, "Sir, where dwell you?" and He invited them to come and see.

And ἐσκήνωσε is not every dwelling, but a dwelling in σκηνῇ, 'a tent' that is but for a time. Not a house to stand for ever, but a tent to be taken down again. Which as it sheweth His Tabernacle of the nature of ours, mortal; so withal, that He came but of an errand, to sojourn till He had done it. A work He had for which He was sent; that being done, He laid His Tabernacle off again.

And even that work itself is in σκηνῶσαι, for it is a word *militare.* Soldiers dwell in tents. As if He were now *factus caro, incola, miles*, as if some battle were toward. And indeed from the beginning, the very third of Genesis, there was war proclaimed between the woman's Seed and the serpent's. (Gen. iii. 15.) An enemy we had, strong and mighty; had, and have still; not one, but many, a whole camp of them. They had prevailed, and led us away "captive under the law of sin." (Rom. vii. 23.) *Dux nobis opus est*, 'a champion we stood in need of' to rescue us. And here we have One now, even *Dux Messias* (Dan. ix. 25) as Daniel calleth Him. He, as this day, came into the camp, set up His pavilion among us. The Tabernacle of God was with men. He might not stay eight days in the camp but He must take *Sacramentum militare;* so He did. And the ceremony of it was to be stricken, and to bleed some small quantity. So He was at His Circumcision, and after He performed the battle at His Passion,

Where, though it cost Him His life, yet the victory fell on His side; "captivity was led captive," (Eph. iv. 8), and we were delivered. His tent ·was but a forerunner to His combat. This for His dwelling. Now the affidavit.

As the word *habitavit* pointeth us to this first day of the feast, and His tent to the middle day when He undertook our quarrel; so *vidimus* now is proper to the last day, the day of manifestation, or Epiphany. He dwelt; and not invisibly or obscurely, but so as He might be and was seen. Even this very first day, *vidimus*, might the shepherds say, 'we saw' His Angels and heard them sing, and then went to Bethlehem and saw Himself. *Vidimus*, might the wise men say; "we saw His Star in the East," (Matt. ii. 2), and we are come to see Himself. This they might say, and truly; for these things were not done *in obscuro.* (Acts xxvi. 26.) But, as we said, this clause is the affidavit, it is inferred as a proof. You tell us of His making, and His dwelling; *quomodo constat?* How shall it appear? *Vidimus* is the best proof that can be; "He saw it, was an eye-witness of what He testified." (John xix. 35.)

And it is not *vidi*, but *vidimus;* more eyes than one. Not he alone, others more saw it besides him. "In the mouth of two or three witnesses"—Peter, James, and he, (*vidimus*) were in the holy Mount together, and saw Him transfigured. (Matt. xvii. 1, 2.) Nay, a whole "cloud of witnesses," (Heb. xii. 1), one hundred and twenty, saw Him taken up into Heaven out of their sight, in the Mount of Olives. (1 John i. 3, and Acts i. 9.) Well might he say, *vidimus.*

And that not *per transennam*, 'at a blush,' passing by; but had a full sight, looked well upon Him, at leisure; did it throughly, for a good time together. It is not ὁρᾷν, but θεάσασθαι, the word whence a theatre is derived: as men with good heed behold things there, so did we intentively all the acts and scenes of His life.

But I ask, what saw they? The flesh peradventure; the Word they could not see. He is God, and "God hath no man ever seen." (St. John i. 18.) True; that they could not, yet His Glory they might and did. Which glory was an infallible demonstration of His Presence there. "Through the veil of His flesh" (Heb. x. 20) such beams He cast, as behind those clouds they might know there was a sun; as that way only could He be made visible to the eyes of flesh, which otherwise could not behold Him.

But it may be it was some wrong, this ; but such as was seen in Moses', or in Stephen's countenance.   He answers that and tells us, It was not *quasi servi,* 'like a servant;' nay, nor *quasi filii,* 'like any adopted sons ;' but this glory was every way such as well might it beseem the Word or only Son, but could agree to no creature, though never so glorious.   To none but Him ; and so being *proprium quarto modo* might be a *medius terminus* in a demonstration.

And if you ask what that glory might be ?   With a word to say to the wind and storm, *Obmutesce,* (Mark iv. 39); and to diseases, *Volo. Mundare,* (Matt. viii. 3); and to death itself, *Tibi dico, Surge.* (Luke vii. 14.)   His miracles they shewed His glory, is expressly said in the next chapter, ver. 11.   The star at His birth, the eclipse at His death, the glory of His changing in the Mount; but above all, His glorious Ascension, and receiving up into Heaven.   All which they saw, as being in the theatre all the while from the epitasis to the very catastrophe.   Therefore he tells us here and again in his Epistle, he writes nothing but "what he saw and beheld and even his hands had handled of the Word of Life." (1 John i. 3.)   We may believe him ; he and his *contestes* suffered many things for the truth of their witness, and the whole world since hath believed this their affidavit.   Now are we past the parenthesis.

But what, is all that a *vidimus?* nothing but a mask to be seen ? came He only to make a glorious show to them all?   No ; but as He came not obscure but was seen, so He came not empty but full and was felt of them that saw Him not.   *Vidimus* is not all—a verse after there is *accepimus ;* to see His glory they receive of His fulness, they and we.

Many are the perfections whereof He is full.   Two only here chosen out, as two streams, 1. Grace, and 2. Truth. With them He cometh, with the fulness of them ; not of one of them, but of both.   Grace referreth to the Son, truth to the Word ; grace is to adopt us, truth to beget us anew ; for "of His own will He hath begotten us by the Word of truth." (James i. 18.)

And these do very fitly follow after glory.   Glory of itself terrifies and makes stand aloof, grace invites; and His glory is such as is full of grace. His mercy, as great as His Majesty full out. A blessed thing it is when these two meet, and they that are in glory are full of grace, too. It is not so with every one that is in glory; but though there be grace, unless there be truth too, all is nothing. For grace, because it is plausible and pleaseth the people, it is affected; there is a taking on grace in face and phrase, but when all is done, it wanteth sound truth. That is right grace that hath truth joined to it. *Verbum gratiæ*, and *verbum charitatis* both, and it is both. Yea, *verbum caro*, His word is not wind, it hath flesh on it; His truth is, as it were, the flesh of His grace. Thus may be the consequence.

But of these two choice is made, as of those our nature stood most in need of. Out of grace we were and without grace, as sinners and in errors wandering up and down; as even the best of our nature did at His coming into the flesh. This is the state He found us in when He came among us.

Against the first, *gratificavit nos in Dilecto*, "He brought us in grace again through His beloved Son." (Eph. i. 6.) *Gratiam pro gratia*, (John i. 16), He saith after straight, "For the grace His Son had with Him, He received us to grace."

Against the latter, He brought us truth to set us in the right way. *Via, Veritas, et Vita*, (John xiv. 6)—*Veritas* between both—*Via et Veritas*, or *Veritas Viæ*, ' the true Way;' *Vita et Veritas*, or *Veritas Vitæ*, the true Life that is Life eternal. We cannot be without either.

This for our need. But within a verse after I find these two set in opposition to the Law, and the Law to them; as if St. John pointed us whereto we should refer them. The Law full of rigour, many threats, and curses in it—Christ bringeth the word of grace, opposeth to that. (John i. 17.) The Law full of empty shadows and ceremonies which truth is set against; *Corpus autem Christus*, "Christ the very Body," (Col. ii. 17), to *Lex habens umbram*, (Heb. x. 1); so, requisite to quit us of the Law—the Law, the Word that married flesh.

The bringing of these two together is a great matter; and together they must be. Grace, take it from truth, and it is *fallax*, 'but a vizor,' but a mere illusion. Truth, sever it from grace, and it is *ingrata*, 'but an unpleasing thing.' Grace and truth kept in sunder, and never met before; but when the Word and flesh met, then "did they meet and kiss each other," (Ps. lxxxv. 10), saith the Prophet, and doth with a whole Psalm celebrate this meeting.

They must meet, and grace be first, as here. We shall never endure the severity of His truth, unless grace come before and allay it. But when grace hath brought us to Him, truth will hold us with Him. By grace we shall accomplish what truth requireth at our hands; that so, receiving grace, and walking in truth, we may come to the third and reward of both, glory.

"Full" of them; and the word would not be passed. We find others full of grace, as His blessed Mother, (Luke i. 28), and as St. Stephen. (Acts vii. 55.) Theirs reacheth not to us; none of them have more than serves for themselves. For, the Spirit is given them but by measure, (John iii. 34); but *plenitudo vasis* in them, 'the fulness of a vessel;' if ye take anything out to pour into another, it is the less for it. But His is *plenitudo fontis*, 'the fulness of a fountain,' which is never drawn dry; *qui implet abyssum et non minoratur*, 'fills a great pool and itself never the less.' Of which fulness they all received, and He never the emptier. We shall not need to go to any other storehouse, or help to supply or fill up Christ with any other, as if He were but half full. He is full, full of both. Our care is to be to make ourselves fit vessels, and there is all.

II. Thus far, *quod Verbum factum caro*. Now, *quid Verbum carni*, the benefit, and that which the benefit ever draweth with it, the duty, *quid caro Verbo?* 1. *Factus caro benefaciet carni*, 'being made flesh He will be a benefactor to it.' "No man ever hated his flesh," (Eph. v. 29), and no more can He us, who are 'flesh of His flesh,' or rather, He of ours. He seeth us daily in Himself, He cannot look upon His flesh but He must think upon us. And God the Father cannot now hate the flesh which the Word is made; which is now taken into one Person with His only Son, and united to the Deity itself. If He love the Word, He must love it too, for the Word is become it; either love both, or hate both. But love it certainly; for, as this day, "when He brought His Son" clothed with it "into the world, He gave express commandment all His Angels should worship

Him," (Heb. i. 6), so clothed, and our flesh in Him—a new dignity which is this day accrued to our nature, to be adored of the blessed Angels. Our nature questionless is set in high favour with God: God send our persons so too, and all shall be well.

Besides, good hope we now have that He being now flesh, all flesh may come to Him to present Him with their requests. Time was when they fled from Him, but *ad factum carnem jam veniet omnis caro.* (Ps. lxv. 2.) For since He dwelt amongst us, all may resort to Him—yea, even sinners; and of them it is said, *Hic recipit peccatores, et comedit cum eis;* "He receiveth them, receiveth them even to His table." (Luke xv. 2.)

A second hope, that seeing He hath made our flesh His Tabernacle, He will not suffer this of ours—the same with that of His—to fall down quite and come to nothing; the same He dwelleth in Himself not to perish utterly; but repair it again and raise it out of the dust. So that *insuper caro nostra requiescet in spe,* "our very body may rest in hope," (Ps. xvi. 9), to be restored again, and "made like to His glorious Body." (Phil. iii. 21.)

A third; that where it was, "Flesh and Blood shall not inherit the Kingdom of God," (1 Cor. xv. 50), it is reversed; flesh and blood shall, for flesh and blood already doth. It is that St. John is about to infer the former verse out of this, viz., "to them gave He power to be made the sons of God," (John i. 12): for, *Ex quo hoc verum est Filium Dei Filium hominis fieri potuisse, non est incredibile, &c.* 'Since sure it is that the Son of God is made the Son of man, it is not incredible but that the sons of men may be made the sons of God.' Not incredible—nay, *securitas nobis data est,* 'a kind of bond is entered, security given.' Seeing this verse is true, so is the last, *dedit potestatem,* "He gave power;" and well might. Why? For "the Word is made flesh," and therefore flesh may have reciprocal hope to be regenerate by the Word and adopted through grace, and so exalted to the glorious dignity of the sons of God.

And because grace and truth do this, we shall fail of neither of them. He is full, and not for Himself; He needs them not. He hath them for us, and hath sufficient. Neither shall be wanting, if we be not wanting to ourselves.

G

His grace shall prevent us, and His truth follow us all the days of our life. (Ps. xxiii. 6.)

III. So we see *quid Verbum carni*, what He hath done for us : now our duty reciprocal, *quid caro Verbo*, what we for Him again. If the Word become flesh, we to take order that flesh of ours that the Word hath taken, we take it not and make it *una caro* with you know whom, (1 Cor. vi. 16), or may read. God forbid ! Know ye not, "the Word is become flesh"? That flesh is then so be preserved, that as he saith, 'We saw the glory,' so may we, 'We saw His flesh as the flesh of the only-begotten Son of God.' Kept with such care, and in such cleanness, as it might be-seem His flesh to be kept. And as much may be said for *habitavit*, the house would be somewhat handsome, as hand-some as we could, that is to receive Him. We blame them that this day received Him in a stable ; take heed we do not worse ourselves.

But the Fathers press a farther matter yet out of *Verbum caro factum ;* that we also are after our manner *verbum carnem facere*, ' to incarnate the word.' We have a word— we may do it too—which is the type or abstract of the very Word, or wisdom of God ; and that is the word which is preached unto us. That word we may, and are to incarnate according to this day's pattern. That we so do. That word is then incarnate, *quando verbum in opus, Scripturas in operas convertimus*, ' when we do what is spoken or written, and turn the vocal word into a real work.' The word with us turneth to nothing but wind. To give it St. John's flesh, and St. James' (Jas. ii. 18) *vidimus*, make it both be felt and seen. Especially, since our Saviour Himself saith, "He reckoneth of this as His second birth, and of everyone that so doth esteemeth as His Mother." (Mat. xii. 48, 49.) That is the duty properly belonging to this day, the day of His birth.

And to look also to *habitavit* as well as *factum est. Fit* sometimes, sometimes somewhat ' is done ;' but *non habitavit*, it vanisheth again, it hath no state in us, it continueth not in us, nor we in it. That it be not only, but remain. By faith *factum est ;* dwell, by perseverance, the true free-hold indeed.

And that this we may, to provide for the fourth ; to use means, to draw from Him that whereof He hath such plenty,

" grace and truth." The breasts that are full have as great
pleasure in being drawn, as the child that draweth them.
Assure ourselves, it is so here. There is *majus desiderium
deplendi* in Him, than *replendi* in us ; more in Him to part
with, than in us to receive. And what means are those?
To go to the word and flesh together. The word itself doth
well, and of the twain the word hath less cause to complain ;
but this at other times. But at this now, we are not to
content ourselves with one alone ; but since He offereth to
communicate Himself both ways, never restrain Him to
one. The word we hear is the abstract of *Verbum ;* the
Sacrament is the antetype of *caro,* His flesh. What better
way than where these are actually joined, actually to partake
them both ? Not either alone, the word or flesh ; but the
word and flesh both, for there they are both. If we regard
habitavit, this is a sure way, we have a plain text for it ; *Qui
manducat carnem in Me manet et Ego in Illo,* " He abides in
Me, and I in Him." (John vi. 56.) If it be grace and truth
we respect, how may we better establish our hearts with
grace, or settle our minds in the truth of His promise, than
by partaking these the conduit-pipes of His grace, and seals
of His truth unto us? Grace and truth now proceeding
not from the Word alone, but even from the flesh thereto
united ; the fountain of the Word flowing into the cistern of
His flesh, and from thence deriving down to us this grace
and truth, to them that partake Him aright.

But setting them aside, the day "the Word was made
flesh" it is most kindly that a memorial be kept, as well of
the flesh as the Word. On the feast of their union, they
would be united ; the day they were joined by Him they
would not be sundered by any ; but we to celebrate both,
in honour of both. For, judge with yourselves how incon-
venient it is to keep a feast in honour of His taking flesh,
and even that day abandon His flesh, and never once take
it. *Verbum et caro* if ever to be joined, *this* day, the day of
their joining. Accordingly then, as well by the act to testify
and represent the Word's making flesh, as to procure He
may dwell in us ; and dwelling replenish us with His grace
and truth. And lastly, that we may hold this feast aright,
and do the duty that properly belongs to it, let us by both
do honour to both, that from both we may receive the
fruit of both ;—grace, to enable us ; truth, to guide us to

the hope of glory. Not to that in the *parenthesis*, that is but *vidimus quasi*; but to the other, *videbimus sicut est*, " to see Him as He is," (1 John iii. 2), and by seeing to be transformed into the same image of glory.

——o——

SERMON VII.

A Sermon Preached before the King's Majesty at Whitehall, on Friday, the Twenty-fifth of December, a.d. mdcxii., being Christmas Day.

At sundry times and in divers manners, God spake in the old time to our Fathers, by the Prophets:
In these last days, He hath spoken to us by His Son, Whom He hath made Heir of all things; by Whom also He made the worlds;
Who, being the Brightness of His glory, and the engraved Form of His Person, and bearing up all things by His mighty word, hath by Himself purged our sins, aud sitteth at the right hand of the Majesty in the highest places. Hebrews i. 1-3.

[*Multifariam, multisque modis olim Deus loquens patribus in Prophetis.*
Novissime diebus istis locutus est nobis in Filio, Quem constituit Heredem universorum, per Quem fecit et sæcula;
Qui cum sit Splendor gloriæ, et Figura substantiæ Ejus, portansque omnia verbo virtutis Suæ, purgationem peccatorum faciens, sedet ad dexteram majestatis in excelsis. Latin Vulg.]

ET erunt novissimi primi, saith our Saviour, "And the last shall be first," (Mat. xix. 30). And this text tells us of a great prerogative of these last days above the first. Of which last days, this is the first day; the day of Christ's birth. For, make a partition of the two times, *olim*, and *dies novissimi*; and this day will be found to end *olim*, and to begin *dies novissimi*; to be the first day of these last days; the very Kalends of Christianity, from whence we begin our era, or Christian computation.

The dignity of this day, and ours in it, is here set out two ways. First by a case of comparison—of comparison between the times past and these now; between the Fathers and us. The point wherein is God's speaking, speaking to both; but in a more excellent manner, and by a far more excellent Person to us, than to them. The end; that so we might know, know and acknowledge, *quæ a Deo data sunt nobis*, "what God hath done for us," and done for us this day. For all the difference is in this day; all the dignity we have above them is by it; that so we may be highly thankful to God for it, and hold the day itself as an high feast.

God is the same in both, He that speaketh to both. 1. Of old to them, 2. of late to us. Thus far, even; they and we. One God, one Speaker, to both. The odds; both spoken to, but not both spoken to alike : not alike in three points. 1. Not in the matter, or parts, of which; 2. not in the form, or manner, after which; 3. not in the persons by whom. 1. To the Fathers He spake πολυμερῶς, "by many pieces;" not entirely. 2. To them, πολυτρόπως, "after sundry fashions;" not uniformly. 3. To them, by His servants, the Prophets; not by His Son.

But when the Apostle cometh to rejoin upon these three, he repeateth not the two first, but pitcheth only on the Person; that He, that the Person by Whom, is without all comparison more honourable and excellent than the Prophets, His servants; (He will do as much to the Angels by and by after;) that look, how much a son is better than a servant, so much our estate above theirs.

II. This for the comparative. But then, fearing it might be we would not conceive high enough of this Son, or weigh Him as He is worthy, he goeth to it, *positive;* and as it were sets up His arms, consisting of eight several coats; or proclaimeth His style, of as many several titles. Which we may reduce to four several combinations. 1. "Son and Heir;" 2. "the Brightness and Character;" 3. "Maker and Supporter of all things;" 4. "That purgeth our sins, and That is set down in the throne." And these again may be abridged to these two : 1. what He is in Himself, 2. and what to us. 1. In Himself, all the rest; 2. to us. 1. "Made Heir," 2. "purgeth our sins," 3. and so cleanseth our nature, that, being so cleansed, He may exalt it. For it is for us, and not for Himself, He taketh up the place mentioned, "at the right hand on high."

III. Then our duty; *bona si sua nôrint,* 'if we can skill

of our own good,' to find our estate greatly dignified by it; and, to honour this day, the beginning of this dignity to us, wherein God gave His Son to speak *vivâ voce* unto us, to purge our sins, and to exalt us to His throne on high.

"God in times past spake to the Fathers;" and His speech was πολυμερὴς, of many several parcels; to several persons, at several times; some at one time, some at another. And as the time grew, so grew their knowledge, piece and piece, of the great mystery this day manifested.

"God in times past," &c. "in many parts spake" concerning His Person. First, one piece; Man He should be "of the woman's seed," That "should bruise the serpent's head," (Gen. iii. 15); and, there was all. Then another piece; of what nation He should be, "of the seed of Abraham." (Gen. xxii. 18.) Then another yet; of what tribe, "of the tribe of Juda." (Gen. xlix. 9, 10.) Then again, a fourth piece, of what family; "of the house of David." (Ps. cxxxii. 11, 12, &c.)

So likewise God, in times past, spake of His offices. To Moses one piece; He should be "a Prophet." (Deut. xviii. 18.) To David another; He should be "a Priest." (Ps. cx. 4.) To Jeremy, a third; He should be "a King, and His Name, *Jehova Justitia nostra.*" (Jer. xxiii. 5, 6.)

And, not to hold you long in this, "God, in times past, in sundry parts spake" concerning this day's work. That came by pieces too. One parcel to Esay, of His birth, (Isa. ix. 6): to Mica, the place of it, (Mic. v. 2): to Daniel, the time of it by weeks. (Dan. ix. 25, 26, &c.) So you see it was by pieces, and by many pieces, they had it. Well said the Apostle that "prophesying is in part," (1 Cor. xiii. 9); one may now in a few hours come to as much as came to them in many hundred years. This for the matter.

Now, for the manner. It was *multiformis.* "God," &c. "many manner ways."

One manner, "by dreams in the night," (Job xxxiii. 15); another manner, by visions. And those again of two manners. 1. Either presented to the outward sense, as Esay vi. (Isa. vi. 1.) Or in an ecstasy represented to the inward, as Dan. x. (Dan. x. 7, &c.) Another yet, by

Urim, in the breast of your Priest. And yet another, by a small still voice, (1 Kings xix. 12), in the ears of the Prophet. And sometime by an Angel speaking in him. (Zech i. 9.) But most-what by His Spirit. And to trouble you no more, very sure it is that as for the matter in many broken pieces, so for the manner in many divers fashions, spake He to them.

But then, if in πολυτρόπως you understand *tropos,* figures; then were they yet many more. The Paschal Lamb, (Exod. xii. 4, 5, &c.), the Scape-goat, (Lev. xvi. 10), the Red Cow, (Numb. xix. 1, 2, &c.), and I know not how many, even a world of them. Many they were, and tropes they were; shadowed out darkly, rather than clearly expressed. Theirs was but candle-light to our day-light, but *vespertina cognitio* in comparison of ours, whom the "day hath visited sprung from on high." (Luke i. 78.) This for the matter and manner. Now for the men.

"God in times past spake by Prophets;" and but by Prophets He spake not, from Moses to John Baptist who was the horizon of the Law and Gospel. I will not stand to run through them all. And now, the Apostle when he is to come to us "in the last days"—when he should oppose three more to match the former three, he doth not; but passeth by the two first, the parts and the manner; leaveth out πολυμερῶς and πολυτρόπως, and so insinuates thereby thus much; that He hath spoken to us entirely without reservation, and uniformly without variation. But those two He waveth, and insisteth only on this last, as the fairest mark of difference, the Prophets and His Son.

The Prophets were "holy men," (2 Pet. i. 21), but *men.* And there is a nature more perfect than that of man, even the nature of God. And in the House of God they were faithful servants, but yet, *servants,* (Heb. iii. 5, and Mat. xxi. 35); and that we know, is but an imperfect condition in comparison of a son. To us in the last days is given, that what we have we have not from any Prophet, though never so excellent, but from the Lord of the Prophets; not from any servant, though in never so great place, but from the Son; and, not from any of the sons of men, but from His own Son, (Mat. xxi. 38), the Son of God. From His mouth we have received notice of God's will; He Himself, *ore tenus,* imparted it to us.

But then, if any ask ; seeing "God in times past," and " God in these last days," is the same God ; He that " spake to the Fathers," and He that "to us," but one Speaker ; why not by His Son at first ? I will give a reason, fit for this place. A decorum was to be kept, and some kind of correspondence with state. That as, at the proceeding of a great Prince before he himself cometh in sight, many there be that go before him, and those of divers degrees, and at last himself doth appear ; so, this Prince that sits in the Throne should not start out at the first and show Himself, but be allowed His train of Patriarchs, and Prophets, to be His *ante ambulones ;* and " in the fulness of time," (Gal. iv. 4), Himself should come with " the fulness of grace and truth," (John i. 14, 16), and establish one entire uniform way to continue for ever.

From this comparison these are the points we learn ; we must *ferri ad perfectionem.* And these are notes of imperfection ; there be too many parts and too many manners in that, to be a perfect state. If the matter were full, no more would be added ; if the manner were perfect, it would no more be altered. Never then to rest in these. Moses himself pointeth us to One after him, by his *Ipsum audite.* (Deut. xviii. 18.) Who is that ? God Himself in the Mount tells us by His *Ipsum audite.* (Matt. xvii. 5.) And when God said it, Moses and Elias were there in the Mount, and resigned up both their several audiences ; Moses for himself, and Elias as well in His own name as in the name of all the Prophets.

This, against the Jews, that will no farther than Moses ; that will rest in the Law. For, *nihil ad perfectum adducit Lex,* 'the Law brings nothing to perfection ;' but *finis Legis Christus.* (Rom. x. 4.) And all prophecy hangs in suspense as imperfect, till the fulfilling of it ; which was done by Christ, to Whom they all gave witness. Now " when that is perfect is come, that that is imperfect must away." (1 Cor. xiii. 10.) Not to rest in them then, but to Christ ; and never rest till we come to Him.

And, as never to rest till we come to Him, so there to rest, when we are come to Him. As soon as His voice hath sounded in our ears, that they itch no more after any new revelations. For, " in Him are all the treasures of wisdom and knowledge." (Col. ii. 3.)

" God spake once and twice" (Ps. xxvi. 11)—a third time He will not speak. This is His last time; He will speak no more. Look for no more pieces, nor fancy no more fashions; *Consummatum est*, (John xix. 30), there are no more to look for. He is " the Truth;" and he that hath found the truth and seeks farther, no remedy he must needs find a lie; he can find nothing else. To get us therefore to Christ, and never be got from Him, but there hold us.

We cannot follow a better pattern than the Apostle here, we see what haste he makes. For as if he were upon thorns till he were with Christ, without any *exordium* or preamble here in the beginning of his Epistle he hits on the points straight; as if all time were lost till he were there. Yea having named the parts and manners of the times past, for very haste to be at Him he forgets both parts and manners, only for desire to be with Him the sooner.

II. And so, with him I haste and pass to the second positive part. Wherein being careful we should take perfect notice of Him, and fearing we would not weigh these words " by His Son" as were meet but hear them slightly and pass them lightly over, the rest of the text he spends in making a commentary of this word Son; that we may consider how great this Party is, and consequently how much it imports us to regard His speech, and to esteem of His feast with no mean account. And to say truth, it was more than needful—considering the meanness of His birth to-day—that He should thus proclaim His style of eight titles, and over the place of it stick them up as so many scutcheons, to give us true notice of the greatness of the Party.

But withal, his meaning was to describe Christ in all points; as indeed these eight contain a perfect description of His natures, His Person, His offices, His agency.

His natures, in the very beginning; *Quem fecit* is man, *Per Quem fecit* is God. Not *quem* only, man alone; but *Per Quem sæcula*, God also. But, for His Divine nature He is more full yet; that He is " His Son, the Splendour of His glory, the Character of His substance, the Maker and Upholder of the world and all in it."

His Person, in this word *semet ipso;* He did it Himself, that is, in His own Person. Himself is ever said of a person.

His offices, in His speaking—His prophecy, by which He

unfoldeth the mysteries of God. In His purging our sins is His Priesthood; and His Kingdom, in the throne of Majesty wherein He sits.

His agency, or *quid ad nos*, in *loctus est nobis*, "to us He speaketh;" and, *purgans peccata nostra*, "our sins He purgeth." *Nobis*, and *nostra;* to us, and for us, He is that He is. All His speaking and doing, *propter nos homines, et propter salutem nostram*, 'for us men and for our salvation,' and our part in Him and His.

We reduced all these eight to two. 1. What in Himself; and what, *referendo* to us. In Himself; what by nature? Son and Heir. What by excellency? Splendour and Character. What by power? Maker and Upholder of all. To us; what in love already performed? "He hath purged our sins." In hope yet expected? He is set and in possession of the throne of glory; which is in our names and to our behoof, and not His own.

His Divine nature hath no less than three to express it. 1. Son, 2. Brightness, and 3. Character. And two to prove it the 1. making, and 2. supporting of all.

I have heretofore remembered you that the high perfections of that nature are such and so many, as no one term will suffice to set it forth; we are glad to borrow from many to do it, and yet but brokenly too. And that though there be not any resemblance translated from the creatures though never so excellent that will hold full essay, yet withal this we are to think, that since the Holy Ghost hath made choice of these terms, they are no idle speculations that are drawn from them.

Of these three then; 1. "Son," 2. "Brightness," 3. "Character." 1. In "Son" there is a true identity of nature; upon it is grounded ὁμοούσιον, 'being of one substance,' even as the Son is with the Father. 2. But the Son cometh after the Father in time, and that a good time: amends is made for that in the next term, "Brightness." For, it is not to be imagined that there ever was or could be a light body, but in the very same instant there must stream from it a brightness. So, upon this is grounded coeternal.

3. But then, there is some inequality between the light body itself and the beam of brightness of it; the beam not full out so clear. This is the imperfection in the term "Brightness." But that is supplied by the next, "Char-

acter;" for that is ever just equal, neither bigger nor lesser than the type or stamp that made it. Upon this then is grounded coequal, and like *per omnia*, ὁμοιούσιος : so like, as "Shew us the Father," (John xiv. 8), saith Philip; why, he that sees the character never desires to see the stamp; if ye see the one ye see the other; "He that seeth Me seeth the Father," (John xiv. 9), Whose express Form I am.

Agreeable to these three, we believe of Him that He is consubstantial, as the "Son;" coeternal, as "the Brightness;" coequal, as "the Character;" against the new heads of the old hydra sprung up again in our days.

This term, "son of God," is sometime communicated to Saints; sometime to Magistrates. Lest we might understand it as we do in Saints, or as we do in Magistrates, he addeth two words; 1. the one, "glory;" 2. the other, "substance." Of which, glory is imparted to others; substance, to none but Him. His glory on earth He imparteth to Magistrates, and they are called "the sons of the Most High." (Ps. lxxxii. 6.) His Heavenly grace, which is glory inchoate, He imparteth to His Saints; and "to them gave He power to be sons of God." (John i. 12.)

But His substance is in neither. For the first, Magistrates, are by *ego dixi;* but He by *Ego genui.* (Ps. ii. 7.) And the second, Saints, to them He giveth privilege, or prerogative, so to be. So they κατ᾽ ἐξουσίαν, but He κατ᾽ οὐσίαν; *per præstantiam* they, *per substantiam* He.

He, "the Brightness of His glory, and Character of His substance;" that is, not in glory only which may be imparted to another, but even in His very substance too itself.

And again, not in substance of the Deity alone, but in that which belongeth to it, the glory also. "Substance" is *Deus*, "glory" is *Dei.* All that He is, and all that He hath—"substance" and "glory," both.

"The Brightness of His glory." He was such a son, as did no way eclipse His Father's glory, but as a beam made it shine more bright. "The Character," the true stamp of His substance; nor He rendered not a broken image as if the stamp had been set on or driven away, but was His very true express Form.

Another mystery yet. These three note a proceeding;

the "Son," from the Father ; the "Brightness," from a light;
"the Character," from the Type ; and so, a second Person.
" I proceeded, and came from the Father," (John xvi. 28) :
—He saith it Himself.

First, a true and natural proceeding from Him as the
Son. Secondly, to take away all conceit of gross or carnal
generation, by a pure and clean proceeding, as *de luce lux,*
in which there is nothing but pure and undefiled. Thirdly,
characterwise from His hypostasis—it is the word in the
text, mark it well ;—not from His οὐσία, that is, not from
His substance at large, but from His determinate personal
Essence ; (for so is hypostasis properly ;)—that is, not from
the Deity or Essence of it which neither begets nor is
begotten, but from a Person in the Deity.

Now these three, if we refer them to *olim,* "the times
past ;" then, as the Son, He is opposed to His servants,
that is, the Prophets. As He is a Beam of light, to the
many parts, as it were many sparks ;—that was all the light
before. As "the Character," or firm impression, to the
many vanishing shadows under the Law.

But if to the present we refer them ; as He is the "Son,"
we shall find no estate but servitude, no adoption but in
Him. As "the Brightness ;" no clear light of knowledge,
nothing but mists and darkness, but by Him. And, as
"the Character ;" no true soundness or sound truth, but
figures and flitting shadows without Him. From Him as
the "Son" receive we grace, whereby we are adopted,
(Eph. i. 5) ; as "the Beam," the clearness of faith whereby
lightened, (John i. 9) ; as "the Character," the true signature
of charity whereby stamped to know ourselves, and be
known of others, that we have heard Him aright, and are
His true disciples.

These three express His Divine nature ; two more, to
prove it. In them His excellency, in these His power.
Which is set out two ways ; 1. in the creation ; *omnia per
Ipsum facta, et sine Ipso nihil,* "all made by Him, nothing
without Him." (John i. 3.) 2. And again, in the preservation, by virtue of His *et Ego usque operor,* (John v. 17), which
is His work to this day ; to continue and uphold in their
being all that He hath made to be. One by His word
spoken ; so, made. The other, by His Law given ; so,
made fast to continue. (Ps. cxlviii. 5, 6.) In a word, all had

been nothing but for Him; and all would fall to nothing without Him.

Now, in that He thus made all and makes all to last, the meetest person He was to make all new—to restore that He had made. And it was a convenience that He should, and it was an inducement that He would undertake the business and go through with it.

All this He is in Himself; yet not so, but in all His splendour and glory He mindeth us. And that, so as He is desirous to bring us to the joint partaking of His inheritance, as "Son;" of His glory, as "the Brightness;" yea, of the very Divine nature, as "the Character of His substance." The ground whereof is laid in *Quem fecit Hæredem*, "Whom He made Heir;" and that was as Man; for *per Quem fecit* we said is God, *Quem fecit* is Man.

"Made Him Heir." Heirs are either born or made; so born by nature, or so made by purchase. He was His Son, and His only Son, and so born His Heir. He was born, and yet He would be made. There is a mystery in this — we are to look to it; it will fall out to concern us. Heir born He was, and so claimeth all as His inheritance, by due of birthright. But it is farther here said, He was "made;" what means this? *Quem fecit?* Nay, *Quem genuit.* That is true; but *Quem fecit* is true likewise. *Fecit Hæredem Qui prius fuit Hæres*, so born and so made too; *Hæres natus,* and *Hæres factus.* So cometh He to a double right—two titles. How so? He needed but one; He would have two. To what end? Not for Himself; for Himself one was enough. Belike, His meaning was to have two, that He might set over one to somebody else. There is the point. He was born Heir for Himself; but "made Heir" for us. *Hæres natus,* that serveth Him; that He retains to Himself. *Hæres factus,* that He disposeth of to us. By this we hold, even by *Quem fecit;* that is our tenure and best hope. He is, and ever was, in the bosom of His Father, as *Hæres natus.* He now is but on our behalf and to our behoof "at the right Hand of His Father," as *Hæres factus.* And now followeth, "He purged our sins."

For He could not bring us to sit with Him in His throne thus purchased, being so spotted and foul as we were, by means of the pollution of our sins. He was then to purge and make clean our nature first, that He might exalt it to partake His purchase, being so cleansed. Where first our case is set down wherein He found us, and wherein we are without Him. A sinner's case, how glorious soever he or she glister in the eyes of men, being in God's eyes as the case of a foul diseased person; and we thereby taught so to conceive of sins as of foul spots without, or of such humours within as go from us by purging. *Inquinamenta carnis et spiritus*, as St. Paul terms them right, "defiling both flesh and spirit," (2 Cor. vii. 1); which unless they be purged, there is no entering into the heavenly Jerusalem where the throne is; into which *nihil inquinatum*, "no polluted thing shall ever enter." (Rev. xxi. 27.)

Exalt us He could not, being in that plight; for love or pity therefore purge us He would. And here now is the top, or highest point of elevation, in this text. "Who being the Brightness,"—or, "though He were the brightness," that is, a Party so excellent in nature, glory, Person, and power; nature as "Son," glory as "Brightness," Person as "Character," power "as Maker and Supporter of all;" Who, though He were all this, did not abhor to come and visit us being in that foul and wretched case. This will teach us, *Domine quid est homo?* "What is man, that Thou shouldest visit him?" (Ps. viii. 4.) Visit him;—not as "the day-spring from on high," (Luke i. 78), doth the earth; but visit him, as if a great prince should go into an hospital, to visit and look on a loathsome diseased creature.

2. And not only visit him, but not refuse the base office to look to his "purging" from that his uncleanness.

3. And thirdly, not cause it to be done by another, but to come and do it in *semet Ipso*, "by His Own Self, in Person."

4. And fourthly, in doing, not to stand by and prescribe, but Himself to minister and make the medicine.

5. And fifthly, to make it Himself, and make it of Himself; *in semet ipso*, and *de semet ipso;* 'to make the medicine, and be the medicine.'

6. And how, or of what? Spots will out with water; some will not with any thing but with blood; "without shedding of blood, there is no taking away sin." (Heb. ix. 22.) And not every blood will serve, but it must be lamb's blood; and "a Lamb without spot." (1 Pet. i. 19.) And

not every lamb neither, but "the Lamb of God," (John i.
29); or, to speak plainly, a Lamb that is God. His blood,
and nothing else, will serve to do this.

7. And seventhly, not any Blood of His ; not of a vein —
one may live still for all that—but His best, most precious,
His heart-blood, which bringeth certain death with it. With
that Blood He was to make the medicine. Die He must,
and His side be opened, that there might issue both the
Water and the Blood that was to be the ingredients of it.
By Himself, His Ownself, and by Himself slain ; by His
death, and by His Blood-shedding, and by no other means;
quis audivit talia? The Physician slain, and of His Flesh
and Blood a receipt made, that the patient might recover !

And now, we may be at our choice whether we will conceive of sin as of some outward soil in the soul ; and then,
the purging of it to be *per viam balnei*, 'needs a bath' with
some cleansing ingredients, as the Prophet (Jer. ii. 22)
speaks of the herb Borith, and this way purged He us ;
made a bath of the water that came out of His side to that
end opened, that from thence might flow " a Fountain for
sin, and for uncleanness " (Zech. xiii. 1)—Water, and mixed
with His Blood ; as forcible to take out the stains of the
soul, as any herb Borith in the world to take away the soil
of the skin.

Or, whether we will conceive of sin as of some inward
pestilent humour in the soul and conscience, casting us into
peril of mortal, or rather immortal, death; then, the purging
of us to be by way of electuary or potion ;—and so He
purgeth our sins too. To that end He hath made an electuary of His own Body, " Take, eat it "—and tempered a
Cup with His own Blood, " Drink ye all of it " (Mat. xxvi.
26, 27)—which by the operation of His eternal Spirit in it
is able effectually to "purge the conscience from dead works"
(Heb. ix. 14) or actual sins, and from the deadly effect of
them ; no balsam or medicine in the world like it.

The sum of all is ; there be two defiling sins, and two
ways He purgeth them. Clean we are from the first, as
washed from the original uncleanness of our nature, and
that, by the laver of regeneration." (Tit. iii. 5.) And whole
we are, as purged within from the actual sins of our persons ;
and that, by "the Cup of the New Testament, which we
bless in His Name," (1 Cor. x. 16) ; and the Blood of

Jesus Christ purgeth us from our sins." (1 John i. 7.) By
both He purgeth us from both. And this for His purging.

"And is set down." Of which we are not to conceive as
of a thing merely touching Him, that His labour being
done He took His rest, and there is all; but that this His
sitting down is a taking possession of that His dear-made
purchase: and that, not in His own Name, He had it
before; He was in glory, and in the self-same glory with
His Father, before ever the world was.

This *hæres factus* pertaineth to us, as done for us; not for
Himself Who needed it not, nor could have any use of it.

These two between them comprehend all, even all we can
wish; 1. to be purged of the one, 2. and to be seized of
the other. They follow well; for to what end purged He
us? To leave us there? No; but for some farther matter,
which though it be last in execution, was first in intention.
Having so cleansed us—not content with that, it was His
purpose farther to bring us to glory; to no less matter than
to sit on His throne with Him, purchased by Him for no
other end.

And these two, "purging," and "sitting down in the
throne," as the alpha and omega, the first and the last of that
He doth for us. And so, in them is all well represented;
"purging our sins," the first; "sitting in the throne," the
last. To purge our sins He began this day, the first day,
the day of His birth; wherein He purified and sanctified, by
His holy Nativity, the original uncleanness of ours. And
'sit in the throne' was His last work, on the last day of His
Ascension; then took He possession in our names, ὡς
πρόδρομος, saith the Apostle, "as forerunner for us." (Heb.
vi. 20.)

The degrees of this exaltation be these. 1. First, a
throne it is, and that is not every seat, but a special, and
chief, and honourable seat. 2. And secondly, of thrones
there be some inferior, as the thrones of justice. This is
the highest, for it is a throne of majesty. 3. Thirdly, it is
in excelsis, and that maketh up all. For the thrones here
below, even of majesty, sooner or later they that sit in them
must come down from them. But "the throne on high,
Thy seat, O God, is for ever and ever," (Ps. xlv. 6); not
fading and transitory, as ours here. 4. Fourthly, in this
throne set He is; and sitting is the site or position of rest,

that is, rest in glory. Here, where most glory, least rest.
5. And fifthly, "on the right hand," (Heb. i. 3), which is
on the throne the best and next place to God Himself.
And by this are we above the angels; for "to which of
them," as the Apostle after deduceth, "said He at any
time, Sit on My right hand?" (Heb. i. 13.) No; but,
stand before Me, as "ministering spirits," all. Or when
they rest, it is on the other hand; the right hand is kept
for us, and possessed already by One in our nature, Who in
this seat will not sit alone, *sed consedere nos secum fecit in
cœlestibus.* (Eph. ii. 6.) Even now, we sit there in Him,
and shall there sit with Him in the end. So He promiseth
in express terms that "we shall sit with Him in His throne,"
(Rev. iii. 21), as He doth in His Father's. And so, not in
the throne will He be above us, but only that He in the
midst, and we on His right hand.

III. Our duty then is, for His excellency to honour
Him; for His power to fear Him; for His love shewed,
reciprocally to love Him again; for His hope promised,
truly to serve Him. God, for His part, would have His
servants the Prophets well used; but however they in times
past were regarded by them, this He makes full account of,
"if He send His Son, we will not fail but reverence Him,"
(Matt. xxi. 37.) Specially, such a Son; of such glory, such
power, and above all of such love towards us, to provoke
ours again. And again, of such ability to reward with
eternal glory, as He will even buy our service at, Who gives
more? and pay us for it to the full with no less wages than
a throne of glory.

This is general. More particular, in three terms He is
set out to us here in the text; 1. Speaking, 2. Purging, and
3. Sitting. As a Prophet, He speaks; as a Priest, purges;
as a King, sits speaking. Our duty is to hear Him, to lay
up His sayings in our hearts. Two marks His word hath
here, 1. *fecit,* and 2. *sustinet;* "made," and "makes continue." Let it have the same in us. In the sermon-time
something is begun to be made in us, but it continueth not;
which sheweth, it is not *verbum virtutis* to us. Again, let
it not be as a "brightness," only to be seen by us; but as
a "character" too, to leave a mark behind it to be seen on
us; and then it is right.

Now, *hodie si vocem,* "to-day if ye will hear His voice"

(Ps. xcv. 7), ye can hear none but *vagitum infantis*, 'such a voice as useth to come from a new-born babe.' And even so He speaks to us, if we can understand. For, even this *Verbum* to be *infans*, and *Tonans* to be *vagiens;* He to send forth such a voice—it speaketh humility, I am sure, and great love that so would humble itself, if we have ears to hear it; when He, That was "the brightness of His Father's glory," should be so eclipsed, He that sits on the throne thus be thrown in a manger.

Prophets spake, but purged not. Purging was ever the Priest's office. It is true, the word He speaks hath a mundifying virtue, *jam mundi estis*, "now ye are clean." It cleanseth then. But, not that only, nor principally. For the medicine which purgeth *ex proprietate*, His flesh and Blood go to it. "By which will we are sanctified, even by the offering of the Body of Jesus." (Heb. x. 10.) "That Blood of Jesus Christ, cleanseth us from all sin." These, the true ingredients into this medicine. But better yet, if both go together. And this day they first came together, the Word and flesh; therefore, of all days, this day they would not be parted. For, will you sever the flesh from the Word that day on which God joined them? God forbid! There is a correspondency between the word and His brightness, and between the Sacrament and His character. The word giveth a light, and His brightness sheweth in it *ad horam*, and not much longer. The parts of the Sacrament they are permanent, and stick by us; they are a remembrance of the characters made in His skin and flesh. And if ye seek to be rid of your sins—"this was broken for you," and "this was shed for you," for that very end, "for the remission of sins." And so ye receive His Person, even *Semet Ipsum;* and in *Semet Ipso*, in His Person it was, "He purged our sins." And so, that a sure way.

Lastly, for sitting; that is His Kingdom, that is kept for *dies novissimorum novissimus*, 'the last day indeed.' That is yet in hope only. The same flesh that cleansed our sins, the same now sitteth on the throne, and so hath both virtues; for the present a power to purge, for the future a power likewise to exalt. The same blood is the blood of Sacrifice for remission of sins, and the blood of the New Testament for the passing to us the bequest, which is the right of His purchase for which He was made Heir. And

the very angels who this day adored Him in our flesh and
it in Him, thereby shewed plainly not the purging only but
the exalting of it also by this day's work. And that to-day,
wherein they sang aloud in the sky, we have cause to make
much of, and to rejoice in it; the day of the greatest
"glory to God, peace to the earth, and good-will towards
men," (Luke ii. 13, 14), that ever rose upon the world.

God grant that we may so hold this first feast with Christian joy, as we may hold that last with like joy, and be
found as cheerful in it !

——o——

SERMON VIII.

A Sermon Preached before the King's Majesty, at
Whitehall, on Saturday, the Twenty-fifth of
December, a.d. mdcxiii., being Christmas-Day.

*Your father Abraham rejoiced to see My day : and he saw it,
and was glad.* John viii. 56.

[*Abraham pater vester exultavit ut videret diem Meum: vidit et
gavisus est.*]

HERE is joy, joy at a sight, at the sight of a day, and
that day Christ's. It is Christ that calleth it here,
diem Meum, "His day;" and no day so properly His, as
His birth-day. So the text comes full upon the day.

But to deduce it point by point.

First, Christ hath a day proper to Him, which in express
terms He calleth here *diem Meum,* "My day."

Secondly, this day to be seen is a day of joy. Double
joy; 1. *Exultavit,* and 2. *Gavisus est,* both in the text.

And thirdly, which is somewhat strange, it was so to the
Patriarch Abraham. Him we find here doing that which we
now are about ; seeing and rejoicing at the sight of Christ's
day ; taking notice of it, and taking joy in it.

Lastly, all this nothing displeasing to our Saviour Christ ;
for it is spoken by Him to the praise of Abraham that did
it, and to the dislike of the Jews that did it not. To them
is this speech ; Christ tells them of Abraham's doing it, and
blames them for not doing the like

And what are we now disposing ourselves to do, but even the very same that is in the text here, to rejoice to see Christ's day?

And a three-fold warrant we have in this verse to do as we do. 1. The Patriarch's doing it. 2. Christ's allowance of the doing of it. 3. And His dislike of the Jews for not doing it.

We have Abraham for our example ; we do but as he did. In his time, Christ's day was a day of joy ; and a day of joy is a feast, and so holden by him we see. Which falls out much to our content. For the same feasts, the same religion. So we find by this, that he and we are of one religion. One in substance, which is Christ ; one in circumstance, which is His day. Christ Himself, Abraham's joy ; nay, His day Abraham's joy too. The same *Meum*, that is, Christ ; the same *diem*, that is, Christmas.

Then, which is another degree, Abraham's example approved of by Christ, and that after somewhat a strange manner ; for it is not here if you mark it, *Exultavit ut videret Me*, but *ut videret diem Meum*. He makes His day the object of all this exultation and joy. His day, I say, and not Himself ; commends Him, that He rejoiced at the sight not of Himself, but of it. Verily, this speech of His is much to the honour of His day ; and the very solemnity of the feast, and all the joy and gladness thereon, may well be thought to have been founded upon this speech of His. Always, if *Exultavit ut videret*, were a praise to Him ; we may be sure, *Exultavit cum videret*, can be no dispraise to us.

Add thirdly, Abraham's example approved by Christ. Not so approved as He leaves it at liberty, they that will may do the like ; but that He reproves them that do it not. For He blames the Jews here for not doing herein as Abraham ; 'Your father Abraham did it, you do it not.' Which is against them that have a spleen at this feast, that think they can joy in Him well enough, and set His day by ; nay, and abrogate it quite ; and in so doing they joy in Him all the better. Nay, love Him, love His feast. Joy not in it, nor in Him neither.

You shall see how they are mistaken. Therefore they do so they tell us, lest " observing days and times " (Gal. iv. 10) they should seem to Judaize. It falls out quite contrary. For who are they whom Christ here blameth ? Are they not Jews? And wherefore blameth He them? for not doing as Abraham. And what did Abraham? rejoice on His day. So upon the point it will fall out that not to rejoice on His day, that is indeed to Judaize, and they little better than these Jews that follow them in it.

Nay, here is another thing yet will grieve them more. Jews they shall be, but none of Abraham's children; no more than these were. Observe it well. It is the occasion of this speech, the very issue Christ takes with them. *Pater noster Abraham* (John viii. 33, 39, 53) was still in their mouths; if, saith Christ, you were his children, (mark that *if*,) ye would *patrissare;* desire what he desired, and joy what he joyed in. Now, My day he so highly esteemed, as glad he was that he might see it; and you that would so fain father yourselves upon him are so far from that, as what he desired absent, ye despise present; what he would have been the better to see, ye are the worse that ye see it. Now then, how are these Abraham's children that have nothing of Abraham in them? Before, at the fortieth verse, "Ye seek to kill Me for telling the truth. This did not Abraham," (John viii. 40), and ye do it. Here now again; "he rejoiced in My day," and ye do it not. Do that he did not, do not that he did—how can these be Abraham's sons? Verily, as it is in Esay, *Abraham nescivit nos;* "Abraham would never know them for his." (Isa. lxiii. 16.) None of his sons, these. Those are his sons that do as he did. And here now come in we. They Jews, but not Abraham's children; we Abraham's children, but not Jews; for as he did, so do we. There is joy with us at the sight of His day; we renew our joy so oft as by the revolution of the year it cometh about. And for this very point we find ourselves the nearer to Abraham, even for the joy of His day. Always sure we are, since 1. Abraham did it, and 2. Christ allowed it, and 3. disallowed the contrary;—by these three we have good warrant to do as we do. To make it a time of joy. And so, a time of joy God make it to us!

Thus it stands for the order. There be in the text three acts specified, from one issuing—from Abraham all. All directed to one mark; falling all upon one object. That object is *diem Meum,* "My day." Of that then first. The three acts be, 1. *Exultavit ut videret;* 2. *Vidit;* and 3. *Gavisus est.* 1. First, would be glad *ut videret,* "that he might see;"

that is, was desirous to see it.   2. Then, had his desire;
"did see it."   3. And lastly, seeing, "took joy" of his
sight.

Of which three the first and last, *desiderium* and *gaudium*,
'desire' and 'joy,' are two affections attending upon love,
and are ever sure signs of it.   Desire, when we want and
have not what we love.   And joy, when we now possess,
or as the term is, enjoy it.   The middle which is sight, that
pertains to faith; faith's light it was he saw it by.   So here
is *fides per charitatem operans*, (Gal. v. 6), Abraham's faith
right.

But I keep the order in the text, I change it not—it
cannot be mended.   All goes by a right line.   1. Desire
first, that is the way to see.   2. Seeing next, that brings
joy.   3. And joy is the end, and a good end it is to end
in joy.

These three with reference; first, to Abraham, and then
after, to ourselves.

I. To find our mark first, that all this desire is to see, all
this joy when it is seen; it is *diem Meum*, "Christ's day."
Christ is God and Man, Son to both.   His day as the Son
of God, or as the Son of man, which of these?

Not as the Son of God—as the Son of God He hath no
day.   Day and night are parts of time; and *egressus Ejus,*
"His goings out are from all eternity." (Mic. v. 2.)   2. If
we would improperly call it a day, no day to be seen: "The
light of it is inaccessible," (1 Tim. vi. 16), not to be ap-
proached to; it would strike any man blind to behold it.
3. If we could see it, and Him in His Deity, yet there is
small joy to see Christ so; small joy to see Him, but by
the light of this day.   All the desire was that He might be;
all the joy, that He was to be seen as the Son of man.   As
the Son of man then; His day so.

But as the Son of man He hath more days than one: so
He saith, "They shall desire to see one day of the Son of
man," (Luke xvii. 22); one of many, any one of them.   But
this here notes some one eminent day, above the rest.   It
is a day with a double article, τὴν ἡμέραν τὴν ἐμήν, "that
day," "that same day;" That, if any one day Mine more
than other, I would by special prerogative call, τὴν ἐμήν,
"Mine indeed."

Now, there be but two such eminent days to stand for

this; 1. The first, and the 2. last. First, of His Genesis; or last, of His Exodus. Genesis, His coming into the world; or Exodus, His going out. That is, the first of His Nativity, or the last of His Passion. Which of these?

Not of His Passion. First, that was none of His. For He saith to them that took Him, *Hæc est hora vestra*, (Luke . xxii. 53), "Yours;"—so theirs it was, not His. Secondly, it was not His day; nay, it was no day neither, but *tenebrarum*, as he there addeth: so night rather than day. But thirdly, without all question, no day of joy. The Heavens are darkened, the earth quaking, the stones renting, every one going their ways, "beating their breasts" for sorrow. That was no sight to rejoice at, that no day to rejoice in.

Then is it of necessity to be His birth-day; that was a day, the Angel calls it to-day; "To-day is born." (Luke ii. 11.) And His day it was, for every man claims a kind of property in His birth-day. Men, in the day of the beginning of their life. As kings, in the day of the beginning of their reigns; as cities, their *palilia* when the trench is first cast; as Churches, their *encænia* when they are first dedicate; so men their γενέθλια, when they first come into the world. It is too plain, this. His day then; and sure, a day of joy withal. Joy in Heaven, joy in earth. In Heaven, for a day of "glory to God on high," (Luke ii. 14); in earth, for a day of "peace here below, and for good-will towards men," (Luke ii. 10)—as ever, nay more than ever was any. The Angel so proclaimed it, *Gaudium omni populo*, a day of "joy to all people;" and proclaimed, why? *Quia hodie natus est.* And this *omni populo*, (Luke ii. 11), as appears now by this text, was not only all people then in being, or after to be; but as Leo well expresseth it, *in præteritas se refudit ætates*, 'the joy of it went back up to the ages past,' up even to Abraham's time, two thousand years and more before ever it came. I know well, this day may be taken for the whole time of His life; but it must be by a figure then. And no man but seeth, that a day doth more literally and properly signify a day, than the time of one's whole life at large. Yet that time too had his beginning on a day; and that day, even for that very beginning, may well challenge a better right, and nearer property in this word "day" than any longer time whatsoever; as the very day whereon He was first seen, first shewed to the world,

as the Son of man; as the very day whereon the first-fruits
of all the joy then, and ever since. Sure I am the Fathers
fix it all upon one day, and upon this day by name. So
Irenæus, Augustine, Cyril set it down, that this day it was.
This day then be it, the day of His birth. So have ye the
object.

II. Now to the three acts; and first, of desire. *Exultavit
ut;* that *ut* is desire. Glad and fain, *ut,* "that" he might
see; that is, he desired, he longed much to see it. *Gaudere
ut* and *vellem ut* expound one another. This day then is
dies desiderii, or *desiderabilis.* To be desired, even of
Abraham; and, if of him, of all. Of the cause, first, Why?
and then, of the manner, How he desired it.

The Cause; why should Abraham so desire to see this
day, two thousand years and more after his days were at an
end, and he in his grave? What was it to him? How
was he concerned in it? We say, *Omnia bonum appetunt*
—what good had he by it? We say again, *Indigentia
desiderii parens*—what need had he of it that he should so
desire it? Yes, Christ's birth he needed; he had good by;
and consequently, His birth-day.

Ye remember Job's Easter; that in all his heaviness this
was *spes in sinu,* his "only comfort and joy," that well yet
—"his Redeemer should rise again" (Job xix. 25) one day.
The joy of Job's Easter, the same is the joy of Abraham's
Christmas; even, that a day should come, wherein his
Redeemer should come into the world. For Abraham's
case was not such, but that a Redeemer he stood in need
of. One he stood in need of, and One he had. You may
read it *totidem verbis,* "Thus saith He that redeems Abraham." (Isa. xxix. 22.) That Party—Him, he needed; and
Him he desired. And desired His day for His sake; *diem*
for *Meum;* the day, for Him That was born on the day.

Will ye hear it from his own mouth? Thus he setteth
down his own case. That very time when he had this day
first shewed him, the first glimpse of it; thus complains he
there of his need, and complaining implies his desire; *Et
ecce ego pulvis et cinis,* "And lo, I am but dust and ashes."
(Gen. xviii. 27.) "Dust" is plain; it refers us to *pulvis es,
et in pulverem,* (Gen. iii. 19); he was that by nature, by his
very creation. But why "ashes?" how come they in?
Ashes he was not made of, that is not natural; that, sure,

refers to somewhat else. Ashes, we know, come of fire; without it they are not made—ever presuppose a fire precedent. So that, besides death to resolve him into dust, he saw a fire to turn him into ashes. He saw it in his vision: "When the sun was down, and it was night, and a great fear or horror fell upon him, he saw *clibanum fumantem*, a fiery furnace." (Gen. xv. 17.) Blame him not, if after such a night he desired to see day, and this day; *dies contra noctem*, "a day to visit him from on high," (Luke i. 78), after so fearful a night as this. But this was but a vision of the night. But when all days and nights should be at an end, he saw there was yet a day to succeed that day, which Enoch taught the world, wherein the "Lord should come with thousands of His saints, to execute judgment upon sinners." (Jude, ver. 14, 15.) Which day, it seems, Abraham took notice of. For speaking to God in the same chapter, he calleth Him by this title, "Judge of the world." (Gen. xviii. 25.) Of which day a visible sign he had before his eyes, waking, in the consuming of the five cities immediately after. No marvel then, though he desired *dies contra diem*, 'a day that should quit him of the fear of that day.' Inasmuch then as dust he was, and ashes he was to be; dust by creation, ashes by condemnation, and both these he confesseth himself liable unto; he needed One, as to restore the ruins of the first, so to prevent the danger of the second. Being in need, he desired; desiring, he was glad to hear of; but more glad would be to see that day that should bring Him into the world. And O, when shall that day be? And sure, the sun must go down with us too? and what fear we shall then be in, or whether we shall see the furnace, I know not; but sure I am, that joyful it will be then to have a comfortable sight and apprehension of the benefit and beginning of this day. When the world shall bid us good-night, then, as St. Augustine expresseth it, *videre in nocte sæculi diem Christi.*

This for the cause why Abraham himself should desire this *ut*, to see this day; why, but for this day Abraham had been but ashes of the furnace. Which sheweth it is a benefit to see this day, and as a benefit desired by him; and as a benefit, and no small benefit, vouchsafed him— the sight of this day. Now for his manner how, how greatly he desired it. We may take measure of the greatness of the day by the greatness of his desire. It was no "day of small things," for *exultavit ut* is no small desire; there is vigour, there is both passion and action in it. The nature of the word *exultavit* is, "he did even fetch a spring for joy" that he should see it. And it is not *exiliit* neither, but *exultavit*. And that is a frequentative; and so he did it more than once. To give a spring, and not once but often; this was much, if all be well considered. For one to do it, one in years, fast upon an hundred as Abraham then was, for such an one to do it, it was very much.

1. Much. First, that he should not contain his affection; not keep it in, but out it must; even break forth into an external act—into a bodily gesture, that all that stood by must see him do it.

2. Into a bodily gesture, I say. But then again, that into such a bodily gesture; a gesture on this fashion. It must needs be he was greatly, yea strangely affected with it, that it made him forget his gravity, and put a kind of indecorum upon his age, at those years to fall on springing. All men will easily know that such as he was, staid, discreet, grave men will never be so exceeding moved as to be brought to fetch a spring, but upon some very exceeding great occasion.

3. Thirdly; to do all this but only in desire and nothing but desire, is yet more strange than the rest. In the fruition, to joy is kindly; but in the desire, altogether unusual. *Exultavit cum videret*, may well be understood; *exultavit ut videret*, not so well. For desire of itself is a restless thing, unquiet, and complaining; but a very affliction of the soul. It makes men, yea the very creature itself saith the Apostle, *ingemiscere*, (which is far from *exultare*,) "to groan for grief," (Rom. viii. 22), not to spring for joy; sad rather than glad, in that way they want their desire. Judge then how great a good is the good of this day that not in the enjoying, but even in the desiring and that against the nature of desire, did put old father Abraham into this passion; and brought from him this act, the act of exultation, and made him even young again.

But I will tell you yet of another as strange. For the same word you shall observe is used of the Baptist, while he was yet but an embryo and in his mother's belly. That at the interview and voice of the blessed Virgin Mary, he then a babe "gave a spring in the womb of Elizabeth his mother." (Luke i. 44.) So that we see both old and young, Abraham and John Baptist, from the eldest in years to the child unborn, it concerns all. All need it, all are bound to be glad of it, all is for the joy and honour of this day.

And this for his first act and first joy, joy of desire, for there be two. There is another in the last word ἐχάρη. As there be two sights, 1. *ut videret*, and 2. *et vidit*, so two joys answerable; either hath his joy. And this first is but John Baptist's forerunner to the second. For all this is but the Apostle's *spe gaudentes* (Rom. xii. 12) yet; but the joy of hope only anticipating the other before it come, and joying as it were that it shall joy when that joyful time shall be.

And with this we must begin, even with desire, and seek to possess our souls of it. This carrieth the next, the eye. For where the desire is, there will the eye be also; and where it is not, no prospect thitherward, no window open that way. Therefore set that, as the needle point, right, and all the rest will follow. For the truth is, therefore we joy not because we see not, and therefore we see not because we desire not. True it is, and pity it is; millions there be never have true sight of Him. Why? they have no desire to Him. We must then begin there with desire, with *ut videret*, or we shall never come to *et vidit*. And for our comfort, the very desire of this day or of any good thing else, if it be true and uncounterfeit, a first degree it is, and it is not lightly to be accounted of. It is not nothing to say—if one can say and say it true, *exultarem et viderem*. For of this desire, *exultarem ut* is, among other one character. Three there be besides; and lightly they go together, and they be *succedanea* as we call them to any good thing which we have not but wish that we had, or that we might have. As, if we cannot repent, cannot abstain, cannot believe, or live as we ought, these come in place, and express yet how we stand inwardly affected toward them—even these four : 1. *exultarem* or *gauderem si ;* 2. *vellem ut ;* 3. *metuo ne ;* 4. *doleo quod non. Gauderem si,* 'glad I would be if it were ;' *vellem ut,* 'and I heartily wish that it were ;' *metuo ne,* 'but sure I doubt it be not ;' and *doleo quod non,* 'sorry I am that it is not.' Characters they be all ; and if they be hearty and true, a sign it is the flax smoketh yet. *Et linum fumigans,* so gracious He is, " the flax if it do but smoke, He will not quench it." (Isa. xlii. 3.) But all the rest, specially if it be this. For there is vigour and vehemency in *exultarem ut.* It is a fervent desire, a kind of hunger and thirst, a *desiderio desideravi*—this *exultarem ut*—I would do any thing, I would give any thing to have a sight of it. And such a desire shall never be frustrate ; it shall see certainly.

Of *exultare ut videas,* the reward shall be *videre ut exultes ;* of desiring that we see not, to see that we desire. We have Abraham, the father, in the text ; take Zachee, the son, for an example of it too. He, out of a desire to see Christ at His coming to Jericho, "and could not for the press," (Luke xix. 3), *exultavit* ' gave a spring,' " got him up into a tree," so as to have a sight of Him. It was so well taken, this very desire, as he not only saw Him, but received Him to his house. And our Saviour pronounceth, this text was fulfilled in him ; " He was even thereby become the son of Abraham." (Luke xix. 9.) For howsoever in things temporal it may be and is oft defeated, in things pertaining to Christ and His sight, *exultavit ut videret* shall ever end, as here it doth, in *et vidit.* And so we pass to the next point of *et vidit.*

It is here first directly avouched, the Patriarchs (and Abraham by name) they did not only desire to see this day, but see it they did. See it, though they did but see it and salute it πόῤῥω "afar off," (Heb. xi. 13) ; or, ὡς ἐν κατόπτρῳ "as in a perspective glass," (1 Cor. xiii. 12) ; yet see it they did. It is but *vidit, vidit, in genere.* Any sight, any descrying will serve to verify the text. I say not they did precisely know the very day of the month, I would not so be understood. But this they did ; they knew and saw *in genere* such a day there should come ; and then come when it would, or what day of the year it would, all joy they wished to that day for the joy it was to bring them. This was enough for them in their estate ; and more particular notice had they had of the month and day, this I am sure, they would never have scraped it out of their Kalendar.

" He saw it." But then, if you ask how he saw it ? Sure, not (as they were mistaken in the text) as if Abraham could not see His day, unless Christ had been in the flesh in the days of Abraham. That is one kind of seeing indeed. For so Simeon saw, "for mine eyes have seen." (Luke ii. 30.) But this text must be true; *vidit Abraham.* Then another there is beside. This is sure; what Simeon saw, the same saw Abraham. What Simeon saw I say, but not as Simeon saw. The same Christ both, and the same day, though not both in the same manner.

But let me tell you, this of Abraham's was the better. And if Simeon had not seen Him in the same manner Abraham did, for all his *viderunt oculi,* (Luke ii. 30), he had been never the nearer. No more than were the Jews here that hurled stones at Him, and so saw Him; but to no benefit, no matter of exultation at all; of condemnation, rather.

Then, if not with his eyes, how? Yes; with his eyes too, though not of the body. Which to conceive, we are to take notice that there is in every man of us two men: (Plato had seen so much and set it down, and it is thought the Apostle took it from him;) 1. an outward, and 2. an inward man. (Rom. vii. 22, and 2 Cor. iv. 16.) Now if there be an inward man, we must allow him senses as a man; he must have eyes. So he hath; "having the eyes of your understanding lightened." (Eph. i. 18.) Here are eyes; by them did Abraham, and even by them and by no other do we see Him.

Those eyes many have beside, but see Him not for want of light. By what light saw he? He was a Prophet, and as a Prophet he might be in the Spirit and have the vision clearly represented before him, *in luce Propheticæ.* But without all question a "faithful" (Gal. iii. 9), man he was, and so certain it is he saw it *in lumine fidei,* 'the light of faith,' which "faith is the clearness or evidence of things not seen," (Heb. xi. 1); (ye know the place;) not seen—nay even of things invisible. In the 27th verse of the same chapter it is said, "Moses was as if he had seen the Invisible." (Heb. xi. 27.) By faith, that was; and in Abraham "the father of the faithful," (Rom. iv. 11), the same faith was. Both saw by the same light, and by it Christ was as verily present unto them, as if they had seen Him this day in the manger with the shepherds; or with Simeon had had Him in their arms, and beheld Him. Thus he, and thus we. For it is all the light he had, or we have to see Him by.

But where was this, and when? The text is enough, so it was, if we rest not in that but would know what the Fathers have conceived of the place and time. This they hold; that he saw His birth at the valley of Mamre, (Gen. xvii. 19); and he saw His Passion in the mount of Moriah. (Gen. xviii. 10.) But this day he saw at Mamre. Then was Christ in Person there, one of the Three; then made Abraham the confession we before spake of. Then is twice mention made of the time of life, which is this time, if ever any. Then Isaac was delivered as a gage, and then was his first feast of joy; down went his fat heifer; so all met at the time just.

And so certainly he then saw it there, as after we see he sware his servant on his thigh. His thigh became *ad sancta Dei evangelia;* he bade his servant "lay his hand on his thigh, and swear by the God of Heaven." (Gen. xxiv. 2, 3.) *Et quid vult Deus Cœli ad femur Abrahæ?* 'What hath the God of Heaven to do with Abraham's thigh?' saith St. Augustine; and his answer is, *nisi quia,* 'but only because he saw certainly the Son of God was from thence to take flesh'—*semen Abrahæ de femore Abrahæ,* and so to make us this blessed day. And this of Christ's *visus;* and now of Abraham's *gavisus,* the end of his sight and desire both.

He that was glad he should see it, must needs be glad when he did see it. If *exultavit ut videret,* then *ut vidit, ut exultavit!* when he saw, how glad a man was he now his desire was accomplished! And "the desire accomplished," saith Solomon, "is a tree of life," (Prov. xiii. 12); and "the tree of life" we know "is in the midst," (Gen. ii. 9), is the very centre of all the joys of Paradise. Now we cannot possibly take a view of these his joys better than out of the promise, which was the very list or brief of all he was either to see or to joy in.

We begin with the blessed joy of *Benedicentur omnes gentes in semine tuo.* (Gen. xxvi. 4). *Benedicentur,* "shall be blessed." And that is of two sorts. 1. Blessed from; and 2. blessed with: and either hath his joys.

Blessed *from,* from *pulvis et cinis,* "dust of the grave and ashes of the furnace." His soul blessed from the *clibanus fumans* which he saw. Moreover also "His flesh should rest in hope," (Ps. xvi. 9), hope of rising again from the dust. Else how could God be called "the God of Abraham"?

"God is not the God of the dead, but of the living." (Mat. xxii. 32.)   Abraham then being dead should live again, and then *Nunc dimittis*, (Luke ii. 29), may he say no less than Simeon.   These two joys first.   And these two fit well the words of joy in the verse.   1. *Exultavit*, that is a motion of the body, for the body's deliverance from dust.   2. *Gavisus*, that is a fruit of the spirit, for the spirit's redemption from the furnace.   These are his two first joys.

Then two more, in blessed *with* or concerning.   Concerning first his two gages, Isaac and Canaan : Isaac, of Christ ; Canaan, of the Kingdom of Heaven.   And this joy was surely great ; and if the joy of the pledge or gage were great, far greater was the joy of the inheritance itself which he so greatly desired.   For both he was, saith the Apostle, and "he bare himself like a stranger here upon earth," (Heb. xi. 13) ; shewing thereby that he sought for another, a better, "an abiding City, whose Builder is God," and that in Heaven.   For that it was no earthly thing which was the object of his joy, nothing but Heaven, thence it may appear, that when God promised him, "his seed should be as the dust of the earth," (Gen. xiii. 16), it never moved him ; it was no object that of his faith or desire, not so much as a *credidit* follows upon it.   But after, in the fifteenth chapter, when God bade him look up, and told him, "they should be as the stars of Heaven," (Gen. xv. 5, 6) ; then presently follows, *Credidit Abraham Deo*, he caught hold of that ; "believed" that straight, and "it was counted to him for righteousness ;" even that his faith touching no dust of the earth, but touching Heaven and Heavenly blessings.   And these are the two next joys of *blessed with ;* and these two answer the two sights ; *ut videret* the pledge, and *et vidit* the inheritance.

Now these four, had they been granted to himself and to his own house, well might it have been *gavisus* with him ; how much more then, that it should by him have his extent and stretch to *omnes familiæ, omnes gentes,* "all kindreds, all nations of the earth," (Gen. xxvi. iv.) ; be *gaudium omni populo,* "be a day of joy to both hemispheres," the joy of generality ; that all the world should be the better for him? And this his fifth, the joy of *omnes gentes.*

And glad might he have been to have received all these by whomsoever, yea though a mere stranger.   That all these

then should come to him, not by any strange party but by
one to come out of his own bowels; that his Seed should be
his Saviour, and out of his root should rise his Redeemer;
all this joy should grow from the fruit of his own body;
that He That *nusquam angelos,* " in no wise them," (Heb.
ii. 16); would take on Him "the seed of Abraham;" this
may I doubt not be reckoned for the sixth, even the joy of
in semine tuo.

Now to *in semine Abrahæ* add *in sinu Abrahæ,* and so
have we seven complete; that "his bosom" should be the
receptacle of all that should enter into bliss.   Whosoever
there entertained, *in sinu Abrahæ* it is to be. (Luke xvi. 23.)
This is the last, that *semen Abrahæ* shall bring us to *sinus
Abrahæ,* and make us partakers of his Heavenly joys there.
But we must begin with *in semine* to-day, that after in His
good time *in sinu* may follow.   And this for *gavisus est,* and
for Abraham.

Now to ourselves.   And the first point is, whether we will
be out with the Jews, or in with Abraham, in the fellowship
of this day's joy.   In with Abraham we sure.   If all be well
weighed, we have greater cause to desire the day than he;
we have more need of it I am sure.   Dust as he, but more
in danger to be made ashes than he, by Manasses' argument
in his prayer.   The benefit of his day and the like, they do
nothing so much concern the just such as Abraham, as
they do sinful Manasses and such as he.   And such are
we; and ever the more sinner, the more it imports him
to love the dawning of this day.   Greater cause we have
than he.

And for our sight, we have that clearer than he by much.
For though we see as he, and he as we, both by the light of
faith; yet he in the faith of prophecy yet to come, we in the
faith of history now past; and there is great odds between
these two.   We have the record of human writers many, but
of Divine all, that this day is come and gone; even of such
as saw Him with the eyes both of the inward and outward
man.

The greater cause and the better sight: then is our joy
also to abound, and be above his.   So it should, sure.   And
we would seem as if it so were; we multiply the days, and
where he had but one we hold twelve together, as if we
would exceed him twelve to one in this joy.   Being then so

bound, joy agreeth well with us at this time. The text invites us to it, the whole strain from the first word to the last. It begins with *exultavit*, and ends in *gavisus est.*

Only, that from whence we take our joy, from thence we take the rules of it, which be three. 1. One of the two parts, *exultavit* and *gavisus est.* 2. One of the end, *diem Meum.* And 3. the last of our pattern, *sicut Abraham pater noster*, to express it as he did.

Here be two sorts; 1. One, exultation, a motion of the body. 2. The other joy, a fruit of the spirit: I am for both. I speak not against *exultavit;* let the body have his part. Reason would the body and the flesh should be allowed their parts, since all the joy is for *corpus aptasti Mihi*, and that *Verbum caro factum est,* "the Word is become flesh;" that Christ hath gotten Him a body. But let not *exultavit* be all, whole and sole. Then we joy but by halves; we lose half our joy, and the better half; for the joy of the spirit is the better part, when all is done. The flesh fades daily; so do the joys of it: the spirit's is "the better part that shall not be taken from us." (Luke x. 42.) That of the spirit should exceed the joy of the outward man, as far as *et vidit* to which it is joined doth exceed *ut videret.* It should so. Well, in the meanwhile I would they might but part equally; at least, not to stay so long, not to make so large allowance of time and cost for the flesh, as we leave little or nothing for the spirit's part. Sure somewhat would be done, some special use of this feast that may tarry by us, when these of the flesh we shall either have forgotten, or remember but with small joy. Time will come, that one lesson in this kind, learned this day and laid up well, will do us more pleasure than all the sports we shall see the whole twelve days after; that we come not behind Abraham half in half.

Our next *caveat* would be, that we look this our joy be for *diem Meum*, and that our joy in *diem* be for *Meum.* For *Meum* is here the substantive, it is Christ ; and *diem* but an accident or adjective to it. That is, that we joy in it, as it is His—Christ's. As His, do we not so? As whose else? To speak plainly, the common sort generally all, some few except, wish for it and joy in it, not as it is Christ's, but as it is somewhat else ; that is, as it is a time of cheer and feasting, as it is a time of sports and revelling. *Exultavit*

I

ut videret—what? why that we shall now fare well. Look you, that is it, as it is *dies epuli*, not *Christi*. What farther? that we shall now see pastimes; that is, as it is *dies ludi*, not *Christi*. Put both together; "down they sat to feast, up they rose to play," (Exod. xxxii. 6); so have you the golden Calf's holiday right. As it is *dies vituli*, not *Christi*. This is not *diem* for *Meum :* in very deed, this is to desire Him for the day, not the day for Him. Christ's day is not desired for Christ, Christ is the least part of His own feast. If it be but matter of the belly, the Jews here could have been entreated to have kept this day so as *dies epuli*. For before, at the sixth chapter, when their bellies were filled, then and never but then, "This is the Prophet, This is He that should come into the world." (John vi. 14.) This was all they then made, all that many now do make of Christ's coming into the world ;—that they may fill their bellies. Never care for *benedicentur* no more than Esau, but for *bene vescentur ;* and if *bene vestientur* too, then all is well.

Or, if it be but shows and matter of sight, Herod he was glad to see Christ too. And it is the same word which is here, glad, and very glad, λίαν ἐχάρη. But why was it? Because "he hoped to have seen him done some strange feats." (Luke xxiii. 8.) This pertaineth rather to Sarah's laughter than Abraham's joy. There is a difference between Sarah's laughter and Abraham's joy. Take heed that we change not Abraham's joy into Sarah's laughter.

Now last, *sicut Abraham*. He is propounded here to us as our pattern ; we to express our joy as he did his upon the day of his sight at the plain of Mamre. So we shall begin right. Two things he did ; first, he got them, the Three, to turn in to him. (Gen. xviii. 3.) The same would Christ do to us this day. That our joy may be suitable, to turn in hither. The beginning of the joy of His day would be in His house ; so the place and the time would agree well. So He saith Himself, *Lætificabo eos in domo Mea ;* the first thing I will do, "I will make them joyful in Mine house." (Isa. lvi. 7.) There first, to satisfy us with the pleasure of His house, wherewith God He knows we are soon satisfied. Well, this is done ; here we are, and much ado too and long it is first, but here we are.

The next was, when they were turned in Abraham said, "Let me set somewhat before you," *ideo enim declinâstis,*

"for even for this are ye turned in hither," (Gen. xviii. 5);
and so made his feast. There is indeed no solemn enter-
tainment or joy without a feast. Christ will be in all respects
as courteous as Abraham. He saith, Let Me set something
before you too, for therefore are you turned in hither; He
invites us to His feast. His Church so doth in His name;
even this day prepares and sets Christ's feast before us,
wherein He offers Himself to us. Not as the object of one
sense only—of sight, as to Abraham in the text; but as the
object of two, sight and taste; *gustate et videte*, (Ps. xxxiv.
8), both. And we may not take the one and leave the other,
but since both be offered, receive both. For we are come
hither for this cause; here then shew your joy in His feast-
day by partaking His feast on His day, the only feast of all
the rest for which the soul is the better. Thus shall we
with joy keep this day aright.

And here now, one day calls another; this day of His
calls to mind another day of His, called so in twenty places
"His day," and called "that day" in plain preference to
this. So to joy this day, as that day we may joy also.
As this His day, because it is the day of His first coming;
so that His likewise, because it is the day of His coming
again. A day, howsoever we do with this, which we must
all see; Abraham, the Jews, we, and all. Only, that we see
that day with joy; that we so demean ourselves in this, as
that also may prove a festival with us, even "the last and
greatest day of the feast" now begun in this. All will be,
how to make that a day of joy to us when we see it: to
have that day rise clear and cheerful to us, will be the
joy of all joys. For here first, as "we see but in part," so
we can joy but in part. As our sight, so our joy, imperfect.
But there "we shall see as we are seen," (1 Cor. xiii. 12);
our sight being perfect, so shall our joy be; perfect sight,
and perfect joy. And besides, that is another manner of
day than this or any day here, a day that shall never go
down; no more shall the joy of it. And it shall not endure
for twelve days, or be a feast of a fortnight; but shall be
from month to month, from jubilee to jubilee, for ever and
ever. To the joy of which feast, or to the feast of which
joy, by &c.

SERMON IX.

A Sermon preached before the King's Majesty at Whitehall, on Sunday, the Twenty-fifth of December, A.D. MDCXIV., being Christmas-day.

Behold, a virgin shall conceive, and bear a Son, and she shall call His name Immanuel.—Isa. vii. 14.

[*Ecce virgo concipiet, et pariet Filium, et vocabitur nomen Ejus Immanuel.*]

OF all the writers of the Old Testament, the Prophet Esay hath the honour to be the first that is vouched in the New. And of all the places this place the honour to be the first of all, even in the first Evangelist, St. Matthew, and in the very first chapter of him. (Matt. i. 23.) We may well think St. Matthew would be careful to make choice of a very prime and pregnant place, to set it as it were in the front of his Gospel. This is much honour St. Matthew doth it.

But the Angel Gabriel doth it more, who takes this verse as it stands, (Luke i. 31), word for word, and makes it serve for his annunciation o. message to the Blessed Virgin without any alteration ; not so much as the *ecce* left out.

The tenor of it is all about a Child to be born, a Child with an *ecce ;* in Whom, and in Whose birth, God should be with us—so with us as never before. On Whose so being with us depends all our well or evil being here, and for ever. For better not to be at all than be without Him ; and having Him we need nothing else, for *in Ipso omnia*, "in Him is all." (Col. i. 17.)

The Eunuch's question falls fitly in here ; "Of whom speaks the Prophet this?" (Acts viii. 34.) Who is His mother? Who the Child? St. Matthew will be as good to us as St. Philip was to him : who, where he enrols it, tells us who the mother, the blessed Virgin ; who the Child, our blessed Saviour. Who else? No virgin ever bare child but she ; no child ever *nobiscum Deus*, and so *Deus*, but He. There is none other to lay claim to it but they.

Ecce hath in it two powers. 1. One for the ear, to awake

it to some matter more than ordinary. 2. Another for the eye, to direct it by pointing to some certainty ; as here to two certain persons, the mother and the Child. And shews us two strange sights in them, *mater virgo*, and *Deus homo ;* ' a virgin to become a mother,' ' God to become man.' A virgin to bear ; God to be born. In both, and in either of them, three points are offered to us. 1. *Ecce concipiet ;* 2. *Ecce pariet ;* 3. *Ecce vocabit nomen.* Our Saviour Christ's first triplicity : 1. The mystery of His holy Incarnation, in *concipiet ;* 2. His holy Nativity, in *pariet ;* 3. His Circumcision, in *vocabit nomen.* And every one of these three makes a several feast. *Ecce concipiet,* the Annunciation ; *et pariet,* this feast of the birth of our Lord ; *et vocabit nomen,* New-year's day, when His name was given.

But we apply it to this feast. So doth St. Matthew in his *inspeximus* of it to the birth of Christ. "The birth of Christ," saith he, "was on this fashion," (Matt. i. 18), and then brings in this record out of Esay. As if this *ecce* did in particular point at this day. As in truth we stand not much upon His conceiving now He is born specially as born He is, *ecce pariet* is the point. For then we see Him, take Him in our arms, then He is "with us" indeed. And when was that ? *Ecce pariet* saith the text ; *Ecce peperit* saith the day, this very day. This is the chief.

But finding them here all, we will deal with them all. 1. Christ as embryo, in His conception. 2. Christ as ἀρτιγέννητον βρέφος, a new-born babe, but yet ἀνώνυμος, ' without a name.' 3. And Christ with his full Christendom, as named ; and named with this name here in the text, the name of " Immanuel."

Of which three, ye may reduce the first two " conceived" and " born" to His nature ; and to make two, to two of the latter make two more, *vocabit* and *nomen,* His name and His vocation—for in His name is His vocation. To bring God to us, to make God with us ; Him to be with us, that we may be with Him for ever. *Nobiscum Deus,* the way ; *nos cum Deo,* the end ; which is, and so may be the end of the text, and of the day, and of us all. Nothing more worthy our sight than this birth, nor more worth our hearing than this name.

I. *Ecce* spreads itself over the whole text—may be repeated at every point of it ; but it first points to *ecce Virgo.* There we may make a stay, there is a block in our way by the Jews. In no one place doth that of the Apostle's speech appear, that "at the reading of the prophecies of Christ the veil is laid over their hearts," (2 Cor. iii. 15); nowhere how true the Proverb is, that 'malice will even blind a man,' as here in this. This verse so dazzles them, as fain would they turn another way, and not see that they do. They see no virgin here: Esay's word *Alma*, say they, is but "a young woman," and not "a virgin" properly. But they say against their own knowledge, in so saying. For first, beside the nature of the word, the very energy gives as much. For it is of *Alam*, and that is "to cover;" and so properly is one that is yet covered, and never yet known; opposed to them that have been uncovered and known, after the Hebrew phrase.

And beside, the use of the word for a virgin in other places. Rebecca then a virgin, called by this name. (Gen. xxiv. 43, 55, 57.) And Miriam then but six years old, called by it likewise. (Exodus ii. 8.)

And beside their own taking of the word, they themselves, the more ancient of them, so in their Targum—this very word *Alamoth* (Cant. ii. 2) they gloss and paraphase it by *Betuloth*, the proper word for virgins; where it stands this day to be seen.

Besides all this, see whither their malice carrieth them by denying this, even to overturn prophecy, and Prophet, and all. For he calls us to see a sign, and that with an *ecce;* and what is that? if it be but a young woman to conceive, and no virgin, where is the sign? what is became of the *ecce?* It is no sign or wonder, unless it be beside the course of nature; and is it any whit beside the course of nature for a young woman to be with child? Therefore take away *Virgo*, and away with the *ecce;* down with the sign. Thus, rather than to bear witness to the truth, sticked they not to expose the word of God, and so God Himself to scorn; make the Prophet, or, as St. Matthew well saith, "God by the Prophet," (Matt. i. 22), to speak idly; give them a sign that is no sign; tell them of a marvel not to be marvelled at.

Reject them then, and read confidently as St. Matthew doth, "Behold a virgin." (Matt. i. 23.) With him rest hardly on the skill and integrity of all the seventy, that more than an hundred years before it came to pass turned it παρ-θένος in Greek, that is "a virgin;" who could skill of their own tongue better than any Kimchi, or Albo, or any Rabbin of them all. This, for *Ecce Virgo.*

And look, what work we had with the Jew about *Ecce Virgo*, the like shall we have with the Gentile about *Virgo concipiet.* To conceive this conceiving, to join these two, a virgin, and yet conceive or bear ; or, conceive and bear, and yet be a virgin. For before the birth, yea before the conceiving come, the virginity is gone. True—in nature ; but this is a sign, and so above nature. And in reason so. But this is *nisi credideritis non intelligetis*, " to be believed, otherwise not to be understood," as a little before was said. For what God can do faith can believe, reason cannot comprehend. But this it can ; that we do God no great favour as well saith St. Augustine, *Si Deum fatemur, &c.* ' If we confess God can do somewhat, which we confess our reason cannot reach.'

The blessed Virgin herself while she stood upon a reason, upon *quia non cognosco virum*, asked, " How it might be ? " (Luke i. 34), but rested in the Angel's resolution, and so let us. Which was of two sorts ; first, that the Holy Ghost should be Agent in it, and "the power of the Most High bring it to pass." (Luke i. 35.) That which of itself seemeth not credible, put the Author to it, put to *ex Spiritu Sancto*, and it will seem not incredible.

Specially, and that is the second, if we set another by it as unlikely as it, and done though ; as this *ecce* of the Virgin's the Angel exemplifies by another *ecce* of Zachary's, in a manner as hard, which yet fell out at the same time. For Elizabeth being barren, first by nature, then by age, and so wanting power to conceive—she was then "gone six months with child." (Luke i. 36.) Now the want of power to conceive is no less material to hinder the conception every way, than want of the soil no less than the want of seed. He that could supply that could also this. He that do it without one, do it without the other. They were cousins, the blessed Virgin and she ; and their signs were so too. One of them made credible by the other.

But I ask St. Paul's question, " Why should it be thought a thing incredible," (Acts xxvi. 8), this to the Gentiles ? If, as their religion taught them, they admitted of Minerva's birth, or Pyrrha's progeny, they need not make strange at this. If they say, The God of nature is not bound to the rules of nature, we say the same. And yet, even in nature, we see it made not altogether incredible. The light passing through a body, the body yet remaining whole—and it is put therefore into the verse to pattern this, *Luce penetratur, &c.* 'The light cometh through the glass, yet the glass is not perished.' No more than the light of Heaven passing through breaketh the glass, no more did the God of Heaven by His passage violate any whit the virginity of His mother; if we will allow God the maker of the light to do as much as the light He hath made.

But I hold ever best to let every thing rest upon his own base, or bottom; natural upon reason, supernatural upon faith. And this is supernatural; in which *tota ratio facti est in potentiâ facientis,* 'the power of the doer is the reason of the thing done.' God is the Doer, *Cujus dicere est facere,* 'to Whom it is as easy to do it as to say it.' As the Angel concluded, so do I; "With God is nothing impossible." (Luke i. 37.) And that of Christ's, "To faith all things are possible." (Mark ix. 23.) And here are both. And where they meet, they make no less a miracle than *Mater* and *Virgo,* or *Deus* and *Homo*—even *fides* and *ratio.* And this, for *Virgo concipiet.*

II. Now to the three particulars; and first, *concipiet.* To make Him man, it is well known there wanted not other ways: from the mould, as Adam; from a rib of flesh, as Eve. No need then of *concipiet.* Yes—for He was not to be man only, but to be "the Son of Man;" the name in the text, *Filius,* and the name that for the most part He giveth Himself, and seemeth most to delight in. But Adam was not son to the mould, nor Eve daughter to Adam. And "a Son" no way but by *concipiet.* And howsoever of the body of man there may engender that which is not of the same kind, yet by way of conception there cometh of man nothing but man; nothing but of the same nature and substance with that he was conceived of.

This we are to hold; to conceive is more than to receive. It is so to receive as we yield somewhat of our own also. A vessel is not said to conceive the liquor that is put into it. Why? because it yieldeth nothing from itself. The blessed Virgin is, and therefore is because she did. She did both give and take. Give of her own substance whereof His body was framed; and take or receive power from the

Holy Ghost, whereby was supplied the office and the efficacy of the masculine seed. This is *concipiet*.

And this word is the bane of divers heresies. That of the Manichee that held He had no true body. That had been *virgo decipiet*, not *concipiet;* not—conceive Him, but deceive us. And that of the Valentinian, revived lately in the Anabaptist, that held He had a true body, but made in Heaven and sent into her. That had been *recipiet*, but not *concipiet;* received Him she had, conceived she had not.

From which His conceiving we may conceive His great love to us-ward. Love, not only condescending to take our nature upon Him, but to take it by the same way and after the same manner that we do, by being conceived. That, and no other better beseeming way. The womb of the Virgin is surely no such place, but He might well have abhorred it. He did not; *pudorem exordii nostri non recusavit*, saith Hilary; 'He refused not that ourselves are ashamed of;' *sed naturæ nostræ contumelias transcurrit*, 'but the very contumelies of our nature (*transcurrit* is too quick a word) He ran through them;' nay He stayed in them, in this first nine months. I say the contumelies of our nature not to be named, they are so mean. So mean indeed as it is verily thought they made those old heretics I named, and others more who yet yielded Him to be Man, to run into such fancies as they did; only to decline those foul indignities as they took them, for the Great God of Heaven to undergo.

This therefore, even this, would He have set down in terms terminant, of *concipiet* and *pariet*. Trusting we would wisely judge of them, and love Him never the less, but the more even for these. Μὴ διὰ τοῦτο ἄτιμος ὅτι διὰ σε ταπεινός: 'Honour Him nevertheless, because He laid down His honour for thy sake.' No; but *quanto ille minus debita, tanto ego magis debitor;* 'the less due He took on Him, the more due from me to Him.' In a word, *quanto pro me vilior, tanto mihi charior;* 'the lower for me, the dearer to me.' It brings to mind King David's *vilior adhuc fiam*, (2 Sam. vi. 22), and how God even for that regarded him the more. *Concipiet et pariet*, to conceive and bring forth in us love, honour, and due regard, even for them. It reaches both.

This sure is matter of love; but came there any good to us by it? There did. For our conception being the root as it were, the very groundsill of our nature; that He might go to the root and repair our nature from the very foundation, thither He went; that what had been there defiled and decayed by the first Adam, might by the second be cleansed and set right again. That had our conception been stained, by Him therefore, *primum ante omnia*, to be restored again. He was not idle all the time He was an embryo—all the nine months He was in the womb; but then and there He even eat out the core of corruption that cleft to our nature and us, and made both us and it an unpleasing object in the sight of God.

And what came of this? We that were abhorred by God, *filii iræ* (Eph. ii. 3), was our title, were by this means made beloved in Him. He cannot, we may be sure, account evil of that nature, that is now become the nature of His own Son—His now no less than ours. Nay farther, given the privilege to the children of such as are in Him, though but of one parent believing, that they are not as the seed of two infidels, but "are in a degree holy," *eo ipso;* and have a farther right to "the laver of regeneration," to sanctify them throughout by "the renewing of the Holy Ghost." (Titus iii. 5.) This honour is to us by the dishonour of Him; this the good by Christ an embryo.

Et pariet; and this no more than needs. There may be *concipiet,* and no *pariet* follow. *Venerunt filii ad partum, &c.*, saith the Prophet, "The children came to the birth, and no strength to deliver." (Isa. xxxvii. 3.) *Pariet* makes all sure.

And *pariet* makes all appear. We could not tell it was *Filium;* knew not what it was, or what it would be. Till He came into the world He was as *thesaurus absconditus;* though we had it, we had it not. But when He was born, when come into the world, we see Him and handle Him; then He was "with us" indeed. "With us".—not as conceived of the same nature with us, but as born and now a Person among us. That which was potential in *concipiet,* made actual by *pariet.*

So that this is the Θεοφανία, when He came forth "as a Bridegroom out of His chamber, or as the Sun from His tabernacle to run His race." (Ps. xix. 5.) And it was with a *visitavit ab alto.* (Luke i. 78.) Thence an angel cried *Ecce,* and sounded it on earth; and a star cried *Ecce,* and proclaimed it from Heaven. Poets in the West write of it; and wise men in the East saw it, and came a long journey upon it to see Him. And what did this *pariet* bring forth? No sooner born, but a multitude of heavenly soldiers sung—"Peace to the earth," (Luke ii. 13)—belike there had been war before, but "peace" now. Nay, more than peace, εὐδοκία: that God had conceived a good liking, was well pleased with men. The same term to men that He useth to Christ Himself, "in whom I am well pleased," (Mat. iii. 17)—εὐδοκία to both. And what would we more? What lack we now? His name.

And now He is born, might we not leave here, and go no farther? *Rem tenemus;* what care we for the name? Yes, we must; for *Christus anonymus* will not serve. Therefore Esay, therefore the angel are careful to bear Him to His baptism, to add His name; the Prophet to intimate it, St. Matthew to interpret it. For though we have said much of Christ an embryo, and Christ a new-born nameless babe, yet nothing to that that followeth—to the *Ecce* of His name.

This name, if it had been of man's giving, I wot well little heed had been to be taken of it. Men set great titles upon empty boxes. Nay, many times the names given by wise men fall out quite contrary. Solomon called his son Rehoboam, "the enlarger of people;" he enlarged them from ten to two. But His name, St. Matthew tells us the Prophet but brought, it was God that sent it. (Mat. i. 22.) And the names of His imposing, there is no surer place in logic than from them. His nominals be reals. As His *dicere, facere,* so His *dici, fieri;* what is said in them comes surely to pass.

Now there were divers names given Him at divers times. To express all His perfections, no one name was enough. There was Jacob's name, Shiloh, (Gen. xlix. 10); that was in respect of His Father, by Whom and from Whom He was sent. There was Paul's name, Messias, Christ; that was, regard had to the Holy Ghost, by or Wherewith He was anointed. (Heb. i. 9.) But what were these? *quid ad nos?* We have no part in them. In this we have; and till this came all was *in nubibus,* as they say. But in this, Immanuel, *Nobiscum Deus,* here come we in first. For in *Immanu* is *anu,* and in *Nobiscum nos.* And this is the first

Nobis, and the first *cum* we find in any name of His; and therefore of all other we are to make much of it. A virgin to bear, God to be born—matter of wonder, but no benefit at all. But when we hear, it is "with us," and for us, that *Ecce* makes us look up to it.

Before I come to it, I would clear a doubt or two of it. 1. One of the name itself; 2. the other of the interpretation, or meaning of the name.

1. It will be said, this was not His name in the end for all this, but Jesus. True: and St. Matthew knew that well enough, for he sets it down so. Yet even in that place he sets it so down, presently he vouches this of Esay of Immanuel, as if Immanuel and Jesus both came to one, as indeed they do; one infers the other. Immanuel, "God with us." Why? to what end? To save us from our sins, and from perishing by them. If there be any odds, it is in Immanuel, which is of larger compass. "God with us" to save us, though that be worth all, yet not that way only, but "with us" other ways besides; and all in Immanuel.

2. "God with us;" why, was He not also with the Patriarchs and Prophets, and Esay himself, as well as with us? He was; but not as well. Some prerogative we must allow this name, if it be but for this *ecce*. No *ecce* belongs to these. Somewhat more to St. Matthew's gospel than to Esay's prophecy. This name must needs imply a secret antithesis to His former being with us. We say nothing in saying, He is now with us, if He be not so with us now as never before. With them in types and figures of Himself; His shadow was with them; but now He Himself. With them He was even thus, in this very *Immanu;* but how? in the future tense, *concipiet pariet;* as things to come are made present to hope. But now, *conceptus est, partus est; re*, not in *spe;* all is past and done. So that now *ita nobiscum ut de nobis;* nay, *ut ipsi nos,* 'So "with us" as even of us now;' of the same substance, nature, flesh and bone that we. "With us" in *concipiet*, conceived as we; "with us" in *pariet*, born as we. Now true as never till now; now so as never so before.

And now, to look into the name. It is compounded, and to be taken in pieces. First, into *Immanu* and *El;* of which, *El* the latter is the more principal by far; for *El* is

God. Now, for any thing yet said in *concipiet* and *pariet*, all is but man with us; not "God with us" till now. By the name we take our first notice that this Child is God. And this is a great addition, and here, lo, is the wonder. For, as for any child of a woman to "eat butter and honey," (Isa. vii. 15), the words that next follow, where is the *Ecce?* But for *El*, for God to do it—that is worth an *Ecce* indeed.

El is God; and not God every way, but as the force of the word is, God in His full strength and virtue; God, *cum plenitudine potestatis* as we say, 'with all that ever He can do;' and that is enough I am sure.

For the other, *Immanu;* though *El* be the more principal, yet I cannot tell whether it or *Immanu* do more concern us. For as in *El* is might, so in *Immanu* is our right to His might, and to all He hath or is worth. By that word we hold, therefore we to lay hold of it. The very standing of it thus before, thus in the first place, toucheth us somewhat. The first thing ever that we look for is *nos, nobis,* and *noster,* the possessives; for they do *mittere in possessionem,* 'put us in possession.' We look for it first, and lo, it stands here first; *nobiscum* first, and then *Deus* after.

I shall not need to tell you that in *nobiscum* there is *mecum;* in *nobiscum* for us all a *mecum* for every one of us. Out of this generality of "with us," in gross, may every one deduce his own particular—with me, and me, and me. For all put together make but *nobiscum.*

The Wise Man out of Immanuel, that is *nobiscum Deus,* doth deduce Ithiel, (Prov. xxx. 1), that is *mecum Deus,* "God with me"—his own private interest. And St. Paul when he had said to the Ephesians of Christ, "Who loved us, and gave Himself for us," (Eph. v. 2), might with good right say to the Galatians, "Who loved me and gave Himself for me." (Gal. ii. 20.)

This *Immanu* is a compound again; we may take it in sunder into *nobis* and *cum;* and so then have we three pieces. 1. *El*, the mighty God; 2. and *anu*, we, poor we,— poor indeed if we have all the world beside if we have not Him to be with us; 3. and *Im*, which is *cum*, and that *cum* in the midst between *nobis* and *Deus*, God and us—to couple God and us; thereby to convey the things of the one to the other. Ours to God; alas, they be not worth the speaking of. Chiefly, then, to convey to us the things of God. For that is worth the while; they are indeed worth the conveying.

This *cum* we shall never conceive to purpose, but *carendo;* the value of "with" no way so well as by without, by stripping of *cum* from *nobis.* And so let *nobis,* "us," stand by ourselves without Him, to see what our case is but for this Immanuel; what, if this virgin's Child had not this day been born us: *nobiscum* after will be the better esteemed. For if this Child be "Immanuel, God with us," then without this Child, this Immanuel, we be without God. "Without Him in this world," (Eph. ii. 12), saith the Apostle; and if without Him in this, without Him in the next; and if without Him there—if it be not *Immanu-el,* it will be *Immanu-hell;* and that and no other place will fall, I fear me, to our share. Without Him, this we are. What with Him? Why, if we have Him, and God by Him, we need no more; *Immanu-el* and *Imanu-all.* All that we can desire is for us to be with Him, with God, and He to be with us; and we from Him, or He from us, never to be parted. We were with Him once before, and we were well; and when we left Him, and He no longer "with us," then began all our misery. Whensoever we go from Him, so shall we be in evil case, and never be well till we be back with Him again.

Then, if this be our case that we cannot be without Him, no remedy then but to get a *cum* by whose means *nobis* and *Deus* may come together again. And Christ is that *Cum* to bring it to pass. The parties are God and we; and now this day He is both. God before eternally, and now to-day Man; and so both, and takes hold of both, and brings both together again. For two natures here are in Him. If conceived and born of a woman, then a man; if God with us, then God. So Esay offered his "sign from the height above, or from the depth beneath," (Is. vii. 11): here it is. "From above," *El;* "from beneath," *anu;* one of us now. And so, His sign from both. And both these natures in the unity of one Person, called by one name, even this name Immanuel.

Vocabit nomen. I told you, in His name is His vocation or office—to be *cum,* to come between that is, to be a Mediator, to make Him that was *contra nos, nobiscum* again. "A mediator is not of one, but God is One." (Gal. iii. 20.)

God and man are two ; and they were two, as they say. Were two, and two will be, till He make them one ; recapitulate and cast up both into one sum ; to knit *anu*, that is "we," and *El*, that is "God," with His *Im*, into one—one word and one thing, *univoce* again.

So upon the point, in these three pieces there be three persons ; so a second kind of Trinity—God, we, and Christ. *El* is God, *anu* we ; for Christ nothing left but *Im*, that is *Cum*, or "with." For it is He that maketh the unity in this Trinity ; maketh God with us, and us with God ; and both, in and by Him, to our eternal comfort and joy.

Thus is He " with us ;" and yet all this is but nature still. But the *nobiscum* of His name bodeth yet a farther matter. For indeed the " with us " of His name is more than the " with us " of His nature. If we make a great matter of that, as great it is and very great, behold the *ecce* of His name is far beyond it. " With us " in His nature, that is " with us " as man—that is short. We are more—sinful men ; a wretched condition added to a nature corrupt. Will He be "with us" in that too ? Else this of nature will smally avail us.

What, in sin ? Nay, " in all things, sin only except." (Heb. iv. 15.) Yea, that is in being " like us," but not in being " with us." For in being " with us " except sin, and except all ; the ridding us of our sin is the only matter, saith Esay after. Therefore to be with us in all things, sin itself not except. St. John's *caro factum est* will not serve, (John i. 14), St. Paul's *fuit peccatum* (2 Cor. v. 21) must come too. In " with us " there too. I say it over again : unity of nature is not enough, He is to be " with us " in unity of Person likewise. So He was. The debtor and surety make but one person in law. That He was, and then He was *Cum*, " with us " thoroughly, as deep in as we.

And this is the proper *Immanu* of His name. And this the *Immanu* indeed. And till He was thus " with us," no name He had ; He was *Christus anonymus*, 'Christ unchristened,' as it were. For His name came not till He became One " with us " in person ; not till His Circumcision ; not, till for us and in our names, He became debtor of the whole Law, principal, forfeiture, and all. To " the hand-writing " (Col. ii. 14) He then signed with the first-fruits of His blood. And then, name the Child, and give

Him this name, "Immanuel." For thus He was a right "Immanuel," truly "with us." "With us" as men; "with us" as sinful men; "with us" in all things, sin itself not excepted.

May I not add this? It is said in the text, "She shall call"—"She," that is, His mother. Why "She"? To let us understand, that she might give Him the name while He undertook this for us. But His Father, till all was discharged and the " hand-writing cancelled," till then He suspended, He gave it Him not. His mother she did, when He dropped a little blood at the sealing of the bond. But He was fain not to drop blood but to sweat blood, and to shed His blood, every drop of it, ere this " with us" were full answered. And then His Father did it too, *dedit Illi nomen super omne nomen,* (Phil. ii. 9) ; then, and not before. His mother now, His Father not till then. But then He had proved Himself fully " with us" *per omnia,* when neither womb nor birth, cratch nor cross, cross nor curse, could pluck Him away from us, or make Him not to be " with us." Then *vocabit illi. nomen,* both she and He ; mother, Father, and all. "With us" to eat " butter and honey" (Isa. vii. 15) seemeth much ; and it is so for God. What say ye to drink " vinegar and gall"? (Ps. lxix. 21, and Mat. xxvii. 48.) That is much more, I am sure ; yet that He did I cannot here say "with us," but for us. Even drunk of the cup with the dregs of the wrath of God, which passed not from Him, that it might pass from us and we not drink it.

This, this is the great " with us ;" for of this follow all the rest. " With us" once thus, and then " with us" in His Oblation on the Altar of the Temple ; "with us" in His Sacrifice on the Altar of the Cross ; " with us " in all the virtues and merits of His life ; " with us " in the satisfaction and satispassion both of His death ; " with us" in His Resurrection, to raise us up from the earth ; " with us " in His Ascension, to exalt us to Heaven ; " with us," even then, when He seemed to be taken from us—that day by His Spirit, as this day by His flesh. *Et ecce vobiscum,* and lo, I am true Immanuel "with you " by the love of My manhood ; "with you " by the power of My Godhead, still " to the end of the world." (Mat. xxviii. 20.)

One more yet. He won it, and he wears this name ; and in it He wears us. And it is both a comfort to us and a glory that so He wears us. That He is not, cannot be named without us; that when He is named, *et nos una Tecum Domine,* 'we also are named with Him.' In *Immanu* is *anu,* and that is we. This is not it, but this; that He hath set us in the forepart of it; *immanu* before *El, Nobiscum* before *Deus.* This note is not out of place in this place, where precedence is made a great matter of; that *Immanu* is before *El;* that is, we first, and God last.

Good manners would in a name compound of Him and us, that He should have stood before us, and it have been *Elimmanu* at least — *Deus nobiscum,* and *Deus* before *nobiscum;* not Immanuel, *nobiscum* before *Deus.* He before us; He the priority of the place in all reason. Booz he placed them so, (Ruth ii. 4), and so should we I dare say, if it had been of our imposing, *Elimmanu.* It had been great arrogancy otherwise. But He giving it Himself would have it stand thus; us set before Him. There is a meaning in it. And what can it be but this? That in the very name we might read that we are dearer to Him than Himself; that He so preferred us, and that His own name doth *præ se ferre* no less, but give out to all the world the *ecce* of St. John's Gospel, *Ecce quomodo dilexit!* (John xi. 36), the *ecce* of his Epistle, *Ecce quantam charitatem habuit!* (1 John iii. 1), "See, how He loved them!" "Behold, how great love He bare to them!" See it in His very name. We are a part of it; we are the forepart of it, and He the latter; He behind, and we before—before Himself, and that by order from Himself: He would have it Immanuel. O! whether was greater, humility or charity in Him! Hard to say whether, but both unspeakable.

Let us examine this *sine nobis,* a little. How came God from us? Nay, ask not that; but how we came from Him. For we went from Him, not He from us; we forsook Him first. Jonas tells us how; "By following lying vanities, we forsook our own mercy." (Jonah ii. 8.)

If we went from Him first, then should it be in reason *nos cum Deo,* not *nobiscum Deus;* we to Him, not He to us. Did we so? No indeed. We sought not Him, He was fain to seek us. *Nos cum Deo,* that would not be; it must be *nobiscum Deus* first, or *nos cum Deo* will never be. This second then; that we began the separation—that long of us; but He begins the reconciliation.

K

Who hath the hurt if God be without us? We, not He. Who gets by *nobiscum*? What gets God by *nobiscum*? Nothing He. What get we? *Multum per omnem modum.* (Rom. iii. 2.) Why then doth He begin, doth He seek to be with us? No reason but *sic dilexit*, and no reason of that.

But when He sought and offered to be with us, did we regard it? Nor that neither. You see, the Prophet here offers Ahaz a sign, bids him ask it; Ahaz would none. (Isa. vii. 12.) And as he to the sign, so we to the *signatum*, 'the thing signified;' care as little for Him or His being "with us,"ᵃ as Ahaz did for His sign. We can be content He in any sort will cease from us, come not at us so long as the world can be with us or we with it; care not for His being with us, till world and all forsake us. How He was fain even to force it on him!

Cast up these then; that He forsakes not, but being forsaken first. That being forsaken, yet He forsakes not though. That He Which should be sought to, seeks first, (Isa. vii. 14), and seeks us by whom He shall get nothing. Yea, when we neglect Him so seeking, when Ahaz will no sign, tells him He will give him one, whether he ask or ask not; that is, will do us good not only without our seeking, but even in a manner against our wills. And tell me, if there be not as much love in *nobiscum*, as in all the rest.

"With us," how we see. Now, "with us" why, or to what end? To more than I have now time to tell you of. Two only I name. 1. One, that of the place—"to save them from their enemies;" as them, so us. Them from Razin and Romely's son; us from the son of Romely, or Romulus, or whomsoever. If He "with us" on our side, then will He be against them that are against us; and that let us never fear neither our own weakness, nor the enemies' strength. For though we be weak and they be strong, yet Immanuel I am sure That is "with us" is stronger than they.

Our fear most-what groweth, both in sin and in danger, that we look upon ourselves as if it were only *nobis;* as if never a *cum;* or that *cum* were not *El*, "the mighty God." As if with that great EL all the inferior *els* were not attendant, Micha-el, and Gabri-el; and if He will, "twelve legions of Angels." (Matt. xxvi. 53.) Or as if He alone with one word of His mouth, one *Ego sum*, could not blow them all

down, (John xviii. 5), could not make them all as those in
the text, as the tails of a couple of firebrands that have spent
themselves, smoke a little, and there is all. No; if He be
"with us," we need not fear what these two, nay not what
all the fire-brands in hell can do against us.

And sure strange it is, the saints of God what courage and
confidence they have taken, from this very name Immanuel.
Go to, saith Esay in the next chapter, "Take your counsel, it
shall be brought to nought; pronounce a decree, it shall not
stand." (Isa. viii. 10.) Why? For Immanuel, "God is with
us;" nothing but this name. For as it is a name, so it is a
whole proposition, if you will. And after, in the fiftieth
chapter, he seeks for enemies; calls them out, "Who will
contend with me?" (Isa. l. 8.) Where is my adversary? let
him come near;—so little doth he fear them. And these
were ghostly enemies; and this was in the point of justification. This for the Prophet.

Now for the Apostle. Never did champion in more
courageous manner cast his glove than doth he to his ghostly
enemies, to "height," to "depth," to "things present," to
"things to come," to all, that none of them "shall be able to
sever him" (Rom. viii. 39) from this *Cum,* from His love.
And in all confidence of *si Deus nobiscum;* in Whom He
makes full account to conquer; nay, conquer will not serve
—more than conquer he, ὑπερνικῶμεν. (Rom. viii. 37.)

The reason is set down, Proverbs xxx., (v. 1), where he
betakes himself to *Ithiel* first, which is but a slip of Immanuel, *Deus mecum;* and then to *Ithiel* straight joins *Ucal,* "I
shall prevail;" not I, but *El* with me. *Ithiel* goeth never
alone; *Ucal* attends it still. Get *Ithiel*—if *Ithiel* be with
us, *Ucal* will not be away, for *Ithiel* and *Ucal* part not.

Is this all? No; there is another in the very body of
the word itself. "With us"—to make us that to God that
He was this day made to man. And this indeed was the
chief end of His being "with us;" to give us a *posse fieri,*
a capacity, "a power to be made the sons of God," (John i.
12), by being "born again of water and of the Spirit;" for
*Originem quam sumpsit ex utero Virginis posuit in fonte
Baptismatis,* 'the same original that Himself took in the
womb of the Virgin to usward, the same hath He placed for
us in the fountain of Baptism to God-ward.' Well therefore
called the womb of the Church σύστοιχον to the Virgin's

womb, with a power given it of *concipiet et pariet filios* to
God.   So His being conceived and born the Son of man
doth conceive and bring forth (*filiatio, filiationem,*) our being
born, our being the sons of God.   His participation of our
human, our participation of His Divine nature.

And shall He be "with us" thus many ways, and shall
not we be with Him—as many I say not, but some, as many
as we can?   We with Him, as He with us?   Specially,
since upon this issue the Prophet puts King Asa, "The
Lord is with you, if you be with Him," (2 Chron. xv. 2)—
with you to save you, if you with Him to serve Him.   It
holds *reciproce*, in all duties of love, as here was love if ever.
"Immanuel, God with us," requires *Immelanu*, 'us with
God,' again.

He "with us" now I hope, for "where two or three are
gathered together in His Name, there is He with them."
(Matt. xviii. 20.)   But that is in His Godhead.   And we
are with Him ; our prayers, our praises are with Him ; but
that is in our spirits whence they come.

These are well, but these are not all we can ; and none
of these, the proper 'with Him' of the day.   That hath a
special *Cum* of itself, peculiar to it.   Namely, that we be so
with Him, as He this day was "with us ; " that was in flesh,
not in spirit only.   That flesh that was conceived and this
day born, (*Corpus aptasti Mihi*), (Ps. xl. 6, and Heb. x. 5),
that body that was this day fitted to Him.   And if we be
not with Him thus, if this His flesh be not "with us," if we
partake it not, which way soever else we be with Him, we
come short of the *Im* of this day.   *Im* otherwise it may be,
but not that way which is proper to this feast.   "Thy land,
O Immanuel," (Isa. viii. 8), saith the Prophet in the next
chapter ; and may not I say, This Thy feast, O Immanuel?
Sure no being with Him so kindly, so pleasing to Him, so
fitting this feast, as to grow into one with Him ; as upon
the same day, so the very same way He did "with us."

This, as it is most proper, so it is the most straight and
near that can be—the surest being withal that can be.
Nihil tam nobiscum tam nostrum, quam alimentum nostrum,
'nothing so with us, so ours, as that we eat and drink down,'
which goeth, and groweth one with us.   For *alimentum et
alitum* do *coalescere in unum*, 'grow into an union ;' and
that union is inseparable ever after.   This then I commend

to you, even the being with Him in the Sacrament of His Body—that Body that was conceived and born, as for other ends so for this specially, to be "with you;" and this day, as for other intents, so even for this, for the Holy Eucharist. This, as the kindliest for the time, as the surest for the manner of being with.

And this is the farthest; and this is all we can come to here—here upon earth. But this is not all; there is a farther to come still. For we are not together; we are parted, He and we. He in Heaven, and we in earth. But it shall not always so be. Beside this day Immanuel hath another day, and that day will come; and when it doth come, He will come and take us to Himself. That as He hath been our Immanuel upon earth, so He may be our Immanuel in Heaven; He with us, and we with Him, there for ever.

This of the Sacrament is a preparative to that; will conceive and bring forth the other. For immediately after He had given them the Holy Eucharist, He prayed straight that they that had so been with Him in the blessed Sacrament —"Father, My will is," My prayer, My last prayer, "that where I am they may be also." (John xvii. 24.)

And He is in Heaven, in the joy and glory there; and there He would have us. So *nobiscum Deus in terris* brings us to *nos cum Deo in Cœlis*, even thither. Thither may it bring us, and thither may we come and there be—He "with us," and we with Him for ever! "Immanuel" is the end of the verse: the same be our end, that so we may be happy and blessed without end!

SERMON X.

A SERMON PREACHED BEFORE THE KING'S MAJESTY AT
WHITEHALL, ON MONDAY, THE TWENTY-FIFTH OF
DECEMBER, A.D. MDCXV., BEING CHRISTMAS-DAY.

*And thou Bethlehem Ephratah art little to be among the
thousands of Judah; yet out of thee shall He come forth
unto me That shall be the Ruler in Israel; Whose goings
forth have been from the beginning, and from everlasting.*
—MICAH v. 2.

[*Et tu Bethlehem Ephrata, parvulus es in millibus Juda: ex te mihi
egredietur Qui sit Dominator in Israel; et egressus Ejus ab initio a
diebus æternitatis.*]

THE Prophet Esay (Isa. vii. 14) had the honour to be
the first that is vouched, and whose words are enrolled
in the New Testament. The Prophet Micah hath the
honour to be the second. That of Esay, *Ecce virgo, &c.* in
the end of the first chapter, (Matt. i. 23, 26); this of Micah,
Et tu Bethlehem, &c. in the beginning of the second of the
first of all the Evangelists, St. Matthew.

They follow one the other; and they follow well, one on
the other. That of Esay, His birth; this of Micah, the
place of His birth. "Behold a Virgin shall bear," saith
Esay; and Bethlehem shall be the place where she shall do
it, saith Micah. His Name, saith Esay, "shall be God with
us;" with us, saith Micah, "to be our Guide" and conduct
us. He with us in Bethlehem in the beginning of the verse,
that we with Him in eternity in the end of it.

We have first a most sure word and warrant of the Evangelist, that "the testimony of Jesus is the spirit of this prophecy," (Rev. xix. 10); that "this day this Scripture was
fulfilled," when "He was born at Bethlehem." (Matt. ii. 1.)
In St. Matthew's steps we tread when we so apply it, and
so treading always sure we are we tread safely. No ἰδίᾳ
ἐπιλύσει, "private interpretation" (2 Pet. i. 20) of our own
head; but Micah by Matthew, the Prophet by the Evangelist—ever the best.

To say truth, there is no applying it to any but to Christ,
none to give it away to from Him.

1. From David to the Son of David, that is to Him, we read not of any other "born at Bethlehem." No record to be shewed but of them two.

But whatever become of that, this is sure; none had ever "His out-goings from everlasting" but He. None, of whom those words can be verified but of Him only, as Who only is the Son of the ever-living God.

3. These might serve; but it is yet more clear, this. For howsoever about Esay's *Ecce virgo* the Jews and we are not of one mind, yet for this here of Micah the coast is clear— the Jews will not quarrel us, touching it; there is on all sides between them and us good agreement.

For upon the coming of the wise men from the East, (Matt. ii. 4), there was a synod of the High-priests and Scribes called at Jerusalem—the very first that we read of in the New Testament—and called by the king, to resolve the point about the place of Christ's birth. (Matt. ii. 5.) And then and there it was resolved *Conciliariter*, that at Bethlehem; and resolved from this very place, for that these words were a known prophecy of the birth of Christ.

Upon which so famous an occasion, this resolution grew so notorious as it did *manare in vulgus ;* the very people could tell this. They argue in the seventh of John (John vii. 42) against our Saviour by it, that He could not be the Christ; for Christ was to come out of Bethlehem, (that was taken as granted,) and He came out of Galilee, as they in error thought, but that was plain *ignoratio elenchi*. For though He were there brought up, He might be born at Bethlehem; and so He was. But so, Priest and people both knew Bethlehem was Christ's *natale solum*, and that this prophecy was the evidence for it.

4. Though these be enough, yet have we a greater witness than all these from Heaven—even the star. For whether this Scripture doth send us thither, the star doth lead us to Bethlehem straight. Never stood still till it came thither, and there it stood directly over the place, (Matt. ii. 9,) as much to say as, "Lo, there He is born." (Ps. lxxxvii. 4.) And in this will we rest, since Micah and Matthew, Prophet and Apostle, Priest and people, Christians and Jews, Heaven and earth are all with us; all testify this text pertains to Christ's birth, and so to this day properly.

It is of a place; and place and time are held weighty

circumstances, specially in matter of fact or story—*Ubi et Quando*, material questions. The Apostles asked them both; *Ubi Domine?* "Where Lord?" (Luke xvii. 37.) *Quando, et quod erit signum?* "When and what shall be the sign?" (Mark xiii. 4.)

Of the time when, some other time may give occasion, if it so please God. Now, of *Ubi Domine?* the place where. There we are to-day; whereto this is a direct answer, Bethlehem is the place. That first.

But then secondly, this circumstance leads us farther, to matter of substance. The place of the birth to the birth itself, and the birth to the Party born, Who is here set forth as a person. He comes forth once and again; He leads, He feeds; all acts of a person entire.

Thirdly, this Person is here said to have two comings forth. 1. *Egreditur ex te*, one. 2. *Egressus Ejus ab æterno*, the other. In which two are expressly set down His two natures. 1. *Ex te*, from Bethlehem, on earth; thence He came according to His manhood. 2. *A diebus æternitatis*, "from everlasting or from eternity;" thence He came according to His Godhead.

And last, to make it a full and complete Christmas in text, besides His place, Person, and natures in these two comings forth, here is His office also, to be ' Ηγούμενος ὅστις ποιμανεῖ, (so doth St. Matthew turn מושל the Prophet's word; I follow no other, for sure I am I cannot follow a better translator :) *Dux qui pascet.* (Mat. ii. 6.) One to 1. lead us and to 2. feed us, and so to conduct us from Bethlehem where this day we come first acquainted with Him, to the state of eternity whence He came out to bring us in; there to live and reign with Him for ever.

So, I. of the Place; II. Person; III. Natures; and IV. Office of Christ. I. The place of His birth, Bethlehem; with her two epithets or twins as it were, 1. *Parvula*, "little;" and 2. *Ephratah*, "fruitful." II. Then, of His Person That did come forth. III. After, of both His natures; 1. As man from Bethlehem; 2. As God from everlasting. IV. Last of His office. 1. To be our guide, to lead us, saith Micah; 2. *Dux, qui pascet*, (Mat. ii. 6); lead us and feed us, saith Matthew, both. And so leading and feeding us, to conduct and bring us to the joys and joyful days of eternity, whither without Him we can never come , and whither till we come, we shall never be as we would be, that is, truly happy indeed. This is His office. And as His office to lead and to feed us, so our duty to be led and to be fed by Him. That follows of itself.

Et tu Bethlehem. A word of the character or manner of the speech. For this verse hath no dependance at all on that went before. The Prophet breaks off the discourse he was in, and breaks into this of Bethlehem here, all of a sudden. This we call an Apostrophe, and it is one of the figures that be stirrers of attention.

For this we find, that while one goes on still with a tale in a continued tenour of speech, attention grows dull, and no readier way to awake it, as the masters of that art tell us, than suddenly to break off the point we were in hand with, and turn us to quite another matter, which with the strangeness will affect the hearer, and make him listen afresh, whether he will or no.

The Prophet doth so in this. He was but the verse before mustering garrisons and laying siege to Jerusalem, and in the midst of his tale falls from that, and presently is at Bethlehem; tells us of a new matter about a Child to be born there. This must needs move attention. Any Apostrophe will do it more or less.

But of all, none to that which is framed in the second person as this is. For it is not a speech of or concerning Bethlehem in the third person, (as that of Esay, "Behold, a Virgin;" so here, 'Behold, out of Bethlehem shall come:') not *enuntiative*. But it is a speech to Bethlehem in the second person; *et tu*, "and thou Bethlehem, out of thee shall there come"—*annuntiative*, which hath more vigour in it. If Esay had said, 'And thou Virgin shalt conceive,' it had been more effectual than "Behold a Virgin shall conceive;" more a great deal.

But more specially yet, if in the second person we turn our speech *ad inanimata*, to things that can neither hear nor understand. Not, that we hold them capable of that which is spoken; but that if in any degree they were so, it is such as surely would move them. Such is the Prophet's here; turns him to the town-walls of Bethlehem, makes a set speech to them, tells them of all this matter; "And thou Bethlehem," to thee be it spoken, "out of thee shall there come." And this is very forcible, and full of life; for it intends that if the very walls and stones in them could hear or could rejoice, there is good cause they should do both; in that there should come out of them One, for Whom Jerusalem and all the cities of Judah, nay, all the world should be the better. Weigh it well, and you shall find there is more in this *et tu*, than is or can be in any *ecce* of them all. And this for *et tu*, the manner of the speech.

I. For the matter, it is an answer to the question, *ubi natus est*, of the wise men, "Where is He that is born?" Born He was, that they knew; where born, that they knew not. The star told them one, the Prophet the other. *Et claritas claritatem clarificat*, and a clear star is made more clear by a prophecy as clear, or clearer than it. For very clear it is, the prophecy, without all circuity noting, naming, and in a manner pointing to it; "And thou Bethlehem."

And because there were two Bethlehems, one in the tribe of Zebulon, (Jos. xix. 15), another in the tribe of Judah; he saith it was "Bethlehem Ephratah" which is that in the tribe of Judah, as St. Matthew, (Matt. ii. 6), rather giving the sense than standing on the words cites it. There can be no error, Rachel's sepulchre was there by, "Rachel was buried at Ephratah—Ephratah, the same is Bethlehem," (Gen. xxxv. 19, and Gen. xlviii. 7), Moses tells us more than a thousand years before. As plain this as plain may be. No oracle of Delphos;—without any equivocation at all.

We have the place. Now what manner place is it? *Et tu Bethlehem, parvula. Parvula*, this "little" doth a little trouble us. Why, it is a sorry poor village, scarce worth an Apostrophe; specially to turn from Jerusalem to turn to it. And as little likelihood, that so great a State as the Guide of the whole world should come creeping out of such a corner—*Locus, et locatum* ever are equal. That birth is sure too big for this place. The Prophet dissembles it not, saw what flesh and blood would except straight; as ever they carry a conceit against some places and persons. And can any great matter come from them? (John vii. 52, and John i. 46.) What, from Bethlehem? What, out of Galilee? Nay, if so great a State, He would come from another manner place than that. *Et tu Jerusalem*, from Jerusalem, Damascus, Cæsarea; from some stately city, much better beseeming Him. These are *dictata carnis*.

First, He denies not "little" it was; and not ὀλίγος but ὀλίγιστος, not *parva,* but *parvula;* "diminutively little." So little, saith the Prophet, that it was not to be reckoned *una de millibus,* not "one of a thousand," for the meanness of it. And the Evangelist makes it rather worse than better; for the Prophet's word *parvula* he turns ἐλαχίστη, that is *minima,* (Matt. ii. 6), even the "very least of all."

This he confesses; but then joins this issue, that though the *tu* be little the *ex te* may be great. *Ex te parvâ egredietur non Parvus.* As little as it is, no little Person shall come out of it. Though it be not *una de millibus* for the meanness, as saith Micah; notwithstanding, He That is to come out of it may be and is, *electus Unus de millibus,* "One of a thousand" (Cant. v. 10) for His choice, for His excellency. Though it not worthy to be "one of the thousands of Judah," it should send forth One That should rule the thousands of Judah, and the ten thousands of Israel. And not of Israel only after the flesh but a handful in comparison of them He should lead, but "the Israel of God," His faithful chosen people all the world over. Indeed, He had answered the objection before He made it, in Ephratah; that "little" it was but "fruitful," and not a little fruitful.

Which two counterpoints make in shew a conflict or contradiction between the Prophet and the Evangelist. The Prophet saith, "Thou art the least;" the Evangelist citing Him saith the clean contrary, "Thou art not the least." (Matt. ii. 6.) *Bethlehem, minima, et non minima;* "least" and "not least"—how may both be? Well enough, both; so both be not said, regard had to one and the same thing.

"Least" saith Micah, and saith true; for the compass of the territory, "least;" for the small number of the inhabitants, "least;" for the thinness and meanness of the buildings, as was seen at Christ's Birth, not able to give lodging to any number, (Luke ii. 7); so "least." But then again, "not least" saith St. Matthew, and saith truly too. Not, in regard of any of the three now mentioned, but of another, able of itself alone to weigh them all down; in that it should yield *Alumnum tam grandem,* 'so great a birth' as the great Messias of the world. One, Whose only coming forth of it was able to make it not the least, nay the greatest and most famous of all the dwellings of Jacob, of the whole land, nay of the whole world then. And thus, not "the least." Though *minima* for the *tu, non minima* for the *ex te; non minima* if it were but for Him, and for nothing else.

What shall we make of this? Nothing but what cometh from it of itself without straining. That with God it is no new thing, (nay very familiar as even the heathen have observed, so familiar as God seems to take delight in it), to bring *maxima de minimis;* 'great out of little,' Christ out of Bethlehem. Which is plain even in nature. How huge an oak from how small an acorn! But that asks great time. From how little a grain of mustard-seed, the very *Bethlehem minima,* "the least of all seeds," (Matt. xiii. 32), how large a plant! of how fair a spread! and that in a little time, a month or two at most.

But we are not in nature now; in this very point here of guides and rulers, therein too it hath been no unusual thing with Him out of small beginnings to raise mighty states. Their first guide, Moses, whence came he? out of a basket of bulrushes, forlorn and floating among the flags, (Exod. ii. 3), taken up even by chance. The great beginner of their monarchy, and not of theirs alone but the two beginners of the two mighty monarchies of the Persians and Romans, Cyrus and Romulus—from the shepherd's scrip, from the sheepcot, all three; those great *magnalia* from *parva mapalia.* And as the kingdoms of the earth from a sheepcot, so His own of the Church from a fisherboat. We may well turn to them with this Apostrophe: And thou sheepcot, out of thee have come mighty monarchs. And thou fisherboat, out of thee four of the chief and principal Apostles. (Matt. iv. 18, 21.)

" Even so Lord," saith our Saviour, "for so is Thy pleasure." (Matt. xi. 26.) And since it is His pleasure so to deal, it is His farther pleasure, and it is our lesson out of this *Bethlehem minima,* even this, *ne minima minimi,* 'that we set not little by that which is little,' unless we will so set by Bethlehem, and by Christ and all. He will not have little places vilified. " Little Zoar," (Gen. xix. 20), will save the body, " little Bethlehem" the soul. Nor have, saith Zachary, *dies parvos,* "little times," (Zech. iv. 10), despised; unless we will despise this day, the feast of humility. Nor have " one of these little ones " (Matt. xviii. 6) offended. Why? for Ephratah may make amends for *parvula, ex te* for *tu.*

This is on God's behalf. On Christ's yet farther, to stay a little upon this "little." For though there want not divers other good congruencies why Christ should come from Bethlehem, rather than from another place. 1. For that it was the town of David, (John vii. 42), and He was the Son of David; and so a place not unmeet for Him to come from even in that respect, being *sedes avita.* Out of thee came David, and well therefore out of thee shall come David's Son; David's Son and David's Lord, both.

2. The surname of Ephratah puts me in mind of another; " Lo, we heard of it at Ephratah," saith the Psalm, (Ps. cxxxii. 6)—there, the first news of the Temple. And, ' Lo, we heard of Him at Ephratah ' to-day by the Angel, (Luke ii. 11),—there the first word of the Lord of the Temple. The Temple was the type of the Church, and that was heard of at Ephratah first; and no ways incongruent that where the Church, there the Head of the Church; Christ, and Christ's Church both at one place.

3. There is a third in the very name of Bethlehem, that is, "the house of bread." For He that was born there was " Bread." But that will be more proper anon at *Qui pascet.*

But these, though they agree well, yet none of them so well as this, that it was *minima*—the very *miniminess* as I may say of it. For in so being, it was a place well suiting with His estate now at His *egredietur ex te,* which was the state of humility, eminent in His, if ever in any birth. Bethlehem was not so "little," but He as "little" as it. Look, what Apostrophe Micah made to the town may we make to Him, and that with better reason; and Thou Bethlehemite, Thou wert as little among the sons of men, as ever was Bethlehem among the villages of Judah. So, *novissimum oppidorum,* as Micah calls it, suits well with *novissimus virorum,* (Isa. liii. 3), as Esay calls Him.

And it was not the place alone, but all were little then. The time, *in solstitio brumali,* ' the deep of winter,' when the days are at the shortest and least. And the people He came of "little." Amos saith, " Who shall raise up Jacob, for he is small? " (Amos vii. 2, 5.) Small ever; but never

so small, never so low brought, as at His coming forth.
Then at the lowest and the very least, as being then brought
under the bondage of a stranger; and he, one of "the
children of Edom" that cried "Down with them, down to
the ground." (Ps. cxxxvii. 7.)   One that made Rachel
mourn in her grave, (Mat. ii. 18), (her grave was there hard
by) for the slaughter of the poor innocents, within a while
after.   So place and time, and people and all, "little;" and
He Himself less than all.

For even in the place, Micah hath not said all; for He is
less yet.   If "little Bethlehem" offended, what could have
been said if he had gone farther, and yet not farther than
St. Luke?   And thou, the stable in the inn at Bethlehem,
and thou the manger in the stable, (Luke ii. 7), *ex te
egredietur*, "out of thee shall He come."   These are beyond *Bethlehem parva*,—less yet; yet thence did He come
too at His entrance into the world.   And all these, nothing
to His going out; another manner of diminution there
than all these.   Such was His humility on this feast of
humility.

And O thou little Bethlehem, and O thou little Bethlehemite, how do you both, both place and person, con-
found the haughtiness of many that yet would be called
Christians, and even near Christ Himself.   There is in
both of you, if it were well taken to heart, enough to prick
the swelling, and let out the apostumed matter of pride
from a many of us, whose look, gesture, gait, and swelling
words of vanity are too big for Bethlehem—whose whole
carriage and course is, as if they were to be saved by one
who came out of the great city Niniveh or Grand Cayre,
rather than out of the little hamlet of Bethlehem.

But all this was done to bring that virtue in credit.   I
find no reason rendered of it but this; that by what manner
of place He made choice of to be born at, He would teach
us what manner of spirits He doth affect, to take up His
residence and to rest in.   "The High and Excellent," saith
Esay, "That inhabits eternity, He also will rest with the
lowly," (Isa. lvii. 15)—with those that be no higher than
Bethlehem in their own eyes.   "To them He looks,"
(Isa. lxvi. 1, 2); "gives grace to them," (Prov. iii. 34); "to
them He reveals what He keeps from the great ones of
this world." (Mat. xi. 25.)   And when He shall sit in all

His glory He shall say, *Quod minimis his, et Mihi.* Say it forward *affirmative,* and say it backward *negative; Quod non minimis his, nec Mihi;* " What to these *minims* to Me ; " " what not to them, not to Me neither." (Matt. xxv. 40, 45.)

To end this point then. For little Bethlehem's sake to love the virtue that is like it, and for the virtue's sake to honour it. Honour it—there is a star over it, there is a Saviour in it. Honour it for That which comes out of it, for the fruit it yields. More good comes] forth out of that poor town, (*mihi* saith the Prophet, " to me ; " *nobis,* may we say, " to us all,") than from all the great and glorious cities in the world. What good, Nazianzen tells us ; *Bethlehem honora parvam, quæ te inducit in Paradisum,* ' it gives us our introduction to Paradise—Bethlehem ;' it gives us a Guide to-day, if we will follow Him, will bring us thither to our original happiness ; nay, farther than so, to the days of eternity. And Him we must follow, and it we must honour — even this virtue, if ever we mean to come there.

II. This for the place. Now for the Person that cometh from this place. For being in speech of a place, he continues in local terms fit for a place, *egredietur ex te. Egredi* is ' to come forth,' and that is properly from or out of a place. And the rather he doth it, because withal it is a term that fitteth His birth well. So the Scripture saith, " Naked came I forth," (Job i. 21), that is, was I born. " The child that first comes forth," (Gen. xxxviii. 28), that is, the first is born. This word is twice repeated. 1. Once, " out of Bethlehem," *ex te.* 2. Another, " from everlasting," *ab æterno.* These two set out to us His two comings forth, that is, His two Nativities ;—nativity is nothing but a coming forth. Those two, His two natures ; since *nativitas est adnaturam via,* ' Nativity is but the way that leads to nature.' 1. *Egredietur ex te* as the Son of man, as David's Son ; 2. *Egressus Ejus ab æterno* as the Son of God, as David's Lord.

III. *Egredietur ex te. Egredietur* is the tense of the time to come. To come, when Micah wrote this, and in the future ; but come, when St. Matthew cited it, and in the præter—" When Jesus was born at Bethlehem." But future and præter both are in time, so this His birth in time.

But the other hath neither future nor præter, neither mood nor tense: nay, no verb at all. It is expressed by a substantive, to shew His subsistence before all time, from all eternity.

2. *Ex* is a place. Out of it He came, so in it He was. And this birth local, as before temporal. So was not His order. That hath no *ex;* that is *ab, ab æterno.* For as eternal, no place contains Him; He is every where—fills both Heaven and earth.

3. *Te;* that place is Bethlehem, a place upon earth. According to which it is said, "There shall come a root out of Jesse," (Esay's term, chap. xi. ver. 1), and out of it "a branch," (Jeremy's, chap. xxiii. ver. 5), thence *germen*, "a flower," or "blossom," (Zachary's, chap. vi. ver. 12), and from it this fruit of Ephratah, the fruit of the virgin's womb. (Luke i. 42.) "Root," "branch," "blossom," and "fruit" —all of the earth, earthly. But there came forth at the same time a star too, to shew He had another more high and heavenly being.

For this of Bethlehem was not His first flight as we say; the other, though it stand behind in the verse, was before that by far. *Ex utero ante luciferum: ante luciferum,* "before the star of His birth—nay, before any morning star came forth," (Ps. cx. 3), He was come forth. *A principio* saith Micah, and it is St. John's. *In principio,* the two first words of his Gospel, long before Moses' *In principio,* the two first words of Genesis. But, to leave no place to doubt of his meaning, he glosseth his *a principio* with *ab æterno,* that is "from everlasting." By which very words, "from eternity," Arius' error of *erat quando non erat* falls to the ground. For *nunquam erat quando non erat æternitas,* 'never was there, call it what you will, when eternity was not.' For as "everlasting" forwards is to *quando tempus non erit amplius,* "there shall be no more time," so "everlasting" backward is to *quando tempus non erat adhuc,* 'when there was yet no time at all.'

Now, let it not trouble you, that this His eternal is the plural number—"outgoings"—as if they were more than one. It is but the Hebrew phrase. They use to express the superlative ever by the substantive of the plural number; to call that man אשרי blessings, whom they mean to be most blessed. So that "outgoings" which is but one, but so high, after such a manner, so past our reach as Esay asks, *Generationem Ejus quis enarrabit,* "Who shall declare His generation?" (Isa. liii. 8), no one, no singular will reach it; and so it is expressed plurally.

So use they also to note out continuance. And so, it sets out to us, the continual emanation or proceeding of Him from His Father ὡς ἀπαύγασμα, the Apostle's word, as a "beam of brightness" (Heb. i. 3) streaming from Him incessantly. Never past—"His generation"—but, as the schoolmen call it, *actus commensuratus æternitati.* For *hodie genui Te* (Ps. ii. 7) is true of every day; yet, because it hath coexistence with many revolutions of time, though it be indeed in itself but one drawn out along, yet according to the many ages it lasteth, it seemeth to multiply itself into many; and so is expressed plurally.

Though, the principal sense always saved, we may refer this plural to both His "outgoings;" both as Son of God before all times, and as Son of man "in the fulness of time." For this latter, though executed in time, had his outgoing (that is the decree for it went forth) *ab æterno.* Even that "out of Bethlehem" He should come; be "the Son of man," "the Saviour of mankind," and their "Guide" to eternity. Even that way also in a sense it may be said, as man He came forth *a principio, a diebus æternitatis; a principio* for the efficacy, *ab æterno* for the decree. From the beginning there went virtue forth of Him, which wrought even then when He was but forthcoming as we say, and not yet come forth. His life, His death, *ab origine mundi.* (Rev. xiii. 8.) So, for the efficacy, *a principio.* As for the decree, that was gone forth from before the foundations of the world, (Eph. i. 4), from all eternity.

IV. So now have we this Party, twice come forth, compound of Bethlehem and eternity. And now we have Him, what shall we do to Him? But first, what shall He do to us? With God, *Officium fundatur in beneficio;* 'He first doth for us, before He require aught of us.' This He shall do for us; He shall be to us,— מושל is the word of the text, St. Matthew turns it Ἡγούμενος. 1. Which in the first and native sense is a guide for the way, *Dux viæ* to lead us: 2. In a second, is a Captain, *Dux militiæ,* to guard us. 3. And to these two by way of paraphrase St. Matthews adds, Ὅστις ποιμανεῖ, *Qui pascet,* "a Guide That shall feed us."

L

1. To lead us in the way. 2. To guard us in the way. 3. To feed us in the way. In these three, His office. From a place, He came to be our Guide to a place. Still he holds on with his local terms he began with. For a guide serves properly to bring one to a place. There is in that word both the office He to perform to us, and the benefit we to receive by Him guiding. And it implieth also our duty to Him again. For if He to lead, we to be led by Him; "He is become the Author of eternal salvation," saith the Apostle, "to them as will obey Him and be guided by Him," (Heb. v. 9), and to none other.

Will ye see, first, the necessity of both those "His comings forth" for this office to be our Guide? *Egredietur ex te*, first. He was to be of us, being to guide us; for being of us, He would the better understand our wants, and have the more compassion on them. (Heb. iv. 15.) Therefore if a Prophet, "A Prophet shall the Lord raise up unto you, from among your brethren," (Deut. xviii. 18);—Moses' *egredietur ex te*. If a Prince, "your noble Ruler shall be of yourselves, even from the midst of you;"—Jeremy. (xxx. 21.) So he, *egredietur ex te*. If a Priest, then "to be taken from men, and be ordained for men, in things pertaining unto God," (Heb. v. 1); the Apostle's *egredietur ex te*. To be every one of these; and these three be the three great guides of mankind.

And again; as meet He should come forth "from eternity," if thither He to bring us. None can bring to a place so well as He that hath been there. There He had been, had "inhabited eternity" saith Esay. (lvii. 15.) Thence He came, and coming thence best knows the way thither again. So neither of His "outgoings" more than needs.

Now to our "Guide." Where the terms of way and of walking and leading meet us so thick, are so frequent all along the Scripture, as plain it is our very life is held as a journey; and we, as the schoolmen term us, *viatores*, 'in state of way-faring men or travellers' all, from our coming into the world to the going out of it again, still going on in the way or out of the way, the one or the other. If so, in a journey two things we have to look to; 1. our *quo*, and 2. our *qua*. 1. *quo*, our end 'whither;' 2. *qua*, our way 'by which.' St. Thomas said well, "Lord, we know not whither

Thou goest ; and how then can we know the way ? " (John
xiv. 5.)   Right ; for *ignoranti quem portum petat nullus
secundus est ventus,* 'no wind is good for him that knows not
for what port he is bound.' He that knows not whither he
goes, wanders, and is never in his way ; is never in it, for he
hath none to be in.

First then, *quo,* ' whither ? '   Now the end of the verse is
our journey's end, " eternity."   Where if we may arrive,
happy we ; that is agreed on presently.   So is not the way
thither.

But yet, this I take is agreed ; that if it be a ready way, we
care the less for a guide ; but if hard to it, then *dux nobis
opus,* ' we need one.'

And sure, the way is not ready to hit ; not so easy a
fool may find it.   It is a foolish imagination so to ween
of it.

By-ways there be divers, many cross paths and turnings
in and out ; and we like enough to miss it, if we venture on
it without a guide.   If there be not one to call to us ever
and anon, as Esay (xxx. 21.) *Hæc est via, ambulate in eâ,*
" This the right way, keep it ; "---if not, you go you know
not whither.

The first point then is to find our own want, to think we
are in case to need a guide.   For if we need none, this text
is superfluous ; "and thou Bethlehem," and Thou Christ,
ye may both well be spared.   If we be able to go the way
without a guide, to be guides to ourselves, nay to be guides
to our guides, then :—the world is come to that now.

Well, he was a wise man and a great counseller that said
when time was, " How can I without a guide ? " (Acts viii.
31) ; and the wise men at this feast were not so well persuaded of their own skill, but they sought and took directions. (Matt. ii. 2.)   Let us follow them.

To get us one then.   And not any one, but one that is
skilful in the way : no one thing need we so to be advised of
as this.   For strange it is, but true it is ; even they that be
blind themselves will take upon them to be guides to others.
You know who said, *Si cæcus cæcum.* (Matt. xv. 14.)   That
si was no vain *si,* no idle supposition ; *usque hodie,* it is done
daily.   But the end there is *in foveam,* a place we would not
come to ; and God keep us from it !

One then that is skilful.   And where shall we have any

so skilful as This, This of ours? He cannot but be so. It
is sure, there were no better guide than the way itself, if the
way could speak to us, and tell us when we were right or
wrong in it. Now He, "He is the Way," (John xiv. 6);
the Way and the End both. As God, He is the End;—the
fruition of the Godhead, the end of our journey. As man,
He is the Way; both Way and Guide too. His doctrine,
our guide; His example, in the whole tract of His life, the
very way thither.

Nothing remaineth but that we now set forward in this
way. For as we daily sing in the *Benedictus*, He came, not
to whet our wits or to file our tongues, but to "guide our
feet into the way." (Luke i. 79.) And into what way? Not
of questions and controversies whereof there is no end, about
which we languish all our life long, but "into the way of
peace," even of those duties about which there is no dis-
agreement. Look but to this feast, it is St. Augustine's
note, *didicerunt Magi, et abierunt; docuerunt Scribæ et re-
manserunt*, 'The wise men they learnt the way and they
went; the Scribes they taught the way, but they tarried still
behind.' O do as did the wise men, *dimittunt Scribas
inaniter lectitare, ipsi pergunt fideliter adorare*, 'Let the
Scribes sit still, and scan and read lectures of the way; on
went the wise men on their way, and performed their worship, the end of their journey'—and so let us. This for
dux viæ.

And this would serve for the way, if there were nothing
but the way, if that were all. But if there be enemies
beset the way to stop our passage, then will not *dux*, "a
guide," serve our turn; we must have *dux*, "a captain"
then, (the second sense of the word ἡγούμενος,) one to guard
us and to make way for us. For we are not only to be led
surely without error, but safely without danger also. Such
a guide we behove to have, as will see us safe at the place
we would be at. And Bethlehem breeds such. Out of little
Bethlehem came he that fetched down great Golias. (1 Sam.
xvii. 49.) And again, out of it this day He That "shall
tread down Satan under our feet." (Rom. xvi. 20.) *Dux
Messias*, Captain Messias, as the Angel in Dan. ix. 25, calls
Him.

And for *Qui pascet*, we may not miss that neither. For
say we be guarded from enemies; yet shall we go our

journey but evil, if we faint by the way for hunger or thirst, and have not to relieve us. He is not a good guide that in that case cannot lead us where we may be purveyed of necessary food for our relief. It is all one to perish out of the way by error, and to perish in the way by want of needful refreshing. St. Matthew therefore, to make Him a complete Guide by way of supply, adds *Qui pascet;* such an One as shall lead *more pastoritio,* ' as a shepherd doth his flock ;' not lead them the way only, but lead them also to "good green pasture, besides the waters of comfort," (Ps. xxiii. 2) ; see they want nothing. *Dux Qui pascet,* or *Pastor Qui ducet:* ` choose you whether, for He is both.

Of all the three, the name of the place He was born in seems to favour this most ; to be ominous toward *Qui pascet. Beth* is a house, *lehem* bread, and *Ephratah* is plenty ; " bread," " plenty." And there was in Bethlehem a well of such water as King David, we read, longed for it, (1 Chron. xi. 17)—the best in all the country. Bethlehem then sure a fit place for *Qui pascet* to be born in, and *Qui pascet* as fit a Person to be born in Bethlehem. He is not meet to be ruler, saith Esay, that saith *in domo mea non est panis.* (Isa. iii. 7.) He can never say that Bethlehem is his house, and that is *domus panis,* and *in domo panis semper est panis.* Never take Him without bread, His house is the house of bread, inasmuch as He Himself is Bread ; that in the house or out of it—wheresoever He is, there is Bethlehem. There can no bread want.

These three abilities then are in Christ our Leader. 1. Skill to be a Guide ; 2. valour to be a Captain ; 3. and for *Qui pascet,* Bethlehem, the house of bread, is His house. Of which, 1. skill serves for direction ; 2. strength for defence ; 3. food for refreshing.

1. *Luce sacerdotalis scientiæ,* ' by the light of His priestly knowledge ;'—so He guides us, " For the priest's lips are to preserve knowledge." (Mal. ii. 7.)

2. And *brachio regalis potentiæ,* ' by the arm of His royal power ;'—so He guards us, for power pertains to the prince principally.

3. And for *Qui pascet,* He is Melchizedek, King and Priest ; ready to bring forth as he did bread and wine. (Gen. xiv. 18.) But in another manner far than he did. The bread and wine Melchizedek brought forth were not

his body and blood; Christ's are. Both *Qui pascet* and *Quo pascet.* As before *Dux et Via,* "the Guide and the Way;" so now here *Pastor et Pabulum,* "the Feeder and the Food," both.

You may see all this represented in the shadows of the Old Testament. There is a book there called Exodus, of Israel's *egredietur* out of Egypt. Therein they had Moses for their guide; and he led them to the borders of the Holy Land, and there he left them; to shew "the law brought nothing to perfection." (Heb. vii. 19.) Then comes Joshua, whom the Epistle to the Hebrews calls Jesus, (Heb. iv. 8), the figure of ours here, and by his conduct they were led and put in possession of the land of promise.

All this but in type of another Testament "after to be made," saith Jeremy, (Jer. xxxi. 31); and "upon better promises," saith the Apostle, (Heb. viii. 6); namely, our spiritual leading through this vale of vanity to the true land of promise, "the Heavenly Jerusalem that is from above," (Gal. iv. 26); whither This our Jesus undertakes to bring all those that will be guided by Him.

Observe but the correspondence between the type and the truth. Moses, when he came to lead the people, found them how? "scattered over all the land of Egypt, to seek stubble for brick," (Exod. v. 12), to build him a city that sought the ruin of them all. Our case right the very pattern of it; when our Guide finds us wandering in vanity, picking up straws, things that shall not profit us; "seeking death in the error of our life," (Wis. i. 12), till we be so happy as to light into His guiding.

Secondly, Moses was to them not alone *dux viæ,* 'a guide for the way;' but when enemies came forth against them, *dux militiæ,* 'a captain for the war.' Christ was so too, and far beyond Moses. For He made us way with the laying down of His life. (Isa. liii. 12.) So did neither Moses nor Joshua. Would die for it, but He would open us a passage to the place He undertook to bring us to. Was *Dux,* a Guide, in His Life; *Dux,* a Captain, in His death.

Thirdly, Moses when they fainted by the way obtained in their hunger manna "from Heaven," (John vi. 32), and in their thirst "water out of the rock for them." Christ is Himself the "true Manna;" Christ, the spiritual Rock.

(1 Cor. x. 4.) Whom He leads He feeds ; carries Bethlehem about Him.

Plain, by the ordaining of His last Sacrament, as the means to re-establish " our hearts with grace," (Heb. xiii. 9), and to repair the decays of our spiritual strength ; even " His own flesh, the Bread of life," (John vi. 33, 48), and " His own blood " " the Cup of salvation." (Ps. cxvi. 13.) Bread made of Himself, the true *Granum frumenti,* " Wheat corn." (John xii. 24.) Wine made of Himself, " the true Vine." (John xv. 1.) Went under the sickle, flail, millstone, and oven, even to be made this Bread ; " trod, or was trodden, in the wine-press alone," (Isa. lxiii. 3), to prepare this Cup for us.

And in this respect it may well be said, Bethlehem was never Bethlehem right, had never the name truly till this day this birth, this Bread was born and brought forth there. Before it was the house of bread, but of the bread that perisheth ; but then of the " Bread that endureth to ever-lasting life." (John vi. 27.) That it might seem *inter alia,* to have been one of the ends of His being born there to make it *Bethlehem veri nominis,* ' Bethlehem truly so called.'

And this is His office. Now all the doubt will be how He can perform this office to us, go before us and be our Guide, seeing He is now in Heaven at His journey's end, and we in earth by the way still. No matter for that. He hath left us first the way traced by the steps of His blessed life, which we keeping us to, sure we are we cannot go amiss. And then, as before He came in the flesh " He led them by the hand of Moses and Aaron," (Ps. lxxvii. 20) —guides chosen and sent by Him—so doth He us now by the hands of those whom the Apostle three several times in one chapter calleth by this very name, 'Ηγουμένους, our " guides," (Heb. xiii. 7, 17, 24), by whom He leads us if He lead us at all. And other leading we are not to look for any ; only to pray they may lead us right, and then all is well.

And they cannot but lead us right, so long as they but teach us to " follow the Lamb whither He goeth." (Rev. xiv. 4.) For their office is but to lay forth before us the way traced by the steps that He went. Those steps, when all is done, are ever our best directions. And I mean to do but so now. As here, not to go a step out of the text, there

are four or five of these steps, as many as we shall well
carry away at once.   And these they be.

The main point is ; it is a place, and so to be gone to.
We take this from the Shepherds directed thither by the
Angel, to resolve of *transeamus usque Bethlehem,* "that we
get us to Bethlehem." (Luke ii. 15.)   There is the rendez-
vous to-day, there He will be first seen and saluted, there
He began with us, there we to begin with Him ; where He
set forth, there our setting forth to be also.   Indeed, there
is no finding Him but there, this feast.   There the shepherds
found Him this day the first ; there the wise men on twelfth-
day, the last.   But thither they came both ; both the shepherds directed by the Angel (Luke ii. 12), and the wise men
guided by the star. (Mat. ii. 9.)   The shepherds—in them,
the Jews ; the wise men—in them the Gentiles.   The shepherds—in them unlettered persons.   The wise men—in
them the profoundest clerks.   The shepherds—in them
mean men.   The wise men — in them great states.   Be
what we will be, at Bethlehem to begin, all.   Thither to go
to Him, thence to set out after Him.   *Transeamus usque
Bethlehem.*

How shall we do that ?   What, shall we go in pilgrimage
to the place ?   We learn a shorter course of the Apostle,
"The righteousness of faith," saith he, "speaketh on this
wise ; say not thou in thy heart, Who shall go over the sea
for me ? that were to bring Christ again into earth.   But
what saith it ?   The word is near thee, in thy mouth, and
in thy heart." (Rom. x. 6, 8.)   And this it is.   Bethlehem
hath here two twins—an epithet, a virtue or two.   Get but
them, get your souls possessed of them, it will save you a
journey.   You shall never stir hence, but be at Bethlehem
standing where you do.

Parvula is the first ; you know, Bethlehem is "little."
And look, what little and low is in quantity, that is little
in our own eyes and lowly in quality.   Get that first,
humility, it is the Bethlehem of virtues where He in great
humility was found this day.   If we begin not there, we
lose our way at the first setting out.   For this is sure ;
where eternity is the *terminus ad quem,* there humility is
the *terminus a quo.*   Humility is the first comma of the
sentence, where eternity is the period, as in this verse it is.
And even here now at the first is Christ like to lose

a great part of His train. The Pharisees are gone, all too big for Bethlehem they; and with them all that are τι μέγα, "some great matter," (Acts viii. 9), in their own sight. Touching whom we may use the Apostrophe; "And thou Bethlehem" are too "little" for these great conceits. None of them will come out of thee, or come at thee by their will—every one of them is a cunning guide himself; and no guide they, but *sequuntur spiritum suum*, "their own bold spirit," (Ezek. xiii. 3), bid Bethlehem farewell; at it they come not. Well, *parvula* is the first.

The next station is to the next virtue, and that is Ephratah, "fruitfulness;"—so it signifies: little it is, but fruitful. Fruitful, first, that it brought forth Him; for He hath brought forth, seen come of Himself saith Esay, *longævum semen*, "a lasting seed," (Isa. liii. 10); the fruit whereof to this day "shaketh like Libanus, and as the green grass covereth all the earth." (Ps. lxxii. 16.) I mean the Christians that were, are, or ever shall be. How great an Ephratah of how little a beginning! It is not only little, but Ephratah too; and by that know it. For indeed, good heed would be taken that we go not to the wrong Bethlehem; not to Bethlehem Zebulon, that is Bethlehem on the sands, (so lay Zebulon by the sea,) "Bethlehem the barren;" but to "Bethlehem Judah," "Bethlehem Ephratah," that is "Bethlehem the Fruitful." That is, to humility to add fruitfulness, I mean plenteousness in all good works. Else it is not Ephratah, not right. Not right repentance unless it be Ephratah, "bring forth fruits of repentance," (Luke iii. 8); nor faith, without "the work of faith;" nor love, "without the labour of love," (1 Thes. i. 3); nor any other virtue without her Ephratah. Ephratah is not the surname of humility only, but even of the rest too—repentance Ephratah, and faith Ephratah; *et sic de cæteris*, if they be true. Else be they but *vites frondosæ*, "leaves and nothing else," (Hos. x. 1); *simulachra virtutum*, and not virtues indeed; of Zebulon, not of Judah; and so, not the right.

Fruitful then, and of what fruit? That is in the very name itself of Bethlehem. Not the fruit of the lips, a few good words, but "the precious fruit of the earth," (James v. 7), as St. James calleth it—*lehem*, "good bread;" that fruit. Such fruit as St. Paul carried to the poor saints at

Jerusalem, (Rom. xv. 28), "alms and offerings." That is the right fruit; *cum signavero fructum hunc,* "it hath the seal on it" for right. Such as the Philippians sent him for supply of his want, whereby he knew they were alive again at the root; in that they thus fructified, yielded this fruit of a "sweet odour and wherewith God was highly pleased," (Phil. iv. 10, 18), as there He tells them.

It was not sure without mystery, that the Temple was first heard of at Ephratah, (Ps. cxxxii. 6), at this "fruitful" place. No more was it, that which the Fathers observe of the trees, that were used about it. Not a post of the Temple, not a spar, nay not as much as a pin, but was made of the wood of a fruit-bearing tree; no barren wood at all in it. No more was it, that the Altar of the Temple was founded on a threshing-floor (2 Sam. xxiv. 25) (Araunah's) where good corn was threshed. All to shew, it would be plenteous in feeding and clothing, and such other pertaining to this of Ephratah. Which, however, they be with us, will be the first and principal point of inquiry at the day of doom; even about feeding and clothing, and other works of mercy. (Matt. xxv. 35, 36, 42, 43.)

Now if we could bring these two together, make a conjunction of them in *Gemini,* it were worth all. For I know not how but if there be in us ought of Ephratah, if we happen to be any thing fruitful but in any degree, away goes *parvula* straight. Straight we cease to be little; we begin to talk of merit and worth, and I wot not what. Indeed, if we be all barren and bare, it may be then and scarce then neither, but peradventure then we grow not high-minded. But so we fall still upon one extreme or other. If fertile, then proud; if humble, then barren. We cannot get to be humble yet not fruitless, or to be fruitful yet keep our humility still. Not Ephratah and *parvula* together. But that is the true Bethlehem, and "there was He born." (Ps. lxxxvii. 4.) And thus far I hope we have been led right, and are in our way.

But leading is not all. Here is *Qui pascet* too, and we may not pass it. For to that He leads us also, *Dux Qui pascet.* We followed a false guide at first that led us to the forbidden fruit, the end whereof was *morte moriemini.* This now will lead us to a food of the nature of the Tree of Life, (Gen. iii. 6), even the Bread of life, (John vi. 48), by eating whereof we shall have life in ourselves, even life immortal. That is His food He leads us to. And if we would forget this, both the Person and the place—the Person, *Qui pascet,* " That shall feed ; " and the place, Bethlehem, "the house of bread," would serve to put us in remembrance of it. Even of the breaking of bread, which the Church as this day ever hath, and still useth as the Childhouse feast.

We speak of the *transeamus usque Bethlehem,* "going thither." That may we even locally do and never go out of this room, inasmuch as here is to be had the "true Bread of life that came down from Heaven." (John vi. 51.) Which is "His flesh" this day born, which "He gave for the life of the world," (John vi. 32, 41, 31), called by Him so, the true Bread, the Bread of Heaven, the Bread of life — and where that Bread is, there is Bethlehem ever. Even *stricte loquendo,* it may be said and said truly, the Church in this sense is very Bethlehem no less than the town itself. For that the town itself never had the name rightly all the while there was but bread made there, bread (*panis hominum*) 'the bread of men.' Not till this Bread was born there, which is *Panis Angelorum,* as the Psalm calleth it, "and man did eat Angels' Food." (Ps. lxxviii. 25.) Then, and never till then, was it Bethlehem ; and that is in the Church, as truly as ever in it. And accordingly the Church takes order we shall never fail of it. There shall ever be this day a Bethlehem to go to—a house wherein there is bread, and this bread. And there shall be Bethlehem, and so near us, and shall we not go to it ? Or, shall we go to it, to the House of Bread, this Bread, and come away without it ? Shall we forsake our Guide leading us to a place so much for our benefit ?

Ubi Domine, was the Apostle's question ; and his answer *Ubi corpus, ibi aquilæ,* "where the body is, there the eagles will be." (Luke xvii. 37.) Let it appear we are so, for here is the "body."

Else do we our duty to Him but by halves. For as our duty to *Dux* is to be led, so our duty to *Qui pascet* is to be fed by Him. To end. And thus *ducendo pascit,* and *pascendo ducit,* 'Leading He feeds us, and feeding He leads us' till He bring us whither? Even to *a principio,* back again to where we were at the beginning ; and at the beginning we were in Paradise. That our beginning shall be our end. Thither He will bring us—nay, to a better estate than so ; to that whereunto, even from Paradise, we should have been translated, to the state of eternity, to the joys and joyful days there ; even to glory, joy, and bliss eternal. To which He bring us, even our blessed Guide, That this day was in Bethlehem born to that end, "Jesus Christ the righteous !" (1 John ii. 1.)

—— o ——

SERMON XI.

A Sermon preached before the King's Majesty at Whitehall, on Wednesday, the Twenty-fifth of December, A.D. MDCXVI., being Christmas-day.

Mercy and Truth shall meet ; Righteousness and Peace shall kiss one another.
Truth shall bud out of the earth ; and Righteousness shall look down from Heaven. Psa. lxxxv. 10, 11.

[*Misericordia et Veritas obviaverunt sibi ; Justitia et Pax osculatæ sunt. Veritas de terra orta est ; et Justitia de Cælo prospexit.*]

I HAVE here read you two verses out of this Psalm, which is one of the Psalms selected of old by the primitive Church, and so still retained by ours as part of our office or service of this day, as being proper and pertinent to the matter of the feast, and so to the feast itself. For the meeting here specified was to be at the birth of the Messias : so saith Rabbi Moses, and other of the Jews. Was at the birth of our Saviour : so say the Fathers with uniform consent, and *eo nomine* have made this a Christmas-day Psalm.

As his manner is, the Psalmist in it under one compriseth the type and the truth both ; by those things which befell the people of the Jews, the Church typical, shadowing out those things which were to befall the Antitype of it, Christ and His Church. For, *primâ et propriâ intentione,* it cannot be denied but the Psalm was first set according to the letter upon the turning back of the captivity of Babel. But the Prophet knew well that was not their worst captivity, nor should be their best delivery. There was another yet behind concerned them more, if they understood their own state aright, which was reserved to the Messias to free them from. To that he points. Even that the Apostle complains of wherein " the soul is led away captive under sin and Satan," (Rom. vii. 23), the very true Babel indeed as which bringeth with it everlasting confusion, from which Christ, the true Zerubbabel, is to set us free—us and them both.

There is a meeting here. A meeting at a birth. A birth that did them in Heaven, Righteousness by name, good to behold. The meeting in *obviaverunt,* the birth in *orta est,* the pleasure to behold it in *prospexit de Cœlo. Prospexit* is to see with delight, as when we look into some pleasant prospect.

A meeting qualified, for the manner. For they do not meet and pass by, but meet and salute as friends with an *osculatæ sunt,* a sign of love begun or renewed.

This meeting is of four. Four which of themselves, *proprie loquendo,* are nothing but attributes or properties of the Divine nature, but are here by the Psalmist brought in and represented to us as so many personages. Personages, I say, inasmuch as they have here personal acts ascribed to them. For to meet, to kiss, to look down, are all of them acts personal. And look, how the Psalmist presents them so we treat of them, in the same terms the text doth.

At a birth, at *orta est,* these four meet here ; at *orta est Veritas,* " the birth of Truth" *de terra,* " from the earth." For two *ortus* there were ; and this, not His *antesæcularis ortus de Cœlo,* ' His birth before all worlds from Heaven,' but His *ortus de terra,* ' His temporal birth from the earth.'

Lastly, the birth of this birth as I may say, the effect it wrought. Of which more there are in the neighbouring verses. Here in these, besides the meeting occasioned by it, there is but one ; that such a spectacle it was as it drew Righteousness itself from Heaven to look at it. Time was when Righteousness would not have done so much ; not have vouchsafed a look hitherward ; therefore *respexit nos Justitia* is good news. That then and ever since she has beheld the earth and the dwellers in it with a far more favourable regard than before. And all for this birth's sake.

And when was all this ? When He that saith of Himself " I am the Truth," (John xiv. 6)—when He was born upon earth; for *orta est Veritas,* and *natus est Christus* will fall out to be one birth. What day soever that was, this meeting was upon it. And that was this day, of all the days of the year. The meeting and the day of this meeting here all one, and the birth of Christ the cause of both. So being this day's work, this day to be dealt with most properly.

Onward we have here four honours of this day, every one of the four giving it a blessing. 1. It is the day of *ortus Veritatis,* 'Truth's birth;' 2. and the same, the day of *occursus Misericordiæ,* 'the meeting here mentioned;' 3. and of *osculum Pacis,* 'the kiss here expressed;' 4. and of *prospectus Justitiæ,* 'Righteousness' gracious respect of us.' These from each of them in several. And generally, the day of reconciling them all.

Holding us to these, we are to speak of the 1. Meeting, the 2. Parties, the 3. Birth, and the 4. Effect here specified to come of it. [I.] Of this meeting in Christ; then, [II.] in Christianity, not to broken off by us but to be renewed, and specially this day.

I. Here is a meeting, and that is no great matter if it be no more. How many meet we as we pass to and fro daily, and how little do we regard it? But that meeting is casual.

Somewhat more there is in set meetings. It was not by hap, not *obviaverunt* simply but *obviaverunt sibi. Sibi* sheweth they had an intent; they came forth on both sides, not to meet any fifth person, but to meet one another.

But not every set meeting is memorable; this is. I find a Psalm here made in remembrance of it. And lightly songs be not made, but *de raro contingentibus;* not of ordinary, but of some special great meetings.

The greatness of a meeting groweth three ways. 1. By the parties who; 2. the occasion whereon; and 3. the end whereto they meet. All three are in this. The parties in the first verse, the occasion and end in the second. The occasion a birth, an occasion oft of making great persons meet; and the end that comes of it, that Righteousness, who is to be our Judge and to give the last sentence upon us, beholds us with an aspect that promises favour.

The occasion and the end we shall touch anon. Now of the parties. If the parties great, the meeting great. The conjunction of the great lights in Heaven, the interview of great States on earth, ever bodes some great matter. Who are the parties here? Four as high, as excellent attributes, as there be any in the Godhead. Or, to keep the style of the text, four as great States as any in the Court of Heaven.

These meet, and in what manner? Great states meet otherwhile in a pitched field. Not so here. This is an *obviaverunt* with an *osculatæ sunt:* they run not one at another as enemies; they run one to another, and kiss as loving friends. And that which makes it memorable indeed is, that these parties in this manner thus meet, who if all were well known were more like to turn tail than to meet. One to run from another; nay, one to run at another to encounter, rather than run one to another to embrace and kiss. Not meet at all; at least not meet thus, standing in such terms as they did.

Mercy and Peace if they two had met, or Truth and Righteousness, they two, it had not been strange. But for those that seem to be in opposition to do it, that is it—that makes this meeting marvellous in our eyes.

Will ye stay a little and take a view of the Parties? Four they are. These four, 1. Mercy, and 2. Truth, 3. Righteousness, and 4. Peace. Which quaternion at the first sight divides itself into two and two. Mercy and Peace, they two pair well; they be *collectaneæ*, as Bernard saith of them in one place, 'bed-fellows,' sleep together; *collactaneæ*, as in another place, 'sucked one milk, one breast' both. And as these two, so the other two, Truth and Righteousness, seem to be of one complexion and disposition, and commonly take part together. Of these Mercy seems to favour us; and Peace no enemy to us nor to any (seeing we must speak of them as of persons) mild and gentle persons both. For Righteousness I know not well what to say: *gestat gladium*, and I fear *non frustra*. (Rom. xiii. 4.) Nor of Truth, who is *vera* and *severa*, 'severe' too otherwhile. These I doubt are not like affected. The reason of my doubt. One of them, Righteousness, it is told here for great news, that she but "looked down hitherwards from Heaven." Before then she would not have done that. A great sign it is of heart-burning, when one will not do so much as look at another—not endure his sight. We cannot promise ourselves much of her. No, nor of Truth. One was so bold in a place to say, *omnis homo mendax*, (Rom. iii. 4), and feared no challenge for it. By that it seems all stands not well with her neither. So then two for us, two against us.

For their order. Mercy is first, and Peace last. With both ends we shall do well enough. God send us to do but so with the midst! Yet this is not amiss that they which favour us less are in the midst; hemmed in on both sides, closed about with those that wish us well; and they between us and them. On the one side, Mercy before; on the other, Peace behind.

Another; that in this double meeting Mercy sorts not herself, goes not to Righteousness; nor Righteousness to her but to Peace. A kind of cross meeting, as it were, there is—the better hope of accord. Mercy and Righteousness have no symbolizing quality at all, no hope of them; but Truth with Mercy hath. There is Truth as well in the promise of Mercy as in the threat of Justice.

And it stands yet better between the other two, Righteousness and Peace. Melchizedek, which is by interpretation "King of Righteousness," the same is "King of Salem, that is, of peace." (Heb. vii. 2.) He That "is after the order of Melchizedek," (Heb. vi. 20), King of both, like enough to set accord between them two—both of them His lieges. This for the view of the Parties.

These meet here; but what is *obviaverunt* without *osculatæ sunt?* Better let them stand in sunder still, and never meet. There seems to be two meetings implied. One *obviaverunt* without, and another with *osculatæ sunt.*

Before they met here, they were parted the one from the other. For they that meet come from divers coasts. Before this meeting they have been in divers quarters, one from the other, and not come together thus a good while.

Their distance in place grew from their distance in affection, estranged one from the other. That they meet not I will not say; but that they meet not thus, ever before. Else, what remarkable thing were there in this meeting, or worth the composing of a Psalm, if it had been familiar with them thus to meet every other, nay any other day.

How came they then asunder that it should be a marvel to see them meet? Since naturally they are not strangers, all four in the bosom of God from all eternity—attributes all four of His undivided Essence. So, not divided of themselves ; not of themselves then. That they were divided, it was about us ; the quarrel ours, that made them part company. Thus I gather it : if at Christ's birth they met, at Adam's fall they parted ; if when Truth was born on earth they came together, when Truth perished from the earth they fell in sunder. That was when the first lie was told, and believed—and that was *nequaquam moriemini,* (Gen. iii. 4)—by Adam, and thereby God much wronged. So that Adam's cause it was, and so ours that first divided Heaven, yea the very attributes in God we see, and so in a sort God Himself. So they parted first. It could not be said by the Apostle that Christ "pacified all things in Heaven and in earth," (Col. i. 20), if there had not in Heaven been somewhat to be taken up.

For all this yet, I deny not but they might and did meet once before. But it was an *obviaverunt* without an *osculatæ sunt ;* never both these till now. Out of Christ and before His birth, they met in opposition ; in Christ and at His birth, did these four lights come to meet and to be in conjunction now. They met before, *obviaverunt ;* but instead of *osculatæ* it was *altercatæ sunt.* While Mercy and Peace would have Adam's and our case relieved, Righteousness and Truth would by no means endure it. The plea is drawn up and reported at large by Bernard in his first Sermon upon the Annunciation. Mercy began, for out of her readiness to do good she is here, she is ever foremost. Her inclination is, or rather she herself is an inclination, to pity such as are in misery, and if she can to relieve them, yea though they deserve it not. For, which is the comfort of the miserable sinner, she looks not to the party, what he is or what he hath done or deserved, but what he suffers, in how woeful and wretched a case he is. And her plea is, *numquid in vanum ?* "What hath God made all men for nought ?" (Ps. lxxxix. 47.) "What profit is in their blood ?" (Ps. xxx. 9.) It will make God's enemies rejoice. (Ps. lxxiv. 18.) Thither it will come, if God cast them clean off. What then, "will He cast them off for ever, will He be no more entreated ? Hath God forgotten to be gracious ?" (Ps. lxxvii. 7, 8.) With these and such like *pii susurri,* as he calls them, did she enter into God's bowels, and make them

M

yearn and melt into compassion. And certainly, if there were none to stand against us, there were hope Mercy had prevailed.

But Truth must be heard too, and she lays in just matter of exception ; pleads, *Deus erat Verbum*, (John i. 1) ; what is God but His Word ? and his word was—as to Adam, *morte morieris*, (Gen. ii. 17), so to his sons, *anima quæ peccaverit*, "the soul that sinneth that soul shall die." (Ezek. xviii. 20.) God may not falsify His word ; His word is the truth. Falsify the truth ? That may not be.

And then steps up Righteousness and seconds her. That God as He is "true in His word," so is He "righteous in all His works." (Psa. cxlv. 17.) So, to *reddere suum cuique*, "to render each his own," to every one that is his due ; and so to the sinner, *stipendium peccati*, "the wages of sin," that is "death." (Rom. vi. 23.) God forbid, the Judge of the world should judge unjustly ! That were, as before to make truth false, so here to do right wrong.

Nay, it went farther, and they made it their own cases. What shall become of me ? said Righteousness. What use of justice if God will do no justice, if He spare sinners ? And what use of me, saith Mercy, if He spare them not ? Hard hold there was, inasmuch as *perii nisi homo moriatur*, said Righteousness, ' I die, if he die not.' And *perii nisi misericordiam consequatur*, said Mercy, ' if he die I die too.' To this it came ; and in those terms brake up the meeting, and away they went one from the other. Truth went into exile, as a stranger upon earth :—*Terras Astræa reliquit*, she confined herself in Heaven, where so aliened she was as she would not so much as look down hither upon us.

Mercy, she stayed below still. *Ubi enim Misericordia esset*, saith Hugo well, *si cum misero non esset ?* ' Where should Mercy be, if with Misery she should not be ? '

As for Peace, she went between both, to see if she could make them meet again in better terms. For without such a meeting, no good to be done for us.

For meet they must, and that in other terms, or it will go wrong with us ; our salvation lies a bleeding all this while. The plea hangs, and we stand as the prisoner at the bar, and know not what shall become of us. For though two be for us, there are two against us, as strong and more stiff than they. So that much depends upon this second meeting, upon the composing or taking up this difference. For these must be at peace between themselves, before they be at peace with us, or we with God. And this is sure; we shall never meet in Heaven, if they meet no more.

And many means were made for this meeting many times, but it would not be. Where stayed it? It was not long of Mercy, she would be easily entreated to give a new meeting —no question of her. Oft did she look up to Heaven, but Righteousness would not look down. Not look? not that? small hope she would be got to meet that would not look that way-ward.

Indeed, all the question is of her. It is Truth and she that hold off, but especially she. Upon the birth you see here is no mention of any in particular but of her, as much to say as the rest might be dealt with; she only it was that stood out. And yet she must be got to meet, or else no meeting.

All the hope is, that she doth not refuse simply never to meet more, but stands upon satisfaction; else Righteousness should not be righteous. Being satisfied, then she will; remaining unsatisfied, so she will not meet.

All stands then on her satisfying; how to devise to give her satisfaction to her mind that so she may be content once more not to meet and argue as ere-while, but to meet and kiss; meet in a joint concurrence to save us, and set us free.

And indeed, *hoc opus*, 'there lies all;' how to set a song of these four parts in good harmony, how to make these meet at a love-day, how to satisfy Justice upon whom all the stay is.

And this, say I, no religion in the world doth or can do but the Christian. No choir sing this Psalm but ours, none make justice meet but it. Consequently, none quiet the conscience soundly but it; consequently, no religion but it. With all religions else at odds they be, and so as they are fain to leave them so; for means in the world have they none how to make them meet. Not able for their lives to tender Justice a satisfaction, that will make her come in. The words next before are, "that glory may dwell in our land." (Psa. lxxxv. 9.) This glory doth dwell in our land indeed. And great cause have we all highly to bless God

That hath made "our lot to fall in so fair a ground." (Psa. xvi. 6.) That we were not born to inherit a lie ; that we were born to keep this feast of this meeting. For bid any of them all but show you the way how to satisfy Justice soundly, and to make her come to this meeting ; how God's word may be true, and His work just, and the sinner find mercy and be saved for all that—they cannot. The Christian only can do it, and none else. All beside for lack of this pass by the wounded man, and let him lie still and bleed to death. (Luke x. 31, 32.)

Bid the Turk. All he can say is, Mahomet's prayer shall be upon you. Mahomet's prayer, what is that ? Say he were that he was not—a just man, a true prophet ; what can his prayers do but move Mercy ? But God's justice, how is that answered ? Who shall satisfy that ? Not prayers ;— Justice is not moved with them, hears them not, goes on to sentence for all them. He can go no further ; he cannot make Justice meet.

Bid the Heathen. He says better yet than the Turk. They saw "that without shedding of blood" there was no satisfying Justice, and so "no remission of sin." (Heb. ix. 22.) To satisfy her, sacrifices they had of beasts. But "it is impossible," as the Apostle well notes, "that the blood of bulls or goats should satisfy for our sins." (Heb. x. 4.) A man sin, and a beast die ! Justice will none of that. What then, will ye go as far as some did, "the fruit of my body for the sin of my soul"? (Mic. vi. 7.) Nor that neither. For if it were the first-born, the first-born was born in sin ; and sin for sin can never satisfy. This meeting will not be there.

Bid the Jew. He can but tell you of his lamb neither. And while time was, that was not amiss ; while it stood in reference to St. John Baptist's Lamb, "the Lamb of God," (John i. 29), this day yeaned, as having the operation, the working, in the virtue of That. That being now past, there is no more in the Jews' than in the Gentiles' sacrifice. Beasts both ; both short of satisfying. So for all that these can do or say, no meeting will there be had.

Only the Christian religion that shows the true way. There is One there thus speaketh to Justice ; "Sacrifice and sin-offerings Thou wouldst not have ; then said I, Lo, I come." (Psa. xl. 6.) He, "of Whom it was written in the volume of the book that He should do that feat," *corpus autem aptasti Mihi,* "make Him a body to do it in," and He will do it. Give Him an *ortus est,* let Him be but born, He will make them meet straight;—Justice and all. For all the world sees, if order could be taken that He, that the Son of God, the Word and Truth eternal would say, "Lo, I come;" would take our nature upon Him, and in it "lay down His soul an offering for sin;" there were good hope of contenting Justice, and that the meeting would go forward. *Deus sanguine in suo,* "God with His blood;"— what sin in the world would not that serve for? What justice in Heaven or earth would not that satisfy? If ye speak of an expiation, a ransom, an ἀντάλλαγμα—Christ's own word—a perfect "commutation," (Matt. xvi. 26), there it is. This had, Justice will meet, embrace, kiss Mercy, shake hands, join now friends; *Inveni enim in quo repropitier,* "I have found that now, wherewith I hold myself fully content and pleased." (Job xxxiii. 24.) This way ye shall make them meet, or else let it alone for ever.

Ver. 11. "Truth shall bud out of the earth; and Righteousness shall look down from Heaven."

And this is it the Christian religion sets before us; how the Son of the Most High God of Heaven and earth took on Him our nature, that in our nature, for our nature, He might make to God (even *stando in terminis justitiæ suæ,* as the schoolmen speak, 'standing on the terms of His most exact strict justice,') a complete, full, every way sufficient satisfaction. And this, lo, makes the meeting. This honour hath the Christian religion above all other; this glory doth dwell in our land; that these four by Christ's birth in it are brought not only to *obviaverunt sibi,* but even to *et osculatæ sunt.*

And if this be the glory, be not they the shame of Christian profession that cherish in their bosoms, and entertain with stipends such as are come to this phrenzy I will call it, to say, what needs any satisfaction? What care we whether Justice meet or no? that is in effect what needs Christ? Cannot God forgive offences to Him made, of His free goodness, of His mere mercy, without putting His Son to all this pain? Fond men! if He would quit His justice or waive His truth, He could; but His justice and truth are to Him as essential, as intrinsically essential, as

His mercy; of equal regard, every way as dear to Him. Justice otherwise remains unsatisfied; and satisfied it must be either on Him or on us. For with beasts or prayers it will not be, and it will hold off till it be. If Justice be not so met with, it will meet with them; and they had better "meet a she-bear robbed of her whelps," (Prov. xvii. 12), than meet Justice out of Christ's presence.

To us they meet this day at the Child-house. For these great lights could not thus meet but they must portend some great matter, as it might be some great birth toward. The astrologers make us believe, that in the horoscope of Christ's Nativity there was a great trigon of I wot not what stars met together. Whether a trigon or no, this tetragon I am sure there was, these were all then in conjunction, all in the ascendant, all above the horizon at once at *orta est* "the birth of" *veritas* "the truth" *de terrâ* "from the earth," the occasion of drawing these four together.

Veritas will fit Christ well Who of Himself said, *Ego sum Veritas*, "I am the Truth." (John xiv. 6.) So is He—not that of the former verse which is but *veritas secunda*, the truth spoken or uttered forth; He the *Veritas prima*, "the first Truth" within. That depends upon this. Then are the words uttered true, when there is an adequation between them and the mind. So 'the first Truth' He is.

The first and last both. For now by His coming He is the adequation of the Word and the Work, the Promise and the Performance. That way He is truth too, the truth of all types, the truth of all prophecies; for " in Him are all the promises yea and Amen," (2 Cor. i. 20)—yea, in the first truth; Amen, in the last. The actual verifying is the truth when all is done, and that He is by His birth.

And as the truth fits His nature, so doth earth man. Of whom God, "earth thou art," (Gen. iii. 19); to whom the Prophet thrice over, "Earth, hear the Word of the Lord," (Jer. xxii. 29); by whom the wise man, *Quid superbis?* "Why should earth be proud?" (Ecclus. x. 9.) *Germinet terra Salvatorem*, "Let this earth bring forth a Saviour," (Isa. xlv. 8)—be the *terra promissionis*, the blessed Virgin, who was in this the land of promise. So was this very place applied by Irenæus in his time, who touched the Apostles' times; so by Lactantius; so by St. Hierom and St. Augustine. Those four meet in this sense, so do the four in the text. *Quid est veritas de terrâ orta? est Christus de fæminâ natus. Quid est Veritas? Filius Dei. Quid terra? Caro nostra.* 'What the truth? Christ. What the earth? our flesh.' In those words they find this feast all.

For *orta est*, it is double; therefore *de terrâ* is well added. Another *ortus* he had *de Cælo;* to wit, His heavenly Divine nature which as "the day sprung from on high," and He in regard of it called *oriens* by Zachary in the New Testament. (Luke i. 78.) But this here is *de terrâ;* for the word properly signifies " the shooting forth of a sprig out of the ground," and He in regard of this *ortus* called "the Branch" (Zech. iii. 8) by Zachary in the Old.

2. And there is more in *orta.* For, it is Rabbi Moses' note, that is properly when it springeth forth of itself, as the field flowers do, without any seed cast in by the hand of man ; so, saith he, should the Messias come, take His nature not only in, but *de,* 'of' the earth. Not bring it with Him from Heaven, the error of the brain-sick Anabaptist, but take it of the earth; be "the woman's seed," "made of a woman," (Gal. iv. 4), "out of the loins of David;" *Virga de radice Jesse,* "the root of Jesse," (Isa. xi. 1)—nothing more plain.

3. And yet more from *orta est.* For that the truth, while it is yet unaccomplished but in promise only, it is but as the seed under ground, hid and covered with earth, as if no such thing were : as soon as ever it is actually accomplished as this day, then does it spring forth as it were, is to be seen above ground ; then *orta est de terrâ,* in very deed.

Of the effect. Now births are and have been divers times the ending of great dissensions, as was this here. For by this birth took end the two great houses ; an union of them by it.

First, by this Truth is gained; Truth will meet now. That truth will come to this Truth, *tanquam minus dignum ad magis dignum,* ' as the abstract to the archetype.' And Truth being now born of our nature, it will never, we may be sure, be against our nature ; being come of the earth, it will be true to his own country ; being made man, will be for man now all he can.

By this means one of the opposites is drawn away from the other ; got to be on our side. It is three to one now. Righteousness is left all alone ; and there is good hope she will not stand out long. For, lo, here is good news; first, that *respexit de Cælo,* "she yet looks down from Heaven now."

So as this birth in earth you see works in Heaven, and by name upon Righteousness there. For though there were none in Heaven but it wrought upon them, yet the Psalm mentions none but Righteousness. For of all, she the least likely; and if she be wrought on, the rest there is no doubt of. How can there? they are all won to us already.

With Righteousness it works two ways; first, "down she looks." Whether it was that she missed Truth, to see what was become of her, and not finding her in Heaven cast her eye to the earth. But there, when she beheld *Verbum caro factum,* "the Word flesh," (John i. 14), the truth freshly sprung there where it had been a strange plant long time before, *aspexit* and *respexit,* she looked and looked again at it. For a sight it was to move, to draw the eye; yea a sight for Heaven to be a spectator of, for the Angels to come down and look at, for Righteousness itself to do so too. Παρακύψαι is the Angel's word in St. Peter, (1 Peter i. 12); διακύψαι is the Septuagint's word here. Both mean one thing. The Greek word is to "look," as we say, "wishly" at it, as if we would look διά, even "through it." The Hebrew word,—that is as if "Righteousness did beat out a window," so desirous was she to behold this sight.

And no marvel; for what could Righteousness desire to see and satisfy herself with, that in Him was not to be seen? A clean birth, a holy life, an innocent death; a Spirit and a mouth without guile, a Soul and a body without sin. In Him she beheld them all. Them, and whatsoever else might yield her full satisfaction. "Lay Judgment to the rule and Righteousness in the balance," nothing oblique will be found in Him, nothing but straight for the rule; nothing *minus habens,* but full weight for the balance.

Thus when "Truth from the earth," then "Righteousness from Heaven." Then, but not before. Before Righteousness had no prospect, no window open this way. She turned away her face, shut her eyes, clapped to the casement, would not abide so much as to look hither—at us, a sort of forlorn sinners; not vouchsafe us once the cast of her eye. The case is now altered. Upon this sight she is not only content in some sort to condescend to do it, but she breaks a window through to do it. And then, and ever since this *orta est,* she looks upon the earth with a good aspect ; and a good aspect in these celestial lights is never without some good influence withal.

But then within a verse after, not only "down she looks," but "down she comes." (Ps. lxxxv. 13.) Such a power attractive is there in this birth. And coming, she doth two things. 1. Meets first; for upon the view of this birth they all ran first and "kissed the Son." 2. And that done, Truth ran to Mercy and embraced her ; and Righteousness to Peace, and "kissed" her. They that had so long been parted, and stood out in difference, now meet and are made friends ; howsoever before removed, *in ortu Veritatis obvia-verunt sibi ;* howsoever before estranged, now *osculatæ sunt.*

And at that birth of His well met they all, in Whom they meet all : the Truth He is, and *per viscera Misericordiæ* He came, "through the tender mercies of our God," (Luke i. 78) ; and He is made to us Righteousness, (1 Cor. i. 30), and He is our Peace. (Eph. ii. 14.) All meet in Him, for indeed all He is ; that no marvel they all four meet where He is That is all four.

And at this meeting Righteousness she was not so off-ward before but she is now as forward, as forward as any of the rest. Mark these three.

1. Lets not Peace prevent her, as Mercy did Truth ; but as Mercy to Truth first, so she first to Peace—as forward as Mercy every way.

2. Nay more forward than Mercy, for Mercy doth but meet Truth, and there is all ; but she as more affectionate not only "meets Peace," but "kisses her." And indeed Righteousness was to do more, even to kiss, that it might be a pledge of forgetting all former unkindness, that we may be sure she is perfectly reconciled now.

3. And one more yet, to shew her the most forward of them all, out of the last verse. At this meeting she follows not, draws not behind, she will not go with them ; she is before, leaves them to come after and bear the train ; she, as David, is before the Ark, puts St. John Baptist from his office for the time ; Righteousness is his forerunner, "Righteousness shall go before," (Ps. lxxxv. 13), tread the way before Him, the foremost now of all the company. By all which ye may know what a look it was she looked with from Heaven.

Thus ye see Christ by His coming "hath pacified the things in Heaven." (Col. i. 20.) A peace of Hosannah is *pax in Cœlis.* There cannot be *pax in terris* till there it be first. But no sooner there it is, but it is peace in earth straight, which accordingly was this day proclaimed by the Angels. (Luke ii. 14.) So by the virtue of this birth, Heaven is at Peace with itself; and Heaven with earth is now at peace. So is earth too with itself, and a fulfilling of the text by this meeting is there too.

The Jews, they represent Truth; to them it belongeth properly. (Rom. ix. 4.) For Truth was where were *eloquia Dei,* "the oracles of God;" and they were with the Jews. The Gentiles they claim by Mercy, that is their virtue. Where was Mercy but where was Misery? and where was Misery but with them that "lay in darkness in the shadow of death"? (Luke i. 79.) And that was the Gentiles' case before this *orta est.* But when "the partition wall was broken down" and the two met in one, then also in a sense Mercy and Truth met together. So these two.

And so the other two likewise. For Righteousness she was where the Law was—for that the rule of Righteousness where the Covenant of the Old Testament was, "Do this and live," the very voice of Justice. But Peace was where Christ was, in the Gospel. *Ipse est Pax nostra,* for "He is our Peace;" Peace and Peace-maker both, *Qui fecit utrumque unum,* That hath made the Law and the Gospel, the Old Testament and the New, to be bound together now both in one volume.

II. Thus we have done with Christ. I would now apply this meeting to ourselves another while. For I ask, did this hold, did these meet only in Christ? Do they not in Christianity likewise? Yes, there too. With Christ came Christianity; look, what in His birth now, in the new birth of every one that shall be the better by it, even the same meeting of the very same virtues all.

Mercy and Truth first to meet. Truth of confession; confession of our sins; which if with fig-leaves we seek to cover and confess not, "there is no truth in us." (1 John i. 8.) And some truth there is to be, at least this truth, or no meeting with Mercy. But when this truth cometh forth, Mercy meeteth it straight. Will ye see the meeting? *Peccavi,* said David—there is Truth. *Transtulit Dominus pec-*

catum, saith Nathan, (2 Sam. xii. 13)—there is Mercy; Mercy and Truth met together. *Homo in terris per Veritatem stimulatus peccâsse se confitebatur, et Deus in Cœlis per Misericordiam flexus confitentis miserebatur.* 'Truth pricked man to confess his sins; and Mercy moved God to pity him confessing,' and sends Mercy to meet Truth.

Will ye go on to the other verse? It holds there too, this. For where a true confession is by man made, *Veritas de terrâ orta est,* "Truth is budded out of the earth." And so it must ere "Righteousness will give us a good look from Heaven." But will, as soon as it is: for when this truth springs freely from the earth to our own condemnation, immediately upon it, Righteousness shews herself from Heaven to our justification. Will ye see this too? "Lord be merciful to me a sinner," (Luke xviii. 13)—there is truth from the earth. *Descendit domum suam justificatus,*—there is Righteousness from Heaven.

But will ye mark, here are two truths, and in either verse one. This latter is the truth of *veritas orta est,* of Christ's religion. And in this treaty it was an article of *Imprimis,* Mercy not to meet any but them that profess the truth of Christ's birth from the earth. Both these were born together; by and by upon the birth of Christ the truth, the other birth also of Christian truth, did flourish and spread itself all over the earth. The whole world before given over, and even grown over with idolatry, quite covered with the mist of error and ignorance, began then to entertain the Christian profession, and by it to "worship God in spirit and truth"—the true religion which is never true, if it have not this meeting. And this meeting it cannot have, if it have not the means of it, *ortus Veritatis de terrâ.*

The same say we likewise for the "Righteousness which looked down" and shewed herself. It was not that of the Law which never came past the top of Mount Sinai, but a new Righteousness cast in a new mould; a Heavenly one which never saw the earth nor the earth it before, before this birth—which is the righteousness of Christ revealed in His Gospel; when that truth sprang, this righteousness looked down upon it.

Now as this of Mercy and Truth enter us; so Truth—not Truth alone, but Truth with Truth's pair—with Righteousness, carry us forward to God. Truth is not enough; not

the truth of religion never so known, never so professed;
not without Righteousness. Truth is but the light to guide
us, Righteousness is the way to bring us thither. A light
is to see by; a way is to go in; so is Righteousness. It
follows straight, *ponet gressus in viâ,* "Righteousness shall
set us in the way" (Ps. lxxxv. 13) of His steps. Steps, that
is the course of life. For *scienti,* by knowledge of the
truth and not *facienti* by the practice of righteousness,
peccatum est illi, saith St. James, (Jas. iv. 17); and *plagæ
multæ,* saith St. James' Master. (Luke xii. 47.) Sin in that
man that serves these two is less pardonable, and more
punishable than in any other.

And then, turn Righteousness to Peace, and they will
not meet barely but more than meet, "kiss" in sign there
is between them more than ordinary affection. *Fac Justitiam et habebis Pacem;* St. Augustine stands much on this.
"Eschew evil and do good," (Ps. xxxiv. 14), saith he—
there is Righteousness. And then " seek Peace," and ye
shall not be long in seeking it; she will come forth herself
to meet Righteousness and kiss her. And this he assures
us as a certain sign to know on the one side true Righteousness, for that tends to Peace not to questions and
brabbles whereof there never will be end; so on the other
side true Peace that kisses Righteousness comes not together like Samson's foxes by the tails, (Jud. xv. 4), by in-
direct means, but clearly and fairly; such means as all the
world will confess to be right and good.

Now mark the order how they stand. Mercy leads to
Truth, and the knowledge of it; and Truth to Righteousness, and the practice of it; and Righteousness to Peace,
and the ways of it—"guides our feet" first "into the way
of Peace." (Luke i. 79.) And such a way shall there
always be, do all the controversy-writers what they can, a
fair way agreed upon of all sides, questioned by none, in
which whoso orders his steps aright " may see the salvation
of our God." Even the way here chalked out before us;
to shew Mercy, and speak Truth; do Righteousness, and
follow Peace. And by this rule proceeding in the points
whereto we are come already, even those truths wherein we
are otherwise minded would in due time be revealed unto
us.

This is Zachary's peace; and this of his well followed in

the end will bring us Simeon's peace, *nunc dimittis in pace,*
(Luke ii. 29) ; to be dismissed, "to depart hence in peace."
And *pax in novissimo,* "peace at the latter end," is worth
all. Peace in the end is a blessed end, and the beginning
of a peace which never shall have end. Mercy our beginning, and Peace our end. This for the meeting ; as in
Christ, so in Christianity or the course of a Christian man's
life.

Now a word for the continuance of this meeting. For I
ask again, met they to part ? By no means ; but as they
be together now, so to continue still. We had much ado
to get them together thus. Now we have them so, let us
keep them so in any wise. For as this meeting made
Christianity first ; so there is nothing mars it but the breaking it off again ; no greater bane to it than the parting of
these.

Let me tell you this : St. Augustine is very earnest upon
this point of the keeping of Righteousness and Peace upon
this Psalm and this verse, and of Truth and Mercy together
in the next, upon *Misericors* and *Verax* against them that
would lay hold on Mercy and let go Truth. O, saith he,
that will not be ; they met together, they will not part now ;
either without either will not be had. And so of the two
others. There be that would have Peace, and pass by
Righteousness. *Tu forte unam habere vis, et alteram non
vis,* saith ye, ' you would gladly have one—Peace ; and for
Righteousness you could be contented to spare it. Ask
any, would you have Peace ? With all my heart, he will
answer. There is no having one without the other ;
osculantur hæ, amant hæ, why they kiss, they love together.'
Si amicam Pacis non amaveris, non amabit te Pax, ' if ye
love not her friend, that is Righteousness, she will none of
your love.' Take that from St. Augustine.

Set this down then ; Christianity is a meeting. One cannot meet. Two there must be, and they may. But it is
not a meeting of two, but of two with two ; so, no less than
four. As Christ Himself was not one nature, so neither
doth Christianity consist in any one virtue ; not under four.
There is a *quaternion* in Christ ; His 1. Essence and His
2. Person, Οὐσία and *Hypostasis, in Divinis.* His 3. Flesh
and His 4. reasonable Soul, *in humanis.* Answerable to
these four are these here, these four to His four.

And as it is a meeting, so a cross meeting of four virtues that seem to be in a kind of opposition, as hath been noted. No matter for that. They will make the better refraction; the cool of one allay the heat, the moist of one temper the drought of the other. The soft virtues need to be quickened, the more forward to be kept from *altum sapere.* So are the elements of which our body, so are the four winds of which our breath doth consist which gives us life. And these in the text have an analogy or correspondence with the elements, observed by the ancients. 1. Truth as the " earth, which is not moved at any time." (Ps. xciii. 1.) 2. *Quasi fluvius pax,* saith Esay, "peace as a water-stream," (Isa. lxvi. 12), "the quills whereof make glad the City of our God." (Ps. xlvi. 4.) 3. Mercy we breathe and live by, no less than we do by air; and 4. Righteousness, she *ventura est judicare sæculum per ignem* (Isa. lxvi 16), in that element.

You may happen to find one of these in Scripture stood much upon, and of the other three nothing said there, but all left out. Conceive of it as a figure, Synecdoche they call it. As ye have here man called earth; yet is he not earth alone, but all the other three elements as well. No more is Christianity any one but by Synecdoche, but in very deed a meeting of them all four.

It deceived the Gnostic, this place; " This is eternal life, to know Thee." (John xvii. 3.) Knowledge, saith he, is it, as if it were all; and so he bade care for nothing else but to know, and knowing live as they list. The Encratite, he was as far gone the other way; he lived straightly, and his tenet was, *Non est curandum quid quisque credat, id curandum modo quod quisque faciat,* ' So that ye hold a straight course of life, it skills not what ye hold in point of faith.' No meeting with these, single virtues all.

Yes, it skills. For both these were wrong, both go for heretics. Christianity is a meeting, and to this meeting there go *pia dogmata* as well as *bona opera*—Righteousness as well as Truth. Err not this error then, to single any out as it were in disgrace of the rest; say not, one will serve the turn,—what should we do with the rest of the four? Take not a figure, and make of it a plain speech; seek not to be saved by Synecdoche. Each of these is a quarter of Christianity, you shall never while you live make it serve for the whole.

The truth is,—sever them, and farewell all. Take any one from the rest, and it is as much as the whole is worth. For, as Bernard well observed, *non sunt virtutes si separentur,* 'upon their separation they cease to be virtues.' For how loose a thing is mercy, if it be quite devoid of justice! We call it foolish pity. And how harsh a thing justice, if it be utterly without all temper of mercy! *Summa injuria* then, that is 'injustice at the highest.' Mercy, take Truth away, what hold is there of it? Who will trust it? Truth, take Mercy from it, it is severity rather than verity. Then Righteousness without Peace, certainly wrong is much better — better than perpetual brabbling. And Peace without Righteousness, better a sword far. This, if you sunder them. But temper these together, and how blessed a mixture! Set a song of all four, and how heavenly a melody!

Entertain them then all four: 1. hope in Mercy; 2. faith in Truth; 3. fear of Righteousness; 4. love of Peace; *O quam præclara concordia!* O how loving a knot! how by all means to be maintained! how great pity to part it!

A little of the time now, when this meeting would be. No time amiss, no day in the year but upon entreaty they will be got to meet. Yet if any one day have a prerogative more than another, of all the days in the year on this day most kindly; the day we hold holy to the memory of this meeting; the day of *orta est,* the occasion of it. In remembrance of the first meeting then, they are apt and willing to meet upon it again; forward ever to meet the day they first met of themselves. But Christ this day born, this day to meet of course. One special end that He was born was that at His birth this meeting might be. If to-day then they should not meet, that were in a sort to evacuate Christ's birth, if there should be a *Veritas orta* without an *obviaverunt sibi;* so that if we procure it not, we had as good keep no feast at all.

What is then the proper work of this day, but still to renew this meeting on it? For Christ's birth we cannot entertain, but all these we must too, necessary attendants upon it every one. They be the virtues of His Nativity, these. At His birth Christ bethought himself of all the virtues which He would have to attend on Him then; and these He made choice of then, and for ever, to be the virtues of this feast.

The sooner and the better to procure this meeting, the Church meets us, as Melchizedek did Abraham, "with bread and wine," but of a higher nature than his far; prepares ever this day a love-feast, whereat they may the rather meet. Where Truth from the earth may look up to Heaven and confess, and Righteousness from Heaven may look down to earth and pardon; where we may shew Mercy in giving where need is; and offer Peace in forgiving where cause is; that so there may be an *obviaverunt,* a "meeting" of all hands.

And even so then let there be. So may our end be as the end of the first verse, in peace; and as the end of the second, in Heaven! So may all the blessings that came to mankind by this meeting, or by the birth of Christ the cause of it, meet in us and remain upon us, till as we now meet together at the birth, so we may then meet in a "perfect man in the measure of the fulness of the age of Christ," (Eph. iv. 13); as meet now at the Lamb's yeaning, so meet then at the Lamb's marriage; "be caught up in the clouds then to meet Him," (1 Thes. iv. 17), and there to reign for ever with Him in His Kingdom of Glory!

SERMON XII.

A Sermon Preached before the King's Majesty, at
Whitehall, on Friday, the Twenty-fifth of
December, a.d. mdcxviii., being Christmas-day.

*And this shall be a sign unto you ; ye shall find the Child
swaddled, and laid in a cratch.*

*And straightway there was with the Angel a multitude of
Heavenly soldiers, praising God, and saying,*

*Glory be to God on high, and peace upon earth, and towards
men good-will.* Luke ii. 12-14.

*Et hoc erit vobis signum: invenietis Infantem pannis involutum, et
positum in præsepio.*

*Et subito facta est cum Angelo multitudo militiæ Cœlestis laudantium
Deum, et dicentium:*

*Gloria in altissimis Deo, et in terra pax hominibus bonæ volun-
tatis.* Latin Vulg.

OF these three verses the points be two ; 1. the Shepherd's
sign, and 2. the Angel's song. The sign is a remain
of *Angelus ad pastores,* 'the Angel's speech to the shepherds.'
We called it, as the Angel himself called it, a sermon;
evangelizo, the word he useth is to "preach."

Of which sermon there are two parts; 1. His birth the
verse before, 2. His finding in this. For this is a double
feast; not only the feast of His Nativity, but the feast of
His Invention also. Therefore the Angel makes not an end
with "unto you is born," but tells them farther; it is not
enough Christ is born, but to take benefit by His birth we
are to find Him. *Natus est* His part, *Invenietis* ours.

Of *natus est* somewhat hath formerly been said. *Invenietis*
now follows and follows well. For what is *natus est* without
invenietis? Such a one there "is born." What shall we be
the better, if we "find" Him not? As good not born, as
not known—to us all one. *Nobis nascitur, cum a nobis
noscitur.* Born He may be before ; but *nobis natus,* 'to us
He is born when to us He is known,' when we find Him ;
and not before. *Christus inventus* is more than *Christus
natus.* Set down *invenietis* then first.

Invenietis leads us to *Hoc erit signum.* For how shall

N

they find Him without a sign? So come we from *Christus natus* to *Christus signatus*. *Natus* "born," to be found; *Signatus*, 'signed or marked,' that He may be found. Born He is, that they know: and when, they know;—*hodie*. And where, they know—in Bethlehem. To Bethlehem they will; but when they come there, how then? In such resort, the town so full of strangers, as "no room in the inns," whither should they turn them? What could they wish, but *O quod erit signum! Natus est;* O that He were *signatus!* O that we had a sign to find Him by!

I. Their wish is honest and good, and pity any that seeks Christ should want a sign to find Him by. The Angel will not suffer that, but before he end his speech he takes order for their sign, and this it is. When ye come to Bethlehem, never search in any house or chamber; in a stable, there shall you find a "Babe swaddled and laid in a manger;" you would little think it, but that is He. And so *signo dato*, 'this sign given,' the sermon ends. For to find Christ is all, all in all.

A sermon would have an anthem of course; it hath so. And one suitable, if it might be. An Angel preached it, and no man; it would be a choir of Angels, and not of men, to sing it. So it is; *Gloria in excelsis*, all the Fathers call it *hymnum Angelicum*, 'the Angels' hymn or anthem.'

II. This is set down in the two latter verses. The 1. choir that sing it, in the former; the 2. song itself, the ditty of it so, in the latter. 1. The choir: in it five. 1. Who? That there were certain Heavenly personages first. 2. In what habit? that in the habit of soldiers to see to. 3. What number? that a great multitude of them. 4. What they did? that they took up this hymn and fell on praising God. 5. And fifthly, when? that they did it instantly upon the speech ended.

2. The song: that consists of three strains. There are in it 1. God, 2. earth, and 3. men; these three first. And then three to these three; 1. glory, 2. peace, 3. good-will. Each sorted to other; 1. glory to God; 2. peace to the earth; 3. to men a good-will.

So have you the sign and the song, the one to balance or counterpoise the other; the song to sing away the sign, to make amends for the manger. The sign very poor and mean, the song exceeding high and heavenly. *Paupertas in imis* the sign, 'poverty at the lowest;' *Gloria in excelsis* the song, "glory at the highest." That well might Leo ask, *Quis est iste Puer tam parvus, tam magnus?* 'What Child is this so little, and so great withal?' *Tam parvus ut in præsepi jaceat, tam maguus ut Ei concinant Angeli;* 'so little as He lies in a cratch, so great though as He hath Angels to sing to Him;'—the whole choir of Heaven to make Him melody. It is a course this, the Holy Ghost began it here at His birth, and after observed it all along, *Sociare ima summis, et insolita solitis temperare;* 'to couple low and high together, and to temper things mean and usual with others as strange every way.'

Out of these we shall learn, 1. First, what our duty is, to find Christ. The Angel presupposes this, that being born we will not leave till we have found Him; till we can say (it was the first word of the first Apostle) Εὑρήκαμεν, "We have found"—found the Messias. (John i. 41.) *Invenietis;* by all means "to find" Christ. 2. Then how to find Him, at what sign. 3. And last, when we have found Him how to salute Him, with what words to praise God for Him. For Him; both for His birth, and for His invention. All considered, His invention to us no less behooful than His Nativity. And this day to be no less solemnized, for *invenietis* His 'finding,' than for *natus est,* "His very birth itself." It is more often found in the first Fathers by the name of *Theophania,* 'His appearance' or being found, than by the name *Genethlia,* 'of being born into the world.' The Angels' *evangelizo* reacheth to both; their *gloria in excelsis* is sung for both.

The work of the day is *invenietis,* to "find" Christ. We shall not be better for *natus est,* if we find him not. Find Him we cannot, if first we find not a sign to find Him by. *Erit vobis signum,* and *hoc erit,* saith the Angel, "a sign ye shall have;" and "this shall be it;" "ye shall find Him swaddled and laid in a manger."

I. Signs never come amiss, but are then so necessary, as we cannot miss them, when we should miss without them; when no sign, no *invenietis,* as here. For if a sign, if this sign had not been given, no *invenietis;* Christ had not been found. Not been found, for never had been sought in such a place. Had not the Angel thither directed the shepherds, had not the star thither pointed the Magi, neither the one nor the other would ever there have sought Him. A *non est inventus* had been returned by both.

And reason; for some kind of proportion there would be between *signum* and *signatum*, and if the sign be a place as here, between *locas* and *locatus*. A chief Person in a chief place, a Lord and Saviour something Lord and Saviour-like. To Bethlehem they will. Set the sign by, let them alone, say nothing to them. When they came thither, they would never go to an inn, or ostrie, but to the very best house in the town. Or if to an inn, to the fairest chamber in it; or to a chamber at least; never to the stable, there to look in the manger for *Christus Dominus*. To the stable we go to look for a horse, to the crib for *bos cognovit et asinus*, (Isa. i. 3)—for one of them; never thither to seek for the Saviour of the world.

Nay, if in their search passing by, by hap they had lighted upon such a birth—a Child so lying; it may be they would have pitied the poor Babe and the mother, but have gone on their way and sought farther. Never, I dare say, taken Him for Christ the Lord. And if one should have bid them, 'Stay, for this is the Child the Angel spake of,' they would have shaken him off and said with as great scorn as they, (1 Sam. x. 27), *Nunquid poterit iste salvare nos*, "What shall this be our Saviour trow?" For *invenietis* is not all, to "find" Him; but finding Him, to apply the Angels' words unto Him; to believe of this Child thus there lying, that He should be Christ the Saviour, *gaudium omni populo*, "the joy of the whole earth." It goes hard, this.

We said when time was, this message was so high as no man meet to bring it but an Angel of Heaven. We say now *ex alio capite*, this sign was so unlikely, no man was meet to give it but an Angel only. And it was well it was an Angel. If it had been any else, His birth would have seemed, as His Resurrection did, λῆρος, "a feigned tale;" no man's affidavit would have been taken for it.

What were the shepherds like to think of this? Sure, thank Him for *natus est*, the news of His "birth," but not for His sign. *Erit signum* they like well, but not *hoc erit*. If He had given them no sign, it would have troubled them. Now the sign given troubles them worse. For this sign they know not what to make of it; it is so poor a one, it is enough to make them half in the mind to give over their journey, as not caring for *invenietis*, whether they find Him or no. If His sign be no better, as good lost as found. Always this is out of the *evangelizo vobis*,—no part of it; for no good news thus to find Him.

And we, if we admit a conference with flesh and blood, when we lay together the sign, and of Whom it is the sign; we find to our thinking a great disparagement, and I know not how, thoughts arise in our hearts, as if some better sign would have done better. The meaning is, we would find Christ fain, but we would find Him in some better place. Half Jews we are all in this point; we would have a Messias in state. *Hoc erit,* "this it shall be," saith the Angel. "Shall be;" but should it be this? No: how should it be? Let us see. Why, this shall be the sign; ye shall find the Child, not in these clouts or cratch, but in a crimson mantle, in a cradle of ivory. That, lo, were somewhat Saviour-like ; *hoc erit signum.*

But in vain take we upon us to teach the Angel ; we would have we know not what. We forget St. Augustine's *distingue tempora ;* as the time is the Angel is right, and a fitter sign could not be assigned. Would we have had Him come in power and great glory? and so He will come, but not now. He that cometh here in clouts, He will come in the clouds one day. But now His coming was for another end, and so to be in another manner. His coming now was, as we say in the Collect, "to visit us in great humility ;" and so, His sign to be according.

Nay then I say, first go to the nature of a sign : if Christ had come in His excellency, that had been no sign, no more than the sun in the firmament shining in his full strength ; *hoc non erit signum.* Contrary to the course of nature it would be, else it is no sign. The sun eclipsed, the sun is sackcloth ; that is *signum in sole,* "the sign indeed." (Luke xxi. 25.) And that is the sign here : "the Sun of Righteousness," (Mal. iv. 2), entering into His eclipse begins to be darkened in His first point, the point of His Nativity. This is the sign say I, and that had been none.

I say again ; it is not only *signum,* that is not all, it is *signum vobis.* We shall do well to look to *vobis.* There is a matter in that, for whom this sign was given ;—not the

persons so much, as the condition.　For if He had been
so gloriously born, such as these should never have been
suffered to come near Him.　But this is a sign for you—
you that keep sheep and such other poor people ; you have
a Saviour too.　He is not the Saviour of great states only, but
even of poor shepherds.　The poorest of the earth may
repair to Him, being no other place but this, and by this
sign to find Him, and so *hoc erit signum vobis.*

I say thirdly, *Vobis*, and take in ourselves too.　So *hoc
erit signum.*　For what praise or thanks had it been for us
to have believed in Him, born in all glorious manner ?
But being thus born with this sign, if now we do it, τοῦτο
χάρις καὶ κλέος, to speak in St. Peter's phrase, "this hath
thanks and praise with God," (1 Pet. ii. 19, 20), and so *hoc
erit signum.*

Fourthly, without regard of them or of us, I say that
even in regard of Himself *hoc erit signum.*　Would there
be a proportion between the sign and the *signatum?*
There is so.　This holds good proportion with the ensuing
course of His life and death.　And all considered, it is
even *signum adæquatum.*　We may well begin with Christ
in the cratch ; we must end with Christ on the Cross.
The cratch is a sign of the Cross.　They that write *de re
rusticâ,* describe the form of making a cratch cross-wise.
The scandal of the cratch is a good preparative to the
scandal of the Cross.　To be swaddled thus as a child, doth
that offend?　What then, when ye shall see Him pinioned
and bound as a malefactor ?　To lie in a manger, is that so
much?　How then, when ye see shall Him hang on the
cross ?　But so,—*primo . . . ne discrepet imum ;* 'that His
beginning and His end may suit well and not disagree,' *sic
oportuit Christum nasci,* 'thus ought Christ to be born,' and
this behoved to be His sign.

But then to remove this scandal, I say fifthly : that the
less glorious, the more glorious ; the less glorious His sign,
the more glorious He.　And even in this respect of His
glory, He was to be born under this sign.　Had He come
in the power and great glory we spake of, what great matter
had it been for Him then to have done things powerful and
glorious ?　But coming in this sort, these same *panni* and
præsepe were an evident sign of the power of His might, in
nothing so manifest as in this, that from so poor a begin-

ning He was able to advance so glorious a work. It was
much from a babe floating in the flags of the Nilus in a
basket of bulrushes, (Exod. ii. 3), Moses, to gather himself a
people, even the nation and kingdom of the Jews, and to
deliver his law. It was infinitely much more from this
Babe here lying in the cratch, to work the bringing in of the
Gentiles, and the turning about of the whole world, and to
publish His Gospel, " the power of God to salvation."
Herein is power, from His cratch to do this. There to lay
Him, and there lying to make so many nations come and
adore Him, as since He hath. That if ever " in His humility His judgment were exalted," (Acts viii. 33), if His
"power were ever made perfect in weakness," (2 Cor. xii. 9),
if ever He shewed that *infirmum Dei fortius est hominibus,*
"God at the weakest is stronger than men in all their strength,"
(1 Cor. i. 25) ; *hoc erit signum,* " in this sign it was."

A sign, *cum externa rejicit, quod sibi sufficit,* ' in that He
casts from Him all outward signs and means, that He is of
Himself all sufficient ;' *et nullo indiget nisi se,* ' and needs
no power but His own.' His cratch and He will bring this
work to pass. His *gloria in excelsis* will be *hoc ipso excelsior,*
' His glory on high, so much the higher for this.' Ever,
but now more than ever ; and in all His signs, but in this
more glorious than in any, nay than in all them. And so
hoc erit signum, " this shall be the sign;" shall be, and should
be both.

But I waive all these, and say sixthly. Make of the
sign what ye will ; it skills not what it be, never so mean.
In the nature of a sign there is nothing but it may be such ;
all is in the thing signified. So it carry us to a rich
signatum and worth the finding, what makes it a matter
how mean the sign be ? We are sent to a crib, not to an
empty crib ; Christ is in it. Be the sign never so simple,
the *signatum* it carries us to makes amends. Any sign with
such a *signatum.*

And I know not the man so squeamish but if, in his
stable and under his manger, there were a treasure hid and
he were sure of it, but thither he would, and pluck up the
planks, and dig and rake for it, and be never a whit
offended with the homeliness of the place. If then Christ
be a treasure, as in Him are "all the treasures of the
wisdom and bounty of God" (Colos. ii. 3), what skills it

what be His sign? With this, with any other, Christ is worth the finding. Though the cratch be not worth the going to, Christ is worth the going for. He is not worthy of Christ that will not go any whither to find Christ.

Lastly, I would fain know why should the shepherds, why should any be ashamed of this sign? the Angels are not. *Non erubescit quis quod prædicat,* 'no man proclaims or preaches of that, makes a hymn of that he is ashamed of.' And indeed, why should the Angels be ashamed to report it, seeing *Christus non est confusus,* "Christ is not ashamed" to wear it? And if He be not so to be found, never let us be so to find Him.

I conclude then. They that will have a Saviour without such a sign, best stay for the Jews' Messias, or get them for their sign to somebody else. The Angel hath none, the Gospel knows none but this. We must take Christ as we find Him, cratch and all. The invention of the cratch, and the invention of Christ fall both upon one feast—this day both : no severing of them. All which I trust by this shew plainly, the sign was well assigned by the Angel. And so I hope we will not let the shepherds go alone, but go along with them too for company, to find Christ, *in hoco signo,* ' by this sign.'

But the cratch is gone many years ago. What is our sign now? Why, what was this sign a sign of? There needs no straining at all—of humility clear; *signum humile, signum humilis.* Not always so, not with us where the highest minds will use the lowest signs; but with Christ, with such in whom is the mind of Christ there is no odds at all. Ye may strike a tally between the sign and the *signatum.* Humility then : we shall find Him by that sign, where we find humility, and not fail; and where that is not, be sure we shall never find Him. This day it is not possible to keep off of this theme; we cannot but we must fall upon it; it is so woven into every text there is no avoiding it. But of all, into the sign, most of all. Such a sign of such humility as never was.

Signs are taken for wonders. "Master, we would fain see a sign," (Mat. xii. 38), that is a miracle. And in this sense it is a sign to wonder at. Indeed, every word here is a wonder. Τὸ βρέφος, an infant; *Verbum infans,* the Word without a word; the eternal Word not able to

speak a word; 1. a wonder sure. 2. And the σπαργα-
νισμὸς, swaddled ; and that a wonder too. "He," that (as
in the thirty-eighth of Job (v. 9) He saith), " taketh the
vast body of the main sea, turns it to and fro, as a little
child, and rolls it about with the swaddling bands of darkness ;"—He to come thus into clouts, Himself ! 3. But
yet, all is well ; all children are so. But *in præsepi*, that
is it, there is the wonder. Children lie not there ; He
doth. There lieth He, the Lord of glory without all glory.
Instead of a palace, a poor stable ; of a cradle of state, a
beast's cratch ; no pillow but a lock of hay ; no hangings
but dust and cobwebs ; no attendants, but *in medio
animalium*, as the Fathers read the third of Habakkuk.
(Hab. iii. 2.) For if the inn were full, the stable was not
empty we may be sure. A sign, this, nay three in one, able
to amaze any.

And " is it true ? " saith Solomon, and makes a wonder
of it : " Will God accept a place in earth to receive Him ? "
(1 Kings viii. 27), when he had built Him a stately
sumptuous Temple, and meant it by that. And is that a
wonder, if in such a Temple ? What is it then, if in a
corner of a stable, in a cratch there ? Will He accept of
that trow ? If He will, *hoc erit signum* indeed. "O Lord,
O Lord," saith King David, his father, rapt with admiration, "how wonderful !" (Ps. viii. 1.) What ? why *minorasti
Eum ab Angelis*, "Thou madest Him lower than the
Angels"—for to Christ doth the Apostle apply that verse
Hebrews ii. 7—"lower than the Angels." Nay, lower yet,
saith Esay in his fifty-third, *Novissimus virorum*, "The
lowest of men." (Isa. liii. 3.) Nay, lower yet, saith the
Angel here, lower than the lowest of men. For a stable, a
cratch is a place for beasts, not for men. So low. Well
may this be said a sign, in this sense, to wonder at. If it
be well looked into, it is able to strike any man into an
ecstasy.

But if we stand but gazing and wondering at this sign, the
Angel will blame us at the Nativity, as they did the Apostles
for the like at His Ascension. (Acts i. 11.) What learn we
by it ?

For *loquitur signis*, 'signs have their speech,' and this is
no dumb sign. What saith it then to us ? Christ, though as
yet He cannot speak as a new-born babe, yet by it He

speaks, and out of His crib, as a pulpit, this day preaches to us ; and His theme is *Discite a Me,* " Learn of Me for I am humble," (Matt. xi. 29)—humble in My birth ye all see. This is the *præcipe* of the *præsepe*, as I may call it, the lesson of Christ's cratch.

A sign it is, but not a sign at large indefinitely, nothing but *hoc erit signum.* But *signum vobis,* " for you," limited to some, not to all. For not to some others, but " to you," and such as you are a sign it is ; a sign it is how to find Him. A sign for whom He was born That thus was born ; to whom He, to whom His birth belongs. Sure, *humilis nascitur humilibus,* ' so He was born, and for them that are so He was born.' Such He was found, and of such He will be found, and of none but such.

But then, as St. Augustine saith well, *Signum vobis, si signum in vobis,* " A sign for you, if a sign in you." For in this sense also it is a sign to sign us with, a signature to make a mark on us. Theirs, in the ninth of Ezekiel, that were saved, they were " marked with the sign of Tau in their foreheads." (Ezek. ix. 4.) That is this very sign, the mark of humility, as being the last and lowest letter of the whole alphabet.

" And this sign shall follow them that believe," (Mark xvi. 17), and by this mark will He know them. By the sign we find Him, by the same will He find us, *invenietis* and *inveniemini,* by one and the same sign both. For *nunquam erit aliud Servatoris signum, aliud servati ;* ' Never He that saves one sign, they that saved another.' At least not a quite contrary, but the same sign both. By the same that Christ found, by the same a Christian : or to speak more nearly to the day, by the same that Christ's birth by the same the Christian's new birth. For as faith is the virtue appropriate to His conception—by faith He was conceived, *Beata quæ credidit,* (Luke i. 45, 48)—so is humility as proper to His Nativity ; in great humility this day was He born and brought into the world. Then, if the sign of Christ's birth be the proper sign of a Christian's new birth, " wherein Christ is fashioned in us anew," (Gal. iv. 19) ; *hoc erit signum,* that they who to faith have not joined humility, (2 Peter i. 5, 6), are not yet come so far as to be babes in Christ, (Matt. xviii. 3) ; not yet, as St. Basil speaks, come to their σπάργανα σωτηρίας, 'their swaddling clouts in the state of salvation.' And what time, trow ye, will these be come to "the measure of the full age in Christ," (Eph. iv. 13), that yet are no farther forward? Many a μεγανήπιος are there among us, if this sign hold.

But then if it be *signum vobis* to some, it is for some others *signum contra vos ;* and that is the proud. For the word of God hath two edges ; and if it go one way thus for humility, it cuts as deep the contrary against pride. And withal, under one leads us to the cause straight, and shews us the malignity of the disease of pride, for the cure whereof this so profound humility was requisite in Christ. There was one when time was took the disease of *ero similis Altissimo,* (Isa. xiv. 14), and he breathed upon our first parents with his *eritis sicut dii,* (Gen. iii. 5), and infected them with it. To make themselves equal with God is plain robbery, (Phil. ii. 6), saith the Apostle. For that robbery of theirs was the Son of God robbed, as I may say, and quite spoiled of His glory. For their puffing up, ἐκένωσε, "He was made empty;" for their lifting up, ἐταπείνωσε, "was He brought thus low," (Phil. ii. 7, 8) ; for their comparing with God, came He to be "compared to the beasts that perish" (Ps. xlix. 12)—lay in the manger, we see.

Never blame the Angel for giving this sign ; he had no other to give. As Christ was born, so was He to tender Him. Ask Christ why He would be so born. Of any other child this could not be asked ; they are born they neither know where nor how. Of Christ it may ; He knew both. For as *oblatus est quia voluit,* (Isa. liii. 7), so *natus est,* " He was so born" because He would so be. And why should He so be? His *Ecce venio,* (Zech. ii. 10), His "coming" was to recover man. Man was to be recovered by the contrary of that by which he perished. By pride he perished, that is confessed. Then, by humility to be recovered, according to the rule, *Contraria curantur contrariis.* So He to come in humility. The pride was high, *eritis sicut dii,* (Gen. iii. 5); the contrary as low, *factus est sicut jumenta,* (Ps. xlix. 12), " as low as they," lie in their cratch.

It is strange this point of Christ in the cratch, how tedious, how harsh it is to be stood on. Harsh—but to none more, nay none so much as to the proud ; and they of all other have least cause to be offended with it, it is they that were the cause of it. They should not, one would think, be offended with their own doing; it is long of them all this. If there they find Him, it is they and none but they that there laid Him. If He be otherwise than He should, their pride is to blame for it. But for it we had found Him in a better place. And fie upon pride, say I, if it were but for this only; enough to make us loathe this vice that laid this so great a disgrace as we count it upon the Son of God.

But marvel not if this be *signum contra* to them a ' sign against them;' they are against it. Well said Bernard, *In signum positum est præsepe Tuum Domine, sed in signum cui a multis contradicitur;* 'Thy cratch, O Lord, is set for a sign, but for a sign which of many is spoken against'—done against I am sure—alluding to that of Simeon at the 34th verse after, (Luke ii. 34), that Christ " should be a sign (and if Christ, His cratch sure) to be spoken against" by many "whose pride," saith the Prophet, "testifies to their faces." (Hos. v. 5.) You may take up the edges of their garments and shew it them, yea that even this day come hither to make a show of it, as it were to affront this sign and the Angel that gave it, come to celebrate the feast of humility in excess of pride. Should the Angel ever have persuaded one of these to have gone into the stable, and have sought their Saviour there? Never. Do but look upon them; you would think they had some other Saviour by themselves that lay in an ivory cradle, and never looked to be saved by Him That this day lay in a manger.

Sure it is no good sign to be *ad oppositum* to this sign. If *signum vobis* to the one, *signum contra vos* to the other. For if humility be the sign of finding Christ, pride must need be the sign of losing Him; and whoso loseth Him is himself even the child of perdition: and therefore look to this sign well.

But humility is not all we find in this sign. The philosopher saith, signs are either indicant or co-indicant. Indicant it is of humility; co-indicant of that which in Him and on His part, as pride on ours, was the cause that made Him stoop to this humility, and that was His love. He left *gloriam in excelsis* for εὐδοκία ἐν ἀνθρώποις, " His glory on high," for " His good-will towards men." It was a sign of love too this. A sign, nay an ensign, His very colours, as in the second of Cant. He terms it, "love His banner or ensign over us." (Cant. ii. 4.) Signal love indeed, that for our sakes refused not first our nature, our mortality—that alone had been love enough— but not the basest estate of our nature, not poverty; poverty, and such poverty as the like was never heard of, *usque ad squalorem et fœtorem stabuli,* to be found where He was found, there to lie.

"Thou didst not abhor the Virgin's womb," so we sing. Thou didst not abhor the beast's manger, so we may sing too; and is not this *hoc erit signum,* a very "ensign of love"?

Two ways take we measure of love. 1. Of *quanti fecit nos,* first, by *quanta fecit pro nobis,* 'how much He made of us,' by 'how much He did for us,'—the ordinary way of the world's measuring.

2. But there is another, and that is, *quanti fecit nos,* by *quantillus factus est pro nobis,* 'how much He made of us,' by 'how little He was made for us.' This latter we hold to be the more, by how much it is easier for Him many times to make great than once to be made little.

3. But then, will ye take in this in the text, *nobis,* to make up a third "for us"? "Us" that even at that time when He shewed so great love to us shewed so little to Him, that if the beasts had not been better to Him than we, He had found no place to be born in? "For us" He came, and we thrust Him out from us and from all place with us, into the place of beasts. And if He had not borrowed their stable, *caruisset tecto,* 'He had no roof to cover Him;' if He had not borrowed their crib, *caruisset lecto,* 'He had lain on the cold ground' at this time of the year. *Nobis* sure is somewhat.

And now to *quanta fecit pro nobis.* For all this was not so much to shew the love in Himself, as to work in God εὐδοκία ἐν ἀνθρώποις, "good-will toward men," the foot of the Angels' song; to regain His Father's love to make Him well-pleased toward men by His humility, with whom for their pride He was justly displeased. Thus unlovely He became to make us beloved, thus poor to make us rich in the grace and favour of God, more worth when the time comes than all the riches of the world.

This, lo, is the co-indicant sign of love, these the colours of it. The cratch is the cradle of His love, no less than of

His humility, and able to provoke our love again. The less He made for us, the more we to make of Him; and that, not so much for that He was made, as for the love by which He was made it. And these two signatures made in us, this sign *erit signum nobis,* and *nobis signum in bonum;* 'a sign it shall be, and to us, and to us for our good.' And this for the sign.

II. Will ye now to this inglorious sign hear a glorious song? to this cratch of humility a hymn of celestial harmony? If the sign mislike you, ye cannot but like the song, and the choir that sing it. The song I shall not be able to reach to; will ye but see the choir? and that shall serve for this time; for by all means before I end I would deal with somewhat that might balance this sign of His low estate.

This the Evangelists never fail to do, ever they look to this point carefully; if they mention aught that may offend, to wipe it away straight and the scandal of it by some other high regard. See you a sort of poor shepherds? Stay, and ye shall see a troop of God's Angels. Hear ye one say, "laid in the cratch" below? Abide, and ye shall hear many sing "Glory on high," in honour of Him that lieth in it.

Vidisti vilia, saith St. Ambrose, *audi mirifica,* 'were the things mean you have seen? Wonderful shall they be ye now shall hear and see both.' *Vilescit præsepe, et ecce Angelicis cantibus honoratur;* 'is the cratch mean? Mean as it is, it is honoured with the music of Angels;' it hath the whole choir of Heaven to sing about it. This also will prove a sign if it be well looked into, a counter-sign to the other; that of His humility, this of His glory.

Surely, seeing the other three Evangelists omitted this sign, one would wonder why St. Luke did not so too. In discretion small credit there was in it, better have concealed it, one would think—a great deal better. But St. Luke knew what he did; he would never have mentioned the sign, but that sure he was when he had laid Him so low he was able to up with Him again, and sing away all the disgrace of the sign with a strange carol, and as strange a choir sent from Heaven to sing it.

I. To the choir then. Who were they? Where the first I pitch on, is the word "Heavenly." For thence they came, and thither they went again. (Luke ii. 15.) *Quid*

præsepi et Cœlo? ' What hath Heaven or Heavenly personages to do here with the cratch?' It would seem,
some celestial thing there is in it; as low as it seems it
reacheth high, as high as Heaven; Heavenly things, and
Heavenly personages both. About it, here comes divers
from Heaven; for it, there goes glory up to Heaven. So
that the sign is also, *signum de Cœlo sursum,* "from on
high," by reason of the choir; as well as "a sign from the
earth beneath," (Isa. vii. 11), in respect of the cratch here.

How appear they? These personages were Angels. It
is said expressly, ver. 15, yet are they here said to be
soldiers. What, shall we have war then? for they are in
the habit of war. True of war; but it is war not that
now is or hereafter should be, but of war that had been
before even to the day of this birth, but now to cease
—witness *pax in terris.* There had been no peace with
Heaven, but plain hostility between earth and it; no
" good-will toward men," but *filii iræ,* " children of wrath
all." (Eph. ii. 3.) Ever since the Cherubim first drew
upon Adam, and with a shaken sword kept the entry of
Paradise, (Gen. iii. 24), ever since in arms till this very day.
Their habit shews what was before, their song what now
should be. By virtue of Christ's Nativity, "peace to earth"
from Heaven, "good-will to men" from God. So now
upon His birth they were to disarm; but before they put
their armour off, yet being in it they would have a *pæan,*
and sing of the new world that was now to ensue. A
sign this and a strange one, this conjunction, *species præli-
antium,* and *voces cantantium,* ' the habit of war,' and ' the
song of peace.' Soldiers make a camp, come to fight; these
make a choir, come to sing. They are not in the habit of
choir-men, yet they sing; they are in the habit of men of
war, yet sing of peace.

What number? A multitude there was of them. First,
for the more authority, that in the mouths of many this
truth might be established—many to witness to. 2. Then
for the better music; if a full choir, many to sound it out.
It was a matter of great weight, so divers to testify it; it
was a matter of high praise, divers therefore to celebrate
and set it forth.

When we hear of a multitude, we fear a confusion. But
you will observe, this multitude was *multitudo militiæ;* no

confused rout. No; but *acies ordinata,* 'a well-ordered army.' There is order in an army, there is order in a choir, there is order among Angels; co-ordinate among themselves, subordinate to their Head and Leader. So a multitude without confusion.

And yet there is a farther matter in this same multitude. For that there were not some few of them but a great many, that was a sign it was no petty Saviour that was born. To have Angels come by one and by two as at the birth of Samson, (Judg. xiii. 15), or Isaac, (Gen. xviii. 2), and others; but the grand Saviour of all by His troops of them, the Lord of Hosts Himself as attended by the whole army.

For at His birth was fulfilled that the Apostle speaks of, Hebrews i. 6, "When He brings His only-begotten Son into the world He saith, Let all the Angels of God worship Him;" let the whole host of Heaven do Him honour, as honour Him here they do. For they "that offer Him praise, honour Him," (Ps. l. 23); and praise they offer Him, the next word is *laudantium.* And even now they do it, even here is this honour done, even to Him in His cratch is it done, and Heaven itself for a while left empty that it may be done. All which is but a sign to shew what a show He could have made if He had listed; that He might have had the " legions " (Matt. xxvi. 53) He speaks of at His death, That had them in such a multitude to-day at His birth. A sign He was not weak, whatever He seemed, That had these military forces, if He would, to take arms for Him. That He was not to be despised, however He appeared. That had these concerts of Angels to sing about His cratch, and to praise Go d for Him.

What did they? "praised God." For Angels to praise God is no new thing. From the beginning it was their oc-cupation so to do. But to praise Him for a Child in a cratch, that lo, is new, a new thing, a new song, and if you will a new sign too. For never the like seen before. Before, in Job, their praise was for the creating, they had that only then to praise Him for, (Job xxxviii. 7); now for the restoring of all things. For the birth of the world then; for the new birth of it now by the birth of Him by Whom the world at first was made, and now *ne perderet quod con-didit,* made again, created anew, and many a new creature in it. To Him sitting in the throne sing they their *Sanctus*

(Isa. vi. 3.) For to Christ was the *Sanctus* sung, saith St. John directly in his twelfth and forty-first. Now to Him here lying in the manger, which is great odds, but indeed to both ; *in imis Puero, in excelsis Deo,* for He was both. And His being both was an *Ecce signum,* if ever there were any upon earth.

And lastly, all this ἐξαίφνης, that "instantly"—no pause between, between Amen and Hallelujah. No sooner the speech ended but straight, as if the word cratch had been their rest, immediately took they up the hymn and begun it. A plain sign that one of these did depend on the other. This the anthem, that properly belongs to that sermon ; and back again this the sermon, that requireth this anthem, and both to the Child in the manger. The ditty meant by Him, and none but Him. For Him this glory, by Him this peace, through Him this good-will. Glory, peace, and good-will, from Him all three. And mark, that the word "cratch" is the last word in the sermon, and the word "glory" the first in the song ; and nothing comes between to part these two. Nothing to part humility below from glory on high. Even as He drew "light out of darkness," (2 Cor. iv. 6), so doth He glory on high from humility below by a sequence. Which when we hear, and hear it from the mouths of Angels, sure we are all that before seemed to tend to His disgrace were but the *Auspicia* of His glory ; all that beneath appear in *ignominia in imis* is pronounced *gloria in excelsis,* and for such celebrated by the whole choir of Heaven. And this for the choir, and for this time.

But I ask, do the Angels praise God for this birth? *Ut quid illis concio, vel cantio,* 'what do they preaching of Him, or praising God for Him?' For them all this is not ; they put it not in the first, but in the second person, *Vobis.* Here is now *Vobis* the third time. 1. *Evangelizo Vobis,* saith the Angel first : 2. *Natus est Vobis,* saith he second, (Luke ii. 10, 11) ; and now *Erit Vobis signum,* third. 1. *Vobis,* the news : 2. *Vobis,* the birth : 3. and *Vobis,* the sign : all three. And who are these *Vobis?* In the song it is expressly set down, *in hominibus,* "for men." What mean the Angels then to make this ado with *laudantium,* and *dicentium,* and it concerns not them at all? What then? the blessed Angels, they rejoice and sing at the good

of others, " at the conversion but of one poor sinner," (Luke
xv. 7): *Hoc Angelicum est.*　As on the other side of the
devil's manner is to howl and to grieve at each others' good ;
if Christ come to save men, to cry, He is come to torment
them, (Mark i. 24) : *Hoc est diabolicum.*

But well ; from this yet that the Angels thus sing whom
in their own particular it concerns not, I rise to make this
inference ; that they whom it concerns are to do it with far
greater reason, and that is ourselves, to whom solely and
wholly this birth and the benefit of this birth redounds.
Shall they for us and not we for us, for ourselves? Shall
we be in at the other three, 1. at the news, 2. at the birth,
and 3. at the sign, and be out at this of *laudantium Deum?*
No, I trust.　The choir of Heaven did it, but to set us in ;
we to bear a part, and it should be a chief part, since the
best part of it is ours.　They but took it up ; we to keep it
up, and never to let it go down or die on our hands, but
from year to year as we have occasion still to renew it.
The Angels began here ; the shepherds they follow and
praise God, " for that they had heard and seen," (Luke ii. 20)
—the sermon they had heard, the sign they had seen.　We
to come in at our turn, and to do the like.

You say well, for that we have heard we may, but not for
any sign we.　Yes, for that too.　The Sacrament we shall
have besides, and of the Sacrament we may well say, *Hoc
erit signum.*　For a sign it is, and by it *invenietis Puerum,*
" ye shall find this Child."　For finding His flesh and blood,
ye cannot miss but find Him too.　And a sign, not much
from this here.　For Christ in the Sacrament is not altogether unlike Christ in the cratch.　To the cratch we may
well liken the husk or outward symbols of it.　Outwardly it
seems little worth but it is rich of contents, as was the crib
this day with Christ in it.　For what are they, but *infirma
et egena elementa,* " weak and poor elements " of themselves?
yet in them find we Christ.　Even as they did this day *in
præsepi jumentorum panem Angelorum,* ' in the beasts' crib
the food of Angels ;' which very food our signs both
represent, and present unto us.

Let me say this farther ; it is the last word in the Sacrament, " this is a sacrifice of praise and thanksgiving," and
the whole text resolves into *laudantium Deum,* " to praise
God ;" and not to praise Him alone, but to praise Him

with this hymn of the Angels. Now being to praise Him
with the Angels' hymn, it behoves to be in or as near the
state of Angels as we can ; of very congruity to be in our
very best state, when they and we to make but one choir.
And when are we so ? If at any time, at that time when we
have newly taken the holy Sacrament of His blessed Body
and most precious Blood—when we come fresh from it.
And as if there were some near alliance between this song
of the Angels and these signs, to shew that the signs or
Sacrament have a special interest in this hymn ; therefore
is it, that even then upon the administration of it hath the
Church ordered this very hymn ever to be sung or said,
whatever day it fall in the whole year. For then sure of
all other times are we on earth most near to Angelic perfection, then meetest to give glory unto God, then at peace
with the whole earth, then a good-will and purpose in us if
ever.

But as the time falleth out we have more inducements
than one. The day itself is one most proper, for it is the
very day this hymn was first sung on. And the celebration
of the Sacrament that is another ; but the Sacrament now
falling on the day, a double. Either of these of itself apart,
but together much more. For the Sacrament, that comes
at other times ; the day, but once a year. On this day
they both meet, and never but on this ; not to slip it then,
but then when it is most proper, most kindly, then to do it.
I would to God we were as meet to do it as the Sacrament
is to do it at, and as the time is to do it on. But as we
may, let us endeavour to do it. So inuring ourselves to
record it as oft as we may, especially when most meetly
we may, here " on earth " among men, that in His good
time we may be counted worthy to do it " on high " with
the Angels in the bliss of Heaven.

SERMON XIII.

A Sermon Preached before the King's Majesty, at Whitehall, on Saturday, the Twenty-fifth of December, a.d. mdcxix., being Christmas-day.

Glory be to God in the high Heavens, and peace upon earth, and towards men good-will. Luke ii. 14.

Gloria in altissimis Deo, et in terra pax, hominibus bonæ voluntatis (*vel, in homines bona voluntas*).

THE anthem of the choir of Heaven for this day. For having the Angel's sermon at twice; 1. Of the Nativity, 2. Of the Invention of Christ, and seen the choir of Angels set with their nature and condition ; there remains nothing but the anthem to make up a full service for the day.

That is it. St. Luke, besides that he is an Evangelist, hath the honour farther that he is the Psalmist of the New Testament : four hymns more hath he added to those of the Old. Of which four, this is so much the more excellent than the rest, in that it is not of any man's setting, though never so skilful ; the ditty and it are both angelical, from the Angels both.

That we praise God with the tongue of Angels, whensoever we praise Him with this, with *Gloria in excelsis.*

The sum of it is, that though all days of the year and for all benefits, yet this day and for this now above all God is highly to be glorified ; more highly than in others—nay, most highly then ; for it is *in altissimis,* " the highest of all."

That Heaven and earth and men are to join in one concert ; Heaven and earth first ; Heaven on high, earth beneath take up one hymn ; both in honour of His birth—both are better by it ; Heaven hath glory, earth peace, by means of it. Heaven hath glory ; *lætentur Cœli.* Earth, peace ; *exultet terra* (Ps. xcvi. 11) at Thy Nativity, O Lord. Warranted by this song, at Thy Nativity, O Lord, let the Heavens rejoice for the glory, let the earth be glad for the peace that come to them by it.

And men, *hominibus,* though they rest and come in last after both, yet they to do it as much, nay much more than both, for God's good-will toward them which brought all this to pass in Heaven and earth both; restoring men to God's favour and grace, and all by means of this Child, their Reconciler to God that hath been, their Pacifier on earth that is, their Glorifier in Heaven that shall be. They therefore if any, nay more than any. And now if ever, nay more than ever, to bear their part in this glorious hymn at the cratch side.

Ita canunt in Nativitate quæ per Nativitatem, 'Thus sing they at His Nativity of those things that came by His Nativity.' Came to Heaven, to earth, to men. Glory to Heaven, peace to earth, grace and favour to men.

To take a song right it behoveth to know the parts of it. And they are easily known; they divide themselves into the number blessed above all numbers, because it is the number of the blessed Trinity; and the mystery of the Trinity do the Fathers find in the parts of it. 1. In God on high, the Father; 2. In peace, *Ipse est Pax nostra,* the Son, (Eph. ii. 14); 3. And in good-will, the Holy Ghost, the essential love and loveknot of the Godhead, and this day of the manhood and it.

Being *Ode natalitia,* if we consider it as a nativity, they that calculate or cast nativities in their calculations stand much upon triplicities, and trigons, and trine aspects. And here they be all, a triplicity of things. 1. Glory, 2. Peace, and 3. Good-will. A trigon of parties; 1. God, 2. Earth, and 3. Men. And a trine aspect, *referendo singula singulis;* 1. To God glory, 2. to earth peace, 3. to men favour, grace, or good-will.

But if, as it is most proper, we consider the parts as in a song, the three will well agree with the scale in music. 1. *In excelsis,* on high, *hypate;* 2. on earth, *nete;* 3. and men, howsoever they come in last, they make *mese,* 'the mean.' Most fitly; for they, as in the midst of both the other, partake of both; 1. their soul from on high, 2. their body from the earth. Not the Heathen but did confess the soul *Divinæ particulam auræ.* And for the body there needs no proof that earth it is; "earth to earth" we hear, we see before our eyes every day.

Of these three parts then asunder. And after, as the nature of a song requireth, of their 1. conjunction, 2. order, and 3. division. 1. Conjunction; glory on high, and in earth peace. 2. Then the order or sequence; but first glory, then peace. 3. And last, the division, sorting them *suum cuique*, 'each to his own.' 1. To God glory : 2. peace to the earth ; 3. εὐδοκία to men. 4. Last of the singing of the hymn, 1. When, the time ; 2. and by whom.

I. There are in this hymn, as the Greeks read and we with them, three rests. The ground of which three are three parties. 1. *In excelsis Deo*, "God on high ;" 2. *In terrâ*, "earth ;" 3. and *hominibus*, "men." To these three other three ; 1. "glory," 2. "peace," 3. "good-will," as it were three streams having their head or spring in Christ's cratch, and spreading themselves thence three sundry ways, having their influence into the three former ; one of these into some one of them. Glory upward *in excelsis;* peace downward to the earth ; good-will to men in the midst between both, compound of both.

You will mark, the Child here is God and Man. God from on high, Man from the earth. To Heaven whence He is God, thither goeth glory ; to earth whence Man, thither peace. Then as God and Man is one Christ, and as the reasonable soul and flesh is one man ; so Christ consisting of these two brings εὐδοκίαν "the fulness of God's favour," the true and real cause of both ; yielding them peace while here on earth, and assuring them of glory when there on high ; as thither on high we trust to be delivered after our time here spent in procuring Heaven glory and earth peace. Thus three rests.

But let me not keep from you that the Latin hath but two rests, and of the Greek some likewise. To two they reduce all, and well. The places are but two ; 1. "on high," 2. and "in earth." The persons but two ; 1. God, 2. and men. So the parts to be but two ; 1. glory on high to God ; 2. peace on earth to men. But then what shall become of good-will ? Good-will is a good word, would not be lost or left out.

No more it shall. And indeed, the diverse reading of that one word makes the parts to be either two or three. The Greeks read it in the nominative case, εὐδοκία, which refers to men ; then there must needs be three, there are two besides. The Latins seem to have read it in the genitive, εὐδοκίας ; but a Σ, but one letter more. And so they make it of the nature of a limitation, "peace on earth to men." What, to men *promiscue*, good and bad, elect and reprobate ? No, but to such as pertain to His εὐδοχία, God's *beneplacitum*, His "good-will" and purpose ; to the children of it.

Εὐδοχία, or εὐδοχίας, nominative or genitive, let it not trouble you. "To men a good-will ;" or "to men of good-will"—no great matter whether, so long as εὐδοχία refers to God and to His "good pleasure," not to men or any will of theirs. And that so it is to be referred, I will use no other witness but Cardinal Tolet himself ; who in his readings at Rome, and in the Pope's own Chapel, and upon this very place confesseth as much, that so is the native signification of the word ; and so and no otherwise to be taken here, but in that sense.

And in that sense being taken, it goes well. Glory from us to Him, peace from Him to us. From men on earth to God on high, glory ; from God on high to men on earth, peace. Men I say, toward whom He is now appeased, and with whom now He is well-pleased ; and both, for this Child's sake here in the cratch, ἐν ᾧ εὐδό-χησα, in Whom He is so absolutely well-pleased, as of the fulness of His favour we all receive. God spake it once, and twice. 1. Once at His Baptism, (Matt. iii. 17) ; 2. and again in the Holy Mount. (Matt. xvii. 5.)

And *hoc erit signum*, this may be a sure sign that He is well-pleased with our nature, that He hath in this Child taken it and united it to His own ; which, if He had not been highly well-pleased, He would never have done. What greater good-will can there be than this ? It passeth the greatest, even that of marriage—union of nature, unity of person.

Then riseth there another doubt, what verb to put to here. For never a verb there is at all. Whether some indicative,—glory is or shall be ; and then it is an hymn of gratulation, and agreeth well with *laudantium*, a praise to God that these now are. Now hath God glory, now earth peace. Men are now received to favour and grace. Thus ; or whether *sit* or *esto* in the *optative ;* and then it is *votum bene ominatum*, 'a vow or wish,' that glory may be to God ; and so to the rest.

I say again here, as before I said, it skilled not then whether nominative or genitive, it skills not now whether indicative or optative. *Tehilla*, a praise it is, and *tephilla*, a wish it may be, do commence. Either is well, but both are best; for both are most true.

By way of gratulation. Glory now is, or shall be to God, for this birth. Before it was not, at least not so as after. Before it was *gloria in excelsis*, but *Deo* was left out. All nations in a manner worshipping the Host of Heaven, the superior bodies; deifying the creature, passing by the Creator quite. *Excelsa* they did, but *Deum in excelsis* they did not. But by this birth now, down should all idolatry go, as down it went wheresoever Christian religion took place. From the creature there, all to the Creator. To none on high, but God on high. The point of glory much mended; God more glory than before.

And the earth more at peace, if you take peace in things spiritual, matters concerning the soul. One only I will mention. There was, as out of Varro St. Augustine reckons them, no less than two hundred sixty and odd several opinions, and that of the wisest then on the earth, touching man's sovereign good, or chief end. The very highest point, and that did most concern them; and least peace, most variance in it. This mist also was scattered, and that point well cleared by Him That was the "Way and the Truth." (John xiv. 6.) That this εὐδοκία here is it; the favour of God it is, and the assurance of it, and nothing but it makes a man truly happy when all is done.

As for the point of God's good-will and favour, that was never in kind till this day. Many favours, much good-will before; never so as when God and man, the Godhead and manhood meet both in one. God never so pleased, as when He was pleased to assume it into one Person with Himself, uniting both with the straightest union that can be. Never that till this day when for εὐδοκία ἐν ἀνθρώποις, "good-will toward men," He forsook *gloriam in excelsis* to come into the cratch for them. So that for God's favour the gratulation is most just; more than both the rest.

Bishop Bradwardine did join a good issue. Let that be the religion, let that prevail as best and most true of all other, that is, *Deo honorabilior*, 'brings more honour to God,' *paci amicabilior*, 'best friend to the earth's peace,' and *homini favorabilior*, 'most favourable to man,' as shewing God better affected to him, and making men better affected

to God, better one to another. That religion is Christian
religion. None sings this hymn in time, in true note, but
it; all other are out. So that we have a compendium of
true religion, and three notes of it, out of the three notes of
the song in this anthem. And this, if it be the indicative,
or by way of gratulation.

II. But I confess it is more usual *per modum voti*, 'by
way of wish,' by *sit* than by *est*. *Sit* doth better become
the Church militant; *est* is more fit for the Church tri-
umphant. "Glory be to God, peace be to the earth," &c.
Exoptando that these may be so; and so being continue
still, and be daily more and more. And so taking it, to the
triplicity again.

First, glory we wish to God. "On high" stands in the
midst, you may either cast it to the first word glory—"glory
on high" and then the point, that is "high glory;" or with
the point after glory, and cast "on high" to God. A third
variety, but easily reconciled if we take in both; "glory on
high to God on high." One "on high" may serve for the
reason why we wish glory to God; for God being *Altissimus*,
"the Most High" as Melchizedek first styled Him, (Gen.
xiv. 18), and glory being the altitude or highest pitch we
can fly or perform, by good reason we wish Him That is
highest the highest thing we have.

But not every glory do we wish, but wish it Him at the
highest. All glory is high, yet is there one glory higher
than another. (1 Cor. xv. 41.) If any be so, that they wish
to God the very height of it, even glory *in altissimis*, as
high as it can go.

Now the more He is glorified, the higher His glory.
Higher if by Heaven and earth, on high and below, by men
and Angels, than by either alone.

This then they wish, when they say "glory be in the
highest;" that high and low, Heaven and earth, (Ps. cxlviii.
1-13), men and Angels would do their parts, to make His
praise glorious, glorious at the highest. On earth, sound it
out far and wide all the world over, to the ends of the earth;
and lift up our voices, and help them with instruments of
all kinds, (Ps. cl. 4, 5), and make them to be heard up to
the very Heavens, that so it may be *in altissimis* indeed.
Yea, that all creatures in both, ravished with the consideration of the great favour and good-will of God in this day's

birth testified, would take occasion to fill their mouths with
the praise of His goodness in resolving, His wisdom in con-
triving, His mercy in promising, His truth in performing
the work of this day, the blessed birth of His Son.

For the work of the day, to make the day of the work a
glorious day, causing it to be attended with a number of
days according to the number of the months of the year, as
no feast else.   Glorious in all places, as well at home with
carols, as in the Church with anthems.   Glorious in all
ages ; even this day, this year, as on the very day on which
He was born.   Glorious in habit, in fare ; but specially, as
we see the Angels here do, with the service of God, the
most solemn service, the highest, the most melodious hymns
we have ; and namely, with this here of the choir of Heaven.
In a word, all the ways we can ; all the ways God can have
any glory from us, to let Him have it ; and have it even at
the height, *in altissimis.*

And good reason we should so wish : Christ lost His
glory by being thus in the cratch.   We took some from
Him ; to wish Him some for it again.   That was *ignominia
in infimis*, to wish Him *gloria in altissimis* in lieu of it.

Again, we get glory by it ; our nature so.   For the glory
we get by God here below, to return some glory to God
there on high.   This is *votum gloriæ ;* this wish we when we
wish *gloria in altissimis.*

The next is *votum pacis ;* they wish peace may be upon
earth.   1. Even Augustus' peace first, that is the first cometh
to our minds when we hear that word, the shutting of Janus,
for that also was a blessed fruit of this birth.   Esay foretold
it, there should then be a bridge from Ashur to Egypt, and
from Canaan to them both, (Isa. xix. 23) ; that is, from
every nation to other, to traffic and to trade together.

That ; but not only that, but the taking down also of the
"partition wall" (Eph. ii. 14) which formerly Moses had
set up between the Jew and the Gentile, the making of
them both one in the body of His flesh ; St. Paul's peace.

And yet farther.   For both these are "peace upon earth,"
of earth with earth.   Augustus can, the world can give that
peace, though many times they will not.   But He speaks
in a place of the "peace which the world cannot give," that
is peace with Heaven.   That there should not be Esay's
bridge only, but Jacob's ladder set up from Bethel to

Heaven, (Gen. xxviii. 12), a peaceable intercourse with that place by the Angels "descending and ascending" between us and them.

And farther yet, peace at home with ourselves, and with our own consciences. "Turn again to thy rest, O my soul," (Ps. cxvi. 7); for in finding Him we shall find rest to our souls.

And last, to answer *gloria in altissimis, pax in novissimis,* peace at the parting, which is worth all; Simeon's peace, a good *nunc dimittis in pace,* "a departing hence in peace." (Luke ii. 29.) And all by means of *viderunt oculi,* "the sight of the salvation" of this day. All these are *in voto pacis.*

The third is, there may be in God a "good-will toward men." And good-will is a kind of peace, but somewhat more with an extent or prorogation, a kind of peace peculiar to men which the other parts of the earth are not capable of. So a further matter to men than bare peace; even δοχεῖν εὖ, to 'think well,' to bear good-will, to be well-pleased with men. And what greater wish can there be than *in Quo complacitum est?* Christ hath no more than ἐν ᾧ εὐδόχησα. (Matt. iii. 17.) It is His high glory, that for His, and this His birth's sake, which we now celebrate, that which is verified of His Person is verified of both His natures; of Him not only as Son of God, but even as Son of man too. And what is verified of Him as Son of man, may be verified also of the sons of men, of all mankind. This wish is at the highest, and more cannot be wished than that this favour to-day begun may still and ever continue to us all. So have you now the three parts of the Angel's wish, *summa votorum,* "glory be to God," &c.

What is now to be done? Three things more; to see the 1. connection copulative, 2. the sequence, 3. and the division. 1. The connection copulative—a blessed couple, Glory and Peace. 2. The sequence: but first Glory and then Peace. 3. The division, which to which. 1. One to God, 2. the other to earth, 3. the third to man.

Glory and Peace are coupled together with an "and"— "and in earth peace;" that Glory would not be sung alone, but Peace together with it. We will not, we may not skip the copulative; that couples together high and low, Heaven and earth, and in them God and man; but that which I respect specially, Glory and Peace must be sung together. If we sing Glory without Peace, we sing but to halves. No Glory on high will be admitted without Peace upon earth. No gift on His Altar, which is a special part of His glory, but "lay down your gift and there leave it, and first go your way and make peace on earth," (Matt. v. 24); and that done come again, and you shall then be accepted to give glory to Heaven, and not before. And O that we would go and do the like, have like regard of His glory that He hath of our peace. But this knot of *Gloria et Pax* is against those that are still ever wrangling with one thing or other, and all for the glory of God forsooth, as if these two could not join—God could not have His glory if the Church were at peace, as if no remedy the Angels' *et* must out.

Glory and Peace; but Glory first, and then Peace. There is much in the order. Glory to be first, else you change the clef,—the clef is in Glory, that the key of the song. That is to be first and before all, Peace to give place to her; Glory is the elder sister. And no *Pax in terris*, unless it be first considered how it will stand with *Gloria in excelsis*. To set Peace before Glory is to set earth above Heaven. Keep the order then, each in her place. So goeth the song; the Child born is God and Man—God from on high, Man from the earth. *Cœlestem primo, dein et terrestrem celebrant*, 'they keep the right order in singing of Him:' we to do the like, Heaven's part ever to be first.

But then next after His glory nothing more dear, more precious, nay nothing so dear, so precious to us then as peace. Set Glory safe, and then by all means *inquire Pacem*, saith the Psalmist, "seek Peace." (Psa. xxxiv. 14.) If she hide herself, seek her out, *et persequere eam*, "and pursue her;" if she fly away, follow her hard. Peace is not sought, no man follows her to make any pursuit; they know not the value of Peace that lose her so easily, that follow her so faintly. Nay, instead of pursuit, persecute her and drive her away, and make the chasing her away the seeking of God's glory. The second thing in the world is Peace; only one, one only before it, the glory of God.

But the air of the song is in the division, wherein each is sorted to his own; God to His, the earth to hers, men to theirs. Justice's division, which makes peace in Heaven and earth, scored here out so plainly, as it is easily seen which pertains to which. And we by all means so to distribute and deal them, and by all means to preserve and hold up this division. Else we change the note which is as much as the whole harmony is worth.

Now in this partition Glory goes whither? Up "on high." To whom there? To God, and none but God. The place and the person are both set forth. "On high"— there is the place. "To God"—there is the Person. Earth is not the place of glory, it is *in excelsis*, "on high;" earth is not on high. Here below it is, as it were the cellar or vault of the world; where though there be *excelsa* and *excelsi*, 'high places' and 'high persons' both, yet the word is ἐν ὑψίστοις, *in altissimis*, and *altissimi* they be not, "there be higher than they." (Eccl. v. 8.)

And as earth is not the place, so man is not the person; for man is upon earth, and is earth. No glory to man then, especially none this day of all days. Glory to him for what? For entertaining Christ and lodging him in a stable? Confusion rather; somewhat to be ashamed of, nothing to glory of. Had men deserved it, some to them; now let God above have the glory of this day.

Yet conceive it aright; we wish it as our duty, not as any longing of His. It were a silly conceit to imagine of God as if He were *avidior gloriæ*, 'did hunger or thirst for our glory.' What is He the better for it? Only nothing we have but that, and so either that or nothing; for nothing but that can He receive from us. But we have nothing to render Him for all His goodness, for His εὐδοκία, but δόξα. Give it Him then, but give it entirely; give it none but Him. *Soli Deo*, saith St. Paul, (1 Tim. i. 17); *Soli*, saith St. Jude; *Soli*, let us all say. "Not unto us, O Lord, not unto us," (Psa. cxv. 1);—it is David, as if he were afraid to touch any part of it. No: but as Paul and Barnabas, rend our clothes, if any "divine honour," (Acts xiv. 14) be forced upon us.

Yet glory we may, I grant, but not this here, *gloria in altissimis*, if we sing to any but Him we sing a false note. Men do so now and then, but the Angels are never out; and thus sing they, and set out glory for God's part.

Let "earth" be content with "peace;" peace is her portion, and a blessed portion if she may well hold it; a fair portion, a rich wish. For I would fain know, what could

be said more to the praise of this portion, than is here in
this song?   First, that in general it reacheth to the whole
earth ; not to men alone, though they have their share too
in whatsoever good cometh to the earth, but it reacheth to
all on earth ; *omni animantium* or *vegetantium generi,* 'to
all the beasts, all the green things on the earth ;' all are the
better for it.

Secondly, what more for the credit of peace than that it
is *votum militare,* 'it comes from the mouths of soldiers' that
were there in their military habit.   Even they sing of peace,
and praise it, and wish it, where they wish any good ; and
know not what better thing to wish to the earth than it.   It
is the earth's happiness, peace ; it flourisheth by it.   "Before
was the earth as the garden of Paradise," saith the Prophet,
"behind it was a waste and barren wilderness, all spoiled and
burnt up." (Joel ii. 3.)

Thirdly, that it is *votum Angelicum,* 'an Angel's wish,'
peace.   They being Heavenly Spirits, wish not any thing at
any time but Heavenly ; so that a Heavenly thing is peace.
And so it is, as Nazianzen here well observed, *pugnas et
dissidia nescire Deum et Angelos,* 'no broils, no brabbles in
Heaven, nothing but peace there.'   And a kind of Heaven
there is upon earth, when there is peace upon earth ; and
justly are they blessed, and rightly are they "called the
children of God," the most blessed that are, or shall be at
any time, that are the procurers of it.   This lo, is the Angels
division they sing.

But here we are like to have no little ado to maintain this ;
as we said before, *huic signo a multis contradicitur,* 'as the
sign so the song is gainsaid of many.'   The devil doth all
he can to mar the Angel's music, to bring in his, his own
black *sanctus,* to procure contempt to God's "glory on
high," (Luke ii. 14), to bring God's glory as low as he can,
to make garboiles upon earth, to work men all evil-will,
mischief, and malice that he can.

And first, to make a confusion in this division, persuades
earth not to stand content with the Angels' partition, but
earth forsooth must have glory, must be dealing with
Heaven's part.   It is well said "to God on high ;" there
be certain gods here below aspire to glory.   And glory we
would allow, but no glory will serve, unless *gloriam altissimis*
be sung to it.   *Sicut Dii* (Gen. iii. 5) cannot be gotten out

of us.   We cannot yet get *Dominus Deus noster Papa*
out of the gloss, no not now after it is reformed.   And
King Herod would be content to be made more than a
man, and to hear (Acts xii. 22). . . . *Nec vox hominem sonat.*
And we beneath are too ready to sing it otherwile, to deify
those that are on high, and give that belongs to " God on
high " to gods below.   Now that earth is thus willing to
entitle herself to Heaven's part, this brings all out of tune.

But in tune or out of tune, to die for it, have it we will.
What the Apostles rent their clothes to put from them,
(Acts xiv. 14), we would rend our skins to pluck to us.   So
greedy are we to be held for gods upon earth.   Nay, earth
is content to thrust from her her own part, that is peace,
to invade God's part, that is glory ; *Et dum gloriam usurpant
pacem turbant,* 'to usurp glory, they lose peace ;' we can
dispense with that.   Shift God's glory how it can, rather
than our own should suffer the least disgrace, away with
peace, *moveatur terra,* 'let all the world be on a welter.'

What comes of this ?   *Pacem contemnentes et gloriam appe-
tentes, et gloriam perdunt et pacem :* even this peace, their
own part, they set light by ; glory, God's part, they gape
after and lose glory and peace both by the means ; and when
they have brought all to confusion, set down by their losses.
For first, by seeking glory, glory is lost.   The heathen man
well observed ; Glory is one of those things that to seek
them is the very next way to lose, and to neglect them the
way to gain they ; *Quærendo amittitur,* no readier way to
miss it than eagerly to seek it.   And again, by seeking glory
peace is lost clear.   Yielding glory to God doth bring with
it *pacem in terris ;* diverting it from Him doth take *pacem de
terris.*   In very deed, "peace upon earth," as it stands
after it, so it hath a dependance upon God's glory ; comes,
as it were, in exchange for it.   *Da gloriam et accipe pacem,*
saith God ; ' let men on earth send glory up to God on
high, and God on high will send down peace to men on
earth,' and will not fail—Heaven's peace for earth's glory.
Whereby we see, if we miss "peace on earth" at any time,
what it is long of.   It is that which makes the Angels here
keep on their armour still.   Upon glory detained from
God, or transferred whither it should not, they are up in
arms straight, have power to take peace from the earth,
till the point of glory be set right again.   The setting

right of which point is the way to recover it. Let Heaven, let God be well served with their part, peace will not long be away. It is coupled to it you see, it followeth close, *Et pax in terris.* So much for that division.

"To men a good-will." For besides earth's peace wherein they enter common, men have a part by themselves which is their prerogative. And first, I would have you to note that here it is entered first into the music of Heaven. In the Angel's hymn in Esay, (Isa. vi. 3), in the Old Testament, men are out there; no mention at all, not a word of them in that. Heaven is in and earth, but no men there. In the Angels' hymn here in the New Testament, here men are in; that all may know that for this Child's sake now made Man, men are now come into the Angels' song, to be a part and a principal part there who before were left out.

A principal part, I say; for mark again, they have never an *et*, they stand by themselves. For both those former resolve into this of men, they the epitome of Heaven and earth; the parties from whom this glory to whom this peace is principally intended to come. Glory to God, glory and peace: why both? for God hath received men to grace, men are now in favour again.

But Heaven and earth, and men and all, resolve into the free grace and good-will of God. How shall they perform either peace or glory, but if there be toward them first? and secondly, but if there be in them this third of good-will? Thence issues God's glory, thence the earth's peace. The fountain of both that, nay of Christ and all. For Him this glory, for Christ; through Him this peace, through Christ. But Christ Himself, whence? Whence, but from the "good-will of God toward men"? From whence also the good-will in men to God, and one to another, if any be in them. That if we go higher yet, even of this birth, God's good-will was the cause; and because His will was men should be restored, therefore His will was Christ should be incarnate and born. Can we go any higher? are we not *in altissimis?* Verily, as we said the humility of the sign was so deep we could not sound it, so may we now that the sublimity of this point is so high we cannot reach it. There is a part of divinity that dazzles; if we look too long on it, we may well lose our sight.

Then to ἐν ἀνθρώποις, last. It may be turned two ways, it will bear both; and for my part I wish no word ever narrowed by a translation, but as much as might be left in the latitude of the original tongue. 1. Ἐν ἀνθρώποις will bear εἰς ἀνθρώπους, *in homines,* ' to or toward men.' So we turn it, and we turn it well. 2. But ἐν ἀνθρώποις, is also *in hominibus,* ' in or among men ; ' ἐν ἀνθρώποις, as well as ἐν ὑψίστοις, and no less properly. And no hurt if we turn it so, *in hominibus,* provided *in* or *erga homines* go first, be sung before it. *In hominibus* so ever, as coming from *in homines.* For then *Donum magnum bonæ voluntatis Dei, bona voluntas in hominibus*—it is Augustine ; ' of the good-will of God towards men a special gift it is, this good-will in men ' to God and man both. The best way is, where there are two to take in both, so we shall be sure to leave out neither.

Yet in their sequence. To or toward men then first, but to or toward them for this Child's sake. In Whom He " is so well-pleased," as for His sake He is pleased first to receive men to pardon, though grievous sinners, and so utterly unworthy of it.

Secondly, He is pleased to reward their works also, otherwise, but for this good-will in God in accepting them, that might justly be excepted to for their many imperfections ; to take them well in worth, though they want worth, and to vouchsafe them a reward, and that a high reward, for " it is your Heavenly Father's good pleasure to give you a kingdom." (Luke xii. 32.)

Thirdly, beyond both these, He is further pleased, in some case to accept even of this εὐδοκία, at our hands ; and though skill and power both fail and be wanting, yet a willing mind if there be, if there be but that, "a man is accepted, according to that he hath, not according to that he hath not." (2 Cor. viii. 12.) Mary Magdalene's *quod potuit fecit,* (Mark xiv. 8); the poor widow's *quod habuit dedit,* (Mark xii. 44), and God wot it was but two mites, yet well taken though—one εὐδοκία by another. That He placeth not acceptance, neither in εὐγνωσία, ' deep capacity of wit,' nor in εὐδηνασία, ' great ability of power ; ' but in εὐδοκία, ' readiness of good-will,' an honest true meaning, an unfeigned hearty desire ; *ut si sit actionis infirmitas, at si sit voluntatis integritas,* ' though there be weakness in the act, yet if there be soundness in the will,' out of His " good-

P

will toward men" He will accept this good-will in men. Nehemiah's " desire to fear Him," (Neh. i. 11), Ezekias' " setting his heart to seek," (2 Kings xx. 3)—the servant's but preparing to do his master's will. (Luke xi. 42, 47.) And even in David's *secundum cor meum*, (1 Sam. xiii. 14), his honest true heart was fairest flower in his garland.

And this, if it were well weighed and digested aright, if Christ, if all that comes by Christ, and that is " all in all," be by His free grace and favour ; if men were but rightly conceited in this point, it would soon bring them out of conceit with their own I wot not what, it would make them truly humble. And it is the humble man that gives God the true glory, that sings this song right, when all is done. This glory that comes to God is δόξα δι' εὐδοκίαν, the first word for the last. With glory it begins, with good-will it ends ; and with good-will it begins, and with glory ends ; as the " first shall be last, and the last first." (Mat. xix. 30.)

But when we have fixed *bona voluntas in homines*, what hurt will it do to wish *bona voluntas in hominibus?* Sure none. *Bona voluntas in homines* is to work this *bonam voluntatem in hominibus*, and that by very course of kind. For *suum simile*, grace to beget his own like is most natural ; *bene placitum Dei*, to beget *bene placitum Deo*, Who out of His good pleasure " worketh in us both to will and to do," (Phil. ii. 13), and Whose only work it is, *Ut respondeat bonæ voluntati Dei bona voluntas hominis*.

What harm then if the Angel should wish it or commend it to men, in whom if it be it comes from that of God merely and from no other. Verily, what is praiseworthy in God cannot but be so in men too. *Summa religionis est, assimilari Ei quem colis,* ' to become like to Him we worship is the pitch of all religion.'

Now an εὐδοκία at the second hand there is in men. The word itself is ascribed to them of Achaia towards the poor saints at Jerusalem, (Rom. xv. 26), to St. Paul towards the Jews, (Rom. x. 1), to the Philippians towards St. Paul, (Phil. i. 15), and in other places.

To wish then in men this εὐδοκία toward God ; which where it is makes men to δοκεῖν εὖ, ' have a good conceit or opinion ' of God, which will bring forth a good affection to God. It is well observed, it is not ἀγαθὴ θέλησις, which is properly Greek for ' good will,' but εὐδοχία, which is rather a ' good thinking,' if we go to the very nature of the word ; but it will come all to one. Only the affection that begins in the opinion is noted for good, and the opinion that is bred in the affection not so.

From that good conceit of God, accepting well whatsoever it pleaseth Him to send; if good receiving it thankfully, if otherwise taking it patiently, ever praising God for all. But no ways entertaining of Him that opinion, for which they cannot but love Him the worse, if as of a tyrant sentencing men to death only for his pleasure, before they have offended him at all. That would prove no εὐδοχία, as it may be handled. And the Apostle tells us, the εὐδοχία that is in God is εὐδοχία ἀγαθωσύνης, (2 Thess. i. 11); it is not but regulate by His goodness, for which ever may there be glory ascribed to Him !

Then, to wish it in men towards men : an εὐδοχία also which, where it is, breeds an inclination to δοχεῖν εὖ, ' to take all in the better part ;' and if possibly we can, and " as much as in us lieth, to have peace with all men." (Rom. xii. 18.) Which if it were on earth, would make Heaven on earth. Peace is not said as glory to be ἐν, but ἐπί, and ἐπί is over ; for indeed it doth but hover aloft over the earth—would light, but cannot otherwhile. The raven can, but the dove cannot, for want of this *bona voluntas in hominibus*, or these *homines bonæ voluntatis*. It finds them not well willing to peace, while every one stands more for his own reputation or other ends, than either for Churches' or country's peace. Banish the opposites of εὐδοχία, envy, malice, and peace will be no stranger upon earth. (Rom. x. 2, and Phil. i. 15.) It would then be ἐν γῇ where it is ἐπί γῆς; the same preposition in both. All depends upon the cadence, εὐδοχία: perform that well, and it will be music for an Angel.

And now ye have heard all the parts, what shall we do with this song? Sing it. But we have no Angels to sing it, and it will be music for an Angel. Angels it would be as at first it was; but when it is not, it will please them well that men sing it whom it most concerns. But if by men, of very congruity, an Angel's song would be by men when in some degree they drew something near to the Angel's estate. At least when nearer than at other times.

And when is that that men on earth come so? At what

time? Sure, if ever men do rise above themselves and approach in any sort near to those blessed spirits; if ever they be in state with Angels and Archangels to laud and magnify His glorious Name; if in all their lives they be in peace and charity, the bond of perfection, the *bona voluntas* we speak of; if at any time it be in men, and they *homines bonæ voluntatis,* upon the taking of the Sacrament it is: at that time, then, or never, they lift up their hearts in true devotion. So then in best case that in all our lives to sing it, if Christ "dwell in our hearts" by faith, if we be "temples of the Holy Ghost."

And that we might be in that case and so sing it, the Church is never unprovided this day of this means of elevating our minds; and it is *operæ pretium,* 'worth the while,' if it were but for that, and there may be joy among the Angels in Heaven to hear their hymn kept still alive. Though there is another congruity for the Sacrament, that the "great mystery of godliness," which is "God manifested in the flesh," (1 Tim. iii. 16), might not be celebrated without the mystery of His flesh; that the day He came among us to be partaker of flesh and blood, we also might be partakers of the flesh and blood which He took from us to give them us again.

But otherwise, this day in this hymn, and this hymn in this day continually have a special interest. Time in music is much. And if we will keep time with the Angels, do it when they do it—this day they did it: and what fitter time to sing it than the day it was first sung, the day of the first singing of it, *Canticum diei, in die cantici?* When should the "hymn of Christ's birth be better sung, than on Christ's birth-day"?

But because it is not *vox* but *votum,* the voice is not all, but the heart's desire and wish it is that God chiefly respecteth, to add that. And what should we wish from our hearts but that the Angels may have their wish, every one may have his due as it is here set out.

And for that *Nihil æquius est, quam ut pro quo quis oret pro eo laboret,* 'what we wish for we should not stand wishing only but endeavour withal it may come to pass, that it be our labour too,' with all our endeavours to procure the glory of Heaven, and the peace of the earth; to find peace in the good-will of God, and to give Him all glory for it,

Who hath appointed peace our portion here, and glory our hope laid up there.

Assuring ourselves, that the same εὐδοκία that was able to bring the Son of God from Heaven into earth, shall have the like power to lift up the sons of men from earth to the glory of Heaven, there with the blessed Angels to sing this glorious hymn eternally. No more of wish then but of fruition, and so of everlasting gratulation.

——o——

SERMON XIV.

A Sermon Preached before the King's Majesty, at Whitehall, on Monday, the Twenty-fifth of December, a.d. mdcxx., being Christmas-day.

When Jesus then was born at Bethlehem in Judea, in the days of Herod the King, behold, there came wise men, from the East to Jerusalem, saying,
Where is the King of the Jews That is born? For we have seen His star in the East, and are come to worship Him.
MATTHEW ii. 1, 2.

Cum ergo natus esset Jesus in Bethlehem Judæ, in diebus Herodis Regis, ecce magi ab Oriente venerunt Jerosolymam, dicentes.
Ubi est Qui natus est Rex Judæorum? Vidimus enim stellam Ejus in Oriente, et venimus adorare Eum.

WE pass now this year from the shepherds and the Angels, to the wise men and their star. This star, and their coming, no less proper to this day than those other were. For though they came not to Jerusalem this day, yet this day *venerunt ab Oriente*, "from the East they came." They set forth this very day. For they came when "Jesus was born," and this day was He born. Howsoever the star brought them not to their journey's end till twelve days hence, yet this day it first shewed itself; how soon Jesus was born, *vidimus stellam*, it appeared straight. For which very appearing, you shall find the Fathers of the East Church do call this first day τὰ ἐπιφάνια, as well as the last. This first, wherein His star appeared and they began their

journey. That last, wherein He appeared Himself, and
their journey was at an end. First and last, an appearing
there was. One begins, the other ends the feast.

We pass from one of them to the other, but from the
less to the greater; for of the twain this is the greater.
Greater in itself, greater to us. Two ways greater in itself.
The other of the shepherds, a poor one, poor and mean.
This of the wise men, a sign of some state, high and
Heavenly.

God bade Ahaz ask a sign; "ask one from here below, or
one from the height above." (Isa. vii. 11.) He would ask
neither, but God gave both. From below, *hoc erit Signum*,
"you shall find the Babe in a manger," (Luke ii. 12)—low
enough. That we have done withal. Now from above,
ecce vidimus Stellam, the sign from Heaven — His new
star.

Besides, to speak uprightly, one might in some sort complain of the privateness of the Angels' appearing. Somewhat obscure it was, few privy to it; passed over in the
night between the Angels and them. And upon it, three or
four shepherds got them into the stable; and what there
they did no man could take notice of.

More famous, and more manifestation-like was this here.
A new light kindled in Heaven, a star never seen before.
The world could not but look up at it, and ask what it
meant. Nothing appeareth there, but "the sound of it
goeth out into all lands, and the news of it to the utmost
parts of the earth." (Ps. xix. 4.)

This made another manner *venerunt*. Upon this came
there to Jerusalem not a rout of Shepherds, but a troop of
great persons. And not from a heath or sheep-common
hard by, but from afar, "from the East," twelve days'
journey off. All Jerusalem rang of it. The King, Priests,
and people busied with it. To this day remembered in all
stories. It cannot be forgotten; "For this was not done
in a corner," (Acts xxvi. 26), this was indeed a manifestation. Better in itself thus.

And for us better—for us all. For we all hold by this.
It was a brack in the former; the sermon was made, and
the anthem sung, and none at it but the shepherds. And
what were they? Jews. What is that to us? This Scripture offereth "more grace." (James iv. 6.) These here that

"came from the East," first they were Gentiles. Gentiles
—that concerns us, for so are we. We may then look out,
if we can see this star. It is ours, it is the Gentiles' star.
We may set our course by it, to seek and find, and worship
Him as well as they.

This is for us all. But there is yet more grace offered to
some in particular. The shepherds were a sort of poor
simple men altogether unlearned. But here come a troop
of men of great place, high account in their country; and
withal of great learned men, their name gives them for no
less. This lo, falls somewhat proper to this place and
presence that will be glad to hear it. It is *faustum et
salutare Sydus* to such; that wealth, worth, or wisdom shall
hinder none, but they may have their parts in Christ's birth,
as well as those of low degree. It is not only *Stella gentium*,
but *Stella magorum*, 'the great men's, the wise men's Star,'
this.

So *quoad nos*, 'for us' it fitteth well. And *quoad se*, 'of
itself' it is fit every way. This star leads us to another
star;—even "the root and generation of David, the bright
morning Star." (Isa. xi. 1; 2 Pet. i. 19; Ps. cx. 3.) He of
whom Zachary saith in the Old Testament, *Ecce Vir, Oriens
nomen Ejus* (Zech. vi. 12); yea, *Oriens ab alto*, saith Zachary
in the New, (Luke i. 78); visits those of the East whence
the day springeth, takes them that are nearest Him, and His
rising works upon the place first that bears His name.
"The wisdom of God, the beginning of all His ways,"
(Prov. viii. 22), is found by wise men of all other, because
they be wise, most fit to find Him.

I. Two verses I have read. In the former after the
matter of the feast first remembered, "When Jesus was
born," accompanied with the two circumstances of place
and time,—the place where, "Bethlehem Judah;" the
time when, "the days of Herod the King"—there is a
memorable accident that then happened set down; a
venerunt, "a coming or arrival" at Jerusalem. And they
that so came were a company of *magi* "from the East."
And this lo, hath the *ecce* on the head of it, *Ecce, venerunt
magi ab Oriente*, "Behold, there came," &c. as the special
point in the text; and so we to make it.

II. In the latter is set down their errand. Both the 1.
occasion, and the 2. end; best expressed by themselves out

of their own *dicentes.* 1. The occasion ; *vidimus stellam,* they had "seen His star." 2. The end ; *venimus adorare,* they are "come to worship Him." *Viderunt, venerunt, adorârunt.*

That they may come to their *finis ultimus* they must have a *medius finis;* that is, to worship, they must find Him where he is.

So they ask *Ubi est?* Not whether He be born, but "where He is born." For born He is they are sure, by the same token they have seen His star. His star is up, that is risen, therefore he is risen too.

So the star in Heaven kindled another star in earth ; St. Peter calls it the "Day-star which riseth in the heart," (2 Peter i. 19), that is faith, which shined and manifested itself by their labour in coming, diligence in enquiring, duty in worshipping.

Christ's birth made manifest to them by the star in Heaven. Their faith, "the star in their hearts," made manifest to Christ and to all by the travel of it, which shewed it manifestly.

That upon the matter there falls a threefold manifestation —you may call them three stars if you please. 1. The star in Heaven. 2. The day-star in their hearts. 3. And Christ Himself, "the bright morning Star," Whom both the other guide us to ; the Star of this morning which makes the day the greatest day in the year.

The sum of all riseth to this, that God hath "opened a door of· faith to the Gentiles," (Acts xiv. 27), and among them to wise men and great men, as well as to the simpler sort. But with this condition, that they say with them, *venite adoremus;* and so come, and seek, and find, and worship Him ; that is, do as these did.

"When Jesus was born," That "when" is now. His birth is the ground of the feast and the cause of our *venimus,* 'our coming together.' Where this we note first : it is the very first time, the first "was born" in the Bible ; "was born" never till now. Here the tide turns, the sense changes from "shall be" to "was." A blessed change. And the day is blessed on which it happened.

Before He was born, it was so sure He should be born as Esay said, *Puer natus est nobis.* (Isa. ix. 6.) But for all that there is some odds between Esay's *natus est* and St.

Matthew's. That was but virtually as good as born, this actually born indeed.

"Jesus Christ yesterday, and to-day, and the same for ever." (Heb. xiii. 8.) "The same," yet not altogether after the same manner. There is as much between Jesus Christ "yesterday," not come, and Jesus Christ "to-day" *cum natus esset*, as is between a state in reversion and one in being.

The Fathers aptly resemble their case, that were the *ante-nati* before Christ, and ours that came after, to the two men that "carried the great cluster of grapes upon a staff between them." (Num. xiii. 23.) Both carried, but he that came behind saw that he carried ; so did not he that went before. The *post-nati* sure are of the surer hand. And so for *cum natus esset*, the day and time, to hold a feast for "when Jesus was born."

Weighty circumstances are ever matter of moment, in a story specially. Three there are in the first verse. 1. The place. 2. The time. 3. The persons. 4. I add a fourth out of the second verse, the occasion. The place *ubi*, "Bethlehem Judah." The time *quando*, "the days of Herod the King." The persons *quibus*, "wise men from the East." The occasion whereupon, a new star appearing. Every one of the four having a several prophecy running of it, and every prophecy a filling of it in these words.

The place. He was born in Bethlehem Judah ; "And thou Bethlehem Judah," saith the prophet Micah, "out of thee shall He come." (Micah v. 2.) And now come He is.

The time. "The days of Herod the King." "The sceptre shall not quite depart from Judah till Shiloh come," (Gen. xlix. 10), said old Father Jacob in his prophecy. Shiloh then is now come. For the sceptre is in Herod's hand, his father an Edomite, his mother an Ishmaelite— Judah clean gone.

The persons. *Magi ab Oriente*, "Kings from the East." The Kings of Arabia and Saba shall come and bring gifts, saith David. (Ps. lxxii. 10.) And Esay specifies them, gold, myrrh, incense. (Isa. lx. 6.) These Kings are come—here they are ; they and their gifts both.

The occasion whereupon. "A star risen." "A star shall rise of Jacob," (Num. xxiv. 17), saith Balaam—no very good man, yet a true prophet in this ; and his prophecy

true, and for such recorded in the Book of Moses. This
" Star," is this morning up, to be seen. Prophecies of all
four, and all four accomplished.

Of the place, of Bethlehem, out of Micah, it hath formerly
been treated. I but touch it and pass it now. It was the
place where David himself was born. And what place more
meet for the Son of David to be born in? It was the place
where was heard the first news of the Temple. And where
could the " Lord of the Temple" more fitly be heard of?
It interpreted *domus panis*, "the house of bread." What
place more proper for Him Who is "the living Bread that
came down from Heaven," (John vi. 51), to give life to the
world? It was the least and the lowest of all "the thousands
of Judah." (Micah v. 2.) What little and low is in things
natural, that lowliness and humility is in spiritual. This
natural birth-place of his showeth his spiritual. Humility is
His place—humility, as I may call it, the Bethlehem of virtues:
where you find it, " Lo, there is He born." So born in us, as
born for us. Pass we Christ's *ubi;* and now to His *quando*.

Of the time. The days of Herod the King. And those
were evil days—days of great affliction to that land. Judah's
" sceptre" clean broken ; not " a lawgiver left between his
feet." Edom, that is Herod the Edomite, cried " Down
with them, down to the ground." (Ps. cxxxvii. 7.) Not so
much as a sort of silly babes but barbarously slain in their
mother's arms—enough to make Rachel mourn as she lay
in her grave. (Jer. xxxi. 15.) Dismal days certainly. Why,
then comes Shiloh ; when man's help farthest off, then
God's nearest. When it is dark, then rises the star.

What one prophecy of Him but came even so, even at
such a time when they were most out of heart, and needed
comfort most? Jacob's, (Gen. xlix. 10), when they were in
Egypt, " the house of bondage." Balaam's, (Num. xxiv.
17), when in the waste and barren wilderness, "among
fiery serpents." Esay's, when they were ready to be over-
run with the two Kings of Syria and Israel. Daniel's, (Dan.
ix. 25), when in Babylon, the land of their captivity.
Aggai's, (Hag. ii. 7-9), when they built the wall with the
trowel in one hand and the sword in the other. As His
prophecies came still, so came He. His prophecies, saith
Peter, as a candle ; Himself as a star—in the dark both. (2
Peter i. 19.) For all the world like the time of the year His

birth fell in ; in the sharpest season, in the deep of winter. As humility His place, so affliction His time. The time and place fit well. For the time of affliction makes the place—makes humility. Which place Christ is born in. I pass this also, and come to the third ; of the persons.

For there stands the *ecce* upon it. Which *ecce* points us to it, as to the chief point of all, as indeed it is. And our chief endeavour to include ourselves, to have our parts in this *venerunt*, in coming to Christ.

Here is a coming, *venerunt*. And they that come, *magi*. In which comers we consider four points; they sustain four persons. 1. Of Gentiles ; 2. Gentiles from the East; 3. great persons, great princes—for so we may be bold to call them, as the prophecy calls them, Kings ; 4. of great learning and wisdom ; so *magi* their name gives them.

"To Bethlehem came the shepherds." Nothing to us— they were Jews. But thither came these too, and they were Gentiles; and in this 'Gentiles,' we. So come we in. "Then hath God also to the Gentiles set open a door of faith." (Acts xiv. 27.) At which door we enter, we with them and they with us, for they and we Gentiles both. The star is *stella Gentium*, ' the Gentiles' star,' and so ours ; and we to direct our course by it. All that ever write call them *Primitias Gentium*, ' the first-fruits;' *Antesignanos*, the 'standard-bearers' to all the Gentiles that came in after. Upon this I beg leave to stand a little, since it is our tenure we hold by.

And that God would thus do, call the Gentles in, there was some little *ecce* still, some small star-light from the beginning.

By way of promise. So much promised by the Patriarchs. Noah ; that " Japhet should at the last dwell in the tents of Shem." (Gen. ix. 27.) Abraham ; that "in his seed," not any one nation, but "all the nations of the earth be blessed." (Gen. xxii. 18.) Jacob ; that Shiloh's coming should be— *expectatio* say some, and some *aggregatio gentium*. (Gen. xlix. 10.) All nations look for Him, all be gathered to Him.

By way of figure. As much was shadowed in the Law, the Tabernacle, and the Temple ; all " figures of things to come." (Heb. x. 1.) The Law : where was it given ? Was it not in " Sinai, a mountain in Arabia," (Gal. iv. 25), saith the Apostle, and so upon heathen ground ? I trust we may have leave to come upon our own ground. And by whom? Was it not by Moses? And we claim to him by alliance. His wife was the daughter of the Priest of Midian, (Exod. ii. 21)—so of a heathen woman ; and his children, heathen of half blood.

The Tabernacle : was not the silk, and gold, and riches it was made of, the spoils of Egypt, and so heathen stuff? (Exod. xii. 36, and xxv. 2, &c.)

The Temple : was it not founded upon the threshing-floor of Ornan the Jebusite, a heathen man? (1 Chron. xxi. 18.) So on heathen soil, and *ædificium cedit solo*. The timber and materials of it, came they not from Hiram's country, a heathen king? (1 Kings v. 10, and vii. 13, &c.) And the chief workman in it, the son of a man of Tyre, heathen also? So the heathen were never wholly out. *Venerunt,* "they came," they made their proffers. Some *ecce*, some little star still.

Now the Prophets, when they came, had we not hold there too? At the same time that God gave Moses to the Jews who wrote of Christ, did He not likewise give Balaam to the Gentiles who in the mountains of the East prophesied of Christ's star, (Num. xxiv. 17), here? Great odds, I know, between the men, none between their prophecies ; both alike true, both their places alike in the library of the Holy Ghost. After that, Jonas. Howsoever his book stand in the volume of the Prophets, yet when time was it was shewed, that in time he was the first of the sixteen Prophets—before, and ancient to them all. And this was a fair star, that His first Prophet of all God sent to Nineveh, the great city of the Gentiles then, (Jonah i. 2); and sent him before He sent any of the other fifteen to His own people then in shew, the people of the Jews.

But even of them He sent to the Jews, saith not Esay directly, " the root of Jesse should be as a standard, all the nations gather unto Him"? (Isa. xi. 10.) Saith not God there, it was too poor a service for Christ to do to Him, to draw to Him a sort of silly shepherds ; He would give him, " as a light to lighten the Gentiles," to bring them, even the very best of them, " from the ends of the earth "? (Isa. xliii. 6.) That " light to lighten the Gentiles," (Isa. xlii. 6), was this star, here ; Simeon had it revealed to him whereto this star referred, and what it meant, (Luke

ii. 32); for it lighted them indeed. And this, standing the first Temple. And saith not Aggai, standing the second Temple, "the desire of all nations should come," (Hag. ii. 8), meaning Christ; the desire not of one nation alone, but even of all? So the Prophets will not be against this *venerunt*, they are all for it.

And was not also this *venerunt* daily sung in their choir —the Psalm of the Nativity? "I will think upon Rahab (that is Egypt) and Babylon, among such as shall know Me. Behold ye the Philistines also, and them of Tyre, with the Morians; lo, there was He born." (Psa. lxxxvii. 4, 5.) "Born," in all those places; that is, His birth concerns them all—all their interest in it. In the Psalm of His Passion: "All the ends of the earth shall remember themselves, and shall turn unto the Lord, and all the kindreds of nations shall worship before Him." (Psa. xxii. 27.) In the Psalm of the Resurrection; that, He should then become "the Head-stone of the corner," (Psa. cxviii. 22), and join both Jews and Gentiles in one coin or angle. And, in the Psalm of His Ascension; that the "princes of the nations should be joined to the people of the God of Abraham." (Psa. xlvii. 9.) And in the Psalm of His Exaltation; "that all Kings should kneel before Him, all nations do Him service." (Psa. lxxii. 11.)

That which then was thus promised to, and by the Patriarchs, shadowed forth in the figures of the Law, the Temple, and the Tabernacle; that which was foresaid by the Prophets, and foresung of in the Psalms, that was this day fulfilled. *Venerunt*, here "they are come;" and *venimus*, "we" in them and with them. Who not only in their own names, but in ours make here their entry; came and sought after, and found and worshipped, their Saviour and ours, the Saviour of the whole world.

A little wicket there was left open before, whereat divers Gentiles did come in. Many a *venit* there was. *Venit* Job in the Patriarch's days, (Job i. 1); *venit* Jethro in Moses', (Exod. xviii. 5), Rahab in Joshua's, (Josh. ii. 1), Ruth in the Judges' time, (Ruth i. 4); Ittai, the King of Gath's son, (2 Sam. xviii. 2), in David's, the Queen of Sheba in Solomon's, (1 Kings x. 1), the widow of Sarepta in Elias', (1 Kings xvii. 9), Naaman the Syrian, in Elisha's time. (2 Kings v. 15.) Each of these in their times had the

favour to be let in. This was but a *venit*, a little wicket for
one or two. Now a *venerunt*, the great gate set wide
open this day for all—for these here with their camels and
dromedaries to enter, and all their carriage.

In the setting down His genealogy, the chapter before,
(Matt. i. 5), that Salmon espoused Rahab the Canaanite, that
Booz likewise Ruth the Moabite, it is plain that Christ
descended according to the flesh of heathen. Descending
of heathen, He will never disdain them of whom He is
descended ; never shut them out, but invite them to His
child-house, as we see this day by His star he did.

And if you mark it of His first sermon, the widow of
Sarepta and Naaman the Syrian were the theme, (Luke iv.
25, 27) ; which made, His sermon was not liked. Yet that
theme He chose purposely. And the Queen of the South,
and the men of Nineveh much in His mouth—He mentioned
them willingly. (Matt. xii. 42, 41.) And to end this point,
He That at His birth now received these of the East, a
little before His death in like sort received Grecians from
the West, to see and to salute Him. (John xii. 20.) And
straight upon it, upon the receiving them brake out and
said, " The hour is come now that the Son of Man is
glorified," (John xii. 23), when East and West are come in
both.

I have a little stood on this, because it is the *ecce* point.
I conclude : the place He was born in, an inn, which is for
all passengers of what country soever, (Luke ii. 7) ; the time
He was born in of the tax, when " all the world came up to
be taxed," (Luke ii. 1) ; the very star which, as the nature
of stars is, is common to all coasts and climates, peculiar to
none ;—all shew that from all coasts they may now come,
that the Gentiles are now to be, as the Apostle in three
pregnant terms delivers it, σύσσωμα, συμμέτοχα, συγκληρόνομα,
" fellow-members, fellow-partners, and fellow-heirs of one
body," (Ephes. iii. 6), co-partners and co-heirs of Christ and
His birth. This for *stella gentium*, 'the Gentiles' star,' so
both theirs and ours.

There came Gentiles, and they came from the East. This
may seem to set us back again, for we are of the West, the
contrary climate. That is no matter. For in that " they
came from the East," there lieth yet farther hope for us,
even from that point of the compass. For that is not only

Gentiles, but "sinners of the Gentiles," (Gal. ii. 15)—
sinners, and that chief sinners. For so were they of the
East; greater, far greater sinners than the rest. For tell
me, what sin was there that came not from thence? There
was the tower set in hand, that should have confronted God;
and of it came Babel, and from it confusion. (Gen. xi. 3.)
2. Thence came all tyranny and oppression among men,
from Nimrod that hunted and ranged over men as over
beasts in a forest. (Gen. x. 9.) 3. Thence all idolatry and
worship of false gods, both in earth from Belus' tomb first;
and in Heaven, from "the star of their god Rempham"
(Acts vii. 43) which St. Stephen speaks of. 4. Thence,
"from the mountains of the East," (Num. xxiii. 7), the pos-
terity of Baalam, false Prophets that love "the wages of
unrighteousness," (2 Pet. ii. 15), and from them all that
naught is. And if in all these it did, it cannot be denied
but that the whole world received their infection that way
from the East.

And herein "appeared the grace of God which bringeth
salvation to all men," (Tit. ii. 11), and to all sinners, as fair
and clear as the star itself; that thence out of the mountains of the East God calleth these to seek, and guided
them to find Christ; that whence the poison first came,
thence might come the triacle; and that as they were
the first that went out, so they should be the first that
came in.

So the East sets us not farther back, but brings us
nearer. For if the East may come which are the greater,
much more may the West which are the less, (Matt. viii.
11); if the seducers, the seduced. From the East to the
West is *a majore ad minus*. That if *venerunt ab Oriente,
venient ab Occidente;* if the greater, much rather the lesser.
This for the star of the Gentiles first, and now the star
of sinners, and chief sinners of the Gentiles, even oriental
sinners.

But they sustain yet a third person, these—to come
nearer, and to make it come nearer us, even to this place.
For great men they were in their countries, of the highest
place and account there, as all stories testify. The Psalm
calls them "Kings of Sheba and Seba," (Ps. lxxii. 10), and
so may we. It may appear by Herod's respect to them, his
calling a synod to resolve them, his privy conference with

them. (Matt. ii. 3, 8.) So may it by their treasures they opened, and by their presents they offered, presents for a King, which give them for no less. So this is now thirdly, *stella magnatum*, 'the star of princes and nobles also.' Yea, *stella regia*, 'the star royal:' Kings themselves have their hold and claim by it.

Christ is not only for russet cloaks, shepherds and such; shews Himself to none but such. But even the grandees, great states such as these, *venerunt*, 'they came' too; and when they came were welcome to Him. For they were sent for and invited by this star, their star properly.

These at His birth, at His welcome into the world; and others such as these at His death, at His going out of it. Then Joseph of Arimathea, an honourable counsellor, bestowed on Him a fair new tomb, (Matt. xxvii. 60); and others came with their "hundred pound of sweet odours." (John xix. 39.) So that coming and going He was beholden to such. The tribe Christ came of was the royal tribe to whom the sceptre belonged; and in the prophecy it follows, "a star shall rise out of Jacob, and a sceptre out of Israel." (Num. xxiv. 17.) To Kings, to sceptres, Christ cannot but be well inclined.

Among His Prophets I find Amos, a herdsman. (Amos i. 1.) True; but I find Esay and Daniel, (Dan. i. 6), both nobly descended, and of the blood royal.

In His descent there are Booz and Jesse, plain countrymen; but there are David and Solomon too, (Mat. i. 6), and a list of Kings withal, that so there may be a mixture of both. It is true St. Paul saith, "You see your calling; not many mighty, not many noble after the flesh." (1 Cor. i. 26.) "Not many" he saith; 'not any' he saith not, he should then have spoken contrary to his own knowledge. Some pertained to this star, went by it. The Lord Deputy of Cyprus, (Acts xiii. 7), the great Judge in Areopagus, (Acts xvii. 34), divers of the nobler sort at Berea, (Acts xvii. 11), and divers of "Cæsar's household," (Phil. iv. 22), came in, and had all their calling by, and from Him.

As likewise the great Lord Treasurer by St. Philip, (Acts viii. 27); and "the elect lady," (2 John i.), by St. John. Those all were of this troop here; under this star all of them, *stella magnatum*. To conclude from our Saviour Christ's own mouth: as there is in Heaven room for poor

Lazarus, so that room was in the bosom of one that was rich, that is of Abraham, a great man, yea a great prince in his time.

1. *Stella gentium;* 2. *Stella peccatorum de gentibus;* 3. *Stella magnatum.* But yet all this while we have not touched *Stella magorum;* not yet dealt with *magi,* the very word of the text, and the chief person they represent. For beside that they were great states, they were also great learned men; and being both, they are styled rather by the name of their skill and learning than by that of their greatness, to point us to the quality in them we are principally to regard.

You shall not need startle when you hear the word *magi,* as if they were such as Simon Magus was. Of later times it sounds not well this name; of old it was a name of great honour, as was the name of *Tyrannus* and *Sophistes,* all in the like case. Evil and unworthy men took them up after, and so they lost their first reputation. But originally *Magus* was a title of high knowledge.

I add of heathen knowledge, and comprehend in it this very knowledge, that they were well seen in the course of Heaven, in the stars and bodies celestial. Their *vidimus stellam* shews as much. "The stars God hath given for signs," (Gen. i. 14), saith the Book of Genesis, even the ordinary. And if them, the extraordinary such as this much more. For signs they are, open the signature who can.

This learning of theirs made them never the farther from Christ we see, it did them no hurt in their coming to Christ. No more than it did Moses, that "he was well learned in all the wisdom of the Egyptians," (Acts vii. 22), saith St. Stephen. Nor no more than it did Solomon, that "he passed all the children of the East in their own learning." (1 Kings iv. 30.) No more than it did Daniel, that "he was brought up and well seen in the cunning of the Chaldeans." (Dan. i. 4.) No more these, than the gold and spoils of Egypt did the Tabernacle hurt, that was hung all over with them.

They that are seen in these learnings of Egypt, of Chaldea, of the East, are not thereby barred at all. This is their star, their guide; a guide apt and proper for them that knew the stars, for them that were learned. Christ

Q

applieth Himself to all, disposes all things; what every one is given to, even by that Christ calleth them. St. Peter, Andrew, James, and John, fishermen, by a draught of fish. These that were studious in the stars, by a star for the purpose.

And note that the apparition to the shepherds was no sooner over, but this star appeared presently, if not the very same hour; that is, both at once. In like manner Christ at first, to shew the glory of His greatness, took and employed fishermen, such as had no bringing up in schools. But it was not long after but learned men came in apace; learned men of all sorts; Zenas in law, (Tit. iii. 13), Luke in physic, (2 Tim. iv. 11), Apollos with his eloquence, (Acts xviii. 24), Dionysius with his philosophy, (Acts xvii. 34), St. Paul with his πολλὰ γράμματα, "much learning," which he had at Tarsus, as famous a University for Asia as Athens was for Greece. Which learning, for all Festus' fancy, "turned not his brains," (Acts xxvi. 24), nor did them any hurt at all.

There is no star or beam of it; there is no truth at all in human learning or philosophy that thwarteth any truth in Divinity, but sorteth well with it and serveth it, and all to honour Him Who saith of Himself *Ego sum Veritas,* "I am the Truth." (John xiv. 6.) None that will hinder this *venerunt,* keep back any wise man, or make him less fit for coming to Christ.

So you see your calling, all four. 1. Gentiles may come; 2. Sinners of the Gentiles may come, yea though they be *peccatorum primi,* 'of the primer sort;' 3. Men of place. 4. Men of gifts, learned and wise may come. *In magis insunt omnes hi,* all are in *venerunt magi.* The star goes before them, guides them all to Christ.

It remaineth that what we may do we will do; that is, "come." For farther than *venerunt* we are not like to come at this time. And though we go no farther it skills not, so we do but that—"come;" even that will serve. For it is all in all. We shall go in the company of wise men, that is once. And if the shepherds were too homely to sort with, these are company for the best; they were company for Cyrus and Darius, and all the great Monarchs of Persia.

Ecce venerunt it is in the text; and indeed, not only the persons, *ecce magi,* but their very coming deserved an *ecce.*

It is an *ecce venerunt*, theirs indeed, if we weigh it well whence they came, and whither. Whence? from the East, their own country. Whither? to Jerusalem, that was to them a strange land: that was somewhat. They came a long journey, no less than twelve days together. They came an uneasy journey, for their way lay through Arabia Petræa, and the craggy rocks of it. And they came a dangerous journey, through Arabia Deserta too, and the black "tents of Kedar" (Ps. cxx. 5) there, then famous for their robberies, and even to this day. And they came now, at the worst season of the year. And all but to do worship at Christ's birth. So great account they made; so highly did they esteem their being at it, as they took all this great travel, and came all this long journey, and came it at this time. Stayed not their coming till the opening of the year, till they might have better weather and way, and have longer days, and so more seasonable and fit to travel in. So desirous were they to come with the first, and to be there as soon as possibly they might; broke through all these difficulties, *Et ecce venerunt*, "And behold, come they did."

And we, what excuse shall we have if we come not? If so short and so easy a way we come not, as from our chambers hither, not to be called away indeed? Shall not our *non venerunt* have an *ecce*, 'Behold, it was stepping but over the threshold, and yet they came not'?

And these were wise men, and never a whit the less wise for so coming; nay never so truly wise in any thing they did, as in so coming. The Holy Ghost recordeth them for wise, *in capite libri*, 'even in the beginning of the New Testament.' Of Christ, when He came into the world, that is, when He was born, the Psalm saith, "In the beginning of the Book it was writ of Him, He said," *Ecce venio*, "Lo I come," (Ps. xl. 7): of these in the same words, when they came to meet Him so born, it is said here in the beginning of the Gospel, *Ecce venerunt*, "Behold they came."

And we, if we believe this, that this was their wisdom, if they and we be wise by one Spirit, by the same principles, we will follow the same star, tread the same way, and so come at last whither they are happily gone before us.

Nay, not only that "come," but this withal; to think and set down with ourselves, that to come to Christ is one of the wisest parts that ever these wise men did, or we or any else can do in all our lives.

And how shall we that do? I know not any more proper way left us, than to come to that which Himself by express order hath left us, as the most special remembrance of Himself to be come to. When He came into the world, saith the Psalm, that is at His birth now, He said, *Ecce venio*, "Lo, I come." What then? "Sacrifice and burnt-offerings Thou wouldst not have, but a body hast Thou ordained Me." (Ps. xl. 6.) Mark, saith the Apostle, "He takes away the first to establish the second," (Heb. x. 9), that is, to establish His body, and the coming to it. By the "offering," breaking and partaking of which "body, we are all sanctified," (Heb. x. 10), so many as shall come to it, For "given it is, for the taking away of our sins." (Matt. xxvi. 28.) Nothing is more fit than at the time His body was ordained Him, and that is to-day, to come to the body so ordained.

And in the old Ritual of the Church we find that on the cover of the canister, wherein was the sacrament of His body, there was a star engraven, to shew us that now the star leads us thither, to His body there.

And what shall I say now, but according as St. John saith, and the star, and the wise men say, "Come." (Rev. xxii. 17.) And He, Whose the star is, and to Whom the wise men came, saith "Come." And let them that are disposed, "Come." And let whosoever will, take of the "Bread of Life, which came down from Heaven" (John vi. 35, 41) this day into Bethlehem, the house of bread. Of which Bread the Church is this day the house, the true Bethlehem, and all the Bethlehem we have now left to come to for the Bread of life,—of that life which we hope for in Heaven. And this our nearest coming that here we can come, till we shall by another *venite* come, unto Him in His Heavenly Kingdom. To which He grant we may come, that this day came to us in earth that we thereby might come to Him and remain with Him for ever, "Jesus Christ the Righteous."

SERMON XV.

A Sermon Preached before the King's Majesty, at
Whitehall, on Wednesday, the Twenty-fifth of
December, a.d. mdcxxii., being Christmas-day.

*Behold there came wise men from the East to Jerusalem,
Saying, Where is the King of the Jews that is born? For we
have seen His star in the East, and are come to worship
Him.* Matthew ii. 1, 2.

[*Ecce magi ab Oriente venerunt Jerosolymam,
Dicentes, Ubi est Qui natus est Rex Judæorum? vidimus enim stellam
Ejus in Oriente, et venimus adorare Eum.* Latin Vulg.]

THERE be in these two verses two principal points, as
was observed when time was; 1. The persons that
arrived at Jerusalem, 2. and their errand. The persons in
the former verse, whereof hath been treated heretofore.
Their errand in the latter, whereof we are now to deal.

Their errand we may best learn from themselves out of
their *dicentes,* &c. Which, in a word, is to worship Him.
Their errand our errand, and the errand of this day.

This text may seem to come a little too soon, before the
time; and should have stayed till the day it was spoken on,
rather than on this day. But if you mark them well, there
are in the verse four words that be *verba diei hujus,* 'proper
and peculiar to this very day.' 1. For first, *natus est* is most
proper to this day of all days, the day of His Nativity. 2.
Secondly, *vidimus stellam;* for on this day it was first seen,
appeared first. 3. Thirdly, *venimus;* for this day they set
forth, began their journey. 4. And last, *adorare Eum;* for
"when He brought His only-begotten Son into the world,
He gave in charge, Let all the Angels of God worship Him."
(Heb. i. 6.) And when the Angels to do it, no time more
proper for us to do it as then. So these four appropriate it
to this day, and none but this.

The main heads of their errand are 1. *Vidimus stellam,* the
occasion; 2. and *Venimus adorare,* the end of their coming.
But for the better conceiving it I will take another course,
to set forth these points to be handled.

I. Their faith first: faith — in that they never ask

'Whether He be,' but "Where He is born;" for that born He is, that they steadfastly believe.

II. Then "the work or service (Phil. ii. 17) of this faith, as St. Paul calleth it; "the touch or trial," " δοκίμιον," (1 Peter i. 7), as St. Peter; the *ostende mihi*, (James ii. 18), as St. James; of this their faith in these five. 1. Their confessing of it in *venerunt dicentes*. *Venerunt*, they were no sooner come, but *dicentes*, they tell it out; confess Him and His birth to be the cause of their coming. 2. Secondly, as confess their faith, so the ground of their faith; *vidimus enim*, for they had "seen" His star; and His star being risen, by it they knew He must be risen too. 3. Thirdly, as St. Paul calls them in Abraham's, *vestigia fidei*, "the steps of their faith," (Rom. iv. 12), in *venimus*, "their coming "— coming such a journey, at such a time, with such speed. 4. Fourthly, when they were come, their diligent enquiring Him out by *ubi est?* for here is the place of it, asking after Him to find where He was. 5. And last, when they had found Him, the end of their seeing, coming, seeking; and all for no other end but to worship Him. Here they say it, at the 11th verse they do it in these two acts; 1. *procidentes*, their "falling down," 2. and *obtulerunt*, their "offering" to Him. Worship Him with their bodies, worship Him with their goods; their worship and ours the true worship of Christ.

The text is of a star, and we may make all run on a star, that so the text and day may be suitable, and Heaven and earth hold a correspondence. St. Peter calls faith "the day-star rising in our hearts," (2 Peter i. 19), which sorts well with the star in the text rising in the sky. That in the sky manifesting itself from above to them; this in their hearts manifesting itself from below to Him, to Christ. Manifesting itself by these five: 1. by *ore fit confessio*, "the confessing of it," (Rom. x. 10); 2. by *fides est substantia*, "the ground of it," (Heb. xi. 1); 3. by *vestigia fidei*, "the steps of it" (Rom. iv. 12) in their painful coming; 4. by their *ubi est?* "careful enquiring;" 5. and last, by *adorare Eum*, "their devout worshipping." These five, as so many beams of faith, the day-star risen in their hearts. To take notice of them. For every one of them is of the nature of a condition, so as if we fail in them, *non lucet nobis stella hæc*, 'we have no part in the light, or conduct of this star.' Neither in *stellam*, "the star itself," nor in *Ejus*, "in Him Whose the star is;" that is, not in Christ neither.

We have now got us a star on earth for that in Heaven, and these both lead us to a third. So as upon the matter three stars we have, and each his proper manifestation. 1. The first in the firmament; that appeared unto them, and in them to us—a figure of St. Paul's ᾽Επεφάνη χάρις, "the grace of God appearing, and bringing salvation to all men," (Tit. ii. 11), Jews and Gentiles and all. 2. The second here on earth is St. Peter's *Lucifer in cordibus;* and this appeared in them, and so must in us. Appeared 1. in their eyes—*vidimus;* 2. in their feet—*venimus;* 3. in their lips—*dicentes ubi est;* 4. in their knees—*procidentes*, "falling down;" 5. in their hands—*obtulerunt*, "by offering." These five every one a beam of this star. 3. The third in Christ Himself, St. John's star. "The generation and root of David, the bright morning Star, Christ." And He, His double appearing. 1. One at this time now, when He appeared in great humility; and we see and come to Him by faith. 2. The other, which we wait for, even "the blessed hope, and appearing of the great God and our Saviour" (Tit. ii. 13) in the majesty of His glory.

These three : 1. The first that manifested Christ to them ; 2. The second that manifested them to Christ; 3. The third Christ Himself, in Whom both these were as it were in conjunction. Christ "the bright morning Star" of that day which shall have no night; the *beatifica visio*, 'the blessed sight' of which day is the *consummatum est* of our hope and happiness for ever.

Of these three stars the first is gone, the third yet to come, the second only is present. We to look to that, and to the five beams of it. That is it must do us all the good, and bring us to the third.

I. St. Luke calleth faith the "door of faith." (Acts xiv. 27.) At this door let us enter. Here is a coming, and "he that cometh to God," and so he that to Christ, "must believe, that Christ is :" so do these. They never ask *an sit*, but *ubi sit ?* Not 'whether,' but "where He is born." They that ask *ubi Qui natus ?* take *natus* for granted, presuppose that born He is. Herein is faith—faith of Christ's being born, the third article of the Christian Creed.

And what believe they of Him? Out of their own words here; 1. first that *natus*, that "born" He is, and so Man He is—His human nature. 1. And as His nature, so His office in *natus est Rex*, "born a King." They believe that too. 3. But *Judæorum* may seem to be a bar; for then, what have they to do with "the King of the Jews"? They be Gentiles, none of His lieges, no relation to Him at all: what do they seeking or worshipping Him? But weigh it well, and it is no bar. For this they seem to believe: He is so *Rex Judæorum*, "King of the Jews," as He is *adorandus a Gentibus*, 'the Gentiles to adore Him.' And though born in Jewry, yet Whose birth concerned them though Gentiles, though born far off in the "mountains of the East." They to have some benefit by Him and His birth, and for that to do Him worship, seeing *officium fundatur in beneficio* ever. 4. As thus born in earth, so a star He hath in Heaven of His own—*stellam Ejus*, "His star;" He the owner of it. Now we know the stars are the stars of Heaven, and He that Lord of them Lord of Heaven too; and so to be adored of them, of us, and of all. St. John puts them together; "the root and generation of David," His earthly; and "the bright morning star," (Rev. xxii. 16), His Heavenly or Divine generation. *Hæc est fides Magorum*, this is the mystery of their faith. In *natus est*, man; in *stellam Ejus*, God. In *Rex*, "a King," though of the Jews, yet the good of Whose Kingdom should extend and stretch itself far and wide to Gentiles and all; and He of all to be adored. This, for *corde creditur*, the day-star itself in their hearts. Now to the beams of this star.

II. Next to *corde creditur* is *ore fit confessio*, "the confession" of this faith. It is in *venerunt dicentes*, they came with it in their mouths. *Venerunt*, they were no sooner come, but they spake of it so freely, to so many, as it came to Herod's ear and troubled him not a little that any King of the Jews should be worshipped beside himself. So then their faith is no bosom-faith, kept to themselves without ever a *dicentes*, without saying any thing of it to any body. No; *credidi, propter quod locutus sum*, "they believed, and therefore they spake." (Psa. cxvi. 10.) The star in their hearts cast one beam out at their mouths. And though Herod, who was but *Rex factus*, could evil brook to hear of

Rex natus,—must needs be offended at it, yet they were not afraid to say it. And though they came from the East, those parts to whom and their King the Jews had long time been captives and their underlings, they were not ashamed neither to tell, that One of the Jews' race they came to seek; and to seek Him to the end " to worship Him." So neither afraid of Herod, nor ashamed of Christ; but professed their errand, and cared not who knew it. This for their confessing Him boldly.

But faith is said by the Apostle to be ὑπόστασις, and so there is a good " ground;" and ἔλεγχος, and so hath a good " reason" for it. (Heb. xi. 1.) This puts the difference between *fidelis* and *credulus*, or as Solomon terms him, *fatuus qui credit omni verbo*, (Pro. xiv. 15); between faith and lightness of belief. Faith hath ever a ground; *vidimus enim,*—an *enim*, a reason for it, and is ready to render it. How came you to believe? *Audivimus enim*, " for we have heard an Angel," (Luke ii. 20), say the shepherds. *Vidimus enim,* " for we have seen a star," say the Magi, and this is a well-grounded faith. We came not of our own heads, we came not before we saw some reason for it— saw that which set us on coming; *Vidimus enim stellam Ejus.*

Vidimus stellam—we can well conceive that; any that will but look up, may see a star. But how could they see the *Ejus* of it, that it was His? Either that it belonged to any, or that He it was it belonged to. This passeth all perspective; no astronomy could shew them this. What by course of nature the stars can produce, that they by course of art or observation may discover. But this birth was above nature. No trigon, triplicity, exaltation could bring it forth. They are but idle that set figures for it. The star should not have been His, but He the star's, if it had gone that way. Some other light then, they saw this *Ejus* by.

Now with us in Divinity there be but two in all; 1. *Vespertina*, and 2. *Matutina lux*. *Vespertina*, 'the owl-light' of our reason or skill is too dim to see it by. No remedy then but it must be as Esay calls it, *matutina lux*, " the morning-light," the light of God's law must certify them of the *Ejus* of it. There, or not at all to be had whom this star did portend.

And in the Law, there we find it in the twenty-fourth of Numbers. (Num. xxiv. 17.) One of their own Prophets that came from whence they came, " from the mountains of the East," was ravished in spirit, " fell in a trance, had his eyes opened," and saw the *Ejus* of it many an hundred years before it rose. Saw *orietur in Jacob*, that there it should " rise," which is as much as *natus est* here. Saw *stella*, that he should be " the bright morning-Star," and so might well have a star to represent Him. Saw *sceptrum in Israel*, which is just as much as *Rex Judæorum*, that it should portend a King there —such a King as should not only " smite the corners of Moab," that is Balak their enemy for the present; but " should reduce and bring under Him all the sons of Seth," that is all the world; for all are now Seth's sons, Cain's were all drowned in the flood. Here now is the *Ejus* of it clear. A Prophet's eye might discern this; never a Chaldean of them all could take it with his astrolabe. Balaam's eyes were open to see it, and he helped to open their eyes by leaving behind him this prophecy to direct them how to apply it, when it should arise to the right *Ejus* of it.

But these had not the law. It is hard to say that the Chaldee paraphrase was extant long before this. They might have had it. Say, they had it not: if Moses was so careful to record this prophecy in his book, it may well be thought that some memory of this so memorable a prediction was left remaining among them of the East, his own country where he was born and brought up. And some help they might have from Daniel too, who lived all his time in Chaldea and Persia, and prophesied among them of such a King, and set the just time of it.

And this, as it is conceived, put the difference between the East and the West. For I ask, was it *vidimus in Oriente* with them? Was it not *vidimus in Occidente?* In the West such a star—it or the fellow of it was seen nigh about that time, or the Roman stories deceive us. Toward the end of Augustus' reign such a star was seen, and much scanning there was about it. Pliny saith it was generally holden, that star to be *faustum sydus*, a 'lucky comet,' and portended good to the world, which few or no comets do. And Virgil, who then lived, would needs take upon him to set down the *ejus* of it, ... *Ecce Dionæi, &c.*—entitled Cæsar to it,

And verily there is no man that can without admiration read his sixth Eclogue, of a birth that time expected, that should be the offspring of the gods, and that should take away their sins. Whereupon it hath gone for current—the East and West, *Vidimus* both.

But by the light of their prophecy, the East, they went straight to the right *Ejus.* And for want of this light the West wandered, and gave it a wrong *ejus ;* as Virgil, applying it to little Salonine : and as evil hap was, while he was making his verses, the poor child died ; and so his star shot, vanished, and came to nothing. Their *vidimus* never came to a *venimus ;* they neither went, nor worshipped Him as these here did.

But by this we see, when all is done, hither we must come for our morning-light ; to this book, to the word of prophecy. All our *vidimus stellam* is as good as nothing without it. That star is past and gone, long since ; " Heaven and earth shall pass, but this word shall not pass." Here on this, we to fix our eye and to ground our faith. Having this, though we neither hear Angel nor see star, we may by the grace of God do full well. For even they that have had both those, have been fain to resolve into this as their last, best, and chiefest point of all. Witness St. Peter : he, saith he, and they with him, " saw Christ's glory, and heard the voice from Heaven in the Holy Mount," (2 Peter i. 17-19). What then ? After both these, *audivimus* and *vidimus*, both senses, he comes to this, *Habemus autem firmiorem, &c.* " We have a more sure word of prophecy " than both these ; *firmiorem*, a " more sure," a more clear, than them both. And *si hîc legimus*— for *legimus* is *vidimus*, ' if here we read it written,' it is enough to ground our faith, and let the star go.

And yet, to end this point ; both these, the star and the prophecy, they are but *circumfusa lux*—without both. Besides these there must be a light within in the eye ; else, we know, for all them nothing will be seen. And that must come from Him, and the enlightening of His Spirit. Take this for a rule ; no knowing of *Ejus absque Eo*, ' of His without Him,' Whose it is. Neither of the star, without Him That created it ; nor of the prophecy, without Him That inspired it. But this third coming too ; He sending the light of His Spirit within into their minds, they then saw clearly, this the star, now the time, He the Child That this day was born.

He That sent these two without, sent also this third within, and then it was *vidimus* indeed. The light of the star in their eyes, the "word of prophecy" in their ears, the beam of His Spirit in their hearts; these three made up a full *vidimus*. And so much for *vidimus stellam Ejus*, the occasion of their coming.

Now to *venimus*, their coming itself. And it follows well. For it is not a star only, but a load-star; and whither should *stella Ejus ducere*, but *ad Eum*? 'Whither lead us, but to Him Whose the star is?' The star to the star's Master.

All this while we have been at *dicentes*, "saying" and seeing; now we shall come to *facientes*, see them do somewhat upon it. It is not saying nor seeing will serve St. James; he will call, and be still calling for *ostende mihi*, "shew me thy faith by some work." (James ii. 18.) And well may he be allowed to call for it this day; it is the day of *vidimus*, appearing, being seen. You have seen His star, let Him now see your star another while. And so they do. Make your faith to be seen; so it is—their faith in the steps of their faith. And so was Abraham's first by coming forth of his country; as these here do, and so "walk in the steps of the faith of Abraham," (Rom. iv. 12), do his first work.

It is not commended to stand "gazing up into Heaven" (Acts i. 11) too long; not on Christ Himself ascending, much less on His star. For they sat not still gazing on the star. Their *vidimus* begat *venimus;* their seeing made them come, come a great journey. *Venimus* is soon said, but a short word; but many a wide and weary step they made before they could come to say *Venimus*, Lo, here "we are come;" come, and at our journey's end. To look a little on it. In this their coming we consider, 1. First, the distance of the place they came from. It was not hard by as the shepherds—but a step to Bethlehem over the fields; this was riding many a hundred miles, and cost them many a day's journey. 2. Secondly, we consider the way that they came, if it be pleasant, or plain and easy; for if it be, it is so much the better. 1. This was nothing pleasant, for through deserts, all the way waste and desolate. 2. Nor secondly, easy either; for over the rocks and crags of both Arabias, specially Petræa, their journey lay. 3. Yet if safe

—but it was not, but exceeding dangerous, as lying through the midst of the "black tents of Kedar," (Cant. i. 5), a nation of thieves and cut-throats; to pass over the hills of robbers, infamous then, and infamous to this day. No passing without great troop or convoy. 4. Last we consider the time of their coming, the season of the year. It was no summer progress. A cold coming they had of it at this time of the year, just the worst time of the year to take a journey, and specially a long journey in. The ways deep, the weather sharp, the days short, the sun farthest off, *in solstitio brumali*, 'the very dead of winter.' *Venimus*, "we are come," if that be one, *venimus*, "we are now come," come at this time, that sure is another.

And these difficulties they overcame, of a wearisome, irksome, troublesome, dangerous, unseasonable journey; and for all this they came. And came it cheerfully and quickly, as appeareth by the speed they made. It was but *vidimus, venimus*, with them; "they saw," and "they came;" no sooner saw, but they set out presently. So as upon the first appearing of the star, as it might be last night, they knew it was Balaam's star; it called them away, they made ready straight to begin their journey this morning. A sign they were highly conceited of His birth, believed some great matter of it, that they took all these pains, made all this haste that they might be there to worship Him with all the possible speed they could. Sorry for nothing so much as that they could not be there soon enough, with the very first, to do it even this day, the day of His birth. All considered, there is more in *venimus* than shews at the first sight. It was not for nothing it was said in the first verse, *ecce venerunt;* their coming hath an *ecce* on it, it well deserves it.

And we, what should we have done? Sure these men of the East shall rise in judgment against the men of the West, (Matt. viii. 11), that is us, and their faith against ours in this point. With them it was but *vidimus, venimus;* with us it would have been but *veniemus* at most. Our fashion is to see and see again before we stir a foot, specially if it be to the worship of Christ. Come such a journey at such a time? No; but fairly have put it off to the spring of the year, till the days longer, and the ways fairer, and the weather warmer, till better travelling to Christ. Our

Epiphany would sure have fallen in Easter-week at the soonest.

But then for the distance, desolateness, tediousness, and the rest, any of them were enough to mar our *venimus* quite. It must be no great way, first, we must come; we love not that. Well fare the shepherds, yet they came but hard by; rather like them than the Magi. Nay, not like them neither. For with us the nearer, lightly the farther off; our proverb is you know, 'The nearer the Church, the farther from God.'

Nor it must not be through no desert, over no Petræa. If rugged or uneven the way, if the weather ill-disposed, if any never so little danger, it is enough to stay us. To Christ we cannot travel, but weather and way and all must be fair. If not, no journey, but sit still and see farther. As indeed, all our religion is rather *vidimus*, a contemplation, than *venimus*, a motion, or stirring to do aught.

But when we do it, we must be allowed leisure. Ever *veniemus*, never *venimus;* ever coming, never come. We love to make no very great haste. To other things perhaps; not to *adorare*, the place of the worship of God. Why should we? Christ is no wild-cat. What talk ye of twelve days? And if it be forty days hence, ye shall be sure to find His Mother and Him; she cannot be churched till then. What needs such haste? The truth is, we conceit Him and His birth but slenderly, and our haste is even thereafter. But if we be at that point, we must be out of this *venimus;* they like enough to leave us behind. Best get us a new Christmas in September; we are not like to come to Christ at this feast. Enough for *venimus*.

But what is *venimus* without *invenimus?* And when they come, they hit not on Him at first. No more must we think, as soon as ever we be come, to find him straight. They are fain to come to their *ubi est?* We must now look back to that. For though it stand before in the verse, here is the right place of it. They saw before they came, and came before they asked; asked before they found, and found before they worshipped. Between *venimus*, "their coming," and *adorare*, "their worshipping," there is the true place of *dicentes, ubi est?*

Where, first, we note a double use of their *dicentes*, these wise men had. 1. As to manifest what they knew, *natus est*, "that He is born," so to confess and ask what they knew not, the place where. We to have the like.

2. Secondly, set down this; that to find where He is, we must learn of these to ask where He is, which we full little set ourselves to do. If we stumble on Him, so it is; but for any asking we trouble not ourselves, but sit still as we say, and let nature work; and so let grace too, and so for us it shall. I wot well, it is said in a place of Esay, "He was found," *a non quærentibus*, "of some that sought Him not," (Isa. lxv. 1), never asked *ubi est?* But it is no good holding by that place. It was their good hap that so did. But trust not to it, it is not every body's case, that. It is better advice you shall read in the Psalm, *hæc est generatio quærentium*, "there is a generation of them that seek Him." (Ps. xxiv. 6.) Of which these were, and of that generation let us be. Regularly there is no promise of *invenietis* but to *quærite*, of finding but to such as "seek." It is not safe to presume to find Him otherwise.

I thought there had been small use now of *ubi est?* Yet there is except we hold the ubiquity, that Christ is *ubi non*, 'any where.' But He is not so. Christ hath His *ubi*, His proper place where He is to be found; and if you miss of that, you miss of Him. And well may we miss, saith Christ Himself, there are so many will take upon them to tell us where, and tell us of so many *ubis*. *Ecce hîc*, "Look you, here He is;" *Ecce illîc*, nay then, "there." *In deserto*, "in the desert." Nay, *in penetralibus*, "in such a privy conventicle," (Matt. xxiv. 23), you shall be sure of Him. And yet He, saith He Himself, in none of them all. There is then yet place for *ubi est?* I speak not of His natural body but of His mystical—that is Christ too.

How shall we then do? Where shall we get this "where" resolved? Where these did. They said it to many, and oft, but gat no answer, till they had got together a convocation of Scribes, and they resolved them of Christ's *ubi*. For they in the East were nothing so wise, or well seen, as we in the West are now grown. We need call no Scribes together, and get them tell us, "where." Every artisan hath a whole Synod of Scribes in his brain, and can tell where Christ is better than any learned man of them all. Yet these were wise men; best learn where they did.

And how did the Scribes resolve it then? Out of Micah. As before to the star they join Balaam's prophecy, so now again to His *orietur*, that such a one should be born, they had put Micah's *et tu Bethlehem,* the place of His birth. Still helping, and giving light as it were to the light of Heaven, by a more clear light, the light of the Sanctuary.

Thus then to do. And to do it ourselves, and not seek Christ *per alium ;* set others about it as Herod did these, and sit still ourselves. For so, we may hap never find Him no more than he did.

And now we have found "where," what then? It is neither in seeking nor finding, *venimus* nor *iuvenimus ;* the end of all, the cause of all is in the last words, *adorare Eum,* " to worship Him." That is all in all, and without it all our seeing, coming, seeking, and finding is to no purpose. The Scribes they could tell, and did tell where He was, but were never the nearer for it, for they worshipped Him not. For this end to seek Him.

This is acknowledged : Herod, in effect, said as much. He would know where He were fain, and if they will bring him word where, he will come too and worship Him, that he will. None of that worship. If he find Him, his worshipping will prove worrying; as did appear by a sort of silly poor lambs that he worried, when he could not have his will on Christ. (Matt. ii. 16.) Thus he at His birth.

And at His death, the other Herod, he sought Him too; but it was that he and his soldiers might make themselves sport with Him. (Luke xxiii. 11.) Such seeking there is otherwhile. And such worshipping; as they in the judgment-hall worshipped Him with *Ave Rex*, and then gave Him a bob blindfold. (John xix. 3.) The world's worship of Him for the most part.

But we may be bold to say, Herod was " a fox." (Luke xiii. 32.) These mean as they say; to worship Him they come, and worship Him they will. Will they so? Be they well advised what they promise, before they know whether they shall find Him in a worshipful taking or no? For full little know they, where and in what case they shall find Him. What, if in a stable, laid there in a manger, and the rest suitable to it ; in as poor and pitiful a plight as ever was any, more like to be abhorred than adored of such persons? Will they be as good as their word, trow? Will they not step back at the sight, repent themselves of their journey, and wish themselves at home again? But so find Him, and so finding Him, worship Him for all that? If they will, verily then great is their faith. This, the clearest beam of all.

"The Queen of the South," (Matt. xii. 42), who was a figure of these Kings of the East, she came as great a journey as these. But when she came, she found a King indeed, King Solomon in all his royalty. Saw a glorious King, and a glorious court about him. Saw him, and heard him; tried him with many hard questions, received satisfaction of them all. This was worth her coming. Weigh what she found, and what these here—as poor and unlikely a birth as could be, ever to prove a King, or any great matter. No sight to comfort them, nor a word for which they any whit the wiser; nothing worth their travel. Weigh these together, and great odds will be found between her faith and theirs. Theirs the greater far.

Well, they will take Him as they find Him, and all this notwithstanding, worship Him for all that. The Star shall make amends for the manger, and for *stella Ejus* they will dispense with *Eum*.

And what is it to worship? Some great matter sure it is, that Heaven and earth, the stars and Prophets, thus do but serve to lead them and conduct us to. For all we see ends in *adorare*. *Scriptura et mundus ad hoc sunt, ut colatur Qui creavit, et adoretur Qui inspiravit;* 'the Scripture and world are but to this end, that He That created the one and inspired the other might be but worshipped.' Such reckoning did these seem to make of it here. And such the great treasurer of the Queen Candace. These came from the mountains in the East; he from the uttermost part of Æthiopia came, (Acts viii. 27), and came for no other end but only this—to worship; and when they had done that, home again. *Tanti est adorare.* Worth the while, worth our coming, if coming we do but that, but worship and nothing else. And so I would have men account of it.

To tell you what it is in particular, I must put you over to the eleventh verse, where it is set down what they did when they worshipped. It is set down in two acts προσκυνεῖν, and προσφέρειν, "falling down," and "offering." Thus did they, thus we to do; we to do the like when we will

R

worship. These two are all, and more than these we find not.

We can worship God but three ways, we have but three things to worship Him withal.   1. The soul He hath inspired; 2. the body He hath ordained us; 3. and the worldly goods He hath vouchsafed to bless us withal.   We to worship Him with all, seeing there is but one reason for all.

If He breathed into us our soul, but framed not our body, but some other did that, neither bow your knee nor uncover your head, but keep on your hats, and sit even as you do hardly.   But if He hath framed that body of yours and every member of it, let Him have the honour both of head and knee, and every member else.

Again, if it be not He That gave us our worldly goods but somebody else, what He gave not, that withhold from Him and spare not.   But if all come from Him, all to return to Him.   If He send all, to be worshipped with all.   And this in good sooth is but *rationabile obsequium*, as the Apostle calleth it. (Rom. xii. 1.)   No more than reason would, we should worship Him with all.

Else if all our worship be inward only, with our hearts and not our hats as some fondly imagine, we give Him but one of three ; we put Him to His thirds, bid Him be content with that, He gets no more but inward worship.   That is out of the text quite.   For though I doubt not but these here performed that also, yet here it is not.   St. Matthew mentions it not, it is not to be seen, no *vidimus* on it.   And the text is a *vidimus*, and of a star ; that is, of an outward visible worship to be seen of all.   There is a *vidimus* upon the worship of the body, it may be seen—*procidentes*.   Let us see you fall down.   So is there upon the worship with our worldly goods, that may be seen and felt—*offerentes*. Let us see whether, and what you offer.   With both which, no less than with the soul, God is to be worshipped. "Glorify God with your bodies, for they are God's," (1 Cor. vi. 20), saith the Apostle.   "Honour God with your substance, for He hath blessed your store," (Prov. iii. 9), saith Solomon.   It is the precept of a wise King, of one there ; it is the practice of more than one, of these three here. Specially now ; for Christ hath now a body, for which to do Him worship with our bodies.   And now He was made poor to make us rich, and so *offerentes* will do well, comes very fit.

To enter farther into these two would be too long, and indeed they be not in our verse here, and so for some other treatise at some other time.

There now remains nothing but to include ourselves, and bear our part with them, and with the Angels, and all who this day adored Him.

This was the load-star of the Magi, and what were they? Gentiles. So are we. But if it must be ours, then we are to go with them; *vade, et fac similiter,* "go, and do likewise." (Luke x. 37.) It is *Stella gentium,* but *idem agentium* 'the Gentiles' star,' but 'such Gentiles as overtake these and keep company with them.' In their *dicentes,* "confessing their faith freely;" in their *vidimus,* "grounding it throughly;" in their *venimus,* "hasting to come to Him speedily;" in their *ubi est?* "enquiring Him out diligently;" and in their *adorare Eum,* "worshipping Him devoutly." *Per omnia* doing as these did; worshipping and thus worshipping, celebrating and thus celebrating the feast of His birth.

We cannot say *vidimus stellam;* the star is gone long since, not now to be seen. Yet I hope for all that, that *venimus adorare,* "we be come thither to worship." It will be the more acceptable, if not seeing it we worship though. It is enough we read of it in the text; we see it there. And indeed as I said, it skills not for the star in the firmament, if the same Day-Star be risen in our hearts that was in theirs, and the same beams of it to be seen, all five. For then we have our part in it no less, nay full out as much as they. And it will bring us whither it brought them, to Christ. Who at His second appearing in glory shall call forth these wise men and all that have ensued the steps of their faith, and that upon the reason specified in the text; for I have seen their star shining and shewing forth itself by the like beams; and as they came to worship Me, so am I come to do them worship. A *venite* then, for a *venimus* now. Their star I have seen, and give them a place above among the stars. They fell down: I will lift them up, and exalt them. And as they offered to Me, so am I come to bestow on them, and to reward them with the endless joy and bliss of My Heavenly Kingdom.

To which, &c.

SERMON XVI.

A Sermon Preached before the King's Majesty, at Whitehall, on Thursday, the Twenty-fifth of December, a.d. mdcxxiii., being Christmas-day.

That in the dispensation of the fulness of the times, He might gather together into one all things, both which are in Heaven, and which are in earth, even in Christ.
Ephesians i. 10.

In dispensatione plenitudinis temporum, instaurare omnia, in Christo, quæ in Cælis, et quæ in terra sunt, in Ipso.

SEEING the text is of seasons, it would not be out of season itself. And though it never be out of season to speak of Christ, yet even Christ hath His seasons. "Your time is always," (John vii. 6), saith He, so is not Mine; I have My seasons. One of which seasons is this, the season of His birth, whereby all were "recapitulate in Heaven and earth," which is the season of the text. And so, this a text of the season.

There is for the most part in each text some one predominant word. That word in this is the word ἀνακεφαλαι-ώσασθαι, here turned "gathering together into one again." To know the nature and full force of it, we may consider it three ways: 1. as it is properly taken: 2. as it is extended; 3. as it is derived.

1. As it is taken properly. So it signifies "to make the foot of an account." We call it the foot, because we write it below at the foot. They of old writ theirs above, over the head, and so called it κεφάλαιον (*in capite libri Scriptum est de me*) (Ps. xl. 7) the sum in the top.

2. As it is extended. So it is "the short recapitulation of a long chapter," the compendium of a book or of some discourse. These are all like the foot of an account, and are usually called the sum of all that hath been said.

3. As it is derived. So shall we have the native sense of it. It comes of κεφάλαιον, and that of κεφαλὴ, Greek for 'a head.' Best expressed in the word 'recapitulate;' that is, to reduce all to a head. Each of these is a gathering together into one, as we read. Which of the three you

take, nay take them all three, you cannot do amiss. They be all true, all tend to edify. Christ is the 1. sum of our account, 2. the shutting up of our discourse, 3. "the Head of the body" (Col. i. 18, and Eph. iv. 15, 16) mystical whereto this gathering here is. We shall make no good audit without Him; no, nor good apology. Whatsoever be the premises, with Christ we must conclude. As we do the year with Christmas, so conclude all with *in Christo*.

The old division is—*ut res, ita tempora rerum.* Here it holds, here are both seasons and things; things for seasons, and seasons for things.

I. Two parts here be. 1. Seasons, first; seasons, more than one. 2. Here is a fulness of them. 3. Here is a dispensation of that fulness. 4. And that by God; "that He," that is God—"that in the dispensation of the fulness of times He might." This is the first part.

II. The "things." For first, here are "all things; things in Heaven, things on earth"—all in both. 2. Of these, a collection or gathering them all together; or rather, a recollection or gathering them together again. 3. A gathering them all into one; all into one *κεφάλαιον,* one "sum;" or all to one *κεφαλὴ,* one "head." And these two are one, and that one is Christ.

You observe, that as the things answer the seasons, and the seasons them, so doth the fulness answer the gathering, and the gathering it. 1. To fill the seasons, to make a fulness of them, here is a gathering. 2. A gathering whereof? Of all in Heaven, and all on earth—a great gathering sure, and able to fill the seasons full up to the brim. 3. But this is not a gathering at the first hand, but a gathering again, that is, a-new at second-hand. 4. A gathering whereto? "To one"—one, either one sum, or one head, both are in the body of the word, and these two are one, and that one is Christ. 5. A gathering, how? that is in the word too: by way of contracting or recapitulation. 6. And when? When God dispensed it; and that is at Christ's birth. 7. Now last, what we are the better by this gathering, what fruit we gather by or from it, what our share is in this sum, which is *summa dividenda.* 8. And then how we may be the better for it, if we divide as God, and when God did it. 9. As God, gather things in Heaven first. 10. When God, and that is this season of the year, the gathering time with God and with us. So shall we dispense the season well.

Find the things, they will bring you to the season; find the fulness of things, you shall find the fulness of seasons. Find the gathering, you shall find the fulness; find Christ, and you shall find the gathering, for the gathering is full and whole in Christ. So, upon the point, find Christ and find all. And this is the first day we can find Him; for this day was He born, and so first to be found by us.

We have heretofore dealt with "the fulness of time;" and now are we to deal with the fulness of season. Time and season are two, and have in all tongues two different words to shew they differ. In Hebrew, ומן and עת; in Greek, χρόνος and καιρὸς; in Latin, *tempus* and *tempestivum.*

And differ they do as much as a time, and a good time. It is time alway, all the year long; so is it not season, but when the good time is. Time is taken at large, any time. Season not so, but is applied to that with which it suits, or for which it serves best. Here it is applied to gathering, the season of gathering.

These seasons be καιρῶν in the plural; for,—*ut res, ita tempora rerum,* 'as the things to be gathered are many, so are the seasons wherein they are to be gathered, many likewise.' Each, his several season to be gathered in.

Now as 'the things,' *res,* have their autumn of maturity, so *tempora,* 'the seasons' have their fulness, and when the things are ripe and ready to be gathered, then is the season full.

Now of these seasons and their fulness there is "a dispensation," an *œconomia,* the word in the text, which is a word of husbandry; a great part whereof consisteth in the skill of seasons, of taking them when they come, allotting the thing to the season, and the season to it.

Which dispensation is here ascribed to God; that He, that is, that God "in Whose hands our times are," saith the Psalm, and our seasons, (Psa. civ. 27, 28; cxlv. 15, 16), both. He that can make them full by giving us kindly seasons, or empty by making them unseasonable, and having made them full is to dispose of them of very right. There is none of these but is sensible in the course of the year, in things upon earth.

But are there seasons for the things on earth and their

fulness, and are there not also seasons for the things in
Heaven and for the filling of them? All for relief of the
bodily wants here below, none for the supply of spiritual
necessities above? All for the body, and never a season
for the soul? If we allow them to the world, shall we not
to the Church, ἀναχεφαλαίωσις or 'abridgment' of the
world? If it be sensible in the natural things, though not
so easily discerned, yet it is as certain in the main revolution of *annus magnus*, 'the great periodical year' of the
world's endurance.

It can never enter into any man to think that the great
Œconomus or 'Steward of this great household,' the world,
should so far forget Himself, but if for all matters He "had
appointed a season," (Eccl. iii. 1), then for the greatest
matter. If for every purpose under Heaven, then for the
highest purpose of all, that as we see concerneth all the
things in Heaven and earth both. Above *salus populi* this
salus mundi, 'the saving the whole world.' Shall not these
have their seasons, and the seasons their fulness there, and
that fulness the due dispensation of all other most worthy
of God, the greatest work of the greatest Person? Set this
down then to begin with: there are seasons, as in our common
year of twelve months, so in the great year, whereof every
day is a year by Daniel's, nay, "a thousand years," (2 Pet.
iii. 8), by St. Peter's calculation.

And which be the seasons, and when, in the common
year? Our Saviour sets them down. 1. The season
"when the earth bringeth forth the blade," (Mark iv. 28);
2. when "the stalk;" 3. when "the ear;" 4. when "the
full corn in the ear." And when the ear is full, and full
ripe, the season is full; then is the season of fulness, the
fulness of season. Then "the reaper fills his hand, and he
that bindeth up the sheaves his bosom." (Psa. cxxix. 7.)
"Then are the barns filled with plenty, and the presses run
over with new wine." (Prov. iii. 10.) And when all is full,
then to gathering we go.

Such like seasons do we find *in anno magno*. 1. The
time of nature, all in the blade; 2. of Moses, in the stalk;
3. of the Prophets, in the ear. 4. And when the full corn?
When but at this great gathering here mentioned? When
all in Heaven, and all in earth gathered, that I think
was the fulness of things, *plenitudo rerum;* and the

fulness of seasons, *plenitudo temporum*, may be allowed for it.

II. This sets us over to the second part, from the seasons to the things; from the fulness of seasons to the gathering of things. And first, whereof, of what things? Of τὰ πάντα, "even all." "All;" and to shew the extent of it, subdivided into "all in Heaven, all in earth;" and that I trow is "all." It was not amiss he should thus sever them, and express things in Heaven by name; else we should little have thought of gathering things there so high. No farther than earth, we; there is all our gathering, and there only. The Apostle points up to Heaven—*sursum corda*, "to lift up our hearts, to set our affections on things there above," (Col. iii. 1, 2), to gather them. There is a gathering of them also.

Of which gathering into one, I know not what the things in Heaven have—the things on earth I am sure have good cause to be glad. In Heaven is all good, and nothing but good. In earth, to say the least, there is much evil. Yet upon the reckoning, Heaven is like to come by the loss; we on earth are sensibly gainers by it. It is a good hearing for us, that both these shall be thus gathered together. For if Heaven and earth be so gathered, it is that Heaven may advance earth higher; and no meaning, that earth should draw it down hither. *Magis dignum semper ad se trahit minus dignum*, is the old rule.

But well: between them both here is a great gathering toward, well expressed by the Apostle in the terms of a sum. For it is *summa summarum*, 'a sum indeed;' Heaven and earth, and the fulness of them both.

All these to be gathered, and well. Gathering God favours, for it ends in unity, to gather into one; and unity God loves, Himself being *principalis unitas*. God favours it sure, Himself is the gatherer. Scattering God favours not; that tends to division, and division upon division. Gathering is good for us; unity preserves, division destroys. *Divisum est*, be it house or be it kingdom, ever ends in *desolabitur.* (Mat. xii. 25.) God "delights not in destruction," (Ez. xxxiii. 11), "would have none to perish." (2 Peter iii. 9.) The kite, he scatters; the hen, how fain would she gather!

But stay awhile, and take with us what kind of gathering. It is not κεφαλαίωσις, 'a gathering;' but ἀνακεφαλαίωσις, "a gathering together again." We must not lose ἀνὰ, there is force in it. It is not a collection, but a recollection. *Re* imports it is a new collection again, the second time. You see it in *recal, return, reduce ;* that is, to call, turn, bring back again.

Now our rule is, ἀνὰ ever presupposeth ἀπὸ. Ἀνακεφαλαίωσις presupposeth ἀποκεφαλαίωσις : that is, a returning to implies a departing from : "a gathering together again," a scattering in sunder before ; "a dispensation," a dissipation. So a dissipation, a departure, a scattering there had been.

Yet one degree more. Ἀπὸ, that is 'from,' ever implies σὺν, that is a former being 'with.' One cannot be said to be gone from, that was never with ; or to fall out, that was never in : one cannot be said to be so again, that was never so before. So then together we were first ; and in sunder we fell after. Which falling in sunder required an ἀνὰ to bring us together again, to restore us to that the second time that we had before lost, to our former estate. It is St. Peter's word "restoring," (Acts iii. 21), the same with St. Paul's "gathering together again" here.

Now these three set forth unto us our threefold estate. 1. 'Together,' σὺν, our first original, which we had in Adam, while he stood with God together. 2. 'In sunder,' ἀπὸ,—there came our misery, by Adam's not keeping his first estate, but scattering from God. 3. But then comes ἀνὰ about, and makes all well again, by bringing us where we were at the first. There was a former capitulation—the articles were broken : then came this recapitulation here anew. An account was cast, but it was mis-cast, and so it is here cast new over again.

But when all is done, ἀνὰ is it we must hold by. The first is gone, all perished by being scattered from. All must be recovered by being gathered to again. Our Separation, our ruin ; our reparation, our ἀνὰ, our 'gathering again ;' and not ours alone, but *salus mundi*, of "all in Heaven all in earth."

But this we may see by the way, 1. what case all were in : 2. what case all are in still, that lie loose and ungathered, and whom ἀνὰ hath not recollected again.

We see what and how gathered. Now *quo?* the next point is, whereto ? Into one. Every thing that is gathered is so. But there is more ones than one. One heap, as of stones; one flock, as of sheep; one pile, as of the materials of a building. All are good; but to take the word in the native sense, the gathering here is either to one κεφάλαιον, "one sum," as many numbers; or to go nearer, to one κεφαλὴ, "one head," as many members—and that is it the Apostle pursueth to the chapter's end. Both these, sum and head, are in the body of the word κεφάλαιον, and they both serve and suit well. The body: the head is as it were the sum of all; all 1. sense, 2. motion, 3. speech, 4. understanding, all recapitulate into the head. This of head or sum fitteth it best. For to speak properly, many heaps, flocks, piles there may be; heads there can be but one. *De ratione capitis est, unum esse.* And so of a sum, but one true sum, were there never so many so divers ways cast.

So then into one, that is not enough; it is not co-adunation will serve. It is recapitulation, and in that word there is *caput;* it is ἀνακεφαλαίωσις, and in that word there is κεφαλὴ, such a reducing all to one, as that one be the head. A headless gathering the Apostle cannot skill of. And indeed, say there were an entire body, and every member in his right place, and all strictly knit together, yet if the head should hap to be away, as good the members all in sunder, for all were to no purpose. So, a head or nothing.

This gathering then, you see, is to the chief member, to the member that wears the crown. Thither, upward, the true gathering goes. There is an union downwards, as of Samson's foxes, that were together by the tails, (Judges xv. 4); that is not the right, but by the head. The oxen that plough are joined together by the head; the foxes that are tied by the tails, they set all on fire. The unity of the head God send us! that is the true unity.

And yet are we not where we should. We may gather upward too, and make a head, and not the right head. That to a head is not enough, if it fall out to be a wrong head, suppose Romely's son. (Isa. vii. 9.) *Humano capiti, &c.* Do but paint, saith the Poet, anybody with a wrong head, it will but move laughter and scorn. The right, the own head it would be. A strange head will not suit, nor do us any stead. The right head then.

And which is the right head he adds? *Recapitulati in Christo*—it is Christ. There, lo, is the right head now. To That let all gather.

And now we are arrived at Christ, we are where we should, our gathering is at the best. All in Heaven, all in earth, gathered together, together again—again into one, one sum whereof Christ is the foot, one body whereof Christ is the Head. Gather then, and be gathered to Him ; gather then, and be gathered with Him. " He that gathereth not with Him scattereth." (Luke xi. 23.)

And so were all, all scattered without Christ, till He came with His ἀνὰ, and got them again together. The seasons were all empty, the things all on heaps.

Things in Heaven from things in earth—Angels with " drawn swords at men." (Gen. iii. 24.) Things on earth from things in Heaven—men at but the sight of an Angel ready to fall down dead. (Judges xiii. 22.) The members from the head, the head from the members, the members one from another : neither union with the head, nor among themselves. *Peccata vestra,* (Jer. v. 25), it was sin that divided between God and them, and divided once and divided ever, divided *in semper divisibilia,* 'till they were quite past all division ;' no longer divided now, but even scattered. The case of the world then.

Scattered in point of religion. Gods scattered all over, " as many gods as cities." (Jer. ii. 28.) All the hosts of Heaven, all the beasts and creeping things of the earth.

Scattered in point of morality or moral philosophy. I know not how many scattered opinions Augustine reckons *de Summo Bono,* the chief point of all.

The Jews scattered from the Gentiles, and the Gentiles from the Jews—a main wall between. (Eph. ii. 14.)

The Gentiles scattered from themselves grossly ; all in fractions, they. Nothing of a body, never a head ; and yet many heads, but never a right one among them all.

No, not the Jews themselves; for " the Tabernacle of David " was then down, and the ruins of it scattered into many sects, as the Prophet Amos complains, (Amos ix. 11), and St. James allegeth it out of him. (Acts xv. 16.) In a word, the whole world then was but a mass of errors, a chaos of confusion, *Tohu* and *Bohu ;* " empty and void " (Gen. i. 2) of all saving grace or truth. Well likened to them that were scattered at the tower of Babel, where no man understood another, (Gen. xi. 7) ; or to the people that were " scattered all over the land of Egypt to gather stubble, to pick up straws." (Exodus v. 12.) All then wandering hither and thither, and seeking "death in the error of their life." (Wisd. i. 12.) By all which you see what need there was of this gathering, this ἀνακεφαλαίωσις.

Now then if, "for the divisions of Reuben, there were great thoughts of heart," (Judges v. 15), as it is in Deborah's song, for but one tribe scattered from the rest, shall there be no thought or course taken for these, such, so general, so many, not divisions but plain dispersions, scattering all abroad? Great pity that all these should lie thus loose and ungathered, as if they were not worth the taking up. He that in John vi. took order for the broken meat, for the fragments, willed them to be gathered ἵνα μή τι ἀπόληται, "that nothing might be lost," (John vi. 12)—no, not of them, He certainly were no good *Œconomus* if He would let all these be lost for lack of gathering.

But could not this gathering be *absque Christo*, in some other? It appears no. Seasons there were more than one, but all empty; proffers were made in them, but nothing full, nor anything near full. A season of the Law unwritten. Then came the Patriarchs. But they had much ado to keep themselves from scattering; they gathered none.

A season of the Law written. Then the Priests and Levites; but the gathering little the fuller for them.

Then came all the Prophets, to no great purpose they neither; some few proselytes they made, that was all. But in the end, all these, as they in the parable of the wounded man, "passed by, looked on him," but let him lie; little was done till the good Samaritan came. (Luke x. 31, 32.) The things in heaven and earth, the generality of them so, in not much better case for all these, could not be recapitulate in the Patriarchs, Moses, the Prophets. So that to this plunge it was come, that the Psalmist even asked God, "Wherefore hast Thou made all men for nought?" (Ps. lxxxix. 47.) It was for Him to come, *Qui venturus erat.* (Heb. x. 37.)

It was time, more than time, when that which was the only known way, when one was scattered from God, how to gather him to God again, which was, "Let Him smell a sacrifice," (1 Sam. xxvi. 19)—when that grew out of season, when that failed. And that it did. "Sacrifice, burnt-offering, burnt-offerings for sin," (sin that made all the scattering), *noluisti,*

that is plain, " Thou wouldst not "—it is Christ now speaketh—" Then said I, Lo, I come." (Psa. xl. 6.)   I, of Whom
it is written, ἐν κεφαλίδι, " in the top or front of the book,
that I should fulfil Thy will," and gather these together
again ; " lo, I come to do it."

By this *Ecce venio* of His a way was found, those that
were thus distracted and scattered before, how to bring
them together again.   What way was that ?   It follows in
the same place what He meant by *Ecce venio.*   He goes it
over again ; " No sacrifice Thou wouldst ;"—no : *corpus
autem aptasti,* " but a body hast Thou ordained Me." (Psa.
xl. 6.)   The incorporating Christ, the ordaining Him a body,
that is the " new and living way, through the veil, that is His
flesh." (Heb. x. 20.)   With that He comes this day, and
gathers all again.

How, or in what manner that ?   The manner is set down
in the word by way of recapitulation.   We are not to conceive there was such " a great sheet," as St. Peter saw, " let
down from Heaven," (Acts x. 11), and that all these were put
into it and so gathered.   No, it was *recapitulando,* ' by reducing to less room,' as we do many diffused matters to a few
heads, as we contract great maps to a small compass, as great
plots to a small module ; for that is properly to recapitulate.
There are two words in the verse set it out well ; 1. πλήρωμα,
2. and κεφάλαιον.   Πλήρωμα, this fulness will come into a
little κεφάλαιον, as the particulars of many leaves come into
a total of not half a line.

If then we be to proceed by way of recapitulation, then
are we to reduce all to heads.   So let us reduce these
things to these two heads ; 1. First, Heaven, and all in it, to
God ; earth, and all in it, to man.   Gather these two into
one, and there is the ἀνακεφαλαίωσις in short.   To conceive
it the better, you shall understand this was on a good way
one-ward, before.   You have heard man called the little
world, the ἀνακεφαλαίωσις of the great one, a compendium
of all the creatures.   And so he is of both.   He participates
with the Angels, and so with things in Heaven, by his soul ;
he participates with the elements, and so with things on
earth, by His body.   The poet had it by the end ; *Fertur
Prometheus, &c.*   That to the making of man's body there
went a piece of every of the creatures.   So there was in man
a kind of recapitulation before.

But that was not full, yet lacked there one thing. All in Heaven were not gathered into man. Of God we say, *Qui es in Cœlis.* He was one of the things in Heaven, and He was out all the while. But if He could be gathered in too, then were it a full gathering indeed. All in Heaven recapitulate into One, that is God ; all in earth recapitulate into one, that is man. Gather these two now, and all are gathered, all the things in either. And now at this last great recollection of God and man, and in them of Heaven and earth, and in them of all in Heaven and earth, are all recapitulate into the unity of One entire Person. And how? Not so as they were gathered at first ; not as the κεφαλαίωσις, 'the first gathering,' so the ἀνακεφαλαίωσις, 'the second gathering.' When things were at the best, God and man were two in number; now God and man are but one Christ. So the gathering nearer than before, so surer than before, so every way better than before.

In man there was one-ward an abridgment of all the rest. Gather God and him into one, and so you have all. There is nothing, not anything, in Heaven or earth left out. Heaven is in and earth, the creatures in Heaven and earth, the Creator of Heaven and earth. All are in now ; all reconciled, as it were, in one mass, all cast into one sum ; recapitulate indeed truly and properly.

Herein is the fulness, that God Himself comes into this κεφάλαιον. The Apostle, where the Psalm saith, " He hath put all things in subjection under His feet ;" it is "manifest," saith the Apostle, "that He was excepted That so put them under." (1 Cor. xv. 27.) But here it is manifest, say we, that He is not excepted That did gather ; but He the very Collector is in this collection Himself and all.

For "God was in Christ reconciling the world." (2 Cor. v. 19.) "The world," that is all things, all in Heaven, all in earth. And in Christ did "dwell the fulness of the Godhead bodily," (Col. ii. 9), when He did so "reconcile them in the body of His flesh." (Col. i. 21, 22.) In a word, certain it is that by virtue of this recapitulation we are one with Christ, Christ as man. God is one with Christ—Christ as God. So in Christ God and man are one. And there is good hope they that are one, will soon be at one ; where unity is, union will be had with no great ado.

And even besides this there is yet another recapitulation ;

that well might it have that name. For if you mark it, it is not recapitation, but recapitulation; and that comes of *capitulum*, which is a diminutive. So was it: *Verbum in principio*, "the eternal," mighty, great "Word" became *Verbum abbreviatum*, (Rom. x. 8), as the Apostle saith, to bring this to pass. He That "the Heavens are but His span," (Isa. xl. 12), abbreviate into a child of a span long; He that *Caput*, "the Head" of men and Angels, principalities, and powers, became *Capitulum;* He that Κεφαλή, Κεφάλαιον, 'a little diminutive Head.' Head? Nay, became the Foot, *Pes computi* the text is, 'the Foot, the lowest part of the account,' and of the lowest account.

And now, because we are in seasons, we speak of seasons. When was this, at what season of the year? when was it that He was so *capite minutus?* Sure never less, never so little, never so minorated, so minimated, I am sure, as now. When was *Ecce venio* fulfilled? We may know that by all the four Sundays in Advent now past, that to-day it is *Ecce venio*. His coming the Psalm expounds by ordaining Him a body, (Ps. xl. 7); a body there was ordained Him in the womb, but to us things are when they appear. That though the Word were made flesh before, yet God was not "manifested in the flesh," came not and "dwelt among us," (John i. 14), visibly to be seen till this day. So that if you ask of *in Christo*, what or when? *In Christo nato*, then was this gathering of things in Heaven and earth.

And in sign it was then, look there comes a choir of Angels down, (Luke ii. 13), there comes a new star forth to represent the things in Heaven, there comes together a sort of shepherds, and there is gathering to them a troop of great princes from the East (Matt. ii. 1) to represent the things on earth, which consist, as these do, of high and low, noble and base, wise and simple; all to celebrate, and make shew of this gathering, of this great πλήρωμα into this small κεφάλαιον. And in their Heavenly hymn (Luke ii. 14) there is mention of this gathering; *in excelsis*, and *in terris* set together, as if all in both were now in full and perfect harmony.

Now when the seasons had travailed with, at last brought forth Him That was the best thing they had, or should ever bring forth, then were they at the best. When "Him in Whom it pleased the Father all fulness should dwell," then were they at the full. The gathering of the things so full as it made *plenitudo rerum*, the gathering of the seasons so full as it made *plenitudo temporum*. And so have we brought both parts, seasons and things together.

The sum is at the foot, the oration at the period, the building at the head-stone, the tide at the full; "the fulness of the Gentiles" (Rom. xi. 25) are come into His Church, "which is His body, the fulness of Him that filleth all in all." (Eph. i. 23.)

But why God in the dispensation of the seasons did so order that at such a year of the world, such a month of the year, such a day of the month, this should fall out just, this is more than I dare take upon me to define. But this I may, that the Christian world hath ever observed divers good congruities of this feast with this text.

The text is of a recapitulation; the feast is so. Twelve months recapitulate to twelve days. Six for the old, in six days was the creation of the old. And when "the old things are past," as many for the new; for "behold all things are new," and "if any be in Christ he is a new creature." (2 Cor. v. 17.) Both these recapitulate in one season equally divided. Equally divided between both, yet so as the days of the last are set before the first, that so *erunt novissimi primi* (Matt. xix. 30) is verified even of the season, and the last first there also.

The text is of a gathering, and that falls fit with the season, and giveth us great cause to admire the high wisdom of God in the dispensation of seasons; that now at this season, when we gather nothing, when nothing groweth to be gathered, there should be a gathering yet and a great one; nay, the greatest gathering that ever was or will be; and so by that means, the poorest and emptiest season in nature become the fullest and richest in grace.

Now we do ourselves in effect express as much as this comes to. For we also make it a season of gathering together, of neighbourly meetings and invitations. Wherein we come together, and both ourselves have, and we make each other partakers of, what we have gathered all the year before.

In which sense also we may call it the season of dispensation; in that we then dispense the blessing God hath sent us, and that is in good house-keeping and hospitality.

And if you will, of fulness too. For the most part do then use to be better filled, and with better fare that are not so full again all the year beside. That one may truly say, there is more fulness in this season than any other. And so it is the season of fulness then; for the " hungry are then filled with good things," (Ps. cvii. 9), then of all the seasons of the year.

And last, there is in the text, and it is the main word in the text, ἀνακεφαλαίωσις, which in the primitive sense is the making the foot of an account; which agreeth well with the foot of the year, for at the foot of the leaf sums used to be set. Set it at the head, or set it at the foot, it is the foot of the old, and the head of the new, and so the fittest season to celebrate it in. For be it head, or be it foot, Christ it is. So recapitulation or gathering, fulness or dispensation, or summing all up, the text is seasonable.

But these I have spoke of are of things on earth. Were it not to be wished, we would endeavour to have some fruition, and to gather some fruit for the Heavenly part from this gathering, this summing up of Christ's?

Christ is but κεφάλαιον, ' a short sum;' but there is in Him πλήρωμα, "a fulness of all." Christ is but the contents of a chapter, some three or four lines, but a great long chapter follows, long and large. For what shall you see in this Shulamite, (Cant. vi. 13), but *chorus castrorum*, legions, whole armies of good things to gather. Such, so great a sum, as twelve days will not serve to cast them up. But yet somewhat let us gather, that the seasons being full, we ourselves be not sent empty away.

The time fails; I will therefore name but one, and that the main word of the text, ἀνακεφαλαίωσις, which referreth properly to 'the making up an account.' The Fathers taking the verse into their considerations, pitch upon it; as St. Jerome, who thinks it chosen of purpose to that end. But the word and thing both we may have good use of, seeing we all are to be accountants, *redde rationem*, (Luke xvi. 2), said to us all, seeing to an account we must all come.

And thus he followeth it, goes no farther than the text for the particulars of our account, makes them consist of *quæ in Cœlis* and *quæ in terris*. Which two, as they are principally taken for the creatures in both, so may they also,

S

and not amiss, be taken for the things done in them both ; specially our gatherings in them referring to either.

Things in Heaven to stand for our good deeds, our alms, fasts, and prayers, that "ascend up thither"—the Angel tells Cornelius so, (Acts x. 4)—and "will receive us up thither into everlasting tabernacles." Of which, gather we as many as we can all our life long.

As for these on earth, we gather but too fast; meaning our evil deeds, which smell of the earth whence they are, and where they were done.

Now when we come to give up our account, it should seem by the word *ἀνὰ*, we had cast them once before and cast them false, that we must to it again, and see if we can find our sums right. There is no danger but in casting our *quæ in Cælis*, our good, lest we cast them over; and our *quæ in terris*, our bad, lest them we cast under. The other way the error is nothing so perilous.

Our *quæ in Cælis*, our good, howsoever our new auditors cast them so as they find God in their debt, for that we have laid out more than ever God required, I doubt will not prove so at the audit. But of our *quæ in terris*, our evil, there is no great fear of overcasting them, their sum will rise but too high if we deceive not ourselves.

But whether it be of both, we shall find ourselves wrong in both, if they be not recapitulate *in Christo*. For our *quæ in Cælis ;* having done all we can, Christ bids us say, *servi inutiles sumus*, (Luke xvii. 10); and so we must say then, and what account can be made of *inutile?* Having suffered all we can, *non sunt condignæ*, (Rom. viii. 18), saith St. Paul ; so both come not home. The good Centurion, he that "built the Synagogue," (Luke vii. 5), nay then St. John Baptist himself, (Luke iii. 16), both cast themselves to a *non sum dignus*, even the best of our nature. That when we have done we must begin again, and cast and cast till we be weary, unless we cast in Christ ; fail still, unless our total of *quæ in Cælis* be recapitulate *in Christo.*

But then come to the other account of *quæ in terris ;* to that there is our fulness, and the fulness of our seasons. Many a broken reckoning shall we find there, such surd numbers, such fractions we shall meet with, we shall not tell how or when to get through, we shall want counters. They are so infinite and intricate withal, that I fear we shall be found in a mighty arrear, a huge debt of thousands and "ten thousand of talents," (Matt. xviii. 24); we shall not tell which way to turn us, nor which way to satisfy it, though all we have were sold, and we ourselves too. To balance this account, Christ is most needful; for, *summis conjunctis,* 'cast both these together,' and Job being our auditor, he finds we shall not be able to "answer God one for a thousand," (Job ix. 3), that he can charge us with. *Sine me nihil potestis facere,* (John xv. 5), if ever, we shall find in this most true. For gather Heaven and earth, and all that is in them altogether, and leave Him out, they will never be able to make our discharge, not the best auditor of them all.

But He out of the fulness of His satisfactions can relieve us that way, to take off, or strike off, a great part of our *onus.* And He can cast in of the fulness of His merits to make up that is found *minus habens,* or defective in ours that way. For the short is, He is both *Pes* and *Caput computi,* the Κεφαλὴ, and the Κεφάλαιον; He is called both in the text. His ἀνακεφαλαίωσις must help us if ever we come to our audit.

But foreseen, that this be no hindrance to our gathering. No: gathering we must be still those of Heaven, spiritual; and turn as much of our earthly as we can into them. And still order the matter so, as "while we have time we be doing good." (Gal. vi. 10.) We shall but evil sum up all in Christ, if we have no particulars to raise our sum of, if we have nothing but what is out of Christ to recapitulate in Christ. To gather, I say, else are we like to have but an empty season of it.

And even to begin now to imitate God in His time when, and in His order how. His time: this is the time, God made His in; now we to take the same time to fall on gathering. His order: this is the order God made His by; He began with Heavenly things, we to keep the same order, follow His method, begin where He begins, begin with the things that have the priority of place in the text, begin with them; make *Regnum Ejus* our *primum quærite,* (Matt. vi. 33), and the things that pertain to it. And not pervert God's order, and be so wholly given to the fulness of the things on earth, that we fall to them first. Nay, I pray God it be not first, and last and all. We shall the better dispense the season, if we gather to prayers, to God's word; if we begin with them, if with the dispensation of His holy mysteries gather to that specially.

For there we do not gather to Christ or of Christ, but we gather Christ Himself; and gathering Him we shall gather the tree and fruit and all upon it. For as there is a recapitulation of all in Heaven and earth in Christ, so there is a recapitulation of all in Christ in the holy Sacrament. You may see it clearly: there is in Christ the Word eternal for things in Heaven; there is also flesh for things on earth. Semblably, the Sacrament consisteth of a Heavenly and of a terrene part, (it is Irenæus' own words); the Heavenly—there the word too, the abstract of the other; the earthly—the element.

And in the elements, you may observe there is a fulness of the seasons of the natural year; of the corn-flour or harvest in the one, bread; of the wine-press or vintage in the other, wine. And in the Heavenly, of the "wheat-corn," (John xii. 24), whereto He compareth Himself — bread, even "the living Bread" (or, "Bread of life"), "that came down from Heaven," (John vi. 50, 51); the true Manna, whereof we may gather each his gomer. And again, of Him, the true Vine as He calls Himself, (John xv. 1.)—the blood of the grapes of that Vine. Both these issuing out of this day's recapitulation, both in *corpus autem aptasti Mihi,* (Ps. xl. 6), of this day.

And the gathering or vintage of these two in the blessed Eucharist, is as I may say a kind of hypostatical union of the sign and the thing signified, so united together as are the two natures of Christ. And even from this Sacramental union do the Fathers borrow their resemblance, to illustrate by it the personal union in Christ; I name Theodoret for the Greek, and Gelasius for the Latin Church, that insist upon it both, and press it against Eutyches. That even as in the Eucharist neither part is evacuate or turned into the other, but abide each still in his former nature and substance, no more is either of Christ's natures annulled, or one of them converted into the other, as Eutyches held, but each nature remaineth still full and whole in his own kind. And backwards; as the two natures in Christ, so the *signum* and *signatum* in the Sacrament, *e converso.* And this latter device, of the substance of the bread and wine to be flown away and gone, and in the room of it a remainder of nothing else but accidents to stay behind, was to them not known, and had it been true, had made for Eutyches and against them. And this for the likeness of union in both.

Now for the word "gathering together in one." It is well known the holy Eucharist itself is called *Synaxis*, by no name more usual in all antiquity, that is, a 'collection or gathering.' For so it is in itself; for at the celebration of it, though we gather to prayer and to preaching, yet that is the principal gathering the Church hath, which is itself called a "collection" (Heb. x. 25) too by the same name from the chief; for "where the body is there the eagles will be gathered," (Luke xvii. 37), and so one *Synaxis* begets another.

And last, there is a "dispensation"—that word in it too, that most clearly. For it is our office, we are styled by the Apostle "dispensers of the mysteries of God," (1 Cor. iv. 1); and in and by them, of all the benefits that came to mankind by this dispensation in the fulness of season of all that are recapitulate in Christ.

Which benefits are too many to deal with. One shall serve as the sum of all; that the very end of the Sacrament is to gather again to God and His favour, if it happen, as oft it doth, we scatter and stray from Him. And to gather us as close and near as *alimentum alito*, that is as near as near may be.

And as to gather us to God, so likewise each to other mutually; expressed lively in the symbols of many grains into the one, and many grapes into the other. The Apostle is plain that we are all "one bread and one body, so many as are partakers of one bread," (1 Cor. x. 17), so moulding us as it were into one loaf altogether. The gathering to God refers still to things in Heaven, this other to men to the things in earth here. All under one head by the common faith; all into one body mystical by mutual charity. So shall we well enter into the dispensing of this season, to begin with.

And even thus to be recollected at this feast by the Holy Communion into that blessed union, is the highest perfection we can in this life aspire unto. We then are at the highest pitch, at the very best we shall ever attain to on earth, what time we newly come from it; gathered to Christ, and by Christ to God; stated in all whatsoever He hath gathered and laid up against His next coming. With which gathering here in this world we must content and stay ourselves, and wait for the consummation of all at His coming again. For there is an *ecce venio* (Rev. xxii. 12) yet to come.

This gathering thus here begun, it is to take end and to have the full accomplishment at the last and great gathering of all, (Matt. xxv. 32), which shall be of the quick and of the dead. When He shall "send His Angels, and they shall gather His elect from all the corners of the earth," (Matt. xxiv. 31), shall "gather the wheat into the barn, and the tares to the fire." (Matt. xiii. 30.) And then, and never till then, shall be the fulness indeed, when God shall be not, as now He is, somewhat in every one, but "all in all." (1 Cor. xv. 28.) *Et tempus non erit amplius,* "and there shall be neither time" nor season "any more." (Rev. x. 6.) No fulness then but the fulness of eternity, and in it the fulness of all joy. To which, in the several seasons of our being "gathered to our fathers," He vouchsafe to bring us; that as the year, so the fulness of our lives may end in a Christmas, a merry joyful feast, as that is! And so God make this to us, in Him, &c.

SERMON XVII.

SERMON PREACHED BEFORE THE KING'S MAJESTY, AT WHITEHALL, ON SATURDAY, THE TWENTY-FIFTH OF DECEMBER, A.D. MDCXXIV., BEING CHRISTMAS-DAY.

I will preach the law, whereof the Lord said to Me : Thou art My Son, this day have I begotten Thee. PSALM ii. 7.

Prædicabo legem, de qua dixit ad Me Dominus : Filius Meus Tu, hodie genui Te.

THIS text, the first word of it is *predicabo,* "I will preach." So here is a Sermon toward. And it is of *Filius—Filius Meus genui Te ;* of the begetting or bringing forth a child. And that *hodie,* "this very day."

And let not this trouble you that it is "begotten" in the

text, and "born" on the day. In all the three tongues one word serves for both. In Latin, *alma Venus genuit ;* Venus did but hear Æneas, yet it is said *genuit.* In Greek γεννη-θέντα ἐκ Μαρίας. He was but born of the Virgin, yet He was said γεννηθείς, *genitus.* And I report me to the masters of the Hebrew tongue, whether the original word in the text bear not, be not as full, nay do not more properly import His birth than His begetting. It is sure it doth. So it may be used, and so we will use it indifferently. And let this serve once for all. We return to our Sermon.

Prædicabo. Here is One saith "He will preach." Hath He a license? Yes: *dixit ad Me,* He was spoken to, or indeed He was commanded. *Amar* is to command. Commanded by whom? By Him That hath lawful authority so to do, *dixit Dominus.* He stepped not up of his own head, He came to it orderly, made no suit for the place, was appointed for it.

What will He preach of? Whence will He take His text? Out of *dixit Dominus,* out of the word of God. And that is right. So do we take ours, for so did He take His. To *dixit Dominus* He held Him, preached not voluntary ; but as He preached the law, so He had a law to preach by, the word of God. *Dixit Dominus.*

And What was His text? *Filius Meus Tu, hodie genui Te.* This text He preached on, as it might be at the bringing forth of a Son. And that, as it should seem by the word *hodie,* "this very day." This day the birth, this day the Sermon. And if so, by the same equity the same text may well be preached on again, whensoever that day comes about by the circling of the year.

It useth to be the first question, I kept it last, Who preacheth? For if we like him we will hear him, else not. Sure He to Whom this is spoken, *Filius Meus Tu,* He it is That saith, *prædicabo.* And He to whom it is said, *Filius Meus Tu,* is Christ. Christ then preacheth. And Christ is worth the hearing. There will lie no exception to the Preacher, that I am sure of.

And indeed so it was most meet that He should. He That was the Lawgiver, most meet to read upon His own law ; He That the Son, most meet to preach upon *Filius Meus Tu ;* He That was born, upon His own birth.

Upon His own birth. And if upon it any day, that day

especially whereon He was born. So is the text. The day He preached on, He was born ; the day He was born, He preached on. No time so kindly to preach *de Filio hodie genito* as *hodie.* So shall you have Christ preach of Christ's Nativity ; and that upon the very day of His Nativity ; which, according to the Christian account, is this day of all the days of the year.

And first I must tell you, this same *hodie* here is said *signanter,* that Christ was " begotten " to-day. For he was " begotten " besides this, had more begettings than one. Two natures He had, and so two Nativities. One eternal, as the Son of God ; the other temporal, as the Son of Man. And as it falls out, this very place here I find vouched for both. Vouched for his begetting as the Son of God by the Apostle, " For to which of the Angels said He at any time, Thou art My Son, this day have I begotten Thee ? " (Heb. i. 5.) Alleging this place to prove His Deity, as One Whose nature was far above, far more excellent than the Angels.

But of the twain, more properly we apply it to this day's birth, His birth as the Son of Man. And for our so apply-ing it, we have the warrant not of one, but of all the Apostles at once, and even of the whole Church assembled in prayer. (Acts iv. 27.) Where to God Himself they say, that the prophecy of this Psalm was fulfilled, when Herod, the High-priests, and the rest took counsel against His holy Child Jesus ; and that we know was at His birth. So applying it to this birth, sure we are we apply it aright.

And indeed it cannot be otherwise. For in the very next words, God bids Him ask, and He " will give Him the heathen, and the uttermost parts of the earth." This must needs be said to Him as the Son of Man, and can no ways be said to Him as the Son of God. As the Son of God He asked not, He needed not ask, He had all ; all *æquo jure* with His Father, as " being in form of God." (Phil. ii. 6.) Nothing was, nothing could be given to Him ; He was not a Person capable of any gift, all was His own. So it was spoken as to the Son of Man, this day born. And so to the Son of Man, this day born we apply it.

I. Of this sermon these be the parts. The matter of it at large, or in general. That it is a law first. Then what manner of law, or how qualified. 1. A law to be preached, as other laws use not to be. 2. A law *de quâ dixit Deus;* where other laws are, *de quâ dixit homo;* which is the reason why it is to be preached. 3. And then, out of the very body of the word in the text, that it is not a law at large, but a statute law, for so is *Elchok,* which but by publishing none can take notice of. A second reason why it is to be preached. And this is the first part.

II. The second is the very text itself, or the body of the law in these words : " Thou art My Son, this day have I begotten Thee." The points in it are five. 1. " Of a Son." 2. Of " My Son," that is, the Son of God. 3. *Genui,* " the Son of God begotten." 4. *Hodie,* the Son of God, " this day begotten." 5. And *Dixit genui,* that is, *dicendo genuit,* " begotten only by saying ; " only said the word, and it was done, and the " Word became flesh." (John i. 14.) This is the second part.

III. The third is the hardest. For it would make one study *Filius Meus Tu,* how this should be a law, as here it is called. It looks not like one. But said it must be, which Christ hath said : a law He calls it, and a law we must find it. Now there be but two laws, as the Apostle tells us, *lex fidei* and *lex factorum,* (Rom. iii. 27) ; if both these ways a law it be, a law we shall find it. And both these ways a law it is.

1. *Lex fidei.* A law limiting what to believe of Him. Of Him, that is, of His Person, His Natures, and His Offices. His Person, out of the words, *Ego* and *Tu.* His Natures, out of *hodie* and *genui.* His Offices, out of *prædicabo* and *legem.*

2. Then *lex factorum.* Setting out first, what He doth for us ; and then what we are to do for Him. What He doth for us, *Filius Meus tu,* to us He conveyeth all filial rights. What we to do for Him, *Filius Meus Tu,* we to return to Him all filial duties. Which duties are comprised in *prædicabo legem.* And *legem,* that law is no more than *Filius Meus Tu,* for *Filius Meus Tu* goes through all, and is all in all. These are the parts. Of these, &c.

I. *Prædicabo legem,* saith Christ. And we like it well that He will preach. But He hath not chosen so good a text ; *legem* were a fitter text for Moses to preach on. We had well hoped, Christ would have preached no law, all Gospel He. That He would have preached down the old

Law, but not have preached up any new. We see it is otherwise. A law He hath to preach, and preach it He will; He saith it Himself, *prædicabo legem.*

So if we will be His auditors, He tells us plainly we must receive a law from His mouth. If we love not to hear of a law, we must go to some other Church; for in Christ's Church there a law is preached. Christ began, we must follow and say every one of us as He saith, *prædicabo legem.*

Nay, there is another point yet more strange. These very words here, *Filius Meus Tu, &c.* are as good Gospel as any in the New Testament; yet are here, as we see, delivered by Him under the term of a law. And we may not change His word, we may not learn Christ how to use His terms. The words are plain, there is no avoiding them; a law He calls it, and a law it is.

First then, to take notice of both these. 1. That Christ will preach a law, and that they that are not for the law, are not for Christ. It was their quarrel above, at the third verse, they would none of Christ for this very cause, that Christ comes preaching the law, and they would live lawless; they would endure no yoke that were "the sons of Belial;" "Belial," that is no yoke; "but what agreement hath Christ with Belial?" (2 Cor. vi. 15.)

And then, that these words *Filius Meus Tu* are a law, and so as a law by Christ preached. So as in the very Gospel itself all is not Gospel, some law among it. The very Gospel hath her law. A law evangelical there is which Christ preached; and as He did, we to do the like. Whereof more is to be said by and by.

In the meantime it is not without danger to let any such conceit take head, as though Christian religion had no law-points in it, consisted only of pure narratives—believe them, and all is well: had but certain *theses* to be held, dogmatical points, matters of opinion. And true it is, such points there be, but they be not all. There is a law besides, and it hath precepts, and they to be preached, learned, and as a law to be obeyed of all.

Look but into the grand commission by which we all preach, which Christ gave at His going out of the world; "Go," saith He, "preach the Gospel to all nations, teaching"—what? "to observe the things that I have commanded you." (Matt. xxviii. 19.) Lo, here is commanding, and here is observing.   So the Gospel consists not only of certain articles to be believed, but of certain commandments also, and they to be observed.   And what is that but *prædicabo legem !*

Now I know not how, but we are fallen clean from the term "Law ;" nay, we are even fallen out with it.   Nothing but Gospel now.   The name of Law we look strangely at ; we shun it in our common talk.   To this it is come, while men seek to live as they list.   Preach them Gospel as much as you will ; but, hear ye, no *prædicabo legem,* no law to be preached, to hold or keep them in.   And we have gospelled it so long that the Christian Law is clean gone with us, we have lost it ; if *prædicabo legem* here get it us not again.   But got it must be, for as Christ preacheth, so must we ; and law it is that Christ preacheth.

I shall tell you, what is come by the drowning of the term " Law."   Religion is even come to be counted *res precaria.* No law—no, no ; but a matter of fair entreaty, gentle persuasion ;   neither *jura,* nor *leges,* but only *consulta patrum,* 'good fatherly counsel,' and nothing else.   *Consilia Evangelica* were a while laid aside ; now there be none else.   All are Evangelical counsels now.   The reverend regard, the legal vigour and power, the penalties of it are not set by.   The rules—no reckoning made of them as of law-writs, none, but only as of physic bills ; if you like them you may use them, if not, lay them by.   And this comes of drowning the term, " Law."   And all, for lack of *prædicabo legem.*

I speak it to this end ; to have the one term retained as well as the other, to have neither term abolished ; but with equal regard, both kept on foot.   They are not so well advised that seek to suppress either name.   If the name once be lost, the thing itself will not long stay, but go after it and be lost too.

They that take them to the one term only, are confuted once a month.   For every month, every first day of every month, this verse faileth not but is read in our ears.   And here a law it is.   And so was the Christian religion called in the very best times of it, *Christiana lex,* 'the Christian law ;' and the Bishops, *Christianæ legis Episcopi,* 'the Bishops of the Christian law.'   And all the ancient Fathers liked the term well, and took it upon them.

To conclude. Gospel it how we will, if the Gospel hath not the *legalia* of it acknowledged, allowed, and preserved to it; if once it lose the force and vigour of a law, it is a sign it declines, it grows weak and unprofitable, (Heb. vii. 18), and that is a sign it will not long last. (Heb. viii. 13.) We must go look our salvation by some other way than by *Filius Meus Tu,* if *Filius Meus Tu* (I say not be not preached, but) be not so preached, as Christ preached it; and Christ preached it as a law. And so much for *legem.*

Now of this law, three things are here said; first, *legem* turns back upon *prædicabo.* And this privilege it hath, that it is *materia predicabilis,* a law which may, nay a law which 'is to be preached.' And that laws use not to be; not to be preached. To be read upon at times privately, but to be preached, not any law but this. But this is, and it serves for a special difference to sever it from other laws, and make it a kind by itself. Even this, that it is to be preached.

To be preached; and that, even to Kings themselves that make laws; to judges themselves that are presumed to be best seen in the law; yet they to learn, they to be learned in this law. *Erudimini* is the word, *qui judicatis terram,* in the tenth verse after.

And the reason is; for this is a law, *de quâ dixit Deus.* And so is none else. And that is a second difference. There is a law *de quâ dixit homo, quam sanxerunt homines,* 'which men among themselves make for themselves,' as by-laws are made. This of a higher nature. This God Himself made, is a law of His own making. *De quâ dixit,* or rather *edixit,* for so is *Amar;* which God enacted first, and then gave commandment, it should be preached.

And to whom? *Dixit ad Me.* Who is that? Christ. First, and before all others to be preached by His Son. His preaching He thought it worth, and gave it Him in charge, and accordingly we see He performed it, and professed *prædicabo,* that He will "preach it."

But the third is a reason why it could not be otherwise, why it could not but be preached. Because as I told you out of the very body of the word, it is not a law at large, but a statute law. And the nature of that law is, without publishing it cannot be known.

God hath His law in the same division that man hath

his; His statute and His common law. "The law of nature
which is written in the hearts of all men," (Rom. ii. 15),
that is the common law of the world.   Of that every man is
to take notice at his peril.   But this law here is no part of
that law; *Filius Meus Tu* is not written in the heart, it
must be preached to the ear.   No light of nature could
reveal it from within—preached from without it must be.
And so and no otherwise come we to the knowledge of it.
The very word gives it for such, which is properly 'a statute'
as this is, enacted and decreed in the High Court of God's
Council above, and reserved "to be revealed in the latter
times," (Eph. iii. 5); and of that we cannot "hear without
a preacher," (Rom. x. 14), and the preaching thereof was
committed to Christ.   He began and we follow.   And so
much for *prædicabo legem, de quâ dixit Dominus ad Me*—the
matter at large.   And now to His text wherein is the letter
of the law itself.

II. I reckoned up to you five particulars in this law.   1.
Filius, a "Son."   2. *Filius Meus*, "My Son," that is, the
Son of God.   3. *Filius Meus genui*, "the Son of God begotten."   4. *Hodie genui*, the Son of God "begotten this
day."   And fifthly, *dixit genui*, that is, *dicendo genuit*, "begotten by saying," as the Word should be.

Of "a Son," first.   Which plainly sheweth it is not the
old, it is a new law this.   The old runs, *Ego sum Dominus*,
which must needs imply, *servus Meus tu*.   This is *Filius
Meus Tu* in another style, which necessarily doth imply,
Ego sum Pater Tuus.   A Father to be the giver of it.   According to the former He saith, *Ego sum Dominus*, and we
say, *Dominus meus Tu*.   According to this latter He saith,
filius Meus Tu, and we say *Pater meus Tu*.   This the better
by far, as far as the condition of a son is better than that of
a servant.   And indeed, the main difference between the
two laws is but this, (1 John iv. 18): Do it, saith the one,
servus Meus tu—the unperfect law of fear and servitude,
(Heb. vii. 19), Do it, saith the other, *filius Meus tu*—the
"perfect law of love and liberty." (James ii. 12.)

Of a Son.   Whose Son?   *Filius Meus*.   And He that
speaks it, that saith *Meus*, is God; and so He to Whom it
is spoken, "the Son of God."   And the Son of God is a
high title, and of a special account.   Solomon before his
crown or sceptre prized that speech of God; "I will

be his Father and he shall be My son." (2 Sam. vii. 14.)

But nothing makes it more clear than this place. The last verse He saith, *Posui te Regem*, "I have set Thee a king :" that He speaks not of, thinks it not fit. But here now, *Filius Meus Tu*—this, lo, preach He will, this He thinks worth the preaching. *Filius Meus Tu* rather than *posui Te Regem*, to be "the Son of God" than to be "a Prince in Sion."

The Son of God ; and "the Son of God begotten." For sons of God there be that are not begotten, they that come in another way, that come by adoption. To beget is an act of nature, and is ever determined in the identity of the same nature with him that did beget. And this putteth the difference.

Otherwise, God speaks of Angels as of His sons ; "when all the sons of God praised Him." (Job xxxviii. 7.) Speaks it of Israel His people ; " out of Egypt have I called My son. (Hos. xi. 1.) Speaks it of rulers and governors ; "ye are all the sons of the Most High." (Ps. lxxxii. 6.) To every of these as much in effect is said as *filius Meus tu.* But to which of them all, "to which of the Angels said He at any time, *genui te*, I have begotten thee ?" Not to any. *Filii* they were but not *geniti*, none of them all. So *filius Meus tu* is communicated to others, but *genui te* to no creature, either in Heaven or earth. Of none is *genui* to be verified in proper terms, but of Christ, and of Christ only.

"Begotten," and "this day begotten ;" *genui* and *hodie genui ;* for begotten He had been before. Another begetting besides this. Two *genuis*. A *genui* before *hodie ; ex utero ante luciferum genui Te*, "said the Lord to my Lord," in the hundredth and tenth Psalm. Twice begotten He was. This day begotten, and begotten *ante luciferum*, "before there was any morning-star," (Ps. cx. 3) ; and so before there was any day at all ; and so before any *quod cognominatur hodie*, any time that "is called to-day."

We are to take notice of both these generations. 1. of *Christus ante luciferum*, and of 2. *lucifer ante Christum.* To take notice of both, but to take hold of this latter. For that *ante luciferum* was not for us ; His second begetting, His *hodie genui*, His this day's begetting is for us, is it we hold by. Not by His "going out from everlasting," (Mic. v. 2); not by His *olim, ante luciferum, ante secula genitus*—none of these. *Hodie genitus* is the law, that we are to preach; that is, not His eternal, but His hodiernal generation. Not as God, of the substance of His Father, begotten before all worlds; but as Man, of the substance of His mother, born in the world; "when in the fulness of time God sent His Son, made of a woman." (Gal. iv. 4.) And that was the *hodie genui* of this day.

Now the speculative Divine pierceth yet deeper, he finds a farther mystery in these two words, *dixit genui*, that is, saith he, *dicendo genuit*. He said He begat, that is, by His very saying He begat. Wherein the very manner of His begetting is set forth unto us.

There is a very near resemblance betwixt *dixit* and *genui*, betwixt begetting and speaking. To beget is to bring forth; so is to speak to bring forth also, to bring forth a word, and Christ you know is called the Word. Now when we speak, either we do it within to ourselves, or without to others. Either of which two may well be compared to a like several begetting.

When we think a word in our thought, and speak it there, within to ourselves, as it were in silence, and never utter it, this if you mark it well is a kind of conceiving or generation; the mind within of itself engendering a word, while yet it is but in notion, kept in, and known to none but to ourselves. And such was the generation of the eternal Word, the Son of God, in the mind of His Father before all worlds; and even to that doth the Apostle apply the *genui* of this verse. (Heb. i. 5.) And this is the first begetting or speaking.

Now as the word yet within us in our thought, when time comes that we will utter it, doth take to itself an airy body, our breath by the vocal instruments being framed into a voice, and becometh audible to the outward sense; and this we call the second begetting or speaking: right so, the eternal Word of God, by *Dominus dixit*, by the very breath of God, the Holy Spirit, which hath His name of *spiro*, 'to breathe,' (*corpus autem aptasti Mihi*), had a body framed Him, (Heb. x. 5), and with that body was brought forth, and came into the world. And so these words, *genui Te*, this very day, the second time, verified of Him. *Genui,* and *dixit genui,* " said, and by saying, begot him ;" for how soon the Angel's voice sounded in the blessed Virgin's ear, instantly was He incarnate in the womb of His mother.

Of both which words, *dixit* and *genui,* we can spare neither. There is good use of both. Of *genui,* to shew the truth of the identity of His nature and substance with His Father That begat Him, and with His mother that bare Him. For to beget, is when one living thing bringeth forth another living thing, of the same nature and kind itself is.

But, I know not how, the term of begetting, the very mention of that word carrieth our conceit to a nature of carnality; therefore is the word *dixit* well set before it, to shew this *genui* was not by any fleshly way, to abstract it from any mixture of carnal uncleanness. That the manner of it was only as the word is purely and spiritually conceived in the mind. The one word, *genui,* noting the truth; the other word, *dixit,* the no way carnal, but pure and inconcrete manner of His generation. And so I have gone over the five terms of this law, or, if you please, the five points of His text.

III. The hardest is yet behind; for it will not sink into our heads how this should be called a law. It seems nothing less; rather a dialogue between a Father and his Son. But a law sure it cannot be. A law runs in the imperative—this is merely narrative, declares somewhat, enjoins nothing, gives not any thing in charge as laws use to do.

Sed non potest solvi Scriptura, (John x. 35), " God must be true in all His sayings," (Rom. iii. 4), Christ may not preach false doctrine. A law He hath called it, and we may not give it any other name.

There be that think this verse is but the preamble, and that the body of the law doth follow and reacheth to the end of the Psalm.

But the better sort are of mind that even this verse, taken by itself, contains in it a law full and whole. Let us see then whether we can find it so.

We pitched upon the Apostle's division of the law, into *lex fidei* and *lex factorum.* If both these be found in it, we may well allow it for a law.

We will begin with *lex fidei,* what we are to believe of

Him. Of Him, that is, of these three : 1. of His Person ;
2. His Natures ; 3. and His Offices.

And then come to *lex factorum.* 1. First, what He doth
for us—the benefit of this law. 2. And then what we are
to do for Him again—our duty out of this law. The former
of which, the benefit, is the Gospel of this law. The latter,
the duty, is the law of this Gospel.

I. Of His person first. That He is of Himself, a Person
subsisting. Plain by the two Persons that are in the text,
Ego and *Tu*, the first and second person in grammar ; and
the same, the first and second Person in Trinity. Here is,
Ego genui, the Person of the Father ; and *Filius Meus Tu*,
the Person of the Son. Here is one begets ; and sure it is
nemo generat seipsum, 'none begets himself,' but he whom
he begets is a person actually distinguished from him that
begets him.

But of these two Persons, this you will mark. That the
first that is named, is *Filius Meus Tu.* He stands first in
the verse before *genui Te.* We hear of *Filius* before ever
we hear of *genui ;* for that is the Person we hold by.
(1 John iv 9.) By nature, *genui Te* should go before *Filius
Meus*, but *quoad nos, Filius Meus* is before *genui ;* to shew
there is no coming to the Father but by Him, no interest
in the Father but from and through Him. This for His
Person.

And in His Person we believe two natures, set down here
in the two words, *hodie* and *genui.* If you do observe, there
is somewhat a strange conjunction of these two words. One
is present, *hodie*, the other is perfectly past, *genui.* In pro-
priety of speech it would be a present act for a present
time, or it would be an act past with an adverb of the time
past ; and not join a time in being, *hodie*, with an action
ended and done, *genui.*

The joining of these two together, the verifying them
both of one and the same person, must needs seem strange.
And indeed could not be made good, but that in that one
Party there are two distinct natures. To either of which,
in a different respect, both may agree and be true, both.
Some little difference there will be about the sorting
of the two words, which to refer to which. But that
will easily be accorded, for they will both meet in the
end.

T

There be that, because *hodie*, the present, is yet in *fieri*, and so not come to be perfect, understand by it His temporal generation as Man which is the less perfect, as subject to the manifold imperfections of our human nature and condition. And then by *genui*, which is in *factum esse*, and so done and perfect, understand His eternal generation as the Son of God, in Whom are absolutely all the perfections of the Deity.

There be other, and they fly a higher pitch and are of a contrary mind, for whatsoever is past is in time say they, and so *genui* is temporal; and that *hodie*—that doth best express His eternal generation, for that nothing is so properly affirmed of eternity itself as is *hodie*. Why? For there all is *hodie;* there is neither *heri* nor *cras*, no 'yester-day' nor 'to-morrow.' All is "to-day," there. Nothing past, nothing to come—all present. Present as it were in one instant or centre, so in the *hodie* of eternity. 'Past and to come' argue time, but if it be eternal, it is neither; all there is present. "To-day" then, sets forth eternity best, say they, which is still present, and in being. But *genui*, that being past, cannot be His eternal at any hand, but must needs stand for His temporal.

But whether of these it be; *genui*, His eternal as perfect, and *hodie* as not yet perfect, His temporal; or *vice versa*, *hodie* represents eternity best, and *genui* time, as being spent and gone; between them both, one way or other, they will shew His begettings. You may weave *hodie* with *genui*, or *genui* with *hodie*, and between them both they will make up the two natures of Him That was the *hodie genitus* of this day. Concerning whom we believe; as first, that He is one entire person and subsists by Himself, so second, that He consists of two distinct natures, eternal and temporal. The one as perfect God, the other as perfect Man.

Now for His offices. Them we have likewise in the two words, *prædicabo* and *legem*. *Prædicabo*, by that it is plain He doth "preach." And that seems strange; for the last news we heard of Him in the verse before was, that He was "set a King in Sion." And the word *legem* imports as much, for laws with us are the King's laws.

A King to preach? Let that alone for the Priests. That is their office; "they shall teach Jacob His judg-

ments, and preach to Israel His law." (Deut. xxxiii. 10.)
But preach He will, as He saith. So *Meus Filius* will
prove a Priest as it seems ; a Priest indeed. And which is
yet more strange, by virtue of these very words, *Filius
Meus Tu.* No words, one would think, to prove Him a
Priest by ; and we should hardly believe it, but that in
Heb. v. 4, the Apostle deduceth His Priesthood from
these very words ; " No man," saith he, " taketh unto him
this honour," that is, the honour of the Priesthood, " but
he that was called of God, as was Aaron." And then he
adds, " No more did Christ, He took not this honour
upon Him, to be our High-priest ; but He that said to Him,
Filius Meus Tu, hodie genui Te, He gave it Him." So that
by virtue of these words, Christ was consecrate a Priest, as
by virtue of the other, *posui Te Regem,* " He was set a King
in Sion."

And the place, Sion, suits well with both. For Mount
Sion had two tops. On the one was the Temple built, on
the other was the King's palace situate. The one for *prædicabo,* the other for *legem.* In one, as King, he makes a law ;
in the other, as Priest, preacheth it. First, *posui Regem,* and
then *prædicabo legem.*

And indeed the Kings that were His types, were mixed
of both. Melchizedek—him the Apostle stands on at large,
in Heb. vii. And if this Psalm be David's, as questionless
it is, for his it is avowed to be, (Acts iv. 25), why then he
preached too. And for Solomon it is too evident, we have
his book of the Preacher. The like may be said of Ezekias,
and the rest by whom this King here was in any sort represented. And by virtue thereof, they all had a greater care
of publishing this law here, than of any of their own laws ;
as, on the contrary, Ahab and his race had more care of
" the keeping the statutes of Omri " (Mic. vi. 16) than they
had of the laws of God.

We believe then for His offices, that He is both King
and Priest. Hath a kingdom to rule, hath a diocese to
preach in. His kingdom, " the heathen to the uttermost
parts of the earth ; " His diocese as large. His auditory
all States, even the highest—Kings and judges ; for *prædicabo legem* concerns them all. And this for *lex fidei,* what it
binds us to believe of Him.

Now for *lex factorum.* First, what shall be done to

them that live by and under this law? They speak of laws of grace: this is indeed a law of grace, nay it is the law of grace; not only as it is opposite to the law of nature, but even because it offereth grace, the greatest grace that ever was. For what greater grace or favour can be done to any, than to have these words, *filius Meus tu*, said unto him? This law doth it; "for to them that receive it it giveth power to be made sons of God." (John i. 12.)

The words seem to be spoken to one person only; but as laws of grace use to be, are to receive ampliation, and to be extended to the most benefit.

Dixit ad Me. Said He it to Him, and said He it to Him alone, and said He it to no other but to Him? No; for He gave it Him in charge to preach it, and to preach it is to say it to others. Therefore it is *dixit ad Me ut ad alios per Me;* 'it was so said to Him, as that by Him it might be said to others.' *Prædicabo* makes it plain.

Prædicabo. When Christ doth preach, He is not to be understood to preach to Himself—no man doth so at any time, but to others more or less, that may be or should be the better for His preaching. For what needed it be preached, if it concern none but Him? if none to have benefit but He? if they that hear it preached shall receive no benefit by it?

So say we of *legem.* This law was not made for Christ, it needed not for Him any law. He was *Filius Meus Tu* φύσει, καὶ οὐ νόμῳ, needed no law to make Him that which by nature He was. The law was for others which by this law were to be made that which by nature they were not, that is, "the sons of God."

Take the very words. You see His text is not in the first person, *Filius Tuus Ego:* His text is, *filius Meus tu.* And who is that *tu?* It cannot be Christ Himself by common intendment. The Father saith to Him, "Thou art My Son." But to whom is it that Christ saith, Thou art my Son? For *filius Meus tu* is His text, that He must preach on; He may not go from the words, or change the tenor of His text. Who is then that son? To whom applieth He His text? To some other certainly.

The Apostle saith, "He was set and sent, that He might bring many sons unto God," (Heb. ii. 10), to whom God also might say, *filius Meus tu.* And Himself likewise saith of Himself in the Prophet; "Behold, here am I, and the children which God hath given Me." (Isa. viii. 18.)

And who be those children? Those, whom He shall regenerate, and beget a-new by His *prædicabo legem,* "the immortal seed," (1 Peter i. 23); for, " of His own good-will begat He us, by the word of truth, that we might be the first-fruits of His creatures." (James i. 18.) These are the children that are here meant. Of whom it shall be said, *quod per Filium filii,* ' that in and by this Son they shall be His sons, all.' And what was said to Christ, shall be said to them and every one of them, *filius Meus tu.*

Of Sion saith the eighty-seventh Psalm, "It shall be said, He was born in her." And that is true, for so He was. But he goes on farther, and saith, "He did remember Himself of Rahab, and Babylon, the Philistines' and the Morians' land, for, lo, there He was born." (Psa. lxxxvii. 4.) "Born there?" How can that be? Yes, born there, and here, and every where, where by this *prædicabo legem,* He begets children to God. The power and virtue of His birth reacheth even thither. Every place that receiveth His law, wherever it be, even there He is born. This for His birth.

To this birth there belongs a birth-right. They talk much of the law as of a birth-right; but, lo, this here is a birth-right indeed, and that *veri nominis,* and amounts to more than a child's part. And it grows out of the double title or interest, which He hath to all that is given Him. For as He is twice a Son, twice begotten, 1. *ante luciferum,* and 2. *hodie;* so hath He a double right grows to Him, expressed in two distinct words in the next verse, 1. one of inheritance, 2. the other of inheritance or purchase; for *Ahuzza* is true Hebrew for a purchase. Of which two one contents Him, His title as Heir. The other He transcribes and sets over to us, which is that of His purchase, as *hodie genitus.*

But we need not so much as to go to the next verse for it. *Filius Meus Tu* will serve; which was said twice to Him. 1. Once at His Baptism, *Hic est Filius Meus.* (Matt. iii. 17.) And so it is likewise at ours, to us; for therein we are made members of Christ, and the children of God. 2. And again, *Hic est Filius Meus,* at His transfiguration in the mount. (Matt. xvii. 5.) And we keeping the law of our Baptism, the same shall be said to us likewise the second time;

and when time comes, we shall also be "transfigured into the glorious image of the Son of God." (Phil. iii. 21.) And this is *lex factorum* on His part, this shall be done for us by Him. This we called the gospel of this law.

And what shall be done for us by Him? Which is the law of duty on our part required, and which we called the law of this gospel, implied in the two first words, *prædicabo* and *legem*. Either word hath his condition. First, if he preach, that we bestow the hearing of Him. And then *legem*, that we know it is "a law" He preacheth, and therefore so, and no otherwise than so, to hear it.

Hear Him preach? That we be entreated to easily. If that be all, we will never stick with Him for that. Nay, God's blessing on His heart! for, as the world goes, we are now all for preaching.

But take *legem* with you too. It is so *prædicabo* as it is *legem*. Preached and so preached as it is law, His sermons are so many law-lectures; His preaching is our law to live by; and law binds and leaves us not to live as we list. And if that which is preached be law, it is to be heard as a law, kept as a law, to be made our *lex factorum*, as well as *lex fidei*. If we hear it otherwise, if we hear it not so, if we lose *legem*, we may let go *prædicabo* too and all.

And here now we break. As a law? Nay, none of that. The hearing we will give Him; but soft, no law, by your leave. Our case is this: so long as it is but *prædicabo*, but preaching, we care not greatly though we hear it; but if it once come to *legem*, to be pressed upon us as "a law," farewell our parts; we give Him over, for law binds, and we will not be bound. Upon the point we are fast at *prædicabo*, and loose at *legem*. Leave Christ His book to preach by, but keep the law in our own hands. But to be short, if we hear it not as a law, here it not but as news; if we bring our sermons "to an end as a tale that is told," (Ps. xc. 9); if that be all, we forfeit all that follows, all our part and portion in *filius Meus*, and *hodie genui*, and all.

Now if you ask what law it is is here meant? No other but the law of these words, *filius Meus tu ;* for *filius Meus tu*, in the body of it, carrieth the law; that contains all filial duties, which is the perfectest law when all is done.

For the law of a son is more than all laws besides. For besides that it is *lex factorum*, that a son will do anything that is to be done, he will farther do it out of filial love and affection, which is worth all. And this law, indeed, is worth the preaching. It is *exibit de Sion lex*, "the law that came from Sion." (Isa. ii. 3).

The "law of Sinai," that begins with *Ego sum Dominus*, it is a law of servitude, a law for the bond-woman and her brood. (Gal. iv. 24.) Never preach it, at least not to children. That law is to give place, and in place thereof is to come the law of Sion, which we preach; the law of the free-woman, and "the children of promise," (Gal. iv. 28); the law of love, of filial love, proceeding not "from the spirit of bondage," but from "the spirit of adoption." (Rom. viii. 15.)

There is *lex factorum* in both; but, as Gregory well expresseth it, *Si servus es, metue plagas*, "if thou be bond, as Ismael, do it out of servile fear, for fear of the whip.' *Si mercenarius, expecta mercedem*; 'if thou be an hireling, as Balaam, do it out of mercenary respect.' *Sed, si filius Meus tu;* then do it out of true natural affection; perform all duties of a kind son to Him That said, *genui te*, as did Isaac the son of the free-woman to Abraham that begot him, "even to the laying down of his life." (Gen. xxii. 9.) None to Timothy, saith St. Paul, "none like minded to him; for as a son with his father, so hath he laboured with me in the Gospel." (Phil. ii. 20, 22.) "So," that is, so freely, so sincerely, so respectfully, as a loving, kind, natural son could do no more. And that is *lex factorum* indeed. And so much for *lex factorum* on our part, what we do for him—the filial duties, the law of this Gospel.

We lack nothing now but the time. And as *legem* is the condition, so *hodie* is the time. We are willed by the Apostle to insist upon this word *hodie*, to call upon men for this duty while it is called "to-day." (Heb. iii. 13, 15.) Not to defer, or to put off, or make a morrow matter of it. We are all inclined to be *crastini* or *perendini*, 'for to-morrow or next day,' or I know not when, but not to be *hodierni*. *Hodie* is no adverb with us, for where shall we find one but will take days for any matter of duty? To look to this *hodie*, and not deceive ourselves, for no time but *hodie* hath any promise — witness *hodie si vocem*, "to-day if you will hear His voice," (Ps. xcv. 7, 8), which every day sounds in our ears.

But *hodie genui* is more than *hodie*, for every day in the year while it lasts is *hodie*, "to-day," but every day is not *hodie genui*. There is but one of them in the whole year, and that is this day. This day then to take, of all other *hodies*, not to let slip the *hodie* of this day. A day whereon this Scripture was fulfilled, whereon *dixit et factum est*, "He said it and did it," whereon this Son was born and given us; a day whereon as it is most kindly preached, so it will be most kindly practised of all others. And so I hold you no longer, but end.

Praying to Him That was the *hodie genitus* of this day, Him That was begotten, and Him by Whom He was begotten, that we may have our parts, as in *prædicabo*, "preaching," so likewise in *legem*, "the law;" in both, *legem fidei*, "to believe aright," and *legem factorum*, "to live according;" that we performing the filial duties required, may obtain the filial rights promised, and may be in the number of those to whom first and last *filius Meus tu* shall be said, to our everlasting comfort, and "to the praise of the glory of His grace," (Ephes. i 6), through Christ our Lord.

INDEX.

U

Sermons for the Church's Year.

Original and Selected. Edited by the REV. W. BENHAM, B.D., *Rector of St. Edmund the King and Martyr, and one of the Six Preachers in the Canterbury Cathedral. Author of " A Short History of the Episcopal Church in America," &c. In 13 Parts, 64 pages, demy 8vo, price 1s. each. Two Volumes, demy 8vo, cloth boards, 6s. each.*

The Series comprises Sermons by the following Eminent Divines.

J. S. M. Anderson.
T. Ainger.
Dean Alford.
Rev. W. Benham.
Bishop Bethell.
Henry Blunt.
Louis Bourdaloue.
Charles Bradley.
Canon Burrowes.
W. Busfield, D.D.
Canon T. W. Butler.
Archbishop of Canterbury.
Bishop of Carlisle.
Dean Chandler.
Derwent Coleridge.
E. Cooper.
Canon C. Dale.
J. V. S. Davies.
Bishop Dehon.
Bishop Dennison.
C. F. De Jessier.
Morgan Dix, D.D.
Archbishop of Dublin.
Bishop of Exeter.
Bishop of Fredericton.
L. H. Gurney.
T. Hambleton.
Archdeacon Hare.
A. W. Hare.
Bishop Heber.

Archdeacon Hoare.
T. J. Holloway, D.D.
Bishop Horne.
W. J. Irons.
Bishop Jackson.
Bishop Jebb.
Bishop Kage.
John Keble.
Dean of Llandaff.
Bishop Wilberforce.
Bishop of London.
W. H. Lewis, D.D.
Bishop of Man.
J. B. Marsden.
F. D. Maurice.
Henry Melville.
W. H. Mill, D.D.
Bishop of Central New York.
R. Parkinson, B.D.
E. B. Pusey, D.D.
T. Rennell, B.D.
S. Richards.
W. Page Roberts.
Bishop Short.
Archbishop Sumner.
Bishop Jeremy Taylor.
Bishop Van Muldert.
Dr. J. Vaughan.
Archdeacon Waterland.
Dean of Wells.

Sermons for Children.
By A. Decoppet, *Pastor of the Reformed Church in Paris. Translated from the French by Marie Taylor. With an Introduction by Mrs. Henry Reeve. Price 3s. 6d.*

GRIFFITH, FARRAN, OKEDEN & WELSH,
Corner of St. Paul's Churchyard, London.

The Preacher's Promptuary of Anecdote

Stories New and Old, Arranged, Classified, and Indexed for the use of Preachers, Teachers, and Catechists. By the REV. W. FRANK SHAW, *Author of "The Mourner's Manual," "Sermon Sketches," &c., &c. Containing* 100 *short and pithy Stories, each pointing some moral or illustrating some doctrine. Crown 8vo, cloth boards, price* 2s. 6d.

"*Its Church tone is irreproachable. . . . A rare attribute of books of anecdotes.*"—LITERARY CHURCHMAN.

"*The selection is good and varied.*"—LITERARY WORLD.

"*Will be found as suitable for the teacher as for the preacher.*"—SCHOOLMISTRESS.

"*Very far from a commonplace collection.*—TABLET.

"*A useful compilation, and will be read with interest.*"—JOHN BULL.

A Manual for the Visitation of the Sick.

By the REV. R. ADAMS. *Containing, besides the ordinary Services for the Visitation of the Sick and others, Special Prayers, Readings, Hymns, &c., for use either by the visitor or the sick persons themselves. There is nothing in this Manual which can be denounced as useless, and the size of the book has been controlled so far as has been possible, without curtailing the usefulness of its contents. Roan limp, price* 3s. 6d.

Great Social Problems of the Day.

Lessons from the Hebrew Prophets for our time. A Series of Sermons by REV. E. A. WASHBURN, D.D. *With Preface by Rev. W. Benham, Editor of "Sermons for the Church's Year." Price* 2s. 6d.

"*Well worth study by Clergymen who have to deal with educated town congregations, as supplying hints for getting out of the usual homiletic groove, and bringing fresh topics, freshly treated, before their hearers.*"—CHURCH TIMES.

"*Remarkable for the power and energy displayed in demonstrating the applicability of divine truth to the social problems of every age.*"—ROCK.

Short History of the Episcopal Church in the United States.

By the REV. W. BENHAM, B.D., F.S.A., *Rector of St. Edmund-the-King, London, and Editor of "Sermons for the Church's Year." With a Portrait of Bishop Seabury (the first American Bishop), engraved from the Portrait in the Vestry of St. Andrews' Church, Aberdeen. Cloth, price* 2s. 6d

---

GRIFFITH, FARRAN, OKEDEN & WELSH,
Corner of St. Paul's Churchyard, London.